INTERPRETING COMMUNICATION RESEARCH

A Case Study Approach

Lawrence R. Frey
Loyola University of Chicago

Carl H. Botan
Purdue University

Paul G. Friedman
University of Kansas

Gary L. Kreps
Northern Illinois University

Prentice Hall
Englewood Cliffs, New Jersey 07632

Library of Congress Cataloging-in-Publication Data

Interpreting communication research : a case study approach / Lawrence
  R. Frey . . . [et al.].
      p. cm.
  Includes bibliographical references and index.
  ISBN 0–13–589110–8
  1. Communication—Research—Methodology—Case studies. I. Frey,
Lawrence R.
P91.3.I58 1992
302.2′072—dc20   91–46277
                                                           CIP

Acquisitions editor: Steve Dalphin
Editorial/production supervision and
  interior design: Fred Dahl, Inkwell
Cover design: Karen Stephens
Manufacturing buyer: Mary Ann Gloriande
Prepress buyer: Kelly Behr
Supplements editor: Sharon Chambliss

© 1992 by Prentice-Hall, Inc.
A Simon & Schuster Company
Englewood Cliffs, New Jersey 07632

Printed in the United States of America
10 9 8 7

ISBN 0-13-589110-8

Prentice-Hall International (UK) Limited, *London*
Prentice-Hall of Australia Pty. Limited, *Sydney*
Prentice-Hall Canada, Inc., *Toronto*
Prentice-Hall Hispanoamericana, S.A., *Mexico*
Prentice-Hall of India Private Limited, *New Delhi*
Prentice-Hall of Japan, Inc., *Tokyo*
Simon & Schuster Asia Pte. Ltd., *Singapore*
Editora Prentice-Hall do Brasil, Ltda., *Rio de Janeiro*

Contents

3: Field Experimental Research, *55*

SECTION II: SURVEY RESEARCH, *85*

Overview of Survey Research, *85*

4: Survey Questionnaire Research, *91*

7: Content Analysis, *194*

Introduction to the Method, *194*

Questions for Examining Content Analysis, *199*

The Illustrative Study, *199*

The Article, *201*
> Lowry, D. T., & Towles, D. E. (1989). Soap opera portrayals of sex, contraception, and sexually transmitted diseases. *Journal of Communication, 39 (2)*, 76–83.

Comments on the Study, *209*

Conclusion, *215*

Questions and Activities to Consider, *215*

Further Readings on Content Analysis, *216*

Examples of Content Analysis, *216*

8: Interaction Analysis, *219*

Introduction to the Method, *219*

Questions for Examining Interaction Analysis, *224*

The Illustrative Study, *225*

The Article, *226*
> Alderton, S. M., & Frey, L. R. (1983). Effects of reactions to arguments on group outcome: The case of group polarization. *Central States Speech Journal, 34,* 88–95.

Comments on the Study, *237*

Conclusion, *241*

Questions and Activities to Consider, *242*

Further Readings on the Study of Conversation, *242*

Examples of Interaction Analysis, *243*

SECTION IV: ETHNOGRAPHY, *247*

Overview of Ethnography, *247*

Ethnographers' Orientation, *248*

Aims of Ethnographic Research, *249*

Conducting Ethnographic Research, *250*

Analyzing and Presenting Ethnographic Data, *252*

9: Ethnographic Observational Research, *255*

Introduction to the Method, *255*

Questions for Examining Ethnographic Observational Research, *260*

Preface

Knowledge about communication usually goes through several stages before the public learns it. Ideas for research begin as "hunches" about patterns in human communication that occur to scholars as they observe people interacting or as they read reports of others' theory and research. They test their ideas by gathering relevant data involving that particular kind of communication phenomenon. They analyze those data and present a report on their investigation to colleagues at their own institutions or at an annual convention of one of the professional organizations in communication. After obtaining feedback on this draft of their work, they revise it and send it off to the editor of a professional journal such as those listed in Chapter 1.

If the article is accepted for publication, it appears in the journal about a year later. Perhaps a year or two after that, a textbook author decides to write a summary of what is known about that particular communication domain and collects a wide range of material on the subject, including that individual journal article. The textbook author paraphrases the whole study—most run from 10 to 25 pages—in about a paragraph, along with a number of others addressing the same general theme.

It takes another year for that textbook to be reviewed and printed; and yet another year may go by before a professor reads and decides to adopt that text for use in his or her college class. Finally, several months later, students learn what that researcher discovered years earlier—at least as the textbook author translated it.

For most students in introductory courses, this procedure is adequate. They are just being introduced to the knowledge a field has to offer, and they have a lot of catching up to do. The textbook author provides an enormous service by collecting and capsulizing all that knowledge. But advanced students in a field of study are severely handicapped if they rely exclusively on textbook material for their knowledge. First, by the time it goes through all the stages we summarized above, the material in those volumes is somewhat out-of-date. Second, the textbook account omits much information about the study that the students might find useful. Third, sometimes the information in the original study is distorted in the condensation process.

Therefore, professionals in the field distinguish between two kinds of information sources: primary sources and secondary sources. Primary sources are research studies that are presented for the first time by the person(s) who conducted the research study, such as books of original research, studies published in journals, and reports of original research presented at conventions. Secondary sources are research reports presented for the second or subsequent time by the person who conducted the research or summaries of research by people other than the original researcher. Textbooks, for example, are secondary sources because the knowledge they present is mediated by the textbook author. To become a true professional in any field, one must become adept at finding and reading primary source material.

However, this step is not an easy one to take. Primary source materials usually must be accessed in a college library, unless you know someone who subscribes to those books and journals or unless you attend a convention yourself. Also, they are not written for the general public, as textbooks are. Their intended audience is the author's peers—other communication professionals. Therefore, they presume a great deal of knowledge on the readers' part. To understand, appreciate, and critically analyze primary source material, you must acquire that information.

Research articles apply research methods to a particular communication content area. Your content area courses provide the required knowledge about particular communication phenomena. A research methods course and books like this one are needed to provide the knowledge about research methods necessary for understanding primary source material.

In 1988, Frey and Botan conducted a national survey to assess the status of instruction in introductory communication research methods. This survey found that many professors who taught the course were dissatisfied with the textbooks written on research methods. Too many textbooks were written for advanced graduate students, which obviously made them difficult for inexperienced students to comprehend; many others were based in psychology or sociology, and virtually ignored research on communication variables. This dissatisfaction led us to write an introductory communication research methods textbook: Frey, L. R., Botan, C. H., Friedman, P. G., & Kreps, G. L. (1991). *Investigating Communication: An Introduction to Research Methods*. Englewood Cliffs, NJ: Prentice Hall (ISBN 0-13-503426-4).

Another important finding from that national survey was that the vast majority of professors who teach communication research methods require students to read and report on research published in scholarly journals. Subsequent conversations with professors revealed that many other communication courses (such as Introduction to Speech Communication, Introduction to Mass Media, Communication Theory, and Interpersonal Communication) require students to read research articles. Professors believe strongly that these research articles are the bread and butter of the communication discipline. Unfazed by the tangle of academic jargon themselves, professors enjoy seeing empirical tests of assumptions about human behavior, debates over competing theories about human behavior, applications of communication insights to the perplexing issues of our times, and expansions of the cutting edge of the field as new dimensions of human social activity are illuminated by research. Since professors want students to appreciate these endeavors, they require students to read primary source material in addition to the required textbooks.

Moreover, professors also commonly require students to write reports on the assigned articles. Our national survey showed that 77% of communication research methods courses require students to complete a research prospectus, while 67% require a completed study. In order to complete these projects successfully, as well as written assignments in many other courses, students must read research reports and write literature reviews.

Conversations with students, however, revealed that as they tackle these assignments, they run into difficulty understanding journal articles. Few research reports are written clearly and in the standard way described in research methods textbooks. The prose is usually inflated and understood only by a few, using words not found in everyday language. The useful material is buried within a mountain of documentation supporting its validity. The readers' knowledge of other published research is taken for granted. To deal with their confusion, students often just skim the contents of the article, and then draw their reports from the "Abstract" at the beginning or from the "Discussion" section at the end and never really comprehend much of what lies between the two. They then vow to avoid all further contact with academic journals.

Professors tend to respond more positively to academic journal articles than do students because they understand the "code" in which these articles are written. Once readers know the purpose and underlying logic of each section within research articles, the value of such articles emerges.

In a sense, academic coursework is intended to prepare students to access and use the primary literature in a field and to teach them how to go on learning the subject matter on their own. To do so, many professors put research articles on reserve in the campus library or in their department offices; they photocopy journal articles to distribute to their classes; they encourage students to join the national communication associations that publish journals; or, they assign each student a different article to read. All of these methods, however, are somewhat awkward and inconvenient.

There is obviously a need to provide students with a better understanding of the research literature, and a more effective means for doing so. While a research methods textbook establishes the foundation for understanding journal articles, there is still a need to provide students with actual examples and analyses of research articles themselves.

This text was born out of this need. The text is aimed primarily at the introductory student, that is, the undergraduate or beginning graduate student who is not yet completely familiar with communication research methods or adept at reading published communication research, but who is prepared to make the shift from reading mainly secondary sources (textbooks) to reading primary sources (original research articles).

We use a case study approach to help students become educated consumers of primary research on communication. "Educated consumers" refers to three subgoals: (1) *motivation*—students will value research articles and want to read them more than they did before reading this book; (2) *understanding*—students will be better able to comprehend a wider range of articles; and (3) *critical analysis*—students will be better able to identify the strengths and limitations of research articles.

We begin in the first chapter by explaining the nature of research and the structure of scholarly research articles, and by posing a generic set of questions students should keep in mind when reading and evaluating articles. The text is then divided into sections that correspond to four major methodologies: experimental research, survey research, textual analysis (which includes rhetorical criticism, content analysis, and interaction analysis), and ethnography. Our intent is to describe these different research methods, including their strengths and limitations, and to show how they are applied within published research. To do so, we first present an overview for each major section, and in the subsequent chapters examine each methodology in more depth. We start each methodology chapter by introducing students to the general procedures researchers use most frequently when employing the specific method being examined. Next, we pose a series of questions specific to the methodology to engage students' "critical thinking" while reading the illustrative article or any other article of that type. An actual article from a scholarly communication journal is then presented with its lines numbered. We refer to these numbered lines in the second half of each chapter when we analyze and evaluate the different sections of the article. To conclude each chapter, we pose questions and activities for students to consider (which can be completed and handed in as assignments), offer some additional reference material that explains in greater depth the specific methodology being examined, and give an annotated bibliography of five additional research articles that use the methodology.

The articles were selected based on a number of criteria. First, all articles focus on an aspect of persuasive communication broadly defined; that is, each deals with how messages of one kind or another influence people. Second, the articles use varied research methods. Each article uses one of the four major kinds of methodologies used to study communication behavior. Some articles employ quantitative methods; others apply more qualitative methods. Some also are concerned more with basic research that tests theory, while others are applied research studies that address specific, "real-world" communication problems. Third, these articles were chosen to represent the broad spectrum of the **communication** discipline, ranging from interpersonal to mediated or mass communication. The articles also examine a number of important contexts in which communication plays an important role, such as health care, legal, and political settings. Fourth, these articles were chosen from different communication journals to illustrate the range of sources for research literature in this field. Fifth, each article is relatively short and is written in a fairly clear manner. We also chose articles dealing with topics of some intrinsic interest to students studying communication. We thought it best to start students off reading intriguing, accessible research which would lead them into pursuing material of greater complexity and academic relevance later on.

We wish to add that these articles are not intended to be model or ideal examples of flawless research. (Actually, we didn't even run across many of these!) The articles selected do represent good research (all were published in refereed communication journals) that illustrate the different methodologies being examined. They are, however, like all research studies, open to being critiqued. For this reason, in fact, we chose an article written by each of the authors of this text because we felt freer to be frankly critical of our own research. We also were able to provide insight into some of the background decisions that were made while conducting the research that do not show up explicitly in the published articles (such as having to reanalyze data because of reviewers' comments).

This text can be used within a wide variety of communication courses. It is most appropriate as a primary or supplementary text for introductory communication research methods courses. This text takes readers one step further toward being appreciative and critical readers of primary research material than our own communication research methods textbook or any other existing textbook does. The case study approach used in this text

allows professors to concentrate more fully on explaining the basic principles of communication research, knowing that students will, in addition,
see how they are applied by practicing researchers in actual research articles. We also believe this text can be profitably assigned in *any* communication course in which the reading of primary research is required. Students
still may be asked to read other, content-specific research articles, but this
book will help them comprehend and critique those articles more effectively.

Finally, like many research projects, this text is a result of a team
effort. We would like to thank Steve Dalphin, Executive Editor of Prentice
Hall for his faith in this project. We also express our sincere appreciation to
Sandra Metts, Illinois State University, and Tom Socha, Old Dominion
University, for their diligent reviews of this text, and to JoAnn Fricke for
secretarial help. Most of all, this text is dedicated to all of our colleagues
who teach, and all of the past, present, and future students who have
studied communication research methods with us at Loyola University of
Chicago, Rutgers University, the University of Kansas, and Northern Illinois University. We sincerely hope this text meets your needs.

Chapter 1

Interpreting Communication Research

INTRODUCTION

As we in academia and people in society at large confront progressively more complex social challenges, we are forced to rely less on our instincts and personal experiences and to develop an increasingly sophisticated understanding of the world in which we live. This shift from a personal, or subjective, knowledge, to a shared, more scientific body of knowledge is made possible by systematic ways of studying phenomena. Research is the systematic process by which we attempt to answer the questions that confront us.

Much communication research has been done. Several of our leading academic journals have been publishing issues quarterly for more than 50 years. From this material, we have learned a great deal about the communication process. Yet there also is little we are absolutely sure about. Why? Because the behavior of human beings is difficult to explain and predict. Many factors have an impact on every instance of human communication. Research on this process inevitably involves a trade-off among several criteria.

For example, if we want to understand a single factor in communication, such as what kinds of arguments yield the greatest persuasion, we must control our research to eliminate all the peripheral factors, such as the appearance of the speaker. To achieve control, therefore, we must make our research conditions somewhat artificial. Do findings in controlled experiments reflect what people do as they naturally interact in everyday life?

Not completely. But to study real-life persuasion situations, we must sacrifice control. Moreover, if we study people in natural conditions, we cannot study enough people to generalize broadly. But if we study a lot of people, we can only investigate a small portion of their communication activities. The list of trade-offs involved in research endeavors could go on and on.

Obviously, there are no "perfect" communication studies. Every instance of research involves trade-offs or choices among various requirements of the design selected as most appropriate for answering the research questions. The decisions researchers make when designing their research studies and the care with which they enact these decisions influence the quality of what they discover. It is insufficient, therefore, to learn simply *what* a researcher has found. That finding is influenced by *how* the research was conducted, and by the trade-offs and inherent limitations involved in what was given up to obtain those results.

The goal of this text is to help you become a knowledgeable and critical consumer of communication research. This necessitates exposure to research methods and actual examples of communication research.

Coursework in academia exposes students to the general principles and concepts in an area of study. The work may not, however, allow for experience or practice in applying these concepts to specific situations students encounter. The **case study approach** provides opportunities to apply general principles to specific situations or examples, called cases. The case study approach asks you to analyze examples in light of important and relevant issues, often phrased as questions. By answering these questions, the case study analyst demonstrates a combination of insight, knowledge, and creativity in identifying and commenting upon relevant issues in the case being examined, in analyzing these issues in light of relevant theory and research, and in devising realistic and appropriate strategies for coping with any problematic situations identified in the case (Kreps & Lederman, 1985).

The case study approach is by no means a new educational tool. It has its roots in the Socratic method of education, where an instructor tells students a story about a problematic situation and queries them about how they might solve the problem. Today, it is used extensively in business, medical, library, social work, and legal education.

We use the case study approach in this text to examine how researchers conduct communication research. The case study approach is particularly well suited for illustrating the principles as well as evaluating the strengths and limitations of instances of contemporary communication inquiry.

We begin each section of this text with a short overview of the methodology being examined. In subsequent chapters we explain in more depth the key features of each methodology. Before presenting each case, we pose a series of questions you should keep in mind when reading and evaluating it. An actual example of a published communication research article is then presented verbatim, and each line of the text is numbered. To make this process manageable and enjoyable, we have tried to select interesting communication research reports that illustrate the methodology being discussed. As mentioned in the Preface, these case studies were selected for a variety of reasons. As a set, they demonstrate some of the breadth and depth of research in the communication discipline. We subsequently analyze each case in light of the principles discussed and the questions posed. We examine the strategic choices made by these communication researchers and sometimes suggest alternatives they could have taken. For the purpose of convenience, we divide these analyses into subheadings that correspond to the traditional format of research articles (introduction, review of the literature, research questions/hypotheses, methods, results, and discussion), and refer to actual line numbers. Finally, we pose some questions and activities for you to consider, suggest some additional readings on each methodology, and briefly describe five additional articles that use each methodology.

We intend this approach to facilitate the following kinds of responses to each article: (1) *understanding*—of the language and the methods used; (2) *appreciation*—of the care taken by the researcher to obtain unbiased findings and of the reasons for undertaking each of the research activities; (3) *connections*—between the article and our explanations of the methodologies, between the article and the material covered in your communication courses, and between the article and the popular literature on this topic (where conclusions often are drawn without being tested and passed off as though they were truth); (4) *criticism*—of the validity of the findings and their generalizability to other contexts and populations, as well as of the choices made by each researcher when designing the study; (5) *creativity*—regarding alternative approaches that could have been taken when doing each research study, and studies that could be done next to follow up on each article; and (6) *application*—of the findings in the article to your own personal life experiences and to general communication problems present in contemporary society.

The remainder of this chapter introduces you to the research process, the nature of communication research, and how to read scholarly communication research articles. The chapters that follow then examine specific research methods used to study communication behavior and present and analyze actual examples of communication research.

THE NATURE OF RESEARCH

Research is a *disciplined* form of inquiry, the process of systematic investigation. Researchers study phenomena in a planned, step-by-step manner and report it so that other inquirers can replicate the process if they choose.

This step-by-step manner involves five stages: conceptualization, planning and designing research, using a research methodology, analyzing data, and reconceptualization.

Conceptualization

The first stage of research is called **conceptualization.** This is where researchers identify a topic worth studying, define the key concepts and variables, review the relevant literature on the topic, and ask a **research question** or pose a **hypothesis** (make a prediction).

The impetus for research typically comes from one of two sources. Some researchers seek to develop, test, clarify, and refine **theory,** which is referred to as **basic** (or pure) **research.** One form of basic research is **deduction,** or "hypothesis testing," in which researchers start with a general proposition (a theory) and deduce from it specific hypotheses to test. Their goal actually is to *disprove* the theory. They articulate hypotheses that, if not supported, will prove the theory wrong. If their hypotheses are confirmed, the theory has one more piece of evidence supporting it. A theory is never "proven" in any single study, however, because only one application of it is tested.

McGuire's (1964) inoculation theory, for example, posits that people can be "inoculated" to resist persuasive messages by providing them with forewarning of the persuasive attack and by giving them arguments to support their position or counterarguments to refute the other person's position. Inoculation theory presumes that refutational arguments should produce more resistance to persuasion than supportive arguments (which only bolster existing attitudes). Benoit (1991) tested this theory by attempting to disprove it. He pointed out that this prediction had only been tested on cultural truisms (culturally shared ideas that seldom, if ever, are challenged and are therefore susceptible to being changed, such as, "You should brush your teeth three times a day"). But the prediction had not been applied to controversial topics where people's positions generally are carefully reasoned from pieces of evidence and therefore difficult to change. He hypothesized that there would be no difference between providing refutational and supportive arguments on resistance to being persuaded about a controversial topic. The results from two studies confirmed this hypothesis, as there were no differences. Benoit's studies thus tested, clarified, and refined inoculation theory.

Another form of basic research is **induction,** or what often is called "grounded theory." Basic researchers who work inductively first examine a situation or behavior and then develop theoretical insights about it. These insights are phrased as tentative theories which deserve further investigation.

Applied research, on the other hand, is conducted for the purpose of solving a particular "real-world," socially relevant problem. Applied researchers start with a perceived problem and conduct a study to solve it. Their research may contribute to theory-testing (that is, if they use a theory to help solve the problem) or to theory-building (if they use the results to build tentative theories and propose hypotheses for future testing).

Acquired Immune Deficiency Syndrome (AIDS), for example, has generated much applied communication research because the best way to stop the spread of this deadly disease is to convince people to avoid engaging in risky behavior. Practitioners often use the mass media, especially television, to present preventive messages. Freimuth, Hammond, Edgar, and Monahan (1990) analyzed television public service announcements (PSAs) about AIDS to see how health communicators have responded to this challenge. They found that most PSAs they examined encouraged people to seek out more information. They went on to argue that these messages should, instead, motivate people to change their behavior. They also proposed some directions for future research, such as studying whether different types of audiences are persuaded by different strategies. Future researchers could pose hypotheses about these differences and test them. This study thus investigated a particular social problem and proposed some viable solutions to help solve it.

While both general theories and particular social problems can provide starting points for research, Miller and Sunnafrank (1984) argue that basic and applied research should be viewed as interdependent and complementary forms of social inquiry. Basic research certainly can be pragmatic, such as when a theory is used to develop a solution to a practical problem. Indeed, Lewin (1951) argued that, "There is nothing so practical as a good theory" (p. 51). Applied research also can be theoretical, such as when a specific situation yields insights with broad theoretical relevance. Kreps, Frey, and O'Hair (1991), therefore, propose that research studies should be categorized and evaluated to the extent that they emphasize theory and/or practice. Some research studies are low on both (probably examples of poor research), some are high on one and low on the other, and some studies are high on both.

Planning and Designing Research

The second stage of research involves carefully planning how to conduct the study. Here researchers decide how to identify, measure, or isolate the variables that they believe to operate within the context, the medium, or the persons involved. A **variable** is a concept that can take on two or more values. There are two types of variables: nominal and continuous. **Nominal variables** are differentiated on the basis of type or category. Television shows, for example, might be divided into comedies or dramas, or into programs for children or adults, live or taped, over-the-air or on cable, and so on. **Continuous variables** (or ordered variables) are assigned meaningful numbers to indicate some relative amount. The variables of height, weight, and number of words spoken per minute are continuous because the higher the score the more the person possesses the variable.

The next step is for researchers to determine how they will define, or **operationalize,** the variables they study in terms that can be *measured* or *identified*. Ray (1991), for example, studied the relationships among communication network roles, job stress, and burnout in educational organizations. One way she operationalized "communication networks" was by giving teachers a roster listing the names of all the other teachers and the principal at their school and having them rate how often they talked with each person using a 5-point scale that ranged from 1 (never) to 5 (several times a day). The higher the score, the more central a person was to the respondent's communication network. This numerical indicator thus served as the operationalization for the variable of communication network.

Communication researchers generally rely on three techniques for measuring variables: questionnaires, interviews, and observations. Examples of each will be illustrated in this text. Of course, these measurement techniques are only effective if they are **valid** (accurate) and **reliable** (consistent from administration to administration). Later we will show how researchers attempt to establish measurement validity and reliability.

Researchers also make ethical decisions as they plan and conduct research. The most important ethical decision is how to treat the human subjects they study. Generally, there are four ethical principles: to benefit the people being studied; to protect their right to privacy; to provide them with free choice; and to treat them with respect (Frey, Botan, Friedman, & Kreps, 1991).

Using a Research Methodology

The third stage of research involves choosing a research methodology and adhering to its requirements. Four methodologies are used frequently by communication researchers: experimental research, survey research, textual analysis, and ethnography.

Experimental research is conducted for the purpose of discovering causal relationships between variables. Experimenters predict and test for the effects of one variable, called the **independent variable,** on another variable, called the **dependent variable.** The next two chapters explain the experimental method and provide two examples, one that is conducted in a laboratory and one that takes place in the field.

Survey research attempts to generalize about a population based on responses from a relatively small number of representative individuals, called a **sample.** The Nielsen ratings, for example, provide estimates of what Americans watch on television based on responses from a relatively small sample (about 2,000 homes). Chapters 4 and 5 explain survey research and provide two examples, one that uses questionnaires and one that uses interviews.

Textual analysis is used to study messages recorded in **texts.** Texts may be written, spoken, electronic, or visual. Chapter 6 explains and provides an example of **rhetorical criticism,** which is used to analyze and evaluate persuasive public messages. Chapter 7 explains and provides an example of **content analysis,** which is used primarily to analyze mass-mediated texts. Chapter 8 looks at and provides an example of **interaction analysis,** the empirical analysis of person-to-person communication.

Finally, **ethnography** is used to study people's behavior in specific, natural settings. Ethnographers try to capture as fully as possible, and from the research participants' perspective, the ways that people use symbols within specific contexts. Chapters 9 and 10 explain and provide two examples of ethnographic research, one that relies on observation and one that uses interviews.

Analyzing and Interpreting Data

An essential component of any research study is gathering and analyzing information, called **data.** There are two types of data: qualitative and quantitative.

Qualitative data take the form of words rather than numbers. Qualitative data are analyzed and presented in the form of case studies, critiques, and sometimes verbal reports. Miles and Huberman (1984) contend that, "Words, especially when they are organized into incidents and stories, have a concrete, vivid, meaningful flavor that often proves far more convincing to a reader—another researcher, a policy-maker, a practitioner—than pages of numbers" (p. 15). Qualitative data are analyzed most often by rhetorical critics and ethnographers.

Quantitative data take the form of numerical indicators that are analyzed by statistical techniques. There are two basic types of statistics: descriptive and inferential. **Descriptive statistics** are used to summarize the information in data, such as reporting the average score (the **mean**) or tabulating and displaying data on a graph. **Inferential statistics** are used to estimate from a sample to a population (such as generalizing from a sample the candidate U.S. voters would choose for president), to test for significant differences between groups (such as differences in self-disclosure between men and women), or to identify significant relationships between variables (such as the relationship between people's ages and communication competence). Quantitative data are analyzed most often by experimental and survey researchers as well as by content analysts and interaction analysts.

Reconceptualization

The final stage of the research process is when researchers use the findings from their investigation to draw conclusions about and to rethink the topic of inquiry. During this stage, researchers examine the significance of the findings with respect to how they answer the research questions or confirm or disconfirm the hypotheses, and how they support or refute theory and previous research. They also suggest how the findings can be used by scholars, practitioners, and/or the general public, and they propose some directions for future research. This stage thus ensures that research is *cyclical,* as researchers end up back at the starting point for yet another investigation, with new questions to ask or new predictions to pose.

THE NATURE OF COMMUNICATION RESEARCH

The need to understand research methods now pervades the field of communication. Communication research is an attempt to *answer questions* about communication in terms of empirical data, to *test assumptions* about communication, and to *infer general principles* from information gathered. Communication research, once narrowly focused on public speaking, now addresses the entire complex process of managing face-to-face and mediated messages and creating meaning.

Communication is one of the largest and fastest growing academic disciplines. It is not unusual, for example, for departments of communication to have several hundred, and up to 1000 or more, majors. The expansion of the field of communication from providing only technical training in public speaking to its current disciplinary status has been made possible by the conduct of research that has yielded an evolving systematic body of knowledge. Communication currently is a full-fledged academic discipline with a content to which scholars apply rigorous scientific principles.

While it is impossible to comprehensively describe all the directions contemporary communication research takes, we want to point out some general ways in which the communication research pie is cut up.

The Goals of Communication Research

Communication research is conducted to achieve three general purposes: to describe communication behavior; to relate communication behavior to other variables; and/or to critique communication behavior.

Researchers who seek to *describe* communication phenomena essentially ask, "What is the nature of communication behavior?" Survey researchers, content analysts, interaction analysts, and ethnographers often seek to describe the communication characteristics of a particular group of people or texts. Hecht, Ribeau, and Alberts (1989), for example, conducted four studies to examine how Afro-Americans perceived interethnic communication with whites. To describe interethnic communication, they asked in one study the research question "What issues do Afro-Americans perceive in satisfying and dissatisfying conversations with whites?" (p. 389).

Researchers who seek to *relate* communication behavior to other variables essentially ask, "How is communication affected by other variables, and how does communication affect other variables?" Experimental researchers, in particular, often predict how **input variables** (variables that exist prior to a communication event, such as the speaker's personality or characteristics of the situation) influence communication, and/or how communication leads to particular outcomes.

Wilson (1990), for example, studied how people form interaction goals in situations. His review of the literature suggested five important interactional goals: (1) compliance goals—the desire to persuade someone to fulfill an obligation; (2) supporting goals—the desire to protect, repair, or enhance an interpersonal relationship; (3) attacking goals—the desire to threaten or damage an interpersonal relationship; (4) image goals—the desire to create or sustain a desired self-presentation; and (5) account-seeking goals—the desire to learn why someone failed to fulfill an obligation. As part of his study, he investigated how features of a situation affect individual differences in interactional goals. He argued that when speakers have "legitimate" power relative to listeners, the listeners should feel obligated to comply with a request, so there should be less use of "polite" strategies, such as supporting and image goals, and more use of attacking goals when a target fails to comply. Therefore, he predicted that, "Individuals report more attacking and fewer supporting and image goals when they seek compliance with obligations from a position of high rather than equal legitimate power" (p. 84). His experiment demonstrated, however, that the independent variable of legitimate power had no effect on the dependent variable of interactional goals.

Researchers who seek to *critique* communication behavior essentially ask, "Was the communication behavior enacted effective (or appropriate, or ethical)?" Rhetorical critics often analyze and evaluate whether and how a communicator used the best available means of persuasion. Murphy (1990), for example, critiqued Robert F. Kennedy's public response to the assassination of Martin Luther King, Jr. He showed how Kennedy made skillful rhetorical choices that encouraged the audience to achieve something worthwhile out of this tragic event.

Levels of Communication

Communication research is often differentiated with regard to the *level* of communication being studied. There are five basic levels of human communication: intrapersonal, interpersonal, group, organizational, and societal.

Intrapersonal communication research focuses on the internal messages we send to ourselves and the cognitive processes we use to develop messages to send to others and to process messages we receive from others. Researchers seek to understand how people create, or **encode,** messages to send to others and how they interpret, or **decode,** others' messages.

Interpersonal communication research investigates interactions between at least two people that are characterized by the mutual awareness of the individuality of the other. This definition distinguishes interpersonal communication from interactions in which other people are treated as objects in an impersonal manner (i.e., conversations with gas station attendants). Researchers are interested, for example, in describing how people manage their interpersonal conversations, such as the communication strategies people use to influence their significant others (i.e., how we persuade others, comfort them, or deceive them). They examine how communication behavior influences important interpersonal outcomes, such as relational satisfaction, development of trust, or disengagement from a relationship.

Group communication research studies interactions that occur among three or more (generally up to fifteen) people as they attempt to achieve shared goals. In a recent review of the relevant literature published during the 1980s, Cragan and Wright (1990) reported that some important lines of small group communication research were studies of small group discussion methods (such as brainstorming), explanations regarding the process of communication in small groups, and the effects of communication on group outcomes (such as decision quality and consensus).

Organizational communication research examines communication that occurs within a social system composed of interdependent groups striving to accomplish commonly recognized goals. Wert-Gray, Center, Brashers, and Meyers' (1991) review of organizational communication research published between 1979 and 1989 in fifteen communication journals found that the majority of the topics investigated were concentrated within five major areas: (1) the relationship between communication and organizational climate and culture; (2) superior-subordinate relations and communication; (3) power, conflict, and politics; (4) information flow within organizations; and (5) public, or external, organizational communication (communication between an organization and its publics).

Societal communication research focuses on communication that occurs within and between large social systems composed of interdependent organizations. There are three forms of societal communication research. First, **public communication** research studies one person (or several) while addressing a relatively large group of people. Rhetorical critics, for example, analyze and evaluate how public communicators create messages to persuade their audiences. Second, **cultural communication** research investigates interactions that occur among members of different cultures or subcultures. Researchers are interested, for example, in describing the communication similarities and differences among members of different cultures, called *intercultural communication,* and among members of the same dominant culture who have different values (say between members of different ethnic, racial, or status groups), called *intracultural communication.* They also assess what occurs when people enter or leave different cultures and subcultures, such as how immigrants are socialized into a new culture. The third form, **mass** or **mediated communication** research, analyzes messages that are processed through particular communication media. Researchers are interested, for example, in how print and television news messages differ, how people use the media to meet particular needs, and the effects of mediated messages (such as how they promote the development of aggressive or prosocial tendencies in children).

Communication Contexts and Populations

Researchers often seek to describe, predict, and critique communication behavior that occurs within some important *contexts* and as performed by certain *populations.* Researchers, for example, investigate communication behavior in such contexts as marriages, families, and educational institutions, as well as health care and legal settings. They also study the communication behavior of populations such as children, gays, handicapped individuals, and the aged. Sometimes, communication within these particular contexts or by these populations is distinctive enough to be the focus of research, and there are domain-specific problems that need to be solved.

SCHOLARLY COMMUNICATION RESEARCH ARTICLES

Research generally can be classified as one of two types: proprietary or scholarly. **Proprietary research** is conducted for, and available only to, a specific audience. General Motors research and development employees, for example, conduct research about automobiles that they do not make available to their competitors or the general public. **Scholarly research,** in contrast, is conducted to promote growth in public knowledge, and, therefore, is available to all members of society. In this text, we are interested in scholarly communication research.

Research also can be classified with regard to whether it is secondary or primary research. **Secondary research** occurs when research findings are presented for the second or subsequent time by the person who conducted the research or when a person reports the results from someone else's research, such as when research findings are reported in newspaper or magazine articles, in textbooks, on television, or over the radio. Most of the research we are exposed to is second-hand information since it does not come from the person who actually conducted the research. **Primary re-**

search, on the other hand, is research reported for the first time by the person who actually conducted it. Primary research is reported in two forms: book-length scholarly *texts* and regularly issued periodicals, usually called **scholarly journals.** Understanding primary research will allow you to judge the validity of the secondary research you are exposed to on a daily basis.

Most scholarly journals are sponsored by academic associations and organizations. These journals print original research studies and sometimes reviews of books and monographs. The communication discipline has many organizations, such as the Speech Communication Association, the International Communication Association, and the World Communication Association, that publish scholarly journals. Figure 1.1 lists some journals published by these organizations as well as some journals published by organizations in other disciplines that frequently include communication research. We divide these journals into those that focus primarily on speech communication, mass communication, and journalism, although many of these journals publish articles that cut across these areas of the discipline. Articles in many of these journals are also referenced in *Communication Abstracts,* a quarterly publication that prints one-paragraph summaries of recent communication articles, and Matlon's (1987) *Index to Journals in Communication Studies Through 1985,* which lists and classifies (by author and topic) every article ever published in some of these journals. There are also many journals in other social science and humanities disciplines, such as business and management, education, history, library and information sciences, linguistics, philosophy, political science, psychology, social work, sociology, and so on, that publish articles of interest to communication scholars.

The process by which journals review manuscripts seeks to assure that only the best articles will be published. Usually authors submit a manuscript to a journal editor who sends it out to be reviewed by two or three **blind reviewers,** usually experts on the particular topic being examined and who publish research regularly. They do not know the identity of the author and all references to the author are removed from the manuscript. The reviewers indicate whether the manuscript should be published as is, revised in light of the feedback they provide and resubmitted, or rejected for publication in that journal. The purpose of this rigorous process is to ensure that only the highest quality articles get published. Indeed, some of the leading journals in communication reject over 90% of the manuscripts submitted to them for publication!

Reading Communication Research Articles

Understanding and evaluating research articles is easier when you know their typical structure and some questions to keep in mind when reading them. While the formats of journal articles vary considerably, most research articles include some traditional, agreed-upon sections. These sections are

FIGURE 1.1
Scholarly Journals That Publish Communication Research

Speech Communication

Argumentation and Advocacy
Bulletin of the Association for Communication Administration
Communication
Communication & Cognition
Communication Education
Communication Quarterly
Communication Monographs
Communication Reports
Communication Research
Communication Research Reports
Communication Studies
Communication Theory
Discourse & Society
Discourse Processes
Group & Organization Management
Health Communication
Human Communication Research
Human Relations
International Journal of Intercultural Relations
Journal of Applied Communication Research
Journal of Communication Inquiry
Journal of Conflict Resolution
Journal of Contemporary Ethnography
Journal of Language and Social Psychology
Journal of Nonverbal Behavior
Journal of Social and Personal Relationships
Journal of Verbal Learning and Verbal Behavior
Language & Communication
Management Communication Quarterly
Mediation Quarterly
National Forensic Journal
Philosophy and Rhetoric
Political Communication and Persuasion
Quarterly Journal of Speech
Rhetoric Society Quarterly
Semiotica
Small Group Research
Southern Communication Journal
Text and Performance Quarterly
Western Journal of Speech Communication
Women's Studies in Communication
World Communication
Written Communication

(continued)

FIGURE 1.1 (*Continued*)

Mass Communication

Cinema Journal
COMM/ENT: A Journal of Communication and Entertainment Law
Communication and the Law
Critical Studies in Mass Communication
Educational Communication and Technology Journal
European Journal of Communication
Federal Communications Law Journal
Feedback
Film History
Film Journal
International Journal of Advertising: The Quarterly Review of Marketing Communications
Journal of Advertising Research
Journal of Broadcasting & Electronic Media
Journal of Communication
Journal of Educational Television and Other Media
Journal of Film and Video
Journal of Mass Media Ethics
Journal of Popular Culture
Jump Cut
Mass Comm Review
Media & Methods
Media and Values
Media Culture & Society
Media Report to Women
Quarterly Review of Film Studies
Quarterly Review of Film & Video
Technology and Culture
Telecommunications Policy
Television/Radio Age

Journalism

American Journalism
Journalism Educator
Journalism History
Journalism Quarterly
Journalism Monographs
Journalism Studies Review
Newspaper Research Journal
Public Opinion Quarterly
Public Relations Quarterly
Public Relations Research Journal
Public Relations Review

either distinguished in an article by appropriate subheadings or else they implicitly guide how an article is written. Here we examine the standard sections of an article and pose some generic questions for each section to keep in mind while reading any research article. (Many of these questions are explained in greater detail throughout the various chapters, and a separate set of questions about each methodology is posed in each chapter.) Many journals also provide an "Abstract," a one-paragraph summary of the article, either in the Table of Contents or at the beginning of the article itself.

Introduction. The introduction of an article usually accomplishes three goals. First, it introduces the reader to the general area, issue, or theme the article will address. Second, it explains the specific purpose of the particular research study. Third, it justifies the significance of the study for scholars, educators, practitioners, and/or the general public. Keep the following questions in mind when reading and evaluating the introduction:

1. Did the researcher explain clearly the *purpose* of the research? Was it apparent what he or she was attempting to do?
2. Was the purpose of the research to *describe, predict,* or *critique* communication behavior, or a combination of these goals? Was this goal appropriate and worthwhile?
3. Did the researcher indicate the potential *significance* of this research study? Was it clear why and how the research could prove useful to communication scholars, educators, communication practitioners, and/ or the general public?

Review of the Literature. The second section of an article reviews previous theory and research related to the topic. The purpose is to summarize in an organized and effective manner what is already known and what is unknown or controversial about the topic. If appropriate, the researcher may start by explaining a theoretical perspective that guides the research. The researcher may then review some general examinations of the topic area and elaborate more fully the methods and findings from studies most relevant to his or her own research. The researcher will also point out at the end of the literature review what gaps still exist in our knowledge and how his or her study seeks to fill these gaps. Keep the following questions in mind when reading and evaluating the review of the literature:

1. Did the researcher use a particular *theoretical perspective* as the basis for the research? Was the researcher trying to develop, test, clarify, or refine a theory by testing a proposition deduced from it (called a deductive approach)? If so, was this theory explained in sufficient depth?

2. If theory was not used as the basis for the research, was the researcher attempting to *develop theory from "the ground up"* (called an inductive approach)? If so, was this approach justified?

3. Did the researcher conduct a *thorough review of the literature?* Was enough research reviewed to provide you with a good foundation for understanding this topic?

4. Did the researcher explain clearly what we know from *previous research* about each of the *variables* of interest and how they are related? Did the researcher provide enough detail about the various studies (such as purpose, methods, findings, and significance)?

5. Was the literature review *organized* in an effective manner (perhaps by using a chronological, topical or problem-solution format)?

6. Did the researcher point out any *gaps* in the research literature that needed to be filled? Was it clear how this study was an extension of previous research?

Research Questions and/or Hypotheses. At the end of the literature review section, or in a separate section, the researcher asks a formal research question or poses a formal hypothesis, or a combination of both. Research questions are asked when researchers investigate a topic about which little is known, called **exploratory research,** or when there are conflicting findings from previous research. Hypotheses are posed when a theory or the review of the literature suggests a tentative answer to a general research question. Keep the following questions in mind when reading and evaluating research questions and/or hypotheses:

1. Did the researcher ask *research questions* or pose *hypotheses?* Did this choice seem appropriate, given what is known about the topic? Did the rationale for the particular research questions and/or hypotheses emerge logically from the review of the literature?

2. If research questions were asked, was this because this was *exploratory research* or because there were *conflicting answers* from the previous research?

3. If hypotheses were posed, was the *relationship between the variables* specified properly? Was it clear, for example, which variable was the independent variable and which was the dependent variable? Was it clear what effects were being proposed?

4. If hypotheses were posed, did each make a *single prediction* or were there *multiple predictions?* If multiple predictions were made in a single hypothesis, is it possible that part of the hypothesis might be confirmed but not the other part? Are the hypotheses phrased such that they will lead to clear rather than confusing answers?

Methods. The methods section explains in a straightforward manner who was studied and how the research was actually conducted. This section is composed of two subsections: subjects (or texts) and procedures. Researchers first explain the criteria and the methods used to select the people (subjects), or the texts they studied and provide relevant information about the sample used (e.g., age of subjects, or length of texts). They then explain in detail the data-gathering procedures they used, including how they operationalized the variables studied through questionnaires, interviews, and/or observations. Keep the following questions in mind when reading and evaluating the methods section:

1. What *criteria* were used to decide from which people or texts data would be gathered for the study? Were these selection criteria appropriate for meeting the research goals?

2. Were *enough subjects or texts* studied to feel confident about the validity of the results?

3. What *method was employed to select* the research participants or texts? Did the researcher study everyone in the population (or every text in the universe) of interest—called a **census**—or was a sample selected? Was this the most effective method possible?

4. If a sample was studied, was it *representative* of the greater population (for people) or universe (for texts) to which the researcher hopes to generalize? Or, did the selection process produce a biased sample, in which case the results can not be generalized back to the population/universe of interest?

5. Was the best *methodology* (experimental, survey, textual analysis, or ethnography, or a combination) used to answer the research questions? What were the advantages and limitations of using this method?

6. Were all the procedures (including the use of questionnaires, interviews, and/or observations to measure variables) explained in a detailed manner? Was sufficient detail provided for another researcher to exactly replicate the study?

7. Did the procedures seem *valid?* Did the measurement techniques seem to measure what they were designed to measure? What evidence was offered?

8. Did the procedures seem *reliable?* Could the measurement techniques, for example, yield consistent results if administered at another time or place? What evidence was offered?

Results. The results section presents the findings from the study. Researchers often show in sequential order how the data obtained answer each of the research questions and/or confirm or disconfirm the hypotheses. This section is a straightforward reporting of the findings, and there usually is little or no attempt to interpret or generalize from these results. Occasionally you will find this section difficult to understand, especially if advanced methods of statistical analysis are used. You should, however, be much better able to comprehend this section of research articles after finishing this book. Keep these questions in mind when reading and evaluating the results section:

1. Were the data obtained in the form of *qualitative* or *quantitative data?* Were these data appropriate for answering the research questions or testing the hypotheses?

2. If *statistics* were used, were the assumptions underlying their use met? Were the proper and most effective statistical procedures used?

3. Were the *results presented* in a clear and organized manner? Did the researcher explain the results for each of the research questions and/or hypotheses that were advanced?

Discussion. The discussion section is where the researcher interprets the meaning and significance of the results. The discussion section typically accomplishes four goals. First, the researcher summarizes and examines the findings from the study in light of the research questions and/or hypotheses, relevant theory, and findings from previous research. Second, the researcher identifies some of the potential problems with the research that may limit the validity of the findings. All research studies have limitations (such as the representativeness of the people studied and the validity of the procedures used) and these should be pointed out. Third, the researcher will point out the significance of the findings for other communication scholars, educators, practitioners, and/or the general public. Finally, the researcher fulfills a heuristic function, using research to generate more research, by proposing some profitable directions for future research. Keep the following questions in mind when reading and evaluating the discussion section:

1. Did the *conclusions* drawn from the research seem valid? Did the researcher build *cogent arguments* regarding these conclusions?

2. Did the researcher identify any *important problems* encountered in conducting the research? How do these problems limit the validity of the conclusions that can be drawn?

3. Did the researcher point out the potential *application* of the findings? Was the *significance* of these conclusions for communication scholars, educators, practitioners, and/or the general public made explicit?

4. Did the researcher fulfill the heuristic function of research by proposing some specific and worthwhile *directions for future research?*

References and Notes. Finally, researchers provide a complete list of all reference material used in the article (and sometimes additional sources that were not used explicitly but influenced the researcher's thinking on the topic). While citation styles may vary (such as the American Psychological Association [APA] stylesheet and the Modern Language Association [MLA] stylesheet), each reference must be complete enough to allow the reader to locate it easily. Researchers also sometimes include notes at the end of an article to explain some of the material in the body of the text. They may, for example, use reference notes to give a formula for a statistical procedure performed on the data.

Keep the following questions in mind when reading and evaluating the bibliography and reference notes:

1. Were all the *works cited in the text* referenced in the bibliography? Were they referenced fully so that any interested reader could locate them easily?
2. Did the bibliography show a good coverage of the *major works* in the area, or is the article too dependent on one or two sources and perhaps ignored other important works?
3. Were the works cited *current?* Did the research reflect the latest developments in the field?
4. Were the works cited generally *primary sources* (original research studies) or *secondary* sources (i.e., textbooks or literature reviews).
5. If *notes* were included, did they clarify and explain some of the material?

CONCLUSION

Research is a way of acquiring knowledge in which we test what we know and seek to find out what we do not know in a planned, systematic manner. The world of research is very much a culture, complete with its own rules and terminology. Learning about any culture takes time, but once we know its code we feel more comfortable operating within it. We hope that by the time you finish this text you will feel more comfortable reading, understanding, interpreting, and evaluating the research produced by members of the communication research culture. We believe that as a knowledgeable consumer of research, you will be better prepared to cope with the challenges that lie ahead in this information age.

ADDITIONAL READINGS ON COMMUNICATION RESEARCH METHODS AND READING RESEARCH

Anderson, J. A. (1987). *Communication research: Issues and methods.* New York: McGraw Hill.

Babbie, E. (1989). *The practice of social research* (5th ed.). Belmont, CA: Wadsworth.

Emmert, P., & Barker, L. L. (1989). *Measurement of communication behavior.* New York: Longman.

Frey, L. R., Botan, C. H., Friedman, P. G., & Kreps, G. L. (1991). *Investigating communication: An introduction to research methods.* Englewood Cliffs, NJ: Prentice Hall.

Hsia, H. J. (1988). *Mass communications research methods: A step-by-step approach.* Hillsdale, NJ: Lawrence Erlbaum.

Katzer, J., Cook, K. H., & Crouch, W. W. (1982). *Evaluating information: A guide for users of social science research* (2nd ed.). Reading, MA: Addison-Wesley.

Leedy, P. D. (1981). *How to read research and understand it.* New York: Macmillan.

Rubin, R. B., Rubin, A. M., & Piele, L. J. (1990). *Communication research: Strategies and sources* (2nd ed.). Belmont, CA: Wadsworth.

Smith, M. J. (1988). *Contemporary communication research methods.* Belmont, CA: Wadsworth.

Tucker, R. K., Weaver, II, R. L., & Berryman-Fink, C. (1981). *Research in speech communication.* Englewood Cliffs, NJ: Prentice Hall.

Wimmer, R. D., & Dominick, J. R. (1991). *Mass media research: An introduction* (3rd ed.). Belmont, CA: Wadsworth.

EXPERIMENTAL RESEARCH

OVERVIEW OF EXPERIMENTAL RESEARCH

The search for causation has long fascinated laypersons and scientists alike. Judges and jurors, for example, examine causes to determine whether defendants are innocent or guilty of crimes committed. Divorced marital partners frequently attempt to pinpoint the factors that caused the breakup of their marriage. And students seek explanations for what went wrong when they receive a low grade on an assignment or examination.

Many scientists also seek causal principles to explain how the world works. They assume that both the physical world and human behavior are ordered in cause-effect patterns and that the principles that govern this order can be discovered. Precise causal explanations have long been the accepted goal of research in the physical sciences. But some critics argue the same precision can never be achieved in the study of human behavior because each person is unique and because most behavior is a result of multiple factors. Social scientists argue, however, that there is substantial regularity in human behavior as indicated by the fact that people behave quite often in highly predictable ways, for instance, stopping at red traffic lights. Andersen (1989) identifies five forces that produce regularities in human communication: (1) natural forces (such as physiology or physics); (2) cultural rules (customs and taboos within a society or organization); (3) personal traits (such as predispositions or habitual patterns); (4) relational patterns (predictable actions engaged in by particular families or small groups); and (5) intentional, goal-oriented behavior.

Social scientists acknowledge that individuals differ. They seek, therefore, to discover causal principles that explain and predict how *groups of people* behave under specific sets of circumstances. To ascertain these causal principles, many conduct systematic, controlled observations, called experiments. Experimentation is a leading methodology used by contemporary communication researchers, one that has produced significant insights. Indeed, Albert Einstein once claimed that, "Development of Western science is based on two great achievements: the invention of the formal logic system [mathematics] and the discovery of the possibility to find out causal relationships by systematic experiment" (Mackay, 1977, p. 51).

Researchers conduct experiments whenever they want to investigate whether and how one variable causes another variable to change. The variable suspected of causing the changes is called the independent variable. The variable expected to change is called the dependent variable. Communication researchers may want to know, for example, whether speeches containing supporting material (the independent variable) in the form of statistical evidence or vivid examples produce more change in people's attitudes toward a topic (the dependent variable); which group discussion procedure (the independent variable), brainstorming or the Delphi Method, produces more creative ideas (the dependent variable) in decision-making group discussions; or whether violence on television shows (the independent variable) causes increases in children's aggression (the dependent variable). In each of these cases, researchers can employ the *experimental method* to discover whether a **causal relationship** exists between the independent and the dependent variables.

ESTABLISHING CAUSATION

To conclude with some assurance that an independent variable influences a dependent variable requires that three conditions be met (Lazarsfeld, 1959). First, the independent variable must *precede* the dependent variable in time. If, for example, communication researchers want to show that watching violent acts on television shows causes certain aggressive behavior in particular children, they must demonstrate that watching violent television shows preceded the development of those children's aggressive acts. If children's aggressive behavior predated their television watching, the causal effect actually might occur the other way around, that is, children's aggressiveness might cause them to watch violent television shows.

Second, to suggest a causal relationship also requires that changes in an independent variable be associated *logically* with changes in a dependent variable. It makes sense that watching violence on television might be related to the development of aggressive behavior in children. On the other hand, it would be capricious to argue that watching violent television shows causes children to use more multisyllabic words. There is no reason to believe these two variables are related in a meaningful manner. Therefore, even if a study happened to find a statistically significant relationship between them, that finding would be considered a **spurious relationship,** a mere coincidence, not an insight into human behavior.

Finally, establishing a causal relationship is only possible if changes in the dependent variable are shown to be the *result* of changes in the independent variable and are not due to some other variable(s). Kerlinger (1973) explains that a scientist "tries systematically to rule out variables that are possible 'causes' of the effects (s)he is studying other than the variable that (s)he has hypothesized to be the 'cause'" (p. 4). Before assuming aggressive behavior in children is explained by their television-watching behavior, researchers also must compare the impact of television with other possible causal factors, such as whether or not they live in a violent social environment (a high- or low-crime area) and the amount and quality of their communication with their parents. Establishing causation thus requires experimental researchers to rule out competing explanations for the changes in a dependent variable, or what are called **alternate causality arguments.**

TYPES OF EXPERIMENTS

Satisfying these three necessary conditions, and particularly the third condition, requires that researchers *control* influences that would compromise the strengths or advantages inherent in the chosen design and influences that would threaten the validity of the conclusions drawn from the experiment. Researchers often control, for example, the environment in which an experiment takes place, the basis on which subjects are assigned to experimental groups, and the amount of time subjects are exposed to the independent variable(s). It is the degree of control exercised by researchers that distinguishes the experimental method from the other methodologies examined in this text.

Control exists on a continuum, and experimental research is divided into three types based on the degree of control present: (1) **full** (or **true**) **experiments,** which exercise the maximum amount of control; (2) **quasi-experiments,** which exercise a moderate amount of control; and (3) **pre-experiments,** which demonstrate little or no control. In the next two chapters, we will explain the requirements for conducting these types of experiments and offer two examples from communication research.

Experiments also can take place in different settings. **Laboratory experiments** take place in a setting created by a researcher, while **field experiments** take place in the natural environment. Full experiments, quasi-experiments, and pre-experiments may be conducted in either the laboratory or the field. Experimental research conducted in a laboratory, however, usually affords researchers greater control; therefore, researchers typically conduct full experiments in a laboratory. Conversely, because of the limitations for exercising control in the natural setting, researchers more often conduct quasi-experiments and pre-experiments in the field. To illustrate the experimental method, therefore, we first examine full experimental laboratory research and then examine field experimental research.

Finally, because causal relationships among variables are generally complex, experimenters often study the effects of more than one independent variable on a dependent variable (and even multiple dependent variables). Attitude change, for example, may be caused not just by a single variable but by numerous variables. Experiments that study the effects of two or more independent variables are called **factorial experiments,** and tell researchers two important things: (1) the effects of each independent variable (called the **main effects**); and (2) the effects of the independent variables working together (called an **interaction effect**). An interaction effect, for example, might show that the persuasive effects of using statistical evidence versus vivid examples in public speeches are affected by individuals' levels of education, such that highly educated people are persuaded most by statistical evidence while less educated people are persuaded most by vivid examples, or that speeches containing both kinds of content are more effective than those that only employ either one. To explain and illustrate the experimental method, the studies we examine in this section only investigate a causal relationship between a single independent variable and a single dependent variable. As you read the following studies, however, think about what other independent variables could have been studied and how they might produce an interaction effect with the independent variable the researchers chose to study.

Chapter 2

Laboratory Full Experimental Research

INTRODUCTION TO THE METHOD

Researchers conduct *full experiments* whenever they study a proposed causal relationship between an independent and dependent variable and are able to exercise a high degree of control. Exercising a high degree of control is accomplished in three ways: (a) manipulating an independent variable; (b) randomly assigning research subjects to experimental conditions; and (c) accounting for the influence of extraneous variables. An experiment is full only when all three procedures are used; if less control is possible, researchers conduct quasi-experiments or pre-experiments.

Manipulating an Independent Variable

In full experiments researchers manipulate an independent variable by controlling subjects' exposure to it. A classic method involves dividing a group of subjects in half and exposing one group to an experimental manipulation (called the **treatment group**) and being sure the other group (called the **control group**) is not. Comparing these two groups on the dependent variable reveals whether the independent variable had its hypothesized effect.

Janis and Mann (1965), for example, wanted to know whether active involvement in *role-playing* (assuming the role of another person) was a more effective persuasive technique than simply *listening* to messages when both were intended to change subjects' attitudes about smoking. They recruited people who were moderate or heavy smokers, and asked half of them to play the role of someone being told (s)he had lung cancer (the treatment group), while the rest of the subjects listened to the same information contained on a taped role-play session (the control group). Attitude questionnaires completed afterwards by everyone in the two groups indicated that the role-playing treatment group became significantly more convinced than the control group that smoking causes lung cancer. People in the treatment group also significantly decreased the number of cigarettes smoked daily, when that dependent variable was measured 8 and 18 months later.

Experimental researchers also often manipulate an independent variable by exposing subjects to different levels of it. "Level" usually refers to a higher or lower amount of a variable. Mongeau (1989), for example, studied the extent to which three independent variables influence persuasion. Two were personality variables: "need for cognition" (defined as the enjoyment derived from engaging in effortful information processing) and "argumentativeness" (defined as a predisposition to advocate positions on controversial issues); the third was a message variable: argument quality. Subjects were first categorized as having high or low needs for cognition and as being either high or low on argumentativeness, based on their responses to two questionnaires. All subjects were then exposed to a persuasive message—advocating that undergraduates should have to pass comprehensive examinations before graduating. Mongeau manipulated the quality of the arguments in the message by providing some subjects with strong arguments and others with weak arguments (amount of argument strength was determined in a previous study). One finding showed that subjects exposed to strong arguments were disposed more favorably toward the message than those who received weak arguments. Only a main effect for argument quality was found in this factorial experiment; an interaction effect was not found, as the relationship between argument quality and attitudes was not affected by individuals' need for cognition or their argumentativeness.

Finally, experimental researchers often combine the two aforementioned manipulations by exposing subjects to different levels of an independent variable, as well as including a control group that does not receive the manipulation. If a researcher wants to know, for example, whether the effectiveness of role-playing for changing attitudes is influenced by monetary incentives, one group of subjects could be paid a monetary reward to role-play (say $20.00), another group could role-play but not receive any monetary reward, and a control group would not role-play at all. Comparing these three groups would demonstrate whether the monetary reward was an important variable and whether role-playing was or was not a persuasive technique.

All researchers who conduct full experiments manipulate, and thereby control, subjects' exposure to an independent variable. Researchers must be assured, however, that an experimental manipulation is what it purports to be. For example, if a researcher wishes to study the effect of a threatening message on compliance, the research subjects must indeed perceive the message as threatening; otherwise, the experimental manipulation is not valid. Experimenters, therefore, will conduct **manipulation checks** to see whether the independent variable manipulation was successful. They might, for example, establish a "threat" level the message must surpass and then ask subjects in the treatment group to rate how threatening they felt the message to be. If their rating was above that level, the researchers substantiate their claim that the variable is what they are testing.

Once the manipulation of the independent variable occurs, researchers measure its effects on the dependent variable through questionnaires, interviews, and/or observations. In some cases, they measure the dependent variable both before the manipulation (called a **pretest**) as well as after (called a **posttest**), and the change in scores from the pretest to the posttest is then compared.

Randomly Assigning Subjects to Experimental Conditions

Measuring the effects of an independent variable manipulation in a full experiment obviously requires a comparison between at least two groups (a treatment group and a control group or two treatment groups). But this comparison is meaningful only to the extent that the experimental groups start off equivalent. What happens if the groups are not equivalent initially? Suppose a researcher is testing whether receiving a threatening message (a scare tactic) produces more compliance than a message promising a reward, but the treatment groups are not equivalent initially with respect to another variable that affects compliance. Let us assume that subjects with a high level of education are persuaded less easily than those with less education. Say one experimental group is composed of college graduates and most subjects in another group have only a high school education, and then a significant difference is found between these two groups. Is the difference due to the different messages or the difference in their levels of education? We can't be sure unless both groups are equivalent at the start.

Subjects' levels of education are relatively easy to measure and to take into account, but in most experiments a whole host of variables can potentially influence the dependent variable, including some of which the researcher may not be aware. Experimental researchers, therefore, must somehow increase the chances that the groups start off equivalent in every conceivable way.

The technique used in full experiments to accomplish this goal is called **random assignment of subjects to groups.** Random assignment allows all research subjects an equal chance of being assigned to any of the different experimental conditions. For example, if a study involves two experimental conditions, subjects can be assigned randomly to one or the other by flipping a coin, putting names in a hat and drawing them out, or by using a table of random numbers.

Random assignment of subjects to groups is the best assurance that all initial differences between subjects will be distributed evenly across experimental conditions. It does not guarantee equivalent groups (even a coin tossed 10 times might come up all heads), but it provides the best statistical odds that the groups will start off equivalent. Hence, random assignment of subjects to groups is a requirement for a full experiment. However, if a researcher wants additional assurance that experimental groups are equivalent initially with respect to particular variables, subjects can be measured on those variables and their scores compared.

Accounting for the Influence of Extraneous Variables

Researchers must try to control for the influence of other variables that might threaten the validity of conclusions about a causal relationship between the independent and dependent variables. Random assignment helps ensure that an experiment's results are not due to initial differences between subjects in the experimental conditions. Researchers also try to control for the influence of extraneous variables in several other ways.

Researchers, for example, often try to control the effects due to their own participation in the research. A researcher may inadvertently influence subjects' responses by encouraging them to respond in a particular way (perhaps with a smile, increased eye contact, or head nods when certain answers are given). To control for this potential problem, researchers often employ assistants unfamiliar with the research hypotheses to run the experiment. They also occasionally employ trained **confederates** (people taught to act consistently in predetermined ways when interacting with subjects). To study how people respond to differently worded requests, for example, researchers might train confederates to ask a number of strangers for a favor in two distinctly different ways. The goal in both cases is to minimize the effects of researchers' behavior on subjects.

Experimenters also take great care to make sure all their research procedures are valid, thereby increasing the *confidence level* of their findings. They often rehearse their research procedures in trial runs, called **pilot studies,** or, as just described, they use manipulation checks to make sure each fulfills its intentions. They also try to minimize the influence of the external environment on subjects' responses. Some researchers even make sure there are no differences in the laboratory rooms used, the time of day the study is conducted, or the sound, light, and temperature to which groups of subjects are exposed.

Finally, and probably most important, experimenters try to account for the effects of **confounding variables** they suspect might influence the relationship between an independent and dependent variable. When studying persuasive messages, for example, the fact that the speaker is male or female may influence subjects' reactions. To account for this possibility, a researcher might tape a male and a female delivering the same speech and show half the subjects the male's speech, the other half the female's. In this way, a potentially confounding variable (gender) becomes another independent variable manipulation to see whether it actually does affect the dependent variable.

These are just some of the ways experimental researchers try to control for the influence of extraneous variables. To assess the degree of causality between variables, they must be confident that changes in the dependent variable are due to changes in the independent variable, not extraneous and unaccounted-for variables.

Strengths and Limitations of the Full Experimental Method

The primary strength of full experiments lies in the extent to which researchers exercise control over the procedures used. This high degree of control, facilitated in a laboratory, maximizes the **internal validity** of full experimental research, or the accuracy of the findings. If the procedures are valid and reliable, then the conclusions that can be drawn from the experiment about causal relationships between independent and dependent variables will be accurate.

Full experimental research is often criticized, however, for its lack of **external validity,** or the degree to which results can be generalized from a particular study to other people and settings. External validity is maximized in three ways: (1) when subjects are representative of the population to which the results are being applied; (2) when research is replicated and leads to consistent findings; and (3) when a study demonstrates **ecological validity,** or reflects real-life circumstances. Critics question most whether laboratory full experimental research is ecologically valid. They argue that the highly controlled procedures used do not reflect real-life circumstances, and thus the findings have limited generalizability.

Laboratory full experimental research, therefore, maximizes internal validity, but sometimes at the expense of external validity. Research methodologists, such as Campbell and Stanley (1963) and Cook and Campbell (1979), argue, however, that internal validity is more important than external validity. After all, why generalize findings that are not accurate? Some experimental researchers also recognize the need to increase the external validity of their findings and frequently conduct experiments in the field (discussed in the next chapter).

QUESTIONS FOR EXAMINING FULL
EXPERIMENTAL RESEARCH

In addition to the general questions posed about research from Chapter 1, several criteria apply specifically to reading and evaluating full experimental research. Keep these questions in mind when reading the following study or any other article that uses a full experimental method.

A. *Evaluating the Hypotheses*

1. How precise are the *hypotheses?* Is each a clearly worded, simple, single cause-effect prediction?

2. Are the hypotheses likely to be borne out? Does the researcher provide a clear *rationale* for the hypothesis based on theory, review of the literature, or logic?

3. Does each hypothesis predict a clear *causal relationship* between the specific independent and dependent variables? Does the hypothesis predict specifically how the independent variable will influence the dependent variable (by increasing or decreasing it), called a **directional causal** relationship, or does the hypothesis predict that the independent variable will influence the dependent variable but does not specify how, called a **nondirectional causal relationship.**

4. Are the hypotheses *interesting* or are they self-evident?

5. Are the hypotheses *significant* or newsworthy? Will the results be worth the effort to obtain them? Will they prove useful in developing a broader theory of communication behavior or in guiding the behavior of an educator, a communication practitioner and/or the general public?

B. *Manipulating the Independent Variable and Measuring the Dependent Variable*

1. How successful was the *manipulation* of the independent variable? Did the researcher conduct a *manipulation check* to determine how well the desired experimental condition(s) was produced? Did the researcher run a *pilot study* to make sure the experimental procedures were effective?

2. Was the manipulation of the independent variable *ecologically valid?* Was it "lifelike" enough to allow the researcher to generalize the findings beyond the confines of this particular experiment?

3. Were the questionnaires, interviews, or observations used to *measure the dependent variable valid* or accurate? If the dependent variable was measured both before and after the manipulation of an independent variable, is it possible that the pretest sensitized subjects to the posttest? That is, could subjects' scores on the posttest be influenced by having taken the pretest?

C. Randomly Assigning Subjects to Experimental Conditions

1. Were subjects *randomly assigned* to the experimental groups? Did everyone studied in the experiment have an equal chance of being assigned to the different experimental conditions?

2. Were *pretests* needed, and if so, used, to determine whether the experimental groups started off relatively equal with respect to one or more important variables?

D. Controlling for the Influence of Extraneous Variables

1. Did the researcher take sufficient precautions to minimize the effects of his or her behavior on subjects' responses, such as the **researcher personal attribute effect**, which occurs when particular characteristics of the researcher (like age or race) affect subjects' responses, or the **researcher unintentional expectancy effect**, which occurs when researchers inadvertently let subjects know what responses they desire? Did the researcher use *research assistants* to conduct the experiment? Were trained *confederates* used if the experiment required a consistent interaction with the subjects?

2. Was the *influence of the environment* controlled or accounted for in the experiment? Was the laboratory setting(s) in which the research was conducted kept consistent for all subjects, thus minimizing its influence on their responses?

3. Might the findings be due to *other events* that occurred between the time subjects experienced the independent variable and when they were measured on the dependent variable? Did any events in the outside environment impinge on subjects in any way?

4. Did the conditions of the study threaten the internal validity of the experiment? For example, people's responses may be biased by the **Hawthorne effect,** the tendency for people to change their behavior when they know they are being observed? Did the fact that subjects had to *volunteer* or agreed to be studied produce a biased sample of people?

5. Were subjects *selected randomly* from the population of interest, thus maximizing the external validity of the research findings?

6. Might the results be due to *statistical regression*, the tendency for subjects selected on the basis of extreme pretest scores (i.e., measuring hippies' liberal tendencies during the 1960s) to "regress" back toward a more average level on subsequent measurements (i.e., finding that these same individuals are much less liberal in the 1990s)?

7. Was there much **subject mortality,** dropping out or loss of subjects during the period of time the study was conducted?

8. Did **maturation**—internal changes within subjects over the course of

the experiment (such as becoming tired or being influenced by other sources)—influence subjects' responses?

9. What precautions were taken to minimize **intersubject bias,** subjects influencing one another's responses (perhaps by being in the same room during the experiment or by talking with future subjects about the experiment)?

10. Were *important extraneous variables* that may confound the findings controlled for? Can you think of anything else that might have influenced the results? Might these variables have been included as additional experimental manipulations (or were they assessed through pretests and their effects factored out by using appropriate statistical procedures)?

THE ILLUSTRATIVE STUDY

The study you will read deals with the general area of "person perception" or "social cognition," that is, how people think about each other and how those thoughts influence social judgments and behavior. Douglas investigates whether anticipating interaction with an unknown person causes people to seek information about that person more vigilantly than usual and, specifically, what type of information they recall about the target person after observing him or her interacting with another.

We tend to judge people hastily, on little information, usually using our stereotypes about their social groups (on such bases as gender, age, job, and family). Occasionally, we are in a situation in which we will interact with a person we have heard about but have never met, like a blind date with someone that a friend has told us about or a friend of a friend who comes to visit. Research shows that we seek and recall more information about an unknown person we expect to interact with than about a person with whom we don't expect interaction.

Suppose we have a chance to observe that person interacting with someone else prior to our meeting. What information would we pay attention to and recall? We can answer this question by comparing people's information-seeking behavior and subsequent recall when they know they will interact with the person *before* observing the interaction, as opposed to knowing immediately *after* observing.

To better understand this aspect of person perception, Douglas conducts a full experiment in a laboratory in which the independent variable, anticipated interaction, is manipulated. The dependent variables are information-seeking and recall.

Anticipated Interaction and Information Seeking

William Douglas
University of Houston

The information that persons possess about others influences social judgments and behavior. Previous analyses have shown that, when expecting to meet with a target, persons recall comparatively more information about the target. Those analyses, however, have provided no indication as to the type of information persons recall nor the range of recall across an action sequence. Moreover, there is no present understanding of the recall performance of persons who observe a target prior to being induced to expect interaction, although such a situation may be common in social contexts. This analysis sought to address these issues. Subjects viewed a videotaped interaction between a female (target) and a male. Subsequent analysis of subjects' recall revealed meaningful between-group differences.

1　A recurrent theme of communication inquiry has been that social information influences persons' attributions and behavior (Berger & Calabrese, 1975; Delia, Clark, & Switzer, 1979; Miller & Steinberg, 1975). Although recent research has illustrated that actors are not
5　habitually engaged in information-seeking (Langer, 1978; Langer & Imber, 1980; Langer & Weinman, 1981; Taylor & Fiske, 1978) and do not necessarily use information optimally (Fischhoff, 1976; Kahneman & Tversky, 1973; Nisbet & Ross, 1980; Tversky & Kahneman, 1973, 1974), there is continuing reason to suppose that, in particular
10　situations, persons do actively seek out information about target others and that such information affects subsequent judgments and communication behavior (Hewes & Planalp, 1982; Kruglanski & Ajzen, 1983; Sillars, 1982).

　　One such situation appears to be when persons *anticipate interac-*
15　*tion* with another (Berger, 1979). Harvey, Yarkin, Lightner, and Town (1980), for example, have reported that subjects who expected to interact with a stranger and who were given the opportunity to view the stranger in a group discussion subsequently recalled more information about that person than did subjects in a "no anticipated inter-
20　action" condition. Similarly, persons have been shown to recall more

Source: Douglas, W. (1985). Anticipated interaction and information seeking. *Human Communication Research, 12,* 243–258. Copyright © 1985 by International Communication Association. Reprinted by permission of Sage Publications, Inc.

William Douglas (Ph.D., Northwestern University, 1982), is assistant professor, School of Communication, University of Houston—University Park, 4800 Calhoun, Houston, TX 77004.

information about persons they expect to date than persons who are not potential dating partners (Berscheid, Graziano, Monson, & Dermer, 1976).

25　　Although these analyses suggest that anticipated interaction induces increased vigilance and, therefore, increased recall of target information, the analyses leave several questions unanswered. Specifically: (1) What kinds of target data do observers typically recall? (2) Relative to persons not expecting to meet with another, do those anticipating interaction attend more closely to the target only (and, so, 30　recall more target data) or is their increased target recall a function of more generally raised attention levels? (3) Does anticipation of future interaction affect input or retrieval of information?

Observation and Information

Although prior research has demonstrated that observers expecting 35　to meet with another have increased target recall, the global (i.e., aggregate) measures of recall used in that research provide no evidence of the kinds of information observers retrieve. During initial encounters, persons consistently exchange information concerning *demographics, experiences, general knowledge,* and *opinions and preferences* 40　(Berger, 1973; Rubin, 1977, 1979). Because both initial observation and initial interaction imply "getting to know" another, observers and interactants are likely to exhibit a general concern for the same kinds of target information. Unlike actors, however, observers have the opportunity to acquire information regarding a target's *interaction be-* 45　*havior* before meeting (Does he or she ask a lot of questions? What sort of language does he or she use?). Moreover, such information may function to reduce observers' behavioral uncertainty (Berger, 1979). Knowing that a target asks few questions, for example, may suggest to an observer that it is necessary to disclose more information than is 50　typical or to be unusually directive in order to sustain interaction with the target. Thus, subsequent analyses examined observers' recall of demographic, experience, general knowledge, opinion/preference, and interaction performance data.

Anticipated Interaction and Information-Seeking

55　Persons prefer to view others in interactive situations (Berger & Douglas, 1981) so that actors other than a target may routinely compete for observers' attention. Because previous studies have consistently tested subjects' retrieval of information clearly associated with a *target* (e.g., his or her dress, nonverbal activity, opinions), they do not 60　detail the extent of observers' recall. That is, previous analyses do not indicate whether the superior recall exhibited by persons expecting

self-target interaction is local to target others or general across interactants.

65 The connectivity of social interaction would seem to mandate that
increased sensitivity to a target be associated with increased sensitivity
to persons interacting with that target. Moreover, although observers
anticipating interaction may be distracted by self-reflection (Harvey et
al., 1980), passive observers typically display such low levels of attention
(Kahneman, 1973; Ross, 1977) that any attention-switching effects
70 (Broadbent, 1958; Norman & Bobrow, 1975; White & Carlston, 1983)
are likely only to attenuate a general disparity between the sequence
recall of persons (not) anticipating interaction. That disparity, however,
may be limited to particular *kinds* of information.

During first encounters, persons appear relatively uninterested
75 in others' general knowledge. Rubin (1977), for example, has reported
that initial interactants asked significantly fewer questions about this
subject than about demographics, opinions, and experiences. Berger
and Kellermann (1983), too, have observed that only 13% of questions
asked during a first meeting were judged to be general information
80 requests. These analyses suggest that information about another's
general knowledge does not reduce interactants' uncertainty. As such,
observers who anticipate interaction are likely to exhibit a similar bias
because their information-seeking, too, is presumed to fulfill an uncertainty reducing function.

85 The absence of prior research makes the case concerning persons' attention to others' interaction behavior less clear. However, because such information seems likely to reduce observers' behavioral
uncertainty, there is reason to suppose that persons anticipating interaction will be comparatively more sensitive to (and, therefore, more
90 able to recall) interactants' conversation behavior.

*(H1) Persons who expect to meet with a target will recall more information
about interactants' demographics, experiences, preferences/opinions, and interaction performance than will persons who do not anticipate interaction.*

Anticipated Interaction and
95 ### the Availability of Information

Observers have been shown to recall more target information when
induced to expect interaction *prior* to viewing a target. Because cognitive schemata are posited to be an attention-directing mechanism
(Streitz, 1982; Tesser, 1978), such effects are likely to accrue from
100 instantiation of different schema by persons in "anticipated" and "no
anticipated interaction" groups. However, because encoding and retrieval are not necessarily governed by the same schema (Flammer &

Tauber, 1982), one cannot be certain whether between-group differences occur at input, retrieval, or both. That is, there is no present
105   understanding of the likely performance of persons who are induced
to anticipate interaction *after* observing a target. Moreover, because
actors often have the opportunity to view others (with whom they do
not expect to interact), retrieval of passively acquired target information may be characteristic of many social encounters.

110   Although input-operative schemata establish an upper limit for
performance on subsequent memory tasks (Moscovitch & Craik,
1976), Anderson and Pichert (1978) have demonstrated that persons'
recall can be altered by postobservation manipulation of schema perspective. In this case, subjects' free recall of a narrative changed in
115   conjunction with a shift in their perspective (a homebuyer and a burg-
lar). Similarly, persons provided different observational goals (impression formation or task learning) process and recall ongoing action
dissimilarly (Cohen, 1981; Cohen & Ebbesen, 1979). Thus, there is
reason to suspect that the recall of persons in traditional conditions
120   differs from that of persons induced to expect interaction after they
have observed a target. Such persons must apply interactive schema to
passively acquired action in memory. As such, some information is
likely to be unavailable.

125   *(H2) The amount and type of information recalled by persons induced to expect interaction after viewing a target will differ from that of passive
observers and persons who expect interaction before viewing a target.*

METHODOLOGY

Subjects

Subjects were 21 males and 34 females enrolled in undergraduate
130   courses at the University of Houston. Within sex, subjects were dis-
persed evenly across conditions; 8 males were assigned to the "expect
interaction before viewing" condition, 6 were assigned to the "expect
interaction after viewing" condition, and 7 males received no instruction they were to meet with the target. Subjects' participation in the
135   study was voluntary and the study was conducted outside of regular
class meetings.

Stimulus Materials

Subjects in each of the experimental conditions viewed a videotaped
portrayal of an initial encounter between a male and a female. The
140   context of an initial interaction was selected because persons have

been shown to hold common expectations regarding the sequence in which information is characteristically exchanged in initial encounters (Berger, Gardner, Clatterbuck, & Schulman, 1976) and to enact similar behaviors during such encounters (Duck, 1980); that is, persons
145   share an "initial interaction" script (Douglas, 1983). In that scripts define between-role relationships (Schank & Abelson, 1977), the presentation of a scripted sequence was designed to minimize the time that subjects spent trying to "figure out" the context and the relationship between the male and female because this is likely to be informa-
150   tion that persons generally possess when observing target others, especially others with whom they expect to interact. Because of these concerns, the meeting was designed to be representative of a typical initial interaction. Thus, the interactants discussed the male's recent trip to Europe, a popular movie, an increase in the female's college
155   tuition, and the male's occupation. No attempt was made to "build into" the sequence specific types of information because this may have produced an interaction judged to be *atypical* of initial encounters so that observers exhibited *atypical* attention levels. Nonetheless, different types of information were exchanged; for example, together with
160   demographic data, the male and female talked about their experiences in Europe, the female disclosed her fear of flying, and both expressed opinions regarding the local economy. The sequence lasted 2 minutes and 20 seconds and was videotaped in color.

Procedures

165   Subject viewed the videotape in groups of 4–6. They were informed that multiple studies concerning initial interactions were being conducted concurrently but that each involved viewing the same videotape. This deception was given verbally and was repeated on the first page of the test booklet. Subjects were randomly assigned to the
170   experimental conditions. Each subject was provided a test booklet and told to read the first page only. Common to all conditions was the following information; (1) multiple studies were being conducted simultaneously, each concerned first encounters, (2) subjects were to see a videotaped reenactment of an actual conversation between a
175   male and a female who had never met before, (3) the persons in the videotape were those involved in the actual conversation, and (4) the conversation took place at a party. Subjects in the expected interaction before viewing condition were also informed they were to interact with the female after viewing the videotape. Subjects were then pre-
180   sented with the videotaped sequence.
        After they had seen the sequence, subjects moved to separate areas of the room. This was designed to reduce the likelihood that

persons would discover they were in the same study. Subjects then
progressed through the test booklet. The following tasks were re-
185 quired of all subjects and were presented in the order they are presented here: (1) indicate on a 0–100, 10-point interval scale the ap-
proximate proportion of the time they had spent attending to the
male and (2) indicate whether they felt the conversation they had seen
was "very abnormal," "abnormal," "somewhat abnormal," "somewhat
190 normal," "normal," or "very normal." At this point, persons in the
expected interaction after viewing condition encountered an insert
informing them they were to interact with the female. Like all other
subjects, they were then required to: (3) indicate all they had seen or
heard about the male that was informative and (4) repeat step 3 in
195 regard to the female. When they had completed all tasks, subjects
returned their booklet to the test administrator. Those who expected
to meet with the female were led from the room individually and
collected in an adjacent area; those who had no expectation of interaction were sent directly to the waiting area. When all subjects in a
200 group had finished all tasks, the group was debriefed as a unit.

RESULTS

Focus of Attention

In order to provide some test of the "anticipated interaction" manipulation, subjects' self-report estimates of the proportion of total view-
205 ing time spent watching the male were entered into a completely
randomized ANOVA. This analysis revealed significant differences
between the groups (no expected interaction mean = 45.0, expected
interaction after viewing mean = 48.3, expected interaction before
reviewing mean = 33.2; $F(2,52) = = 13.66$, $p < .001$). A subsequent
210 Newman-Keuls multiple comparison test demonstrated that persons
who anticipated interaction with the female prior to viewing the videotape reported spending less time watching the male (and, by inference, more time watching the female) than did persons in either of
the other conditions.

215   ### Sequence Normality

In order to ensure t ıat the videotaped sequence was not perceived as
atypical of initial interactions, thus prompting subjects to become unusually attentive, the subjects' ratings of sequence normality were entered as the dependent variable in a second ANOVA. This analysis
220 revealed no significant between-group differences ($F < 1$). Moreover,
the three cell means ranged from a low of 4.3 to a high of 4.5; that is,
all groups rated the sequence as "somewhat normal" to "normal."

Sequence Recall

All items that subjects had indicated to be informative regarding the
225   interactants were typed on to cards and given to two independent
judges. The judges were required to assign each item to one of five
categories; information concerning interactants' (1) demographics,
(2) personal experiences, (3) opinions and preferences, (4) interaction
performance, and (5) general knowledge. The judges were instructed
230   to keep separate any items they concluded could not be appropriately
classified.

Interjudge agreement on this task (number of agreements divided by number of decisions) was .97 for items concerning the
female (n of items = 270) and .98 for items concerning the male (n of
235   items = 242). Neither judge assigned any item to the "cannot be
classified" category and judges conferred in cases of disagreement.
Thus, 512 items of data clustered into five categories were incorporated into subsequent analyses.

Two sets of dependent measures were generated; (1) the num-
240   ber of female-related items referenced by each subject (one for each
information category) and (2) the number of male-related items referenced by each subject (one for each information category). Because
so few items were assigned to the "general knowledge" (female = 5,
male = 14) and "interaction performance" categories (female = 7,
245   male = 8), those categories were excluded from further analyses.
Thus, data concerning the female's and male's demographics, experiences, opinions and preferences were entered as the dependent variables in a completely randomized MANOVA.

This analysis revealed significant multivariate effects (Pillais's
250   F[12, 96] = 3.99, p < .001). Inspection of the univariate tests showed
significant between-group differences in regard to subjects' recall of (1)
female demographic items (F[2, 52] = 8.09, p. = .001, η^2 = .24) and (2)
female and *male opinion/preference* items (female items, F[2, 52] = 6.44,
p = .003, η^2 = .20; male items, F[2, 52] = 7.56, p = .001, η^2 = .23).
255   A series of Newman-Keuls multiple comparison tests showed
that (1) persons who anticipated meeting the female *prior* to viewing
the videotape recalled more target demographic items than other
subjects, and (2) subjects in the expected interaction before viewing
and expected interaction after viewing groups recalled more female
260   *and* more male opinion/preference items than their counterparts in
the no expected interaction condition.

In summary, this analysis revealed that: (1) Most of the information (93.3%) retrieved by subjects concerned interactants' demographics (40.4%), experiences (27.1%), and opinions and preferences
265   (25.8%); (2) relative to persons in the other groups, those in the
expected interaction before viewing condition recalled more target

TABLE 1
Female Data by Information Category

Category		N of Items
(1)	Demographic	
	College attending	43
	Degree major	23
	College classification	15
	Hometown	17
	Cultural heritage	20
	Total	118
(2)	Personal Experiences	
	Vacation	29
	Tuition increase	19
	Movies seen	6
	Summer residence	9
	Total	63
(3)	Opinions/Preferences	
	Fear of flying	24
	Value of education	18
	Like of alcohol	16
	Anxiety of job-hunting	8
	Actors (dis)liked	3
	Movies (dis)liked	2
	Enjoys travelling	6
	Total	77
(4)	Interaction Performance	
	Initiated conversation	4
	Language used	3
	Total	7
(5)	General Knowledge	
	History of Europe	2
	Local economy	3
	Total	5
Total		270

(i.e., female) demographic information; (3) relative to passive observers, those anticipating interaction (both prior and subsequent to viewing the videotape) recalled more items concerning the target's
270 opinions and preferences and the male's opinions and preferences; (4) recall of experience data was uninfluenced by the independent variable; and (5) subjects in all conditions exhibited poor recall of general knowledge and interaction performance data.

DISCUSSION

275 Most generally, these results suggest that observers' target uncertainty is influenced primarily by demographic and opinion/preference information. Although subjects recalled information concerning the in-

teractants' experiences, retrieval of such data did not vary across conditions. Further, items assigned to the general knowledge and in-
280   teraction performance categories accounted for only 6.7% of all items
listed (female, 4.4%; male, 9.1%). Examination of information-seeking
during initial encounters further supports the suggestion that uncertainty reduction is contingent upon persons' ability to access demographic and opinion/preference information. Berger and Keller-
285   mann (1983), for example, have reported that approximately 50% of
initial interactants' questions were inquiries for demographic and
attitudinal information. Moreover, examination of subjects' self-
reports showed that 87% of question-asking strategies dealing with
information content could be classified as attempts to acquire either

TABLE 2
Male Data by Information Category

Category	N of Items
(1) Demographic	
Lack of college education	36
Occupation	28
Employer	21
Hometown	4
Total	89
(2) Personal Experiences	
Vacation	45
Movies seen	13
Applied for new job	9
Spending in Europe	9
Total	76
(3) Opinions/Preferences	
Unhappy in job	14
Movies liked	10
Concern for money	11
Bored by flying	8
Enjoys travel	4
Actors (dis)liked	4
Like of alcohol	4
Total	55
(4) Interaction Performance	
Offered a drink	5
Did not initiate conversation	2
Language used	1
Total	8
(5) General Knowledge	
Events/places in Europe	8
Local unemployment	6
Total	14
Total	242

TABLE 3
Number of Items Listed—Group Means and Standard Deviations

	Anticipated Interaction					
	(1) Before		(2) After		(3) None	
Target: Female						
(a) Demographic	2.95	(1.13)	1.72	(1.02)	1.83	(0.92)
(b) Experience	1.16	(0.83)	1.00	(1.03)	1.28	(0.96)
(c) Preference	1.58	(1.02)	1.83	(0.92)	0.78	(0.81)
Target: Male						
(a) Demographic	1.89	(0.81)	1.50	(0.79)	1.28	(1.02)
(b) Experience	1.53	(1.26)	1.56	(1.04)	1.11	(0.68)
(c) Preference	1.37	(1.16)	1.33	(1.08)	0.28	(0.46)
	n = 19		n = 18		n = 18	

290 biographic/demographic or attitude/opinion information about a partner.

More specifically, the analysis suggests the effects of anticipated interaction are relatively limited. Usual comparisons of persons expecting interaction with those not expecting interaction would have
295 argued that persons who observe others with whom they do not anticipate interaction have less complete recall of demographic *and* opinion/preference information for both targets and targets' cointerlocutors. The performance of subjects in the expected interaction *after* viewing group, however, shows that information concerning interac-
300 tants' opinions and preferences can be retrieved even when input is not goal-driven. Their recall of opinion preference information was equal to that of subjects in the expected interaction before viewing group and both groups outperformed their counterparts in the no expected interaction condition.
305 This suggests, too, that demographic and opinion/preference information are obtained in different ways. Perhaps because it has such high attributional value (Berger, 1979), personal information may be acquired automatically and remain available, even to passive observers. Acquisition of demographic information, meanwhile, ap-
310 pears to require effort. Recall of such information was significantly improved only when subjects were induced to expect interaction before viewing the videotape. Compared to other observers, therefore, those anticipating interaction appear to seek out more vigorously demographic information only, particularly that associated with a target.
315 This analysis provided no evidence that the superior target recall routinely shown by persons expecting to encounter another derives from increased attention to the target only. Instead, conversa-

tional memory appears to be sequence-based so that information concerning a target is conjoined to similar information (i.e., con-
320   tiguously exchanged information) concerning a target's cointerac-tants. Persons retrieved (or failed to retrieve) opinion/preference in-formation in consistent ways across interactants. Moreover, although analysis of subjects' recall of demographic information revealed sig-nificant between-group differences only in regard to the female, per-
325   sons in the expected interaction before viewing group also tended to recall more male-related demographic items.

Subjects' recall of experience information was stable across con-ditions. This was unexpected because such information has potential conversational value (suggesting topics of discussion), especially to
330   persons anticipating interaction. Kellermann and Broetzmann (1984), however, have demonstrated that during initial encounters talk con-cerning personal experiences is extended, commonly involving de-clarative statements, questioning, discussion, evaluation, and explana-tion. Interactants in this study talked of their experiences in a similar
335   way. Conversation of the male's vacation, for example, was initiated by the male as a statement of fact (I went to Europe this summer); this was followed by an inquiry/discussion phase (Did you spend any time in Paris? Did you go to the Louvre?); the conversation about this issue terminated with the pair making general evaluative statements (We
340   really enjoyed it) accompanied by some explanation (because the life style was very different). Such prolonged discussion may have made information about the interactants' experiences sufficiently salient to be resistant to treatment effects. Nonetheless, because the videotaped sequence was judged typical of first meetings, acquisition of informa-
345   tion concerning targets' experiences may be generally invariate.

Participants in the analysis recalled few items associated with either the female's or the male's general knowledge and interaction behavior. Observers' inattention to general knowledge information is consistent with persons' information seeking *during* first encounters
350   (Berger & Kellermann, 1983; Rubin, 1977), suggesting that social targets typically are not defined along evaluative dimensions associ-ated with expertise. As such, interactants' uncertainty, conversation behavior, and liking for others (Berger & Calabrese, 1975) are un-likely to be contingent upon estimates of targets' general knowledge.
355   Only 2.9% of all items recalled (female, 2.6%; male, 3.3%) were assigned to the interaction performance category. Although this per-haps indicates that observers' judgments are unaffected by targets' linguistic selections and conversation behavior, depressed recall of such information may be a methodological artifact. Participants were
360   informed that the videotaped sequence was a *reenactment* of an actual conversation. Because no effort was made to convince subjects of the sequence's immediacy, participants may have dismissed the interac-

tants' paralinguistic activity as not indicative of their characteristic (i.e., real life) performance.

365   In summary, this analysis provides further and more detailed support for the suggestion that, when anticipating interaction with another, observers are induced to become more vigilant. Persons expecting to meet with another appear not to attend exclusively to the target. Instead, their sequence recall is more generally complete than 370 that of passive observers. In particular, would-be interactants appear to reduce their uncertainty by seeking out information concerning a target's demographics and opinions and preferences, although demographic information is unavailable in memory when expectation of interaction does not precede observation.

REFERENCES

Anderson, R. C. & Pichert, J. W. (1978). Recall for previously unrecalled information following a shift in perspective. *Journal of Verbal Learning and Verbal Behavior, 17*, 1–12.

Berger, C. R. (1973). *The acquaintance process revisited: Explorations in initial interaction.* Paper presented at the annual convention of the Speech Communication Association, New York.

Berger, C. R. (1975). Proactive and retroactive attribution processes in interpersonal communications. *Human Communication Research, 2*, 33–50.

Berger, C. R. (1979). Beyond initial interaction: Uncertainty, understanding, and the development of interpersonal relationships. In H. Giles & R. St. Clair (Eds.), *Language and social psychology.* Oxford: Basil Blackwell.

Berger, C. R. & Calabrese, R. J. (1975). Some explorations in initial interactions and beyond: Toward a developmental theory of interpersonal communication. *Human Communication Research, 1*, 99–112.

Berger, C. R. & Douglas, W. (1981). Studies in interpersonal epistemology: III. Anticipated interaction, self-monitoring, and observational context selection. *Communication Monographs, 48*, 183–196.

Berger, C. R., Gardner, R. R., Clatterbuck, G. W., & Schulman, L. A. (1976). Perceptions in information sequencing in relationship development. *Human Communication Research, 3*, 29–46.

Berger, C. R. & Kellerman, K. (1983). To ask or not to ask: Is that a question? In R. Bostrom (Ed.), *Communication yearbook 7.* Beverly Hills, CA: Sage.

Berscheid, E., Graziano, W., Monson, T., & Dermer, M. (1976). Outcome dependency: Attention, attribution, and attraction. *Journal of Personality and Social Psychology, 34*, 978–989.

Broadbent, D. E. (1958). *Perception and communication.* New York: Pergamon Press.

Cohen, C. E. (1981). Goals and schemata in person perception: Making sense from the stream of behavior. In N. Cantor & J. H. Kihlstrom (Eds.),

Personality, cognition, and social interaction. Hillsdale, NJ: Lawrence Erlbaum.

Cohen, C. E. & Ebbesen, E. B. (1979). Observational goals and schema selection: A theoretical framework for behavior perception. *Journal of Experimental Social Psychology, 15,* 305–329.

Delia, J. G., Clark, R. A., & Switzer, D. E. (1979). The content of informal conversations as a function of interactants' interpersonal cognitive complexity. *Communication Monographs, 46,* 274–281.

Douglas, W. (1983). Scripts and self-monitoring: When does being a high self-monitor really make a difference? *Human Communication Research, 10,* 81–96.

Duck, S. W. (1980). Personal relationships research in the 1980's: Towards an understanding of complex human sociality. *Western Speech, 44,* 114–119.

Fischhoff, B. (1976). Attribution theory and judgment under uncertainty. In J. H. Harvey, W. Ickes, & R. F. Kidd (eds.), *News directions in attribution research* (Vol. 1). Hillsdale, NJ: Lawrence Erlbaum.

Flammer, A. & Tauber, M. (1982). Changing the reader's perspective. In G. E. Stelmach & P. A. Vroon (Eds.), *Advances in psychology* (Vol. 8). New York: North-Holland Publishing.

Harvey, J. H., Yarkin, K. L., Lightner, J. M., & Town, J. P. (1980). Unsolicited interpretation and recall of interpersonal events. *Journal of Personality and Social Psychology, 38,* 551–568.

Hewes, D. E. & Planalp, S. (1982). There is nothing as useful as a good theory: The influence of social knowledge on interpersonal communication. In M. E. Roloff & C. R. Berger (Eds.), *Social cognition and communication.* Beverly Hills, CA: Sage.

Kahneman, D. (1973). *Attention and effort.* Englewood Cliffs, NJ: Prentice-Hall.

Kahneman, D. & Tversky, A. (1973). On the psychology of prediction. *Psychological Review, 80,* 237–251.

Kellermann, K., & Berger, C. R. (1984). *Affect and the acquisition of social information: Sit back, relax, and tell me about yourself.* Paper presented at the annual convention of the International Communication Association, San Francisco.

Kellermann, K., & Broetzmann, S. (1984). *The sequential structure of initial interaction.* Paper presented at the annual convention of the Speech Communication Association, Chicago.

Kruglanski, A. W. & Ajzen, I. (1983). Bias and error in human judgment. *European Journal of Social Psychology, 10,* 1–44.

Langer, E. J. (1978). Rethinking the role of thought in social interaction. In J. H. Harvey, W. Ickes, & R. F. Kidd (Eds.), *New directions in attribution research* (Vol. 2). Hillsdale, NJ: Lawrence Erlbaum.

Langer, E. J. & Imber, L. G. (1980). Role of mindlessness in the perception of deviance. *Journal of Personality and Social Psychology, 39,* 360–367.

Langer, E. J. & Weinman, C. (1981). When thinking disrupts intellectual performance: Mindfulness on an overlearned task. *Personality and Social Psychology Bulletin, 7,* 240–243.

Miller, D. T., Norman, S. A., & Wright, E. (1978). Distortion in person perception as a consequence of effective control. *Journal of Personality and Social Psychology, 36,* 598–607.

Miller, G. R. & Steinberg, M. (1975). *Between people: A new analysis of interpersonal communication.* Chicago: Science Research Associates.

Moscovitch, M. & Craik, F. (1976). Depth of processing, retrieval cues, and uniqueness of encoding as factors in recall. *Journal of Verbal Learning and Verbal Behavior, 15,* 447–458.

Nisbett, R. E. & Ross, L. (1980). *Human inference: Strategies and shortcomings of social judgment.* Englewood Cliffs, NJ: Prentice-Hall.

Norman, D. A. & Bobrow, D. G. (1975). On data-limited processes. *Cognitive Psychology, 7,* 44–64.

Ross, L. (1977). The intuitive psychologist and his shortcomings: Distortions in the attribution process. In L. Berkowitz (Ed.), *Advances in experimental social psychology* (Vol. 10). New York: Academic Press.

Rubin, R. B. (1977). The role of context in information seeking and impression formation. *Communication Monographs, 44,* 81–90.

Rubin, R. B. (1979). The effect of context on information seeking across the span of initial interactions. *Communication Quarterly, 27,* 13–20.

Schank, R. C. & Abelson, R. F. (1977). *Scripts, plans, goals, and understanding.* New York: John Wiley.

Sillars, A. L. (1982). Attribution and communication: Are people "naive scientists" or just naive? In M. E. Roloff & C. R. Berger (Eds.), *Social cognition and communication.* Beverly Hills, CA: Sage.

Streitz, N. A. (1982). The role of problem orientations and goals in text comprehension and recall. In G. E. Stelmach & P. A. Vroon (Eds.), *Advances in psychology* (Vol. 8). New York: North-Holland Publishing.

Taylor, S. E. & Fiske, S. T. (1978). Salience, attention, and attribution: Top of the head phenomena. In L. Berkowitz (Ed.), *Advances in experimental social psychology* (Vol. 11). New York: Academic Press.

Tesser, A. (1978). Self-generated attitude change. In L. Berkowitz (Ed.), *Advances in experimental social psychology* (Vol. 1). New York: Academic Press.

Tversky, A. & Kahneman, D. (1973). Availability: A heuristic for judging frequency and probability. *Cognitive Psychology, 5,* 207–232.

Tversky, A. & Kahneman, D. (1974). Judgment under uncertainty: Heuristics and biases. *Science, 185,* 1124–1131.

White, J. D. & Carlston, D. E. (1983). Consequences of schemata for attention, impressions, and recall in complex social interactions. *Journal of Personality and Social Psychology, 45,* 538–549.

COMMENTS ON THE STUDY

Introduction, Review of the Literature, and Hypotheses

Douglas begins by framing his experiment within the context of prior research (1–32). He shows how previous research established a causal link between anticipated interaction and increased vigilance in information-seeking (14–23). Previous research, however, failed to answer some important questions about the relationship between anticipated interaction and other aspects of information-seeking and recall. These questions include what *types* of information observers recall; whether *observation* of a target person with whom one expects to interact leads only to heightened information-seeking about the target or whether it raises one's *general* attention level (thereby leading people to pay more attention to both interactants); and how *anticipated future interaction* affects information recall (24–32).

Douglas also wants his study to contribute to developing communication *theory*. Therefore, he advances two *hypotheses* based on three theoretical perspectives (34–126). The first theory, *uncertainty reduction* (see Berger & Calabrese, 1975), maintains that one important purpose of communication is to reduce uncertainty. If this is correct, situations that heighten participants' uncertainty (such as initial interactions) will lead to increased information-seeking in order to reduce that uncertainty. Douglas' first hypothesis predicts, therefore, that those who expect to interact with a person will recall more information that reduces uncertainty about the person (such as demographics, experiences, preferences/opinions, and interaction performance) than about someone with whom they do not anticipate interaction (91–93).

Second, *cognitive schemata theory* maintains that communication is driven by different situation-based schemata, or conceptual frames of reference. We use a different cognitive schema when interacting with a good friend, for example, than when we interact with a potential employee, and, consequently, we are bound to recall different information from these encounters. The third theory, *memory* or *recall theory*, suggests that what we remember depends upon whether circumstances make recalling information important (for instance, being told that we will be spending time in the future with someone we just met). If these theories are correct, Douglas' second hypothesis—which predicts that people will differ in the amount and type of information they recall based on whether they expected interaction *prior* to or *after* observing the target, and from those who do not expect interaction *at all* (124–126)—will be borne out.

This experiment is thus well grounded in contemporary theory and research. (Like most researchers, Douglas assumes readers know these theoretical perspectives, too.) This experiment attempts to extend our knowledge of communication theory and the causal effects of anticipated interaction on information-seeking.

Method

The subjects for this study were 65 students enrolled in undergraduate courses who volunteered for the experiment (129–136). These subjects, therefore, were not selected randomly from the population they represent (all adults, we presume), which, unfortunately, is true of most social science research. This is a **convenience** and **volunteer sample,** a sample of subjects—university students—who were easy to obtain and agreed to take part. Such samples are quite common. Indeed, Applebaum (1985) reports that 65.5% of published communication research uses samples from the college population.

We know from previous research, however, that volunteer subjects usually differ from nonvolunteer subjects in several ways. They have greater intellectual ability, interest, motivation, need for approval, and sociability, as well as less authoritarianism (Rosenthal, 1965). Findings from this group of subjects thus may not apply to the general population.

Subjects were assigned randomly to one of three conditions: expected interaction before viewing, expected interaction after viewing, and no expected interaction (130–134). This experiment, therefore, employs two treatment groups as well as a control group that does not receive the independent variable manipulation. Subjects were balanced across the experimental conditions with regard to gender, thereby negating the potential confounding effects from this variable.

Creative procedures were used in this study to elicit genuine responses from the subjects. They were brought into the laboratory setting and given a test booklet and told to read only the first page. Everyone received identical introductory information, except one-third of the subjects were told they would interact with the female in the videotape they were about to see (165–180). Subjects were then shown a two-minute videotape of the first meeting between a male and a female. After watching the tape, subjects moved to separate areas of the room and answered "distraction" questions irrelevant to the study about what portion of the viewing time they spent attending to the male and whether the conversation was "normal." At this point, another third of the subjects were told they would interact with the female from the videotape. Finally, subjects were asked questions about the dependent variable, to determine what they recalled about both interactants (181–195).

Douglas claims the script for the taped interaction was "typical" (138–163), so the subjects' responses were valid. Do you agree? Would people observing a brief videotape in a college laboratory experiment think and respond to it the same way they would if they were to be present when the same conversation took place at a real party? Do people "typically" get to overhear a two-minute conversation before meeting someone? In most first encounters, the parties speak to one another and are too self-conscious to note and recall much of what is said to them. So ecological validity is questionable.

Perhaps a more ecologically valid procedure would be to arrange for subjects to actually meet each other in a waiting room or at a "get-acquainted" reception. But then all the subjects would not have identical experiences. Another measurement limitation is the researcher's interest in what subjects recalled about the interactants' verbal behavior while ignoring impressions gleaned from their nonverbal behaviors. We know the latter have a large effect on person perception.

We must also wonder whether watching the videotape in groups of 4 to 6 created any *intersubject bias.* It could be that subjects influenced one another to pay more or less attention to the videotape. (If you are watching a movie and someone else in front of you looks away or laughs, you may be more inclined to do the same.) A more effective, although more time-consuming, method would have been to have each of the subjects watch the videotape alone.

We also must wonder whether there is a potential *confounding effect* due to the target's gender in this experiment. Douglas counterbalanced the experimental conditions with respect to males and females, but the antici-pated interaction manipulation concerned only the female in the vid-eotape. It is possible that men and women differ on how much attention they pay to females, which would influence the time they spent watching the target and the amount and type of information they recalled. Douglas did not analyze whether there were any differences between male and female subjects' recall, so we will never know whether the gender of the target person interacted with the gender of the subjects to influence the results. The experimental manipulation would have been more consistent if all the subjects would have anticipated interacting with a same-gender target. Or, if cross-gender perception is an important variable, then the gender of the target could have been manipulated.

We can be relatively assured, however, that the procedures probably produced little if any of the researcher effect that occurs when researchers influence subjects' responses. Because the experimenter (probably Douglas himself, although this is never indicated) provided and solicited all relevant information in a test booklet, he probably had little effect on the subjects.

Results

Douglas begins the results section by claiming that the anticipated interac-tion manipulation was successful (203–214). A statistical analysis called **Analysis of Variance** (ANOVA, or *F*-test) was used to determine whether there were significant differences between the treatment groups. All statistical analyses of differences between groups tell researchers the probability of obtaining the difference due to chance/error. If the analysis indicates differences are due to chance only 5% of the time (or less)—the **.05 probability level** (p = .05) is the minimum level of probability accepted in the social sciences—the findings are assumed to be due to the actual differences that exist between the groups. In this case, the analysis demonstrates that subjects who anticipated interaction spent significantly less time watching the male (and, by inference, significantly more time watching the female target with whom they expected to interact) than subjects in the other two conditions (p < .001). Douglas also reports that subjects in the three experimental conditions did not differ significantly in their ratings of how normal the videotaped interaction was, and that they perceived it as somewhere between "somewhat normal" and "normal" (216–222).

The manipulation check of the normalcy of the videotape is convincing. But the check for the manipulation of the anticipated interaction is only indirect. Just because subjects reported that they spent more time watching the target does not mean that they actually thought they would interact with her (perhaps they suspected this was a research ploy). Maybe Douglas should have asked them after the experiment was over (during the **debriefing** stage, when the entire experiment is explained to subjects [199–200]) if they really believed they would have to interact with the target. Still, it is reasonable to conclude that subjects in the anticipated interaction conditions did believe they would be interacting with the target.

Each piece of information the subjects recalled was typed onto cards and given to two independent judges who assigned each item to one of five categories: demographics, personal experiences, opinions/preferences, interaction performance, and general knowledge (224–231). These categories are not defined in the article, although the judges had little difficulty categorizing the informational items, since they agreed on 97% of the items for the female and 98% for the male (232–235). This high level of agreement indicates their placement of items into categories was consistent or *reliable*. It is helpful to have specific examples of each category provided in Table 1 and Table 2.

The statistical analyses performed on the data (239–273) show that most of the information recalled by subjects concerned demographics, experiences, and opinions/preferences, while general knowledge and interaction performance data were not easily recalled. Further, subjects who expected interaction before viewing recalled significantly more of the target's *demographic* information than subjects in the other two conditions. Both groups anticipating interaction recalled significantly more of *both* the female's and the male's *opinions and preferences* than subjects in the control group. Finally, recall of *experience* data was not affected by the anticipated interaction manipulation.

Discussion

The findings from this study shed light on communication theory by determining the effects of anticipated interaction on information-seeking and recall. Specifically, Douglas explains in the discussion section that observers *reduce their uncertainty* upon first meeting someone by concentrating primarily on learning demographic and opinion/preference information (275–291). There are few differences in the recall of information for those who expect interaction before or after observing. Persons in the group expecting interaction before viewing were more vigilant only in their recall of demographic information. Finally, subjects who expect interaction with an observed target person, in contrast to those who do not, pay more attention to both the target and the person with whom they interact, thus demonstrating that *anticipated interaction heightens general awareness* (315–326).

Douglas concludes the article by pointing out some limitations of the internal validity of the study (355–364). He does not, however, suggest directions for future research. What, specifically, do researchers need to study next about the process of person perception in initial interaction, or, more specifically, about the effects of anticipated interaction on information-seeking and recall? Perhaps researchers should investigate whether a target's and subject's gender influences information-seeking and recall, or whether subjects who evaluate a new person favorably or expect to *be* evaluated favorably seek and recall more information than those who form negative opinions or expect to be evaluated negatively. Studying what people recall about initial interactions more than a few minutes later (say an hour, a day, or a week later) would also be interesting.

Conclusion

Douglas' research gives us an opportunity to examine closely the full experimental method conducted in a laboratory setting. When researchers manipulate subjects' exposure to an independent variable, measure its effects on a dependent variable, randomly assign subjects to experimental conditions, and attempt to control for the influence of extraneous or potentially confounding variables, the full experimental method is a powerful technique for investigating the causal links between variables.

QUESTIONS AND ACTIVITIES TO CONSIDER

1. What is one apparent strength and one weakness, as indicated in this study, of using the full experimental method to study communication behavior?

2. This chapter has shown that experiments are potentially affected by lots of internal validity threats. Can you think of any additional internal validity threats, not discussed in this chapter, that may have affected Douglas' experiment?

3. As mentioned in this chapter, laboratory experiments are often criticized for not being ecologically valid, or "lifelike" enough. How realistic do you believe Douglas' experiment is? It seems rare, for example that we meet someone for the first time and know absolutely nothing about him/her. We almost always know "of" someone from friends, family, or classmates. What do you think of Douglas' experimental design in light of this point? How might it have been made more realistic?

4. What does any other communication theory you have studied suggest about initial interactions? Pose a hypothesis that would apply if this theory were true.

5. Notice what goes through your mind when you first meet a person. After a few minutes, write down what you recall. What do these two experiences suggest about other research questions to investigate in the field of person perception?

6. Do you think Douglas' experiment was worth conducting? Does it have any application or utility to communication scholars, educators, or to people's lives?

7. We have provided one or two suggestions for future research on antici- pated interaction and information-seeking. Pick your own or one of our suggestions for future experimental research in this area and design a full experiment.

8. Finally, conduct a full experiment to investigate this (or any other) as- pect of communication behavior. Compare the effect of an independent variable on an expected outcome (the dependent variable). Randomly assign ten of your classmates to one of the two conditions, and then measure them and compare their scores to see whether the hypothe- sized differences occur. What problems did you encounter in conduct- ing this research that threaten the internal validity of your conclusions?

FURTHER READINGS ON FULL EXPERIMENTAL RESEARCH

Aronson, E., & Carlsmith, J. M. (1968). Experimentation in social psychology. In G. Lindzey & E. Aronson (Eds.), *Handbook of social psychology: Vol. II. Research methods* (2nd ed., pp. 1–79). Reading, MA: Addison-Wesley.

Campbell, D. T., & Stanley, J. C. (1963). *Experimental and quasi-experimental designs for research.* Chicago: Rand McNally.

Hsia, H. J. (1988). *Mass communications research methods: A step-by-step approach.* Hills- dale, NJ: Lawrence Erlbaum.

Kirk, R. E. (1968). *Experimental design: Procedures for the behavioral sciences.* Belmont, CA: Brooks/Cole.

Myers, J. L. (1972). *Fundamentals of experimental design.* Boston: Allyn & Bacon.

Poole, M. S., & McPhee, R. D. (1985). Methodology in interpersonal communication research. In M. L. Knapp & G. R. Miller (Eds.), *Handbook of interpersonal communication* (pp. 100–170). Beverly Hills, CA: Sage.

EXAMPLES OF FULL LABORATORY EXPERIMENTAL RESEARCH

Hiltz, S. R., Johnson, K., & Turoff, M. (1986). Experiments in group decision making: Communication processes and outcomes in face-to-face versus computerized conferences. *Human Communication Research, 13,* 225–252.
This study assessed the effects of the independent variables of group and task type on the type of communication engaged in by group members and the quality of group decisions (the dependent variables). Subjects were assigned randomly to one of two modes of communication (face-to-face or computerized conferencing) and given two tasks to solve (a qualitative human relations task and a scientific ranking task with a criterion solution). The findings showed that, although group decisions were equally good in the two modes, the groups were less likely to reach agreement in the computerized conferencing mode. There also were many more communication units produced in the face-to-face groups, although there were more types of task-oriented communication associated with decision quality in the computerized conferences.

Hirokawa, R. Y. (1985). Discussion procedures and decision-making performance: A test of a functional perspective. *Human Communication Research, 12,* 203–224.
This experiment tested whether satisfaction of critical task-achievement functions (such as identification of realistic alternative courses of action) or type of discussion procedures (the independent variables) accounted better for group decision-making performance (the dependent variable). Subjects were assigned randomly to a three-person group and to one of four discussion procedures (reflective-thinking, single-question, ideal-solution, and free discussion) and given a task to solve. The group discussions were then rated by observers with regard to meeting four critical task-achievement functions as well as the quality of the group decision. The results provided support for the "functional" perspective as discussion format had no effect, but the satisfaction of certain requisite conditions was related to group decision-making success.

Hoffner, C., Cantor, J., & Thorson, E. (1989). Children's responses to conflicting auditory and visual features of a televised narrative. *Human Communication Research, 16,* 256–278.
These researchers randomly assigned subjects at three age levels (5–6, 8–9, and 10–12 years) to view one of two videotapes of a children's story (either kind or cruel behavior of a woman toward a cat) that was presented in one of

three formats: audio-only, video-only, or audio-visual mismatch (two conditions). Group differences on these independent variables were then assessed on the dependent variables of personality assessments of the central character, a recognition memory test, and awareness of auditory-visual discrepancy (for subjects in the two audio-visual mismatch conditions). The findings indicated that there are predictable age differences in children's processing of television, with younger children being less likely than older viewers to form an integrated understanding of a televised story, especially when there is conflicting auditory and visual narrative content.

Jordan, J. M., & Roloff, M. E. (1990). Acquiring assistance from others: The effect of indirect request and relational intimacy on verbal compliance. *Human Communication Research, 16*, 519–555.

This experiment examined the effects of using different types of requests as mediated by relational intimacy (the independent variables) on attaining assistance (the dependent variable). Subjects were assigned randomly to focus on either an intimate relationship, a friend, a non-intimate relationship, or a stranger. They then received one of three request forms that varied in terms of directness (question + imperative, need assertion, or resource inquiry), and were asked to write a response to the request. Responses were rated by coders with regard to verbal compliance to measure the attainment of assistance. The results demonstrated an interaction effect between the independent variables, as directness was more effective at eliciting verbal compliance at higher levels of intimacy.

Neuendorf, K. A., & Fennell, T. (1988). A social facilitation view of the generation of humor and mirth reactions: Effects of a laugh track. *Central States Speech Journal, 39*, 37–48.

These researchers studied whether a laugh track in a movie socially facilitates humorous reactions. Subjects were assigned randomly to watch a comedy (*Nobody's Perfekt*) that contained either a laugh track or no laugh track (the independent variable). Subjects' were videotaped without their knowledge and their humorous reactions (the dependent variable) were coded by observers at 57 predetermined laugh points (where a "canned laugh" had been inserted in the laugh track condition) using a 5-point scale, ranging from no humor reaction to loud laughter (the dependent variable). The results showed that those in the laugh track group exhibited significantly more mirthful behavior but did not evaluate the film as significantly funnier than those in the control condition.

Chapter 3

Field Experimental Research

INTRODUCTION TO THE METHOD

Some research questions necessitate searching for causal relationships between variables in places where people naturally interact, such as in their homes, community groups, or organizations. A *field experiment* is an experiment conducted in a natural setting.

Field research rarely permits the amount of control necessary for conducting a full experiment. It may not be possible, for example, to manipulate the independent variable, assign subjects randomly to experimental groups, or even be able to compare two groups. Just because a full experiment is not possible, however, does not mean that researchers cannot conduct an experiment to discover the causal relationship between an independent and dependent variable. They can, but compromises must be made. In such cases, they conduct *quasi-experiments*, studies that incorporate a moderate degree of control, or *pre-experiments*, investigations with a low degree of control. Two issues determine which type of field experiment is conducted: (1) whether the independent variable can be manipulated or must be observed; and (2) whether one experimental group or multiple groups are studied.

Manipulation Versus Observation
of the Independent Variable

We know from the last chapter that full experiments *always* require a researcher to *manipulate* the independent variable. Quasi-experiments and pre-experiments *may or may not* involve such a manipulation.

Some field experiments manipulate subjects' exposure to the independent variable. Dillard (1990), for example, conducted a field experiment to assess whether the quantity of behavior called for by the acceptance of an initial request (the independent variable) affects the likelihood of compliance with a later request (the dependent variable). Twelve trained experimenters walked around a ten-block city area and knocked on doors. They varied the extent of their requests to the person who answered the door in one of two ways: asking him or her to spend 5 or 10 minutes addressing 10 envelopes, or to spend 20 to 25 minutes addressing 35 envelopes. One to three weeks later a different experimenter returned to those homes where a person had accepted the first request, and asked him or her to help construct a hiking trail outside the municipality in which the study was conducted. The two initial request sizes were then compared on the rate of compliance to the second request. Dillard's field experiment thus manipulated subjects' exposure to two levels of an independent variable.

Field experiments, however, often do not allow a researcher direct control of the independent variable. In such cases, quasi-experiments or pre-experiments are used to *observe* the effects of an independent variable that the researcher did not manipulate on a dependent variable.

Researchers typically observe the effects of an independent variable in two situations. In the first, subjects are exposed to a planned manipulation, but that manipulation is not controlled directly by the researcher. Bach (1989), for example, conducted a field experiment to study the effects of organizational members' communication links with others (the independent variable) on their adoption of an organizational innovation (the dependent variable). She chose a medical clinic in the northern Rocky Mountains that was about to experience a change in its billing process, which consisted of a pocket-sized booklet containing daily log sheets on which a physician's hospital work could be recorded. She assessed physicians' and physician assistants' communication network links within the organization (by having them indicate how many times they exchanged work, social, or innovative information with every other member of the organization within a two-week period) both before and two weeks after the new recording procedure was introduced. Adoption of the procedure was measured by both the time of the initial adoption and the extensiveness of adoption over a 90-day time period. While Bach did not control how often the physicians interacted, she was able to observe the effects of their communication network links on the dependent variable of innovation adoption.

Researchers also can observe different levels of an independent variable that have already occurred naturally in the field. Motley and Smith (1989), for example, conducted a field experiment to assess the effects of similarity in temperament of interviewers and applicants (the independent variable) on hiring decisions (the dependent variable). The experiment was conducted within a personnel office of a large institution, that of the Associated Students of the University of California at Davis (ASUCD). Interviewers were assessed as being one of four temperament types (sensing-perceiving, sensing-judging, intuitive-thinking, or intuitive-feeling). Applicants were assigned to the interviewers according to normal ASUCD personnel procedures, and their temperament type was assessed at the end of the interview. It was then possible to categorize the interviews, after they were completed, into three temperament-matched categories: identical, independent, and opposite. These three groups were then compared with regard to hiring decisions. Although Motley and Smith could not manipulate the interviewer-applicant match, they were able to measure the effects of different levels of this naturally occurring independent variable.

All experiments study the effects of an independent variable on a dependent variable. However, while full experiments always manipulate the independent variable, quasi-experiments and pre-experiments either manipulate it or observe its effects.

Single Versus Multiple Experimental Groups

Full experiments *always* demand at least two groups, either a treatment and a control group, or two treatment groups. Field experiments *often* employ two or more groups. Sykes (1983), for example, conducted a large-scale field experiment to assess the effects of proximity and similarity on the frequency of interaction of strangers and acquaintances who varied by social class. He did so by assigning the bunk and classroom locations of six units of naval apprentice trainees to three experimental conditions: maximum *segregation* by social class, maximum *integration* by social class, and *randomized* location by social class. Trainees were required by the Navy to be in their living quarters between the hours of 3:30 and 9:30 P.M., when they could talk, do personal chores, or do as they wished. Observers circulated through these areas at designated times and coded whether apprentices were or were not interacting (speaking and apparent listening as indicated by nonverbal gestures) and, if so, with whom. Comparisons between these three groups showed that proximity had a stronger effect on the frequency of interaction than similarity of social classes.

Full experiments require not only two or more groups, but also subjects who are *assigned randomly* to conditions. Most research conducted in the field *does not* allow researchers to randomize subjects into conditions. In quasi-experiments and pre-experiments, there is *no* random assignment of subjects to conditions. These researchers are less sure, therefore, about the causal effects of the independent variable on the dependent variable because initial differences between the groups cannot be ruled out.

There is, however, an important difference between quasi-experiments and pre-experiments when studying multiple groups. Quasi-experiments use *pretests*, measurements of subjects prior to a manipulation, to assess whether the groups start off equivalent with regard to the dependent variable and/or other important variables that might confound the results. Pretests are not as effective as random assignment, however, because they only assess whether subjects are different on the variables tested, whereas random assignment is the best guarantee of producing equivalent groups across *all* variables. For that reason, using pretests instead of random assignment produces *quasi-equivalent* experimental groups. Pre-experiments, on the other hand, do not use pretests to assess whether the groups start off equivalent. Pre-experiments, therefore, could easily start with *nonequivalent* experimental groups.

Finally, while full experiments require at least two groups for comparison, quasi-experiments and pre-experiments may study only one group. Reardon, Sussman, and Flay (1989), for example, studied how a group of adolescents from two Southern California schools rejected peer pressure to smoke cigarettes. They asked each adolescent to indicate how he or she would respond to eight hypothetical situations created by the researchers. The situations varied in relationship (friend versus acquaintance), number of people present (dyad versus group), and amount of pressure (first versus second exertion of pressure). They then had observers code the type of non-compliant responses adolescents gave, and found that the strategies varied by condition. Note that only one group was studied in this field experiment.

There is, however, a crucial difference between quasi-experiments and pre-experiments when studying one group. Quasi-experiments use procedures to establish an **intragroup baseline comparison.** One way to do this is to use multiple *pretests* and multiple *posttests* (a measurement after exposure to a manipulation) (for example: pretest, pretest, treatment, posttest, posttest). If, for example, a researcher conducts a quasi-experiment to study whether a training program in an organization improves managers' communication skills, he or she would give the managers at least two pretests prior to the training program, and at least two posttests following it. If there are no changes between the pretest scores but there is a difference between the pretest and the posttest scores, the researcher can be fairly confident that the training program has had an effect. Another way to establish an intragroup baseline comparison is by observing multiple exposures to different levels of an independent variable that occurs naturally and assessing the dependent variable after each exposure ($X_1, O_1, X_2, O_2, X_1, O_3, X_2, O_4$, where X_1 and X_2 are two different levels of an independent variable and O is an observation). For example, if a researcher categorizes salespersons' calls as either threat conditions or promise conditions and observes their effects on sales after each exposure to a threat and after each exposure to a promise, an intragroup baseline comparison can be established.

Pre-experiments, on the other hand, use only one pretest and one posttest (O_1, X, O_2) or only a posttest for a single level of an independent variable (X, O$_1$) when studying one group. Without an intragroup baseline comparison, researchers cannot presume a causal relationship exists.

In conclusion, field experiments are either full experiments, quasi-experiments, or pre-experiments, depending on how much control over the variables and their measurement the natural setting allows. The major differences between full experiments, quasi-experiments, and pre-experiments are summarized in Figure 3.1.

Strengths and Limitations of Field Experiments

Field experiments have their own strengths and weaknesses relative to laboratory experiments. Laboratory experiments enable researchers to exercise a great deal of control (and thereby assure *internal validity*) by manipulating an independent variable, assigning subjects randomly to experimental conditions, and minimizing the influence of extraneous variables on the outcomes of the experiment. Yet, the very high level of control the researcher has over the laboratory setting also often tends to make this research rather artificial. Subjects in laboratory situations may not perform the way they normally would in a real setting, thereby limiting the *external validity* of the research, the extent to which the findings can be generalized to the real world.

To increase the realism and external validity of research, field experiments are conducted in natural settings. Because subjects in most laboratory experiments have no history together, for example, their communication behavior may not be comparable to that of people interacting as they really would in everyday life. Field researchers, at times, are able to conduct full experiments, thereby maximizing both the internal and external validity of their research. More often, however, conducting experiments in the

FIGURE 3.1

A Comparison of Full Experiments, Quasi-experiments and Pre-experiments

Type of Experiment	Manipulation of Independent Variable	Random Assignment	Experimental Groups	Control of Extraneous Variables
Full experiment	Manipulate	Yes	Equivalent	High
Quasi-experiment	Manipulate or observe	No	Quasi-equivalent or multiple intragroup comparisons	Moderate
Pre-experiment	Manipulate or observe	No	Nonequivalent or no comparison group	Low

Source: Lawrence R. Frey, Carl H. Botan, Paul G. Friedman & Gary L. Kreps, *Investigating Communication: An Introduction to Research Methods*, p. 165, copyright © 1991 by Prentice Hall, Inc. Reprinted by permission of Prentice Hall, Inc.

field decreases the amount of control researchers can have, leading them to design quasi-experiments or pre-experiments. The moderate and low control demonstrated in quasi-experiments and pre-experiments, respectively, limit the confidence that can be placed in the causal relationships discovered.

QUESTIONS FOR EXAMINING FIELD EXPERIMENTAL RESEARCH

In addition to the general questions posed about research and many of the criteria used to evaluate full laboratory experiments, several criteria apply specifically to reading and evaluating field experimental research. Keep these questions in mind when reading the following study or any other article that employs a field experimental design.

A. The Field Setting

1. Did the *purpose of the experiment* lend itself best to conducting research in the *field,* or would a laboratory experiment be better for assessing the causal relationship between the independent and dependent variables?

2. What was the *setting* for the experiment? Was the specific setting chosen appropriate for meeting the goals of the experiment? Was the setting somewhat representative of a larger set of situations, so communication behavior there is likely to be typical of a general kind of interaction, or is it atypical or even unique?

3. How did the natural setting influence the researcher's *control* over the experiment? With little control, how can the researcher be sure the conditions or groups being studied are the kind required for testing the research hypotheses?

4. How did the researcher account for or overcome *uncontrolled influences* on the data being collected?

B. Independent and Dependent Variables

1. Were the independent and dependent variables *operationalized and measured* in a *valid* manner?

2. Was the independent variable *manipulated* or *observed* by the researcher?

3. If observed, did the researcher *precisely measure* subjects' exposure to the independent variable?

C. Field Experimental Procedures

1. How were subjects *selected* from the larger population they are to represent for the experiment? Was a *random* procedure, where every member

of the population has an equal chance of being selected, used or was a *nonrandom* procedure, where every member of the population does not have an equal chance of being selected, used? Did the selection process *bias* the sample in any way?

2. Was a *full experimental, quasi-experimental,* or *pre-experimental design* used in the field experiment? How do elements in the experimental design maximize or limit the confidence that can be placed in the causal relationships discovered?

3. Did the experimental design in this study incorporate the *normal communication behavior* of the potential subjects in their natural contexts or did it influence subjects' normal activities?

4. If a quasi-experimental or pre-experimental design was used, was only *one* group studied or was there a *second* treatment or control group used for comparison purposes? If not, how might one have been studied?

5. If there were two experimental groups, were *pretests* used to make sure that subjects in the two groups started off *quasi-equivalent* with respect to the dependent variable or other important variables? If pretests were not used, how confident can we be about any differences found between the experimental groups?

6. If only one experimental group was used, were *multiple pretests* used to provide an *intragroup baseline comparison?* If not, how confident can we be about any causal relationships found?

7. How did the researcher account for or control the threats to validity stemming from *irrelevant variables,* such as the researcher's behavior, the research procedures, and subjects' biases, examined in the previous chapter?

THE ILLUSTRATIVE STUDY

The study you will read in this chapter is a field experiment conducted in a natural setting with a real organization, the University of Southern California Faculty Senate. The USC Faculty Senate deliberates about issues and problems members bring before it and makes decisions or policies about how the university should respond to them. The experiment examines communication behavior used by members of this organization while solving real tasks and making real decisions. This experiment thus studies communication events that occurred naturally, rather than events contrived by a researcher in a controlled laboratory setting.

Kreps' field experiment tests a theoretical proposition derived from Weick's (1969) model of how organizations process information. Specifically, the model predicts a **positive relationship** between the equivocality (complexity, ambiguity, and unpredictability) of the problems confronting organizations and the kinds of communication required by organizational members to solve these problems. That is, the more complex the problem, the more communication will be required to solve it. Weick suggests that communication exchanges among organization members (referred to as "cycles") help reduce the equivocality of complex problems by enabling members to share relevant information and develop strategies (rules) for responding to the problems.

Structurally, a communication cycle is a *double-interact*—a three-part interpersonal communication exchange—that begins with an *act* (such as a question or a policy statement), is followed by a *response* (feedback to the act, such as an answer to a question or a comment accepting or rejecting the policy statement), and concludes with an *adjustment* (a comment that acknowledges the response, such as providing additional information about the original policy statement). As an example of a communication cycle, imagine a doctor and a patient communicating in a diagnostic interview. The doctor might initiate the cycle by requesting information from the patient (an act) about why he or she is seeking medical attention, such as the question, "What seems to be bothering you?" The patient answers the doctor's query (a response) with, "I've been having stomach pains off and on all day." The doctor might respond (an adjustment) with, "Well, let's run some tests to see what is causing these abdominal pains." This three-part exchange (act-response-adjustment) reduces some of the equivocality in their encounter by providing the doctor with information about the patient's condition and letting the patient know that the doctor is going to investigate the source of the pain. An ongoing series of communication cycles will provide the doctor and the patient with additional diagnostic information. Each communication cycle helps to reduce the equivocality or clarify the nature of the problem the interactants are seeking to solve.

When confronting relatively simple problems (low equivocal informational inputs), members of organizations typically rely on "rules" established in the past for responding to such problems and need not engage in many communication cycles to solve them. The more equivocal the problems, however, the more communication cycles needed to cope with them.

For example, in the doctor-patient interview just described, if the patient's health problem was relatively routine (of low equivocality), such as an upset stomach caused by an already diagnosed ulcer, the doctor could assess the health problem with relatively few communication cycles with the patient and use preset rules to prescribe appropriate treatment for it. But if the patient's health problem was complex and the symptoms were unfamiliar to the physician (of high equivocality), the doctor and patient would have to engage in many communication cycles to diagnose and treat it.

Kreps' field experiment, therefore, investigates Weick's theory by testing a hypothesis based on it about the relationship between the amount of information equivocality (the independent variable) and the performance of communication cycles (the dependent variable). Specifically, the experiment examines the differences between high- and low-equivocality topics on the number of communication cycles performed in the deliberations by the faculty senate.

A Field Experimental Test and Revaluation of Weick's Model of Organizing

Gary L. Kreps
Purdue University—Calumet

A field experimental test of the central assumption of Karl Weick's model of organizing is reported. Weick's model posits a direct relationship between the levels of informational equivocality input into human organizations and the frequency and types of communication behaviors performed by organization members in response to the informational inputs. The field experiment investigated the information processing behaviors of an intact, on-going academic organization, the University of Southern California Faculty Senate, over a period of one academic year. The relationship between the equivocality of Faculty Senate motions and the type and frequency of communication behavior performed by Faculty Senate members was assessed. The results of this field experimental test of Weick's model of organizing lend support to Weick's model. As the level of informational equivocality was manipulated in the field experiment from low equivocality Senate motions to high equivocality Senate motions a marked increase in communication behavior cycles performed by Faculty Senate members was measured, and found to be statistically significant in a one-tailed t *test.*

1   Karl Weick (1969) presents an innovative, behavior-oriented model of human organizations, stressing human communicative interactions as the central phenomena of organizing in his book *The Social Psychology of Organizing.* Weick's model of organizing is, in fact, a communication
5   model, depicting the manner in which human organizations interact within their informational environment to produce and preserve an on-going state of organization. Organizations are represented as being constantly in the process of organizing by coping with informational complexity and ambiguity. "Organizing is directed toward re-
10   moving equivocality from the informational environment," (Weick, 1969, p. 40). The model of organizing describes how organizations

Source: Kreps, G. L. (1980). A field experimental test and evaluation of Weick's model of organizing. In D. Nimmo (Ed.), *Communication yearbook 4* (pp. 389–398). New Brunswick, NJ: Transaction Books. Reprinted by permission of Transaction Books.

remove equivocality from their informational environments through the performance of interlocked communication behavior cycles, double interacts (act-response-adjustment). These equivocality reducing
15 communication behavior cycles allow organizations to adjust and react appropriately to the ever-changing information inputs confronting them, ultimately allowing organizational survival through adaptation. In this way, Weick represents human communication interactions as integral adaptive mechanisms for organizational perpetuation.
20   Weick's communication interaction emphasis in his model of organization makes the model an attractive perspective for organizational communication researchers and theorists to adopt. In addition to the marked communication emphasis of Weick's model of organizing, Bantz and Smith (1974) point out attributes of the model of
25 potential appeal to human communication research; some of these aspects of Weick's model of organizing that are most amenable to communication research and theory include the concepts: (1) that a single set of variables may be applicable at all levels of communicative behavior (the systems notion), (2) that a single unified model can be
30 created that will describe communicative behavior in a variety of settings, (3) that activity may be more important than structure in explaining the communicative process, and (4) that communicative acts are central to social processes (Bantz and Smith, 1974, p. 171). These aspects of Weick's model of organizing make it a potentially powerful
35 and heuristic perspective for organizational communication inquiry.
        The purpose of the study reported herein was to test the central communication relationship posited by Weick in his model of organizing to determine the adequacy of the model for organizational communication inquiry. Weick (1969, p. 92) claims a direct relationship
40 between the level of informational equivocality input into an organization and the frequency of communication behavior cycles performed by the organization in response to the input. As the equivocality of the organization's informational environment increases, the more the organization needs to reduce the equivocality to manageable levels. The
45 organization performs as many communication behavior cycles as is necessary to process the optimum amount of equivocality out of the informational environment. In essence, this study will examine whether organizations perform more communication behavior cycles, double interacts, in informational situations of high equivocality than
50 they do in situations of low equivocality.
        Bantz and Smith (1974) report the only in-depth analysis and test of Weick's model of organizing since the publication of *The Social Psychology of Organizing* in 1969. They do an excellent job of explaining, analyzing, and critiquing Weick's model, but their experimental
55 test of the crucial communication relationships posited by Weick, al-

though elegant and carefully performed and analyzed, is less than satisfying. Their test results suggest there is no direct relationship between informational equivocality and the frequency of communication behavior cycles performed by the organization. These results
60   may be a product of several methodological and research design problems encountered in their experimental test.

Bantz and Smith (1974) operationalize communication behavior cycles, their dependent variable, inappropriately in terms of the numbers of adjective choices made by ad hoc groups in response to 18 ten-
65   word passages of differing levels of equivocality. Communication behavior cycles are interlocked communication behaviors performed by organizational members. Weick (1969, p. 46) describes these interlocked communication behaviors as double interacts. Adjective choices are not double interacts. A more advantageous way to opera-
70   tionalize communication behavior cycles in organizations would be to identify the double interacts in the communicative interaction of organization members.

Another problem in Bantz and Smith's (1974) experimental test is the unrepresentativeness of their experimental manipulation in
75   comparison with actual tasks facing on-going organizations. In the study, the experimental manipulation was to have subjects choose adjectives in response to written passages. This manipulation does not seem accurately to reflect organizational tasks undertaken in actual organizations. In the same vein, the subject selection process in the
80   Bantz and Smith test created artificial "laboratory" organizations that were not representative of actual organizations. The groups used in their study were composed of researcher-selected ad hoc groups. These groups had no past history together prior to the experiment; they were chosen specifically for the experimental test. This is atypical
85   from actual organizations that have organization members who have developed interpersonal relationships and have learned to coordinate their activities over time. As organization members work together over time, they develop repertoires of communication experiences that they can call on in helping them respond to organizational tasks.
90   This notion of using past experiences to aid organization members in coping with organizational tasks is crucial to Weick's model of organizing. In addition, the ad hoc groups used by Bantz and Smith lack many of the on-going features of intact organizations, and this problem can make the behaviors of these groups unrepresentative of the
95   behaviors of actual organizations. It is most difficult for an ad hoc group to demonstrate the process of organizing; as people work together over time they develop the abilities to coordinate their activities and exhibit organization.

The present study attempts to correct some of the weaknesses

100   discussed in Bantz and Smith's test of Weick's model of organizing. At
the same time, the present test of Weick's model is not nearly as
ambitious or as encompassing as was the test performed by Bantz and
Smith. They tested the relationship between informational equivocality and communication behavior cycles, as well as the frequency of
105   communication behavior cycles performed in each of the three phases
of Weick's model of organizing, enactment-selection-retention. The
present test of Weick's model of organizing only tests the relationship
between informational equivocality and communication behavior cycles, and does not concern itself with the three phases of the model.
110   Rather than identifying each of the phases of organizing, and evaluating the use of communication behavior cycles in each phase, this study
examines the use of behavior cycles throughout the informational
situation being examined. The present test of Weick's model was not
designed to test the validity of the phases of Weick's model, instead it
115   was designed to test the more basic issue of the relationship between
informational equivocality and communication behavior cycles.

METHOD

The present study employed a field experimental test of organizational communication response to informational equivocality. "A field
120   experiment is a research study in a realistic situation in which one or
more independent variables are manipulated by the experimenter
under as carefully controlled conditions as the situation will permit"
(Kerlinger, 1973, p. 401). Field experimental tests allow the experi-
mentalist the realism of field research, enhancing the representative-
125   ness of the study, while retaining much of the precision and control of
laboratory experiments. The realistic organizational field setting utilized in this study was the University of Southern California Faculty
Senate. The Faculty Senate is an intact, on-going organization whose
task is to provide faculty representation in university government.
130   The Faculty Senate achieves its organizational tasks through the related actions of proposing Senate motions impacting on university
government, discussing and voting on these motions, and passing
them on to other levels of the university government. The relationship between the equivocality of Senate motions and the form of
135   communication response performed by the Faculty Senate was examined as a means of testing the central communication assumption of
Weick's model of organizing.
        One independent variable was manipulated in this field experi-
ment, and one dependent variable was measured in response to the
140   experimental manipulation. The independent variable, informational

equivocality, has two levels—low equivocality and high equivocality. The dependent variable measured in this study was communication behavior cycles. The research hypothesis posits a direct relationship between increases in the independent variable—informational
145   equivocality—and increases in the dependent variable—communication behavior cycles. The research hypothesis is: As the equivocality of informational inputs increases (from low equivocality to high equivocality), the number of communication behavior cycles performed will increase in the same direction. This hypothesis reflects the central
150   assumption in Weick's model of organizing, concerning the relationship between informational equivocality and communication behaviors exhibited by the organization.

      A one-group repeated trials design was used in this field experiment. "In the one-group repeated trials design, as the name indicates,
155   one group is given different treatments at different times or is measured at different times" (Kerlinger, 1973, p. 362). The different treatments measured were the different Senate motions acted on by the Senate during the 1977–78 academic year. During this nine-month period the Senate was confronted with 24 motions. These 24
160   motions were measured for their levels of informational equivocality, while the Faculty Senate interaction in response to each of these motions was measured for the frequency of communication behavior cycles performed.

      Unobtrusive data-gathering techniques were used to obtain the
165   primary data base for this study. Unobtrusive research methods are used to provide the researcher with data that "do not require the cooperation of a respondent and do not themselves contaminate the response" (Webb, Campbell, Schwartz, & Sechrest, 1969, p. 2). Private institutional records of the Faculty Senate were made available to the
170   researcher, including audiotaped transcripts of all Senate meetings, photocopies of all Senate motions, photocopies of Faculty Senate minutes, and additional peripheral Faculty Senate documents. All of the institutional records used in the study are part of the normal working documents of the Faculty Senate and in no way interfered with the
175   normal working interaction of the organization under study. Unobtrusive techniques were used to gather written and audio transcripts of Faculty Senate motions and interaction in response to these motions, which comprised much of the raw data for the field experimental test.
180   The independent variable, informational equivocality, was operationalized through an analysis of the level of equivocality of each of the 24 motions. Survey methods were used to measure the levels of information equivocality of the motions. Questionnaires were distributed to a 42% sample (n = 40) of Faculty Senators. Each Senator respondent

185   rated each of the motions—which were reprinted on the questionnaire
       exactly as they had appeared on the Faculty Senate motion form
       originally presented to the Senate for consideration—on three seman-
       tic differential-type scales representing three of the underlying dimen-
       sions of informational equivocality as explained by Weick. These three
190   scales were: complicated–uncomplicated, unpredictable–predictable,
       and ambiguous–unambiguous. The motions rated by the respondents
       as being high in complexity, unpredictability, and ambiguity on these
       scales were considered high equivocality motions and the motions
       rated as being low in complexity, unpredictability, and ambiguity on
195   these scales were considered low equivocality motions, thereby com-
       posing the high equivocality and low equivocality levels of the indepen-
       dent variable, informational equivocality.

            The dependent variable, communication behavior cycles, was
       operationalized through a content analysis of the Faculty Senate's ver-
200   bal interaction in response to the Senate motions judged as being high
       equivocality and low equivocality motions. A content analytic pro-
       cedure developed by Scheidel and Crowell (1966) was modified and
       used to identify all communication behavior cycles, double interacts,
       occurring in the Faculty Senate verbal interaction on each of the mo-
205   tions. Weick's description of double interacts in terms of *act, response,*
       and *adjustment* is strikingly similar to the Scheidel and Crowell opera-
       tional definition for double interacts: "that event in which any partici-
       pant (X) initiates a comment which is followed by a comment from
       any other participant (Y) which in turn is followed immediately by a
210   further comment from the first participant" (1966, p. 274).

            A problem with the Scheidel and Crowell operationalization is its
       representation of double interacts as merely a linear progression of
       messages with each series of three comments being separate from
       every other series of three comments. This operationalization does
215   not account for the processual aspects of group interaction, where
       there is communicative interdependency between all group members
       and their messages. Verbal interaction in small groups is processual
       and cyclical, with each message and each message-sender performing
       a variety of roles and functions within the group. Therefore the
220   Scheidel and Crowell content analytic operationalization of double
       interacts in group communication has been modified to encompass
       the processual nature of group communication.

            In the modified operationalization of double interacts, all com-
       ments by group members can be classified as *acts* in the double inter-
225   act cycle if they precede any other two comments by group members.
       All verbal comments can be considered to be *responses* in the double
       interact cycle if they follow a verbal comment by another group mem-
       ber, and are in turn themselves followed by a verbal comment by a

group member. Similarly, all verbal comments by group members can
230   be considered to be *adjustments* in the double interact cycle if they
follow two previous comments by group members. In essence, this
means the total number of double interacts in any group interaction
will be the total number of verbal comments by group members
minus two comments (double interacts = n − 2).
235   All verbal comments by group members during the Faculty Senate's discussion of a Senate motion judged as being either high or low
in equivocality were content analyzed to enumerate double interacts
per motion. Faculty Senate interaction was content analyzed from the
point of introduction of the motion to the Faculty Senate, through the
240   Senate's discussion of the motion, until the Senate culminates interaction on the motion with a formal vote or show of hands that marks the
final dispensation of the motion by the Faculty Senate.

RESULTS

The statistical analyses indicate that the level of equivocality of the
245   Faculty Senate motions *does* account for the variation in the number of
double interacts performed by the Faculty Senate members. Based on
the field experimental test conducted, it is reasonable to reject the
null hypothesis in favor of the research hypothesis.
The independent variable, informational equivocality, was sepa-
250   rated into the two levels of high and low equivocality by selecting the
five highest- and five lowest-rated Senate motions rated by the Faculty
Senators on the questionnaire. Questionnaires were distributed to a
42% sample of Faculty Senate members (n = 40), eliciting a 57%
response rate (n = 24).
255   Each of the motions were rated by the Senators on the three
scales representing informational equivocality. The mean scores for
these three scales represented the ratings of equivocality per-motion
by each Senator. Table 1 reports the descriptive statistics for the ratings of informational equivocality on each of the twenty-four motions
260   by the Senators. Table 2 reports the motions selected for the high
equivocality and the low equivocality levels of the independent variable, informational equivocality.
The dependent variable, communication behavior cycles, were
enumerated through a double interact content analytic procedure. All
265   double interacts were identified in the Senate's group interaction on
each Senate motion identified as being high and low in informational
equivocality. Table 3 reports the total number of double interacts
measured per-motion.
To evaluate the reliability of the content analytic measures ob-

TABLE 1

Descriptive Statistics for Equivocality Ratings of Senate Motions

Motion	Mean	Mode	Min	Max	Med	Std Dev	Variance	Skewness	Kurtosis
1	2.3	2.0	1.0	5.5	2.0	1.2	1.50	1.00	0.6
2	3.9	2.0	1.0	7.0	4.0	1.9	3.60	0.04	−1.3
3	1.0	1.0	1.0	1.7	1.0	0.1	0.02	4.80	23.0
4	3.4	2.3	1.0	6.0	3.1	1.3	1.70	0.40	−0.7
5	2.9	1.0	1.0	7.0	2.3	1.8	3.30	1.10	0.5
6	3.6	4.0	1.0	7.0	3.9	1.8	3.20	0.30	−0.9
7	2.3	1.0	1.0	7.0	1.6	1.8	3.10	1.50	1.5
8	3.5	2.3	1.0	7.0	3.4	1.8	3.20	0.50	−0.7
9	3.7	2.0	1.0	7.0	3.3	1.7	3.00	0.20	−1.0
10	5.1	7.0	1.3	7.0	4.8	1.6	2.70	−0.40	−0.2
11	3.7	4.0	1.0	6.0	4.0	1.5	2.30	−0.30	−0.9
12	2.9	1.0	1.0	7.0	2.3	2.0	4.10	0.80	−0.5
13	2.8	1.0	1.0	5.0	2.4	1.5	2.10	0.10	−1.6
14	2.8	2.0	1.0	7.0	2.4	1.3	1.80	1.60	3.5
15	3.5	1.0	1.0	7.0	3.0	2.0	4.10	0.40	−1.1
16	2.3	1.0	1.0	5.0	2.0	1.3	1.60	0.70	−0.3
17	3.0	2.0	1.0	7.0	2.6	1.6	2.60	1.30	1.4
18	3.8	2.0	2.0	7.0	3.6	1.4	2.00	0.90	0.5
19	2.8	2.0	1.0	7.0	2.7	1.4	1.90	1.10	2.6
20	2.8	2.0	1.0	7.0	2.1	1.4	2.00	1.30	2.1
21	2.6	2.0	1.0	5.0	2.4	1.1	1.20	0.30	−0.6
22	3.0	1.0	1.0	5.7	3.1	1.5	2.20	0.10	−1.2
23	1.6	1.0	1.0	5.3	1.1	1.2	1.50	2.50	5.6
24	3.0	2.0	1.0	7.0	2.6	1.5	2.20	0.90	0.6

TABLE 2
Motions Selected for Low and High Levels of Informational Equivocality

Low Equivocality Level		High Equivocality Level	
Motion	Mean	Motion	Mean
1	2.3	2	3.9
3	1.0	9	3.7
7	2.3	10	5.1
16	2.3	11	3.7
23	1.6	18	3.8

270　tained in operationalizing the dependent variable, communication behavior cycles, a measure of interrater reliability was obtained. An additional content analyst was trained to perform the double interact content analytic procedure. This analyst performed the double interact content analysis on a random sample of the Faculty Senate group
275　interaction. A composite reliability formula, reported by Holsti (1968, p. 137), was used to obtain a composite reliability score of .94. Table 4 reports the composite reliability equation.

A one-tailed t test was performed on the data to assess the probability of obtaining the increase measured in the number of com-
280　munication behavior cycles under conditions of high equivocality over the number of communication behavior cycles measured under conditions of low equivocality. The t test indicated the difference between the population means was significant at the .05 level. The one-tailed probability for the obtained t value was less than .02. Table 5 reports
285　the results of the t test of mean differences.

TABLE 3
Double Interacts Per Motion

Low Equivocality Motions		High Equivocality Motions	
Motion	Double Interacts	Motion	Double Interacts
1	11	2	25
3	3	9	15
7	10	10	74
16	5	11	165
23	6	18	91
Total	35	Total	370
Mean	7	Mean	74

TABLE 4
Composite Reliability Formula

$$\text{Composite Reliability} = \frac{N \ (\text{average inter–judge agreement})}{1 + (N - 1) \ (\text{average inter–judge agreement})}$$

$$\text{Composite Reliability} = \frac{2 \ (.89)}{1 + (2 - 1) \ (.89)} = \frac{1.78}{1.89} = .94$$

TABLE 5
T-Test of Mean Difference

t-Value	Degrees of Freedom	2-Tailed Probability	1-Tailed Probability
−2.49	8	.038	.019
		p < .05	p < .02

An Omega Square test of the strength of association indicated that the independent variable, informational equivocality, accounted for 34% of the variance in the dependent variable, communication behavior cycles.

DISCUSSION

Karl Weick (1969) asserts, in his model of organizing, that the equivocality of informational inputs into an organization is directly related to the number of communication behavior cycles the organization members perform in the process of organizing. The results of this field experiment strongly support Weick's assertion. As the level of informational equivocality was manipulated in the field experiment from low equivocality Senate motions to high equivocality Senate motions a marked increase in the number of communication behavior cycles (double interacts) performed by Faculty Senators was observed and measured. This increase in communication behavior cycles during situations of high equivocality over situations of low equivocality was found to be statistically significant at a .05 alpha level.

In addition to statistical significance, the results of this field experiment may have heuristic theoretical significance for the development of organizational communication research and theory. By adding empirical support to Weick's model of organizing, increased evidence is provided for a human communication-based approach to studying organizational phenomena. In this study human communication is examined as a central variable in organizational adapta-

310 tion to its informational environment and shown to be strongly related to the organization's task and performance. Weick's model of
organizing, and this empirical test of his model, support a human
communication oriented approach to the study of organizations.

The Faculty Senate demonstrated the relationship between pat-
315 terns of communication behavior performed in organizations and the
informational aspects of organizational tasks. In high equivocality informational situations the Faculty Senate attempted to process the
equivocal informational input down to less equivocal, more predictable information, to enable the organization to react to the input in a
320 more effective manner. The Senate processed these equivocal informational inputs into more manageable levels of equivocality through
the performance of communication behavior cycles. Weick (1969)
contends that the performance of each communication behavior cycle
removes some equivocality from the informational input and the or-
325 ganization members will perform as many of these communication
behavior cycles as is necessary to whittle down the equivocality of the
input to an optimal, workable level of equivocality for the organization to respond to. The Faculty Senate demonstrated the use of communication behavior cycles to process high equivocality inputs by per-
330 forming many double interacts in response to high equivocality
Senate motions.

In low equivocality informational situations there was less need
for the Senate to process the informational input, since the input was
already at a low level of equivocality and thereby in a manageable
335 informational form. Accordingly, the Faculty Senate performed fewer
communication behavior cycles (double interacts) in response to low
equivocality Senate motions than they had in response to high equivocality Senate motions. This supports Weick's premise that human
communication is an adaptive mechanism for social organizations,
340 where the performance of communication behaviors allows the organization to adapt and adjust to the equivocality of its informational
environment and tasks.

The findings of this study indicate a systematic relationship between the informational aspects of organizational tasks and the or-
345 ganizational member's communication behaviors in coping with these
organizational tasks. Human communication is shown to be a crucial
organizational process in the performance of organizational tasks and
the accomplishment of organizational goals. As a crucial organizational process human communication should be a rich heuristic area
350 for organizational research and theory building. Weick's model of
organizing and this test of Weick's model signifies the utility of inte-
grating a human communication approach to research and theory
with an organizational approach to research and theory. By focusing

355 on the communication processes performed within organizations, organizational researchers may begin to understand more clearly the processual development of organization.

This test of the central assumption of Weick's model of organizing lends support to the validation of the model. Replications of this study using several different intact on-going organizational popula-
360 tions as research subjects will help clarify the strength (external validity) of the present study, as well as impact the validation of Weick's model. Future replications might include additional message variables in their content analysis of communication behavior cycles. Different types of double interacts may be identified by focusing on message
365 content, as well as message patterns in analyzing group interaction for communication behavior cycles, leading to more in-depth conclusions about the nature of organizational communication in response to informational inputs.

Since the field experimental study reported here does not really
370 test the entirety of Weick's model of organizing, testing only its central assumption, future research can begin to test empirically the model more completely than the present research. This study does not test Weick's phases of the organizing process, nor does this field experiment deal with the organizational use of communication assembly
375 rules that Weick illustrates as performing the function of determining the appropriate communication process the organization needs to perform to elicit organization. Future research may enlarge on this present test of Weick's model by operationalizing communication assembly rules and the phases of enactment, selection, and retention,
380 subjecting these additional aspects of Weick's model to empirical tests.

Several recommendations for organizational practitioners can be derived from this test of Weick's model. Supervisors should always allow adequate communication contact between organization members when processing equivocal information inputs. To remain viable
385 and efficient organizations must process information with the same degree of equivocality as is present in the input itself. This means if organizations handle equivocal inputs as if they were unequivocal (without constructing appropriate communication behavior cycles), fatal mistakes are likely to occur because the organization would be
390 unable to process the equivocal inputs into understandable information, and probably react inappropriately to the inputs. If organizations handle unequivocal inputs as though they were equivocal (by performing a variety of double interacts) they will probably waste organizational energy and atrophy. Organizations can only exist to
395 the degree they can accurately register the level of equivocality in information inputs, construct appropriate communication behavior cycles in response to the inputs, and process the equivocal inputs into

desired organizational outputs. Management can facilitate organizational adaptation to informational equivocality by fostering interaction between organization members on difficult organizational tasks. Workers should be encouraged to ask questions when processing difficult information inputs, and groups of workers should be used to deal with tasks too complex for individuals to comprehend and perform easily.

Management should concentrate less on individual organization members' behaviors, and more on the interlocked communication behaviors of groups of organizational actors, because the process of control within organizations is accomplished through relationships between individuals, rather than by individuals. Training programs can be developed in organizations stressing teamwork; daily and weekly meetings between organization members can be arranged; problem-solving organizational groups can be formed to provide the interlocked communication behaviors necessary for organizational adaptation. The communications between organization members become crucial processes in organizational survival, and as such should become recognized as indispensable organizational activities. The recognition of the importance of human interaction to organizational survival can aid organizational adaptation by encouraging concern for the adequacy and accuracy of interaction in organizations. From this perspective it becomes the responsibility of all organization members to communicate actively on the job, giving and receiving messages in response to informational inputs.

At the end of his book, *The Social Psychology of Organizing,* Weick hesitantly proposes "some implications for practice that would hold if the proposed model is verified to any degree" (1969, p. 105). Since the present field experimental test does lend verification to Weick's model of organizing, these implications for organizational practitioners may be of interest. Weick's (1969) five golden rules for organizational practice are presented: "1. *Don't panic in the face of disorder*" (p. 106). Organizations must react to informational inputs with the same degree of equivocality as was input; therefore it is necessary for organizations to react in disorderly ways (performing many communication behavior cycles) in response to highly equivocal inputs. "2. *You never do one thing all at once*" (p. 106). Organizations accomplish their tasks through the performance of interlocked behaviors and processes. "3. *Chaotic action is preferable to orderly inaction.*" (p. 107). Only through the performance of interlocked communication behaviors can organizing be accomplished. "4. *The most important decisions are often the least apparent*" (p. 107). It is more critical to decide what an organization knows about an input, than to decide what to do about an input, because rules for organizational action derive from organizational knowledge and ex-

perience. "5. *You should coordinate processes rather than groups*" (p. 108).
The focus in organizing is on interlocked behaviors rather than on
structural groups. Who performs different functions in an organiza-
445   tion is often immaterial, only that the interrelated processes of organizing must be performed for organizational adaptation to occur.
These five rules for organizational practice suggest a process-oriented
perspective for organizational management, where the emphasis is on
patterns of organizational communication. The Weickian manager is
450   concerned with coordinating interrelated communication processes.

REFERENCES

Bantz, C. R. & Smith, D. H. A critique and experimental test of Weick's model
of organizing. *Communication Monographs*, 1974, 44, 171–184.

Holsti, O. R. *Content analysis for the social sciences and humanities.* Reading,
Mass.: Addison-Wesley Publishing Company, 1968.

Kerlinger, F. N. *Foundations of behavioral research.* New York: Holt Rinehart &
Winston, 1973.

Scheidel, T. M. & Crowell, L. Feedback in small group communication. *Quarterly Journal of Speech*, 1966, 52, 273–78.

Webb, E., Campbell, D. T., Schwartz, R. D., & Sechrest, L. *Unobtrusive measures: nonreactive research in the social sciences.* Chicago: Rand McNally
College Publishing Company, 1969.

Weick, K. *The social psychology of organizing.* Reading, Mass.: Addison-Wesley,
1969.

COMMENTS ON THE STUDY

Introduction, Review of the Literature, and Hypothesis

Kreps sets the stage for this study in the introduction to the article (1–116)
by first describing Weick's model, its relevance to communication, and the
primary purpose of the experiment, which is to test a central assumption of
the model about the relationship between informational equivocality and
communication cycles. This field experiment, therefore, is a good example
of *basic research,* the purpose of which is to test a hypothesis derived from
a theory. Applied research, in contrast, whether conducted in a laboratory
or in the field, is designed to solve a practical problem.

Kreps also justifies the need for this study by critiquing the only
previous test of Weick's model (Bantz & Smith, 1974), which found no
direct relationship between equivocality and communication cycles (51–
116). Kreps argues that the results of Bantz and Smith's study may be
erroneous because of three major flaws in their research design.

First, he argues that their study used an *inadequate operationalization,* or measurement, of communication cycles (62–72). Bantz and Smith asked ad hoc groups to choose adjectives in response to 18 ten-word passages, and used the number of adjectives chosen as the measurement of equivocality. Kreps points out that this procedure does not capture what Weick meant by "communication behavior cycles," which are interlocked communication behaviors of act, response, and adjustment.

Second, Kreps argues that Bantz and Smith used an *unrealistic experimental* manipulation of the independent variable of equivocality (73–79). Choosing adjectives in response to written passages, he claims, is artificial, not a real organizational task, and, therefore, does not reflect or even simulate the way members of an actual organization would respond to different informational inputs.

Third, Kreps claims that Bantz and Smith used a sample of subjects that *did not represent* organizational members (79–98). The sample was composed of ad hoc groups who had never worked together before they were selected by these researchers. Members of newly formed groups, however, are unlikely to demonstrate the kinds of activities members of established organizations learn over time.

Kreps thus justifies his experiment as both a test of Weick's theory of organizing and as an attempt to correct the flaws inherent in the only previous in-depth analysis and test of this theory. His purpose is to examine a prediction derived from a theory within a natural environment and to assess the validity of findings from previous research.

Method

Let's examine the key elements of the research design in this field experiment. First, Kreps used tape recordings of the 24 motions discussed by the Faculty Senate during a nine-month period (164–179). These tape recordings were *natural* organizational records used by the Senate secretary to compose senate minutes (all sessions were recorded for that purpose), so Kreps did not affect the subjects' behavior. We do not know, however, whether the recording process induced the *Hawthorne effect.* Kreps then had a sample of 40 members from the Faculty Senate rate the equivocality of the 24 motions on three semantic differential scales (180–197). A **semantic differential scale** has polar-opposite referents at each end of the scale and seven undefined points in between (for example, good ___:___:___:___: ___:___:___ bad). In this case, the poles of each semantic differential item represented the underlying dimensions of informational equivocality: (1) complicated–uncomplicated; (2) unpredictable–predictable; and (3) ambiguous–unambiguous. The independent variable of *information equivocality* was then divided into high and low levels by choosing the five highest rated motions and the five lowest rated motions, respectively.

This operationalization and measurement of information equivocality appears to be straightforward. There are, however, some concerns about these procedures. First, Kreps claims that the independent variable was *manipulated* in this field experiment (138–141), but it was not. Instead, he observed the natural occurrence of the two levels of this independent variable after they had occurred. Since manipulation versus observation of the independent variable separates full experiments from quasi-experiments and pre-experiments, we know that this was not a full experiment. It could be that none, or all, of the motions were highly equivocal. If so, his data would be biased.

Second, only a sample (42%) of the Senators rated the motions, and we are left wondering why a *census* (a study of all members of the population, in this case, Senators) was not conducted. Moreover, we do not know whether the sample of Senators was selected *randomly,* where each member of the population has an equal chance of being selected for the sample. Random sampling is the best guarantee that a sample is representative of the population from which it is drawn because all variables should be distributed evenly across conditions. This experiment actually used a *nonrandom* sample, so we cannot be certain that these subjects were truly *representative* of the Senate as a whole. Perhaps those who volunteered would rate the motions in a biased way.

Finally, the Senators who rated the motions did so after already discussing and voting on them earlier in the year. Their post hoc, or after-the-fact, equivocality evaluations might have been influenced by their memories of the Senate discussions of the motions. They may, for example, have attributed high equivocality to motions that necessitated a lot of discussion, whereas prediscussion ratings might have resulted in a low equivocality rating for the very same motions. If this bias existed, the equivocality measurement would be invalid and produce fallacious results. This potential problem would have been difficult to overcome, however, since the study required analyzing the actual motions handled by the Senate, and it was important to have the Senators themselves rate the equivocality of the motions. (After all, equivocality is in the eye of the beholder.) Perhaps Kreps could have provided a validity check by asking objective observers (those who have no stake in the research) or even previous Senate members who had not been involved in these discussions to also judge the equivocality of the motions and then analyze whether there were any differences between the observers' and the Senators' ratings.

The dependent variable, *communication cycles,* was operationalized and measured by identifying the number of double-interacts performed with respect to the different motions discussed. Kreps himself *content-analyzed* the tape recordings of the faculty senate discussions by counting every three consecutive messages in the recorded discussions to identify communicative acts, responses, and adjustments (198–242). Every message that was followed by two other messages was considered an *act*. Every message that was preceded by one message and followed by another was considered a *response*. Every message that was preceded by two other messages was considered an *adjustment*. Kreps measured the *reliability* of the content analytic procedure by training another person to code a random sample of the discussions. Codings like these are generally considered reliable if the coders agree 70%, or .70, of the time. Comparing the two codings yielded a reliability score of .94, indicating that the content analysis was highly reliable (269–277).

This measurement of communication cycles seems effective, but some questions must be raised. First, why did Kreps himself code the communication? To avoid any potential bias, researchers typically ask objective observers to code communication behavior. Second, why did only one observer, rather than two or more, code a portion of the discussions? What percentage of the recordings was coded by this observer? Why didn't the observer code all the data? Even though the reliability figure is very high, some important information about these procedures is missing from this article, and we are left to wonder whether the most effective procedures were used. Third, this is strictly a *structural* content analytic procedure, counting the *number* of messages rather than analyzing their actual content. By failing to examine the actual content of the discourse, it is likely that certain messages were miscast as acts, responses, or adjustments. A better operationalization might have been to conduct a *functional* content analysis of the discussions by identifying the specific purposes of the messages and then classifying them as either acts, responses, and adjustments, or something else irrelevant to the motion on the floor at the time.

The methodology employed by Kreps in this field experiment constitutes a "one-group, repeated trials design" (153–158), in which one group is given different treatments at different times or is measured at different times. This is an example, then, of a *quasi-experiment* because the researcher: (1) *observed* levels of an independent variable that occurred naturally as opposed to manipulating subjects' exposure to them; (2) studied only *one* group of subjects; and (3) established an *intragroup baseline comparison* by observing the dependent variable (the number of communication behaviors performed) after each occurrence of one of two levels of the independent variable.

Results

This study tested the hypothesis that as the equivocality of informational inputs increases (from low equivocality to high equivocality), the number of messages performed increases. Kreps compared the number of communication cycles performed by the faculty senate members while discussing high equivocality motions to the number of communication cycles performed while discussing low equivocality motions. To assess the significance of the differences (the probability that they occurred by chance or error) between the number of communication cycles performed in these two conditions (278–285), Kreps employed a one-tailed **t-test.** A one-tailed t-test is used when a **directional hypothesis** is advanced (one that specifies the type of relationship between variables or the direction of the differences between groups, such as in this study), while a two-tailed t-test is used when a **nondirectional hypothesis** is posed (one that proposes a relationship between variables or a difference between groups but does not specify its direction). The one-tailed t-test indicates that the differences found between the two equivocality conditions had less than a 2% probability of occurring due to chance or error. Since this exceeds the .05 level of probability usually used in social science research, the differences between these groups are *statistically significant.* The **null hypothesis** (predicting no differences between these groups), therefore, can be rejected and the research hypothesis is accepted. An additional test of **statistical power,** the Omega Square Test of the *strength of association,* demonstrates that 34% of the dependent variable—communication behavior cycles—can be explained by the independent variable of informational equivocality (286–289). This is a relatively high level of observed variance accounted for in this experiment, although 66% is left unexplained. What other variables do you think might explain the number of communication cycles performed by the Senate members? An example might be the time in the meeting—near the beginning or the end—when the motion was introduced.

Discussion

In discussing the results of this study, Kreps asserts that the differences found between the independent treatment groups validate Weick's model and its corresponding assumption about the relationship between information equivocality and communication cycles (291–302). This field quasi-experiment thus discovered a causal relationship between an independent variable and a dependent variable.

It must be pointed out, however, that the statistical analysis performed on the data (the t-test) only assessed differences between high and low equivocal conditions. It does *not* indicate whether there is a positive relationship or correlation between these two variables, whereby the number of communication cycles performed increases systematically as the informational equivocality increases. Kreps could have assessed this relationship if he simply had used the ratings of all 24 motions to represent different degrees of equivocality, rather than selecting only the 5 highest and 5 lowest rated motions (constituting less than 42% of his database) and dividing them into high and low conditions.

Kreps realizes, of course, that no single experiment can establish a generalization about a causal relationship between variables. Only after research has been *replicated* can such a conclusion be drawn. Accordingly, Kreps fulfills the heuristic function of research by suggesting that future experiments should: (1) study different kinds of intact organizations, since this study only examined one specific organization and the results may not be generalizable to other organizations; and (2) measure double-interacts in a different way, since this study provided only a structural and not a functional content analysis of communication cycles (358–368). We would add that the findings from this quasi-experiment need to be verified in a full experiment, both in a laboratory and in the field, where subjects are assigned randomly and exposed to both high or low equivocal messages manipulated by the researcher, and the number of communication cycles performed is measured.

The article concludes by recommending how the findings can be used by organizational communication practitioners (381–450). One important recommendation is that organizational members need to be given plenty of time to discuss complex questions. The other recommendation is that communication is a process of *interaction,* so management should concentrate less on individuals' behavior and more on the interlocked communication behaviors of groups and organizations, such as by developing training programs that stress dialogue and teamwork. The discussion section thus explains both the theoretical and practical significance of the experiment and establishes directions for future research.

CONCLUSION

Kreps' research illustrates the value of conducting a field experiment to examine causal relationships between variables in a natural setting. The quasi-experimental design used in this study enabled the researcher to adapt to the constraints of the field, enhancing the ecological validity of experimental research, while maintaining some of the control demanded by experimental research designs for discovering causal relationships between variables.

QUESTIONS AND ACTIVITIES TO CONSIDER

1. What is one apparent strength and one weakness of conducting field experiments as opposed to laboratory experiments as illustrated in this study?

2. What are the crucial differences between full experiments, quasi-experiments, and pre-experiments? What are the advantages of conducting a full experiment over a quasi-experiment or a pre-experiment?

What are the advantages of conducting a quasi-experiment over a pre-experiment? Why are quasi-experiments and pre-experiments ever conducted?

3. How is the purpose of this study more representative of basic research than applied research? How might an applied research study related to Weick's theory be designed?

4. Does Kreps' experiment fully overcome the design flaws he suggests are in Bantz and Smith's (1974) research? Does his operationalization of communication cycles represent the interactive nature of double-interacts? Are the experimental conditions in his study representative of activities performed by members in most organizations? Are the subjects in this study representative of most organizational members?

5. Design a full experiment to test the central assumption of Weick's model of organizing in a natural setting or in a laboratory. How would you operationalize information equivocality and communication cycles? What advantages are there to testing this proposition with a full experiment as opposed to a quasi-experiment or a pre-experiment?

FURTHER READINGS ON FIELD EXPERIMENTAL RESEARCH

Bickman, L., & Henchy, T. (1972). *Beyond the laboratory: Field research in social psychology.* New York: McGraw Hill.

Campbell, D. T. (1957). Factors relevant to the validity of experiments in social settings. *Psychological Bulletin, 54,* 297–312.

Campbell, D. T., & Stanley, J. C. (1966). *Experimental and quasi-experimental designs for research.* Chicago: Rand McNally.

Cook, T. D., & Campbell, D. T. (1976). The design and conduct of quasi-experiments and true experiments in field settings. In M. Dunnette (Ed.), *Handbook of industrial and organizational psychology* (pp. 228–293). Skokie, IL: Rand McNally.

Cook, T. D., & Campbell, D. T. (1979). *Quasi-experimentation: Design & analysis issues for field settings.* Boston: Houghton Mifflin.

Frey, L., O'Hair, D., & Kreps, G. L. (1990). Applied communication methodology. In D. O'Hair & G. L. Kreps (Eds.), *Applied communication theory and research* (pp. 23–56). Hillsdale, NJ: Lawrence Erlbaum.

EXAMPLES OF FIELD EXPERIMENTAL RESEARCH

Burgoon, M., Parrott, R., Burgoon, J. K., Birk, T., Pfau, M., & Coker, R. (1990). Primary care physicians' selection of verbal compliance-gaining strategies. *Health Communication, 2,* 13–27.

This field experiment assessed physicians' ratings of how likely they were to use 17 compliance-gaining strategies. Sixty-nine primary care physicians practicing internal medicine and family care in metropolitan areas were asked to recall one of six situations within the last six months in which they had attempted to persuade a patient to follow a particular treatment regimen. The researchers created the six situations by manipulating the independent variables of the severity of the medical problem (severe, moderately threatening, and nonthreatening) and the sequence of compliance-gaining attempt (first versus second attempt). Differences among these situations were examined with respect to the compliance-gaining strategies used.

Guinan, P. J., & Scudder, J. N. (1989). Client-oriented interactional behaviors for professional-client settings. *Human Communication Research, 15*, 444–462.

This field experiment examined whether professionals' performance (the independent variable) affected their communication behavior with clients (the dependent variable). Computer systems developers, ranked as high- and low-performing based on ratings by their managers, read a case study describing a typical set of problems encountered by a small, privately held company. They then role-played a first interview with a confederate who pretended to be the office manager and a "typical" naive end-user (someone who did not know what [s]he wanted or needed from the information system and had unrealistic expectations of system capabilities). Audiotapes of the interviews were coded with respect to the number of times a developer used a specific communication behavior (such as metacommunication or metaphors), and differences between the two types of professionals were compared.

Miller, K. I., & Monge, P. R. (1985). Social information and employee anxiety about organizational change. *Human Communication Research, 11*, 365–386.

This field quasi-experiment examined the effects of social information, individual needs, and job characteristics (the independent variables) on employee anxiety about organizational change (the dependent variable). Subjects from a company that was moving to a new building were exposed to one of six informational conditions. The information promoted positive or negative needs, positive or negative descriptions of the change, and positive or negative interpretations of the descriptions in terms of needs. They were also exposed to a control condition during a presentation that was part of the training for the relocation. The effects of the independent variables on the dependent variable were then assessed.

Pfau, M., Kenski, H. C., & Sorenson, J. (1990). Efficacy of inoculation strategies in promoting resistance to political attack messages: Application to direct mail. *Communication Monographs, 57*, 25–43.

This field full experiment examined the potential for the direct-mail communication channel to combat the persuasiveness of political attack messages. Potential voters in a metropolitan area during the 1988 presidential campaign randomly received one of four political messages (the independent variable) through the mail: inoculation, inoculation-plus-reinforcement, post hoc refutation, or control. They then received a follow-up attack message during interviews in their homes. Finally, attitudes toward the candidate and the position supported in the attack message and the likelihood of voting for the candidate were assessed (the dependent variables).

Zalesny, M. D., & Farace, R. V. (1986). A field study of social information processing: Mean differences and variance differences. *Human Communication Research, 13*, 268–290.

This field quasi-experiment assessed the effects of informational influence (the independent variable) on work environment perceptions (the dependent variable) in a sample of state government employees who were relocating to an open office environment. The researchers manipulated the information employees received from three of the agency's newsletters. The first newsletter examined the general physical appearances of the traditional and the new, open-plan offices; the second discussed the visual and acoustical privacy of the new offices; and the third examined the "meaning" conveyed by the physical environment of the new offices with regard to the work group's norms and expectations about privacy. Differences between those sampled prior to each issue (the control group) and those sampled after distribution of each newsletter (the treatment group) were compared.

SURVEY RESEARCH

OVERVIEW OF SURVEY RESEARCH

A variety of research questions have been addressed through survey research. Examples include What communication strategies do men and women use on dates to influence their partners' sexual behavior, and are these strategies related to actual premarital sexual behavior (Christopher & Frandsen, 1990)? What variables are associated with stress in the workplace, and do certain types of communication, such as social support and participation in decision making, help to reduce burnout (Miller, Zook, & Ellis, 1989)? What images do people have of their local daily newspapers (Lavrakas & Holley, 1989)? How have videocassette recorders (VCRs) influenced family interaction, and what pre-existing family relationships and media orientations determine the use of the VCR and its role in the family (Morgan, Alexander, Shanahan, & Harris, 1990)?

The *survey method* is a commonly used social science research strategy that involves selecting individual respondents, asking them questions, analyzing their responses, and then inferring how the findings apply to large groups of people. Survey research in communication uses individuals' self-reports to describe their communication behavior.

STRENGTHS AND LIMITATIONS OF SURVEY RESEARCH

The major strength of survey research is learning how large groups, even whole populations of people, think about something. Surveys make it unnecessary to obtain self-reports from everyone in a population, since the findings from a representative sample can be generalized to a population with extreme accuracy. Surveys also obtain information from the "horse's mouth" by asking people directly what they think and feel.

In addition to scholarly research, surveys are also used to conduct problem-solving or applied research. Surveys are used, for example, to conduct political polls, evaluations of new programs, and market research. Indeed, Looney (1991) claims that market research has developed into a $2.5 billion business, and that surveys "determine what type of car we will drive, the kinds of food we will eat, the pain-killers we take, the deodorants, toothpaste, soap and perfume we use" (sect. 5., p. 1).

There are, however, some limitations to survey research. First, inferences about a population based on data collected from a sample are never absolutely accurate. Conclusions about a population can only be stated as *probabilities*, as assessments of how good an estimate is. This is because a sample drawn from a population never reflects exactly that population.

Second, people generally are able to report attitudes and beliefs that are relatively stable, but they generally are not able to recall attitudes or feelings that existed previously. The same may be said for behavior. People can recall recent and unusual behavior much more readily than they can recall distant and routinized behavior, particularly when frequencies are requested. This is why so many self-report measures of conflict and persuasion tactics ask, "How likely are you to do each of the following . . ." These directions move respondents toward "beliefs about their communication behavior" rather than toward recalling how often they have done each of the tactics.

Third, many individual differences affect survey responses. Some people, for example, monitor their behavior more closely than others, and some people are more articulate and provide more in-depth answers than others.

Fourth, survey researchers often find that people will not answer questions honestly. This is particularly true when researchers ask questions about intimate topics or about socially unacceptable behavior.

Finally, Margolis (1991) argues that surveys often fail to capture people's responses to complex phenomena, such as their feelings toward a presidential candidate, because questions often are posed in relatively simplistic ways, such as by asking yes or no questions.

SURVEY RESEARCH PROCEDURES

Two crucial components to survey research are: the selection of respondents and the techniques used to acquire self-report data.

Selecting Survey Respondents

Findings from survey research are used to describe how a **population**—everyone who possesses a certain characteristic of interest—thinks, or how a characteristic (called an attribute) is distributed among them. Sometimes it is possible to survey an entire population, which is called a *census.* A researcher, for example, might interview all the employees of a small, family-owned business.

Most of the time, however, survey researchers cannot contact every member of a population, so they usually collect information from a subgroup, called a *sample,* and then report how likely what they find applies or *generalizes* to the whole population. To generalize results from a sample to a population, the research must be *externally valid.* What determines whether survey results are externally valid?

First, researchers must choose an appropriate population from which to sample. The population obviously must match the research question. If researchers want to learn the communication abilities large organizations seek in the people they hire, do you think they should survey the top managers who set hiring policy or the campus recruiters who interview job candidates? Each might give different answers. The population chosen must be evaluated by considering how well it allows the researcher to answer the questions asked.

Second, a researcher must identify the **sampling frame,** or the part of the population that actually can be reached. Ideally, the sampling frame consists of all members of the population of interest, but this is seldom the case. Suppose, for example, a researcher wants to know what members of a community think about a new communication curriculum in a public school. The population of interest is all members of the community, but it is unlikely that a complete list of all community residents exists from which to draw a sample. The researcher might use the tax roll, phone book, or direct mail lists, or even conduct door-to-door interviews, but none of these sampling frames would include everyone in the population. They probably exclude, for example, homeless people, as well as families that have moved into town since the last tax season, phone book publication, or door-to-door canvass. They would also exclude people who were temporarily out of town while the survey was being conducted, as well as those who have no phone, have an unlisted phone, or pay no taxes. Such omissions make the sampling frame an incomplete list of the population, and the subsequent sample may be a biased one.

Third, the method of selecting the sample is crucial to the external validity of the research. Sampling methods are either random or nonrandom. **Random sampling** methods assure that each member of the population or sampling frame has an equal opportunity for being included in the sample. For example, a **simple random sample** is one in which each person in the sampling frame is assigned a consecutive number, and then individuals are selected from this list if their assigned numbers are chosen randomly until the size of the desired sample is obtained. A **stratification sample** categorizes members of a population (such as students at a university) along a characteristic (such as freshman, sophomores, juniors, and seniors), and then samples randomly from each category in proportion to its representation in the population. Researchers typically use random number tables generated by a computer program to assure everyone an equal chance of being selected. Random sampling does not guarantee a representative sample, but it does give the best assurance of representativeness.

Nonrandom sampling methods, on the other hand, do not guarantee an equal chance of including all potential subjects. For example, surveying a **convenience sample,** say everyone who passes by on a paticular street in downtown Chicago, does not guarantee everyone in the population (Chicago residents) an equal chance of being selected. A **volunteer sample**—using respondents who *choose* to participate in the survey—also does not necessarily represent the population of interest because research shows that volunteers and nonvolunteers differ in some important ways.

Another general sampling rule is that the larger the sample, the better. However, having a random sample is even more important. The value of random sampling is that any characteristics of the respondents that might influence the data, such as their political opinion or susceptibility to persuasion, may be assumed to be distributed evenly across the sample. Random sampling methods also allow researchers to calculate the amount of **sampling error,** the extent to which a sample differs from its population. Researchers can determine the **confidence level,** the degree of assurance in generalizing from a sample to a population (the 95% confidence level is typically used), and the **confidence interval,** the range of scores associated with the confidence level (for instance, the "margin of error," such as plus or minus 4%, in political polls). Surveys using random sampling, therefore, provide the most generalizable results.

Because sampling is crucial to evaluating the results of a study that uses the survey approach, we urge you to keep the following questions in mind when reading *all* survey research:

1. Was an appropriate *population* and *sample* used to answer the research question?
2. Was there bias in the *sampling frame* of this study? If so, how might the

choice of subjects have skewed the results and, therefore, limited how generalizable they are?

3. Was a *random* procedure used to select the sample?

4. Was a sufficient *number* of people surveyed? (Random samples of the United States, such as those done by political pollsters or media ratings companies, typically use about 2000 people because after that the reduction in error is minimal.)

5. Is there a *response bias* in the sample? Could there be differences between those who participated and those who did not? (For example, if the population is known to be 80% white and 20% nonwhite, does the sample reflect the same proportion? If 80% of the respondents are nonwhite, the study may surface an issue of greater interest to a minority community than to the community as a whole.) Are responses clustered from one part of the geographic area covered? One gender? One age group?

Data-Gathering Techniques in Survey Research

Responses to messages occur internally in people's minds. To study them, researchers have two alternatives. They may study external indicators of these internal states (such as eye contact, applause volume, transcripts of conversation, voting records, or written documents), or they may ask people what they are feeling and thinking. Using external indicators assumes that observed behavior is a more valid indicator of how people think, feel, or behave than what people themselves report. Survey researchers disagree. They argue that an action may reflect more than one inner state, such as a smile which stems from pleasure for some people and from embarrassment for others. Also, researchers cannot observe many important aspects of communication behavior—private interactions within families, for instance. So survey researchers prefer to rely upon people's *self-reports* of their own behavior and feelings.

Survey researchers use two principal techniques to gather self-reports: written questionnaires and interviews. A **questionnaire** presents printed questions to evoke written responses from people, while an **interview** provides spoken questions to evoke oral responses from people. The choice of a questionnaire or an interview is influenced by the research questions being asked and how effective each technique is for eliciting valid answers to those questions. Questionnaires and interviews also have inherent relative strengths and weaknesses, which are examined in the next two chapters.

To conclude, survey research is a common form of communication research because it lends itself to measuring how large groups perceive communication phenomena. Like other methodologies, its strengths and weaknesses have to be understood to become an effective consumer (or producer) of survey research. In the following chapters we provide two examples of communication survey research that help to illustrate some of these strengths and weaknesses. The first is an example of using *mail* questionnaires, while the second uses an *interview* approach.

Chapter 4

Survey Questionnaire Research

INTRODUCTION TO THE METHOD

Good survey research, like all research, must reasonably convince readers that the conclusions drawn are accurate—that they are *valid*. Survey researchers draw conclusions by asking people questions about their attitudes and behaviors. The findings from survey research, therefore, are only as valid as the questions themselves, the procedures used to ask them, and the people asked. Here we first discuss some general issues researchers consider when constructing items for both questionnaires and interviews. We then explain some survey administration procedures and the importance of response rates that can apply to both written and oral questionnaires. We conclude by examining the relative advantages and limitations of using questionnaires in survey research.

Designing Survey Questions

Fink and Kosecoff (1985) point out that in survey research, "The content is the message" (p. 23). That is, the questions researchers ask determine the answers they will receive. Survey researchers, therefore, must take great care when constructing questions.

First, questions must be phrased so that they produce *reliable*, or consistent, answers from respondents. A reliable measurement of a person's political beliefs, for example, is consistent from measurement to measurement. If a question yields three different opinions within a few hours, there is no way of knowing which is correct.

Second, questions must be phrased so they produce *valid* answers from respondents. For survey research, this means that the questions must be interpreted by all respondents the same way they were intended by the researcher and then answered accurately. It is irrelevant if a researcher believes a question is worded clearly or correctly if respondents interpret it differently. For example, if some respondents interpret a question as asking for their own personal opinion while others believe it is asking about how people in general think, their answers would not be comparable.

Ambiguous and confusing questions yield invalid results. For example, a questionnaire that uses many multisyllable words and compound sentences may confuse respondents and lead them to answer something other than what the researcher sought to learn. Similarly, a **double-barreled** question, one that asks about more than one issue, such as "Are you apprehensive about giving a public speech and writing a term paper?", is confusing because we do not know whether the answer applies only to one referent or to both of them. Questions must also not be **leading**—they should not lead respondents to answer in certain ways. A question with emotionally charged wording, such as "What do you think of Candidate X's vicious attacks on Candidate Y's personal life?", will get different responses from one written with more neutral wording, such as "What do you think of Candidate X's comment '_____' about Candidate Y's personal life?"

Survey researchers must be audience-centered—they must write or speak as their respondents require, not as they themselves prefer. This may mean that they have to modify an existing questionnaire to suit a specialized population they wish to study, such as children or members of other cultures.

Third, researchers ask questions to obtain a *measure* of respondents' views. The kind of measurement sought will determine in what form questions are asked. There are four general kinds, or levels, of measurement: nominal, ordinal, interval, and ratio.

Questions that use **nominal measurements** ask respondents to choose between different, mutually exclusive symbolic categories, such as "Will you vote for candidate X or candidate Y?" or "Did you vote in the last election: Yes or No?" Questions that use **ordinal measurements** ask respondents to rank a variable along some dimension, such as "Rank the members of your task group on leadership from highest to lowest." There is no assumption that the distance between the points on an ordinal scale are equal. Questions that use **interval measurements** ask respondents to rate a variable on a numerical scale where the distances between the points on the scale are assumed to be equal. In the social sciences, including communication, researchers often use scales to measure a person's agreement or disagreement with a statement, and they assume that the distances between the points on this scale are equal. This assumption applies, for example, when a researcher asks, "Indicate how you feel about the statement, 'I do not fear giving a public speech,' using the following scale: (1) Strongly Agree; (2) Agree; (3) Neither Agree nor Disagree; (4) Disagree; or (5) Strongly Disagree." Finally, some questions call for **ratio measurements.** These are similar to interval measurements except that they possess an absolute zero point, meaning that the variable does not exist when it reaches zero. For instance, the question "How many hours a day do you watch television?" uses ratio measurement.

The choice of a measurement scale depends on many factors, but generally ratio and interval scales yield more information than ordinal and nominal scales. Knowing how many phone calls a salesclerk made during the last month (a ratio measurement), for example, yields researchers more information than asking whether he or she made any calls at all (a nominal measurement).

Fourth, researchers must decide what *type* of questions to ask. **Closed questions** ask respondents to choose between specified answer categories. The simplest closed question is a yes/no or true/false question. Other researchers use ordinal, interval, or ratio levels of measurement to construct closed questions. Allen and Shaw (1990), for example, conducted a survey to examine the relationship among elementary and secondary teachers' communication competencies and supervisors' evaluations of teachers' effectiveness and the cognitive, affective, and behavioral learning occurring in their classes. Part of the questionnaire asked administrators to evaluate several elements of teachers' oral communication (such as clarifying assignments) on a 5-point scale ranging from "very poor" to "exceptional." Restricting respondents to such standardized responses promotes consistency between respondents.

Open questions, on the other hand, allow respondents to answer in their own words. Sorensen, Plax, and Kearney (1989), for example, surveyed experienced elementary and secondary teachers to see what types of compliance-gaining strategies they use. They presented the teachers with four hypothetical scenarios of student misbehavior (such as a student who demonstrated apathy). Rather than offering a menu of predetermined strategies, they asked the teachers "to please write what you think you would say to get the particular student to do what you want him/her to do," and to "feel free to write as many different things you think you would say" (p. 107). They then developed a coding scheme to categorize the various responses. (See Chapter 7 for a discussion of coding schemes.) The choice of closed or open questions, or a mixture of both, depends on whether the researcher is interested in preferences among a limited set of response types or in the terms respondents use when given free choice.

Fifth, researchers must decide on the *strategic sequencing* of questions, or what is called the **question format.** Three possibilities are the tunnel, funnel, and inverted funnel formats. The **tunnel format** asks respondents a series of consistent or similarly organized questions, the **funnel format** starts with broad, open questions followed by narrower, closed questions, and the **inverted funnel format** begins with narrow, closed questions and builds to broader, open questions.

Finally, researchers must be wary of a **response set,** which occurs when all questions are worded in the same "direction," or polarity, and respondents choose only one end of the scale. For example, when all the items are worded in a positive manner, respondents may get in the habit, or set, of selecting an "Agree" response and gradually put less effort into answering the questions. This response bias reduces the internal validity because people's answers will not be based on what they actually think about each question, but on how the preceding questions were worded. To solve this potential problem, researchers mix up the questions so that respondents are forced to use different ends of the scale if they wish to be consistent.

Questionnaire Administration Procedures

Survey researchers are faced with some choices regarding the procedures used to administer questionnaires. **Researcher-administered questionnaires,** for example, are given in person by researchers or their assistants, while **self-administered questionnaires** ask respondents to complete the questionnaire by themselves at their own discretion. Researcher-administered questionnaires are typically used when a researcher has direct, face-to-face access to respondents, such as college classroom students. Self-administered questionnaires generally are used when researchers conduct a mail survey.

Survey researchers also must decide whether their research calls for a single administration or multiple administrations. **Cross-sectional surveys,** the kind used most frequently, describe respondents' characteristics only at one point in time, so they require only a single administration. **Longitudinal surveys,** ones administered more than once, are necessary if researchers want to assess changes over time. Rubin, Graham, and Mignerey (1990), for example, conducted a longitudinal survey to study the development of communication competence during the course of students' college years. Students completed a communication competence questionnaire each year for four years. The findings showed that communication competence decreased significantly during sophomore year, the "sophomore slump," but then increased during junior and senior years. A cross-sectional survey obviously is not capable of detecting such trends.

Regardless of the procedure used, consistency in questionnaire administration is necessary to assure that all respondents answer the questionnaire under the same conditions. Consistency is generally enhanced in two ways. First, researchers must provide clear instructions for completing a written questionnaire. Second, respondents generally must be treated the same way if their answers are to be comparable. They should, for example, have the same length of time to answer a questionnaire. If important differences exist in surveying technique from one respondent to another, the validity of the results may be questionable.

Response Rate

The **response rate** is the number of usable questionnaires or interviews divided by the total number of people sampled. The response rate is crucial for evaluating survey research, for if there are important differences between those who did and did not respond, the results of the survey are not valid.

Researchers thus strive to maximize response rates if their research findings are to be valid. They will, for example, send a follow-up mailing for mail surveys. It can be just a simple postcard reminding nonrespondents to complete the survey, or it can include another cover letter and questionnaire. Researchers must be very sure that the method used to decide who gets a reminder does not compromise the anonymity of the respondents. Usually this is achieved by assigning each respondent in the initial mailing a number, which is checked off when a response with that number is received; no record of names is kept. Numbers not checked off are sent the reminder.

There is, however, no generally accepted minimum response rate. Fowler (1988) points out that the Office of Management and Budget of the federal government generally will not fund a survey unless it is likely to yield a response rate in excess of 75%. This is an ideal standard, and may be quite possible for interview surveys and researcher-administered questionnaire surveys, but mail surveys often produce a far lower percentage. One problem may be that more and more people are simply refusing to complete surveys. Looney (1991) reports that some recent studies showed that about 35% of people refused to cooperate with survey researchers.

Choosing Survey Questionnaires or Interviews

The choice of a questionnaire or an interview survey depends on the purposes of the research, the population being studied, the type and content of the questions, the desired response rate, and the available resources.

First, the population being studied makes a difference. Questionnaires demand that the potential respondents have sufficient reading and writing skills. Mail questionnaires also demand that the research is of high interest to the members of the population; otherwise, they may not answer them.

Second, Fowler (1988) argues that questionnaires generally lend themselves to closed questions while interviews lend themselves better to open questions. If detailed answers are desired, interviews are generally more effective.

Third, questionnaires are generally more suitable for studying sensitive topics, such as deviant behavior. Questionnaires can assure respondents anonymity, which may produce more honest and accurate answers.

Fourth, the desired response rate is an important concern. Researcher-administered questionnaires typically yield high response rates, but interviews generally yield a much higher response rate than mailed questionnaires. Yu and Cooper (1983), for example, studied response rates from 497 studies and found that the average response rate for all mail surveys was only 47.3%.

Finally, researchers must weigh the available resources, such as time, costs, and facilities. Mail questionnaires generally cost the least; telephone interviews are the next most expensive when the cost of training and paying interviewers is included; and face-to-face interviews are usually the most expensive. However, waiting for mail questionnaires to be returned usually requires more time than telephone interviews.

QUESTIONS FOR EXAMINING SURVEY QUESTIONNAIRE RESEARCH

In addition to the general questions posed about research and the questions concerning the selection of survey respondents, several criteria apply specifically to reading and evaluating survey questionnaire research. Keep these questions in mind when reading the following article, or any article that employs the survey questionnaire method.

A. Choice of the Questionnaire Method

1. Was a *questionnaire the best choice* for meeting the purposes of the research? What specific advantages were offered by a questionnaire, and what limitations, if any, existed?

2. Were there any unique *respondent attributes* (such as reading and writing levels) that affected their ability to complete a questionnaire?

B. Question Design

1. Did the questions actually measure what they claim to? What support did the author provide for their *validity*?

2. Were the *instructions* to respondents about how to answer the questions brief and unambiguous?

3. Were the *questions worded* clearly?

4. Were *double-barreled* questions avoided?

5. Were *leading* questions avoided?

6. Was the choice of *closed* or *open* questions, or a combination, appropriate and effective?

7. Were the variables measured by the optimal *level of measurement* (nominal, ordinal, interval, or ratio)?

C. Questionnaire Administration

1. Were the questionnaires completed in a *group* setting or done *individually?* If done in a group setting, might the presence of others have biased respondents' answers?

2. Were respondents guaranteed *anonymity?* Can the researcher connect responses to the individuals who provided them? If so, might this have influenced the answers given or the response rate?

3. Did the purpose of the research necessitate a *cross-sectional* or a *longitudinal* survey design? If a cross-sectional survey was conducted, did it capture accurately the respondents' points of view, or might the results reflect unique events occurring at that point in time? If a longitudinal survey was conducted, was there much attrition (loss of respondents) over time?

4. Was the *response rate* sufficient for the purposes of the research? Did the researcher use follow-up mailings or phone calls to boost the response rate?

THE ILLUSTRATIVE STUDY

The study you will read in this chapter examines whether two groups of workers differ in their trust of their labor union versus the messages they receive from their union. The authors also wanted to know whether demographic factors, such as voluntary union membership, gender, and race, affect workers' trust. To do this, they conducted a mail questionnaire survey of employees of one district of the United States Post Office.

Do Workers Trust Labor Unions and Their Messages?

Carl H. Botan
Lawrence R. Frey

This study investigated differences between workers' attributions of trustworthiness toward their labor union and its messages, as influenced by affiliation behavior and several demographic variables of interest. A complete metropolitan postal district open shop, numbering 4,225, was surveyed. Results demonstrated significant differences between workers' trust of their labor union and their labor union's messages, favoring the union over its messages. In addition, results demonstrate that affiliation behavior, race, age, and seniority significantly affect perceived trustworthiness of the labor union and its messages. Finally, regression analyses found differences between union and non-union members on several demographic variables as predictors of trust. The implications of these results for organizational communication research in general, and research on labor unions specifically, are discussed.

1   In their annual reviews of organizational communication research, Falcione and Greenbaum identify five types of organizations in which communication has been studied: (1) industrial organizations, (2) governmental organizations, (3) educational organizations, (4) health-
5   care organizations, and (5) other service organizations (i.e., banks, public utility companies, department stores, etc.).[1] One significant institution which exists within all of these organizational settings, and has been virtually ignored within the relevant literature, is organized labor. With approximately 106.8 million members in the total U.S.
10   labor force,[2] 19.7 percent, or 21,043,000, are labor union members.[3]

Source: Botan, C. H., & Frey, L. R. (1983). Do workers trust labor unions and their messages? *Communication Monographs, 50,* 233–244. Reprinted by permission of the Speech Communication Association.

Carl H. Botan is a doctoral student in speech communication, theatre, and journalism and Lawrence R. Frey is assistant professor of speech communication, theatre, and journalism at Wayne State University. The majority of funding for this project was provided by the Detroit District Area Local of the American Postal Workers Union.

[1]Raymond L. Falcione and Howard H. Greenbaum, *Organizational Communication: Abstracts, Analysis and Overview,* 5 vols, (Beverly Hills, CA: Sage Publications, 1974, 1975, 1976, 1977, and 1980).

[2]*Monthly Labor Review* (Washington, D.C.: U.S. Department of Labor, Bureau of Labor Statistics), 104 (1981), 71.

[3]*Handbook of Labor Statistics* (Washington, D.C.: U.S. Department of Labor, Bureau of Labor Statistics, 1980), p. 412.

The study of the labor force, and labor unions in particular, is therefore significant for organizational communication research.

The study of the labor union as an organizational entity is well grounded in organizational communication theory. Hawes, in his re-
15   view of books on organizational communication, discovered that authors tended to assume the existence of "an organized organization" and treated communication as a variable contained within such organizations. As an alternative to accepting this assumption, he suggested that organizing be regarded primarily as a phenomenon emerg-
20   ing from communication.[4] Redding, however, noted that "there are different and complementary advantages to be obtained if we admit the possibility of communication being studied *both* as a phenomenon occurring 'within' an organizational entity (e.g., General Motors) *and* as a phenomenon contributing to the emerging entity we are forced to
25   label 'organization.'"[5] Because labor unions represent direct attempts to organize workers, the study of this organizational context is potentially capable of addressing communication from both perspectives, as product and process.

One profitable method for studying the "system of communica-
30   tion" which produces and is produced by organizations and institutions is the use of a "receiver orientation," a perspective which entails examining how individuals perceive, attribute meaning, and respond to communication attempts directed at them.[6] As Dennis, Goldhaber, and Yates noted in their overview of organizational communication
35   theory and research, most surveys developed in the 1970s employed a receiver orientation to assess effectively respondents' perceptions of

[4]Leonard C. Hawes, "Social Collectivities as Communication: Perspective on Organizational Behavior," *Quarterly Journal of Speech*, 60 (1974), 497–502.

[5]W. Charles Redding, "Organizational Communication Theory and Research: An Overview," in *Communication Yearbook 3*, ed. Dan Nimmo (New Brunswick, NJ: International Communication Association/Transaction Books, 1979), p. 329.

[6]Chester I. Barnard maintained that a "system of communication within an organizational setting *must* be approached from a receiver orientation. See *The Functions of the Executive* (Cambridge, MA: Harvard University Press, 1938). However, Frederick M. Jablin questions the desirability of using a receiver orientation for the study of organizational communication. In particular, he cites the concern that subjective, perceptual measures do not necessarily correlate with objective measures. See, "Organizational Communication Theory and Research: An Overview of Communication Climate and Network Analysis," in *Communication Yearbook 4*, ed. Dan Nimmo (New Brunswick, NJ: Transaction Books, 1977), pp. 328–47. Nevertheless, Jablin acknowledges that numerous scholars have argued/found that the characteristics that perceptual measures explore directly affect the behavior of organizational participants; see p. 331. Hence, Japlin's position leads us to take exception with Barnard's position, and we maintain only that a receiver orientation is one fruitful method, but not the sole method, for studying organizational communication.

communication topics, channels, sources, interpersonal relationships, feedback, and outcomes.[7]

40   This study constitutes a preliminary investigation into the virtually unexplored area of communicative behavior within labor unions from a receiver orientation. Specifically, this study investigated three things: (1) whether significant differences exist between workers' trust of their union as an entity and their union's messages; (2) whether significant differences exist between union and non-union

45   workers' trust of their labor union and/or its messages; and (3) the effects of two sets of demographic variables on workers' trust of their labor union and/or its messages—those demographic variables consistently shown to be of significance to organizational communication research within various organizational contexts, and those demo-

50   graphic variables important to the labor union context. The following discussion reviews the literature relevant to, and the rationale for the selection of, these research variables.

REVIEW OF RELEVANT LITERATURE

Empirical research within the field of labor unions is surprisingly

55   limited. There has not been a significant change since 1965, when Redding noted that "only a tiny fraction of behavioral research of any kind has dealt directly with labor unions."[8] What little research does exist about communication within labor unions can be classified into three broad areas: (1) training programs, including instruction in

60   such communication skills as public speaking, parliamentary procedure, discussion, etc.; (2) labor-management interactions within such formal settings as mediation, arbitration, negotiation, and bargaining; and (3) intra-union communication.[9] The third area, intra-union communication studies, concerned with patterns of com-

[7]Harry S. Dennis III, Gerald M. Goldhaber, and Michael P. Yates, "Organizational Communication Theory and Research: An Overview of Research Methods," in *Communication Yearbook 2*, ed. Brent D. Ruben (New Brunswick, NJ: International Communication Association/Transaction Books, 1978), pp. 224–69.

[8]W. Charles Redding, "The Empirical Study of Human Communication in Business and Industry," in *Frontiers of Speech-Communication Research*, ed. Paul E. Reid (Syracuse, NY: Syracuse University Press, 1965), p. 80.

[9]Mark L. Knapp and James C. McCroskey identified one additional area in which research on communication and labor unions could be classified—*surveys of communication needs*, in "Communication Research and the American Labor Union," *Journal of Communication*, 18 (1968), 160–72. However, because such surveys assess union members' perceptions of communication directed toward them by union officials, we have classified this as a form of intra-union communication.

65   munication internal to labor unions, is most relevant to this particular
       study.

       While the area of intra-union communication has been investi-
       gated the least, a small number of studies attempt to analyze patterns
       of communication within the labor union setting. One avenue for
70   such research concerns the assessment of communication needs and
       desires of union members. Dee, in a series of articles, identifies sev-
       eral types of factors that influence which communication channels
       operated and what communication needs were fulfilled within each
       labor union local.[10] Tompkins reports what he terms a "seman-
75   tic/information distance" between union officers and rank and file
       members of a particular labor union, a distance which he thought
       resulted from the poor vertical communication patterns he found
       within that union.[11]

       The consensus of what research does exist on intra-union com-
80   munication is that the communication needs of workers are not being
       adequately met by labor unions. A U.S. Department of Labor study
       reports that 69.7 percent of labor union members agreed that "more
       feedback from the union" should be the highest priority of their labor
       union, second only to the perceived need for improvements in griev-
85   ance handling.[12] As Spinrad argues, the most serious problem in the
       majority of labor unions is that of effective communication.[13]

       This problem may result from lack of interest in assessing intra-
       union communication patterns. As Dee concludes, "In the past, labor
       has paid relatively little attention to its internal communication ac-
90   tivities."[14]

       From a speech communication perspective, the use of a receiver
       orientation necessitates not only studying how people perceive others
       and institutions, but more importantly, how they perceive message

[10]See James P. Dee, "Written Communication in the Trade Union Local," *Journal of Communication,* 9 (1959), 99–109; James P. Dee, "Oral Communication in the Trade Union," *Journal of Communication,* 10 (1960), 77–86; James P. Dee, "Channels of Talk in the Union Local," *Today's Speech,* 10 (1962), 7–8; and James P. Dee, "Communication Needs of the Active Union Member," *Journal of Communication,* 18 (1968), 65–72.

[11]Phillip K. Tompkins, "An Analysis of Communication Between Selected Units of a National Labor Union," Diss. Purdue University 1962. For a summary and evaluation of subsequent research on Tompkins' concept of "semantic/information distance," see Frederic M. Jablin, "Superior-Subordinate Communication: The State of the Art," *Psychological Bulletin,* 86 (1979), 1201–22.

[12]Thomas P. Kochan, "How American Workers View Labor Unions," *Monthly Labor Review,* 102 (1979), 23–32.

[13]William Spinrad, "Correlates of Trade Union Participation: A Summary of the Literature," *American Sociological Review,* 25 (1960), 237–44.

[14]Dee, "Written Communication in the Trade Union Local," p. 100.

attempts directed at them. The first independent variable for this study is therefore directed at understanding how workers view their labor union and its communication attempts and whether significant differences exist between these two perceptions.

The second independent variable for this study concerns the effects of workers' affiliation behavior with a labor union on their perceptions of their labor union as an entity and/or their labor union's messages. Numerous sources have suggested that desire for membership in a labor union is primarily a function of perceived economic advantages.[15] However, while workers do view labor unions as good for their bread and butter interests,[16] the fact that union membership is dwindling and workers are voting against union certification in record numbers[17] indicates that choosing or rejecting union membership is too complex a behavior to be accounted for by any single factor. Clearly, in addition to economic considerations, a number of attitudinal factors influence this decision-making process.[18] Rather than trying to assert a causal link between attitudes and affiliation behavior, however, this study investigates whether significant differences exist between union and non-union workers' attitudes toward their labor union and/or its messages.

While there are multiple indicators for assessing attitudes toward institutions and/or their messages, this study focused upon workers' perceptions of the *trustworthiness* of their labor union and/or

[15]See Tove Hellend Hamner, "Relationships Between Local Union Characteristics and Workers' Behavior and Attitudes," *Academy of Management Journal*, 21 (1978), 560–78; George Strauss, "Union Bargaining Strength: Goliath or Paper Tiger," *The Annals of the American Academy of Political and Social Sciences*, 350 (1963), 86–94; and Chester A. Schriesheim, "Job Satisfaction, Attitudes Toward Unions, and Voting in a Union Representation Election," *Journal of Applied Psychology*, 63 (1978), 584–92.

[16]See Julius G. Getman, Stephen B. Goldberg, and Jeanne B. Herman, *Union Representation: Law and Reality* (New York: Russell Sage Foundation, 1976), as cited in Kochan; Schreisheim; and Kochan.

[17]The American Labor movement has dwindled from 25.5 percent of the nation's labor force in 1953 to 19.7 percent of the nation's non-agricultural labor force in 1978, as cited in *Handbook of Labor Statistics* (Washington, D.C.: U.S. Department of Labor, Bureau of Labor Statistics, 1980), p. 412. On a related front, American workers are voting against union representation in record numbers. In the twelve month period which ended September 30, 1980, labor unions won only 45 percent of the 8,043 representation elections held, as cited in Urban C. Lehner, "Unions Rekindle Organizing Efforts With New Tactics to Lure Members," *Wall Street Journal*, 28 July, 1980, sec. 2, p. 1.

[18]See Clay W. Hamner and Frank J. Smith, "Work Attitudes as Predictors of Unionization Activity," *Journal of Applied Psychology*, 63 (1978), 415–21; and Russell L. Smith and Anne H. Hopkins, "Public Employee Attitudes Toward Unions," *Industrial and Labor Relations Review*, 32 (1979), 484–95.

its messages. The investigation of trust and its implications for behavior is warranted because trust has received widespread attention in
the speech communication and social psychology disciplines.[19] As
120   Golembiewski and McConkie point out, "The burgeoning literature
pounds home one major point: trust acts as a salient factor in determining the character of a huge range of relationships."[20]

Of particular importance for this study, trust has been shown to
influence significantly communicative behavior within organizational
125   settings. Specifically, McGregor, in his discussion about how to reduce
differences between management and employees, argued that trust
induces communication while distrust retards communication.[21] Gibb
maintains that the degree of trust affects the quality and degree of
communication within organizations, with increases in trust leading to
130   more timely feedback, more effective communication, and construc-
tive action.[22] Crockett, Gaetner, and Dufur argue that trust is *the* basis
for effective delegation, two-level communication, giving and receiving feedback, and team spirit.[23] Roberts and O'Reilly report a study of
four organizations where they find trust to be a significant predictor
135   of reception of information between superiors and subordinates.[24]
Finally, with regard to labor relations, Nigro finds trust to be among
the most important components of effective labor relations and collective bargaining.[25]

The review of the literature above demonstrates that trust influ-
140   ences a wide range of organizationally-relevant variables. Furthermore, because labor unions are direct attempts both to organize and

---

[19]For a review of the relevance of trust to the speech communication discipline,
see W. Barnett Pearce, "Trust in Interpersonal Communication," *Speech Monographs*, 41
(1974), 236–44. For a substantive review of social psychological research on trust, see
Robert T. Golembiewski and Mark McConkie, "The Centrality of Interpersonal Trust
in Group Processes," in *Theories of Group Processes*, ed. Cary L. Cooper (London: John
Wiley, 1975), pp. 131–85.

[20]Golembiewski and McConkie, p. 131.

[21]Douglas McGregor, *The Professional Manager* (New York: McGraw-Hill, 1967).

[22]Jack R. Gibb, "Climate for Trust Formation," in *T-Group Theory and Laboratory
Method*, ed. Leland P. Bradford, Jack R. Gibb, and Kenneth D. Benne (New York: John
Wiley, 1964), pp. 279–309.

[23]B. Crockett, B. Gaetner, and M. Dufur, "OD in Large Systems," NTL Conference on New Technology in Organization Development, Washington, D.C., 1972, as
cited in Golembiewski and McConkie, pp. 159–60.

[24]Karlene H. Roberts and Charles A. O'Reilly III, "Failure in Upward Communication in Organizations: Three Possible Culprits," *Academy of Management Journal*,
17 (1974), 205–15.

[25]F. A. Nigro, *Management-Employee Relations in the Public Service* (Chicago: Public
Personnel Association, 1969), as cited in Golembiewski and McConkie, p. 131.

service workers, the study of how workers perceive these organizational communication variables operating potentially provides an indication of how labor unions use communication as a product and,
145   concurrently, how communication contributes to the process of organizing workers. Because the review of the literature indicates that
trust is a common denominator of these organizational communication variables, understanding how workers trust their labor union
and/or its messages provides an initial overview of how communica-
150   tion operates within labor unions.

Based upon the discussion above, the following research question and hypothesis were advanced:

Q_1: *Do workers differ with respect to trust of their labor union as an organizational
entity and trust of their labor union's messages?*

155   H_1: *Labor union members will demonstrate a significantly greater degree of trust in
their labor union and/or its messages than will nonlabor union members.*

One profitable method for studying organizational communication from a receiver orientation entails examining differences which
result from a host of demographic variables. Such studies must seek
160   to understand the relationship between demographic variables and
workers' perceptions of the organizational messages they receive.

The first set of demographic variables employed are those which
emerge from previous organizational communication research as significant receiver-oriented variables which influence communication-
165   oriented variables: age/seniority, race, and gender. Falcione and
Greenbaum report that 26 percent of all articles within the area of
"intergroup communication" (the second largest category of organizational communication research[26]) are concerned with the effects of
"age, race, and sex."[27] Furthermore, these variables have been pri-
170   marily employed to investigate relatively new areas of research (i.e.,
female managers' attitudes, black versus white leaders' attitudes,
etc.).[28] The findings from such studies point to the importance of
these demographic variables as significant predictors of such things as
communication attitudes and communication satisfaction within
175   various organizational settings. We believe that the relative impor-

[26]Falcione and Greenbaum, Vol. 5, p. 29.

[27]Falcione and Greenbaum, Vol. 5, p. 49.

[28]For example, see Paul J. Andrisani and Mitchell B. Shapiro, "Women's Atti-
tudes Toward Their Jobs: Some Longitudinal Data on a National Sample," *Personnel
Psychology*, 31 (1978), 15–34; and Kathryn Bartol, Charles L. Evans, and Melvin T. Stith,
"Black Versus White Leaders: A Comparative Review of the Literature," *Academy of
Management Review*, 3 (1978), 293–304.

tance given these variables within the relevant literature and their significant influence upon organizational communication justifies their selection as independent variables which cut across organizational contexts.

180   These demographic variables are also important to the labor union context. On a theoretical level, in a political arena relatively well integrated with regard to demographic variables of age/seniority, race, and gender, messages from the union must appeal to, and be understood by, a wide range of workers with different backgrounds,
185   characteristics, and needs. The investigation of these demographic variables thus provides some indication of the effectiveness of labor unions' use of communication in the process of organizing workers. With respect to relevant research, age has been shown to be a significant predictor of attitudinal militancy[29] and voting in a union cer-
190   tification election.[30] Race has been shown to influence attitudes toward labor unions[31] and voting in a union certification election.[32] Finally, it is surprising that research which investigates females' attitudes toward labor unions and/or their messages is almost nonexistent, given the increasing influence which females are having upon
195   the general work force and labor unions in particular.[33] However, what research does exist demonstrates that female labor unionists are not satisfied with the information they receive from their elected officials.[34]

The second set of demographic variables are those which are
200   firmly embedded within the labor union context itself: previous union membership and presence of a union member in the family.

[29]See Joseph A. Alutto and James A. Belasco, "Determinants of Attitudinal Militancy Among Nurses and Teachers," *Industrial and Labor Relations Review*, 24 (1974), 216–27.

[30]See Harry S. Farber and Daniel H. Saks, "Why Workers Want Unions: The Role of Relative Wages and Job Characteristics," *Journal of Political Economy*, 88 (1980), 349–69.

[31]See Kochan.

[32]See Farber and Saks; and Kochan.

[33]The percentage of women who are employed is expected by the government to increase from the current figure of 51 percent to 56.4–63.2 percent by the year 1990, as cited in Ronald E. Kutscher, "New Economic Projections Through 1990—An Overview," *Monthly Labor Review*, 104 (1981), 9–17. In terms of labor union membership, females represented 23.44 percent of the membership in 1978, or 5,106,000 total female union members, as cited in *Handbook of Labor Statistics* (Washington, D.C.: U.S. Department of Labor, Bureau of Labor Statistics, 1980), p. 412.

[34]See Barbara Wertheimer and Anne Nelson, *Trade Union Women* (New York: Praeger Publishers, 1975); and Marilyn S. Boyd, *Women's Liberation Ideology and Union Participation: A Study* (Saratoga, CA: Century Twenty One Publishers, 1981).

Research has demonstrated that workers with past union experience[35] and workers within labor union families[36] are more willing to join public employee labor unions than those workers without such
205   experience or family background.

Based upon the discussion above, the following hypotheses were advanced:

H_2: *Male workers will demonstrate a significantly greater degree of trust in their labor union and/or its messages than will female workers.*
210   H_3: *Black workers will demonstrate a significantly greater degree of trust in their labor union and/or its messages than will white workers.*
        H_4: *Workers who (a) have previously been labor union members, or (b) have a union member in their family will demonstrate a significantly greater degree of trust in their labor union and/or its messages than will workers who (a) have*
215   *not previously been labor union members, or (b) do not have a union member in their family.*
        H_5: *There will be a significant positive correlation between workers' age and seniority with respect to attributions of trustworthiness toward their labor union and its messages.*

220   **METHOD**

Subjects

In order to study the effects of affiliation behavior on workers' trust of their labor union and/or its messages, an *open shop* was selected for this study. An open shop is one in which there is a labor union and a
225   contract; however, employees are *not* required to join the labor union or pay for their representation. Therefore, economic considerations are not the crucial factors in workers' decisions to join a labor union within an open shop.

A metropolitan post office district was selected for this study, in
230   which approximately 3,600 employees are labor union members while approximately 625 are non-union members, more than a 5.5-to-1 ratio in favor of the union.

Independent Variables

Eight independent variables were used in this study. Subjects were
235   identified with respect to: (1) *questionnaire* answered (whether subjects

[35]See Lewis V. Immundo, Jr., "Why Federal Government Employees Join Unions: A Study of AFGE Local 1138," *Journal of Collective Negotiations*, 4 (1975), 319–28.

[36]See Helen J. Christrup, "Why Do Government Employees Join Unions?" *Personnel Administration*, 29 (1966), 49–54.

were responding to a questionnaire about the union itself [*union*] or a questionnaire about its messages [*messages*]); (2) *affiliation* (*union member* or *non-union member*); (3) *gender;* (4) *race* (*black* or *white*); (5) *previous union membership* (*yes* or *no*) (6) *presence of a union member in the family*
240 (*yes* or *no*); (7) *age:* and (8) *seniority.*

Dependent Variable

The Giffin Trust Differential was used as the dependent measure of trust.[37] This instrument measures three factors: *character,* or attributions about the reliability and intentions of a referent; *expertness,* or
245 attributions about a referent with respect to knowledge; and *dynamism,* or attributions about a referent with regard to degree of activity.[38] Each factor is assessed by nine items on a seven-point semantic differential; hence, the range of scores for each factor is potentially from 9 to 63. The questionnaire used was a slight modification of the Giffin
250 instrument.[39]

Procedure

The Giffin Trust Differential was mailed to all bargaining unit employees of the metropolitan postal district. Mailings contained a cover sheet explaining the purpose of the study, an instruction sheet, a
255 demographic questionnaire, the Giffin Trust Differential, and a postage-paid return envelope. Half of the labor union and non-union members were asked to complete the trust instrument with respect to the statement, "The union is ____"; while the other half of the labor union and non-union members were asked to complete the trust in-
260 strument using the referent, "Written and spoken messages I have received from the union have been ____."

[37]For his conceptualization of trust, see Kim Giffin, "The Contributions of Studies of Source Credibility to a Theory of Interpersonal Trust in the Communication Process," *Psychological Bulletin,* 68 (1967), 104–20; Kim Giffin, "Interpersonal Trust in Small Group Communication," *Quarterly Journal of Speech,* 53 (1967), 224–34; and Kim Giffin and Bobby Patton, "Personal Trust in Human Interaction," in *Basic Readings in Interpersonal Communication,* ed. Kim Giffin and Bobby Patton (New York: Harper and Row, 1971) pp. 375–94. For his measurement of interpersonal trust, see Kim Giffin, *The Trust Differential,* (Lawrence: University of Kansas, 1968); and Kim Giffin, *The Conceptualization and Measurement of Interpersonal Trust* (Lawrence: University of Kansas, 1969).

[38]For a discussion of the relationship between these three factors and the construct of source credibility, see Kim Giffin, "The Contributions of Studies of Source Credibility."

[39]The modification involved the substitution of the term *outgoing* for the term *extroverted,* as subjects demonstrated difficulty understanding the latter term in pretesting. The modification produced no significant differences between the modified Giffin Trust Differential and the original instrument ($t = .69$, $df = 13$).

In total, 866 questionnaires were returned, of which 710 were sufficiently complete for use in this study. Of the 710 questionnaires used, 585 labor union members and 125 non-union members were 265 represented; 366 females and 344 males were represented; and 434 blacks and 260 whites were represented.

Data Treatment[40]

Because the dependent measures of trust were highly correlated (*expertness* with *character*, .85; *expertness* with *dynamism*, .83; and *character* 270 with *dynamism*, .76), the effects of the independent variables of *questionnaire, affiliation, race, previous,* and *family* were analyzed through the use of a multivariate analysis of variance (MANOVA), using Wilks Lambda criterion, with specific effects ($p < .05$) further explored via univariate tests.[41] The independent variables of *age* and *seniority* were 275 analyzed through the use of Pearson Product-Moment correlations with respect to the dependent measures of trust. As a final analysis, all independent variables, except *questionnaire*, were entered into multiple regression analyses for the purpose of establishing the relative weights of each independent variable.[42]

280 **RESULTS**

MANOVA

The tests of significance for overall effects demonstrated that *questionnaire* was significant (Wilks Lambda = .96, F[3, 631] = 8.20, $p < .001$), *affiliation* was significant (Wilks Lambda = .96, F[3, 631] = 8.47, $p <$ 285 .001), and *race* was significant (Wilks Lambda = .97, F[3, 631] = 5.99, $p = .001$).

Univariate tests on the *questionnaire* variable indicated significant effects for *character*, (F[1, 633] = 9.47, $p = .002$, eta^2 = .014), and marginal significance for *dynamism*, (F[1, 633] = 3.34, $p = .068$, eta^2 = 290 .005). In both cases, the union was perceived as significantly higher than the union's messages. For *character*, the mean for the *union* condi-

[40]The authors are grateful to Dorris Allen for her help with the statistical analyses for this study.

[41]The MANOVA program, as well as the subsequent univariate tests, sums over the questionnaires. In such cases, we refer to the dependent variable as perceptions of the *union and its messages.*

[42]The equipment limitations were such that inclusion of the continuous variables of age and seniority in the MANOVA program was prohibited. Hence, a regression equation was employed for the purpose of establishing the relative weights of the independent variables.

TABLE 1
Means and Standard Deviations for Dependent Variables
by Affiliation Condition

	Union Members	Non-Union Members
Character	X = 45.22	X = 40.09
	SD = 12.03	SD = 11.52
Expertness	X = 42.26	X = 36.09
	SD = 12.92	SD = 13.12
Dynamism	X = 40.31	X = 33.22
	SD = 12.83	SD = 12.55

tion was 44.27 (SD = 12.10) as opposed to the *message* condition mean of 41.68 (SD = 13.24). For *dynamism,* the mean for the *union* condition was 38.87 (SD = 13.07) as opposed to the *message* condition mean of 37.09 (SD = 13.79).

Univariate tests on the *affiliation* variable indicated significant effects for all three of the dependent measures: *character,* (F[1, 633] = 23.41, $p < .001$, $eta^2 = 0.4$; *expertness,* (F[1, 633] = 20.08, $p < .001$, $eta^2 = 0.31$); and *dynamism,* (F[1, 633] = 21.29, $p < .001$, $eta^2 = .033$). As Table 1 indicates, the means for the *union members* were significantly higher than the means for the *non-union members* for all dependent measures.

Univariate tests on the *race* variable indicated significant effects for *expertness,* (F[1, 633] = 6.77, $p = .009$, $eta^2 = .011$), and marginal significance for *character,* (F[1, 633] = 3.58, $p = .059$, $eta^2 = .006$). In both cases, blacks had a higher trust of their union and its messages than did whites. For *expertness,* the mean for *blacks* was 41.53 (SD = 12.85) as opposed to the mean for *whites* of 39.84 (SD = 13.68). For *character,* the mean for *blacks* was 43.36 (SD = 12.57) as opposed to the mean for *whites* of 42.41 (SD = 13.15).

No other independent variables were statistically significant, nor any two-way interactions between independent variables. Therefore, hypotheses 1 and 3 were supported while hypotheses 2 and 4 were not.

Correlations

Pearson Product-Moment correlations were run for the variables of *age* and *seniority* with respect to the dependent measures. As predicted in hypothesis 5, *age* and *seniority* were positively correlated with each of the trust dimensions at the .002 level of probability or less. Specifically, *age* was positively correlated with *character* (r = .20, $r^2 = .04$), *expertness* (r = .16, $r^2 = .03$), and *dynamism* (r = .18, $r^2 = 0.3$); while

seniority was positively correlated with *character* (r = .16, r^2 = .03), *expertness* (r = .13, r^2 = .02), and *dynamism* (r = .12, r^2 = .01). While the results supported the hypothesis, it must be noted that the cor-
325   relations are in the low range.

Regression Analyses

All independent variables, except *questionnaire*, were first entered into a multiple regression analysis. The results indicated that *affiliation* (beta = .042, r = .21, r^2 = .04) and *age* (beta = .03, r = .27, r^2 = .07)
330   were the only two variables which carried significant weight in the equation.

   All independent variables, except *questionnaire*, were then entered into separate multiple regression analyses for *union* and *non-union members*. With regard to *union members*, only *age* (beta = .17, r =
335   .18, r^2 = .03) carried significant weight in the equation. However, with regard to *non-union members*, four variables were found to carry significant weight in the equation: *age* (beta = .21, r = .24, r^2 = .06); *race* (beta = −.18, r = .19, r^2 = .04); *gender* (beta = .16, r = .29, r^2 = .08); and *previous* (beta = −.16, r = .32, r^2 = .03).

340   **DISCUSSION**

This study investigated workers' attitudes toward their labor union and its messages with respect to trustworthiness. The findings demonstrated that significant attributional differences exist with respect to perceived trust for: (1) the labor union versus the labor union's
345   messages; (2) labor union members versus non-union members; and (3) some of the demographic variables studied. The importance of these findings are discussed with respect to the study of communication within the labor union context and organizational communication research in general.
350   The findings from this study demonstrate that workers differ significantly with respect to perceptions of their labor union as an entity versus their labor union's messages with regard to the character dimension of the trust instrument. It appears that the labor union in general has a reservoir of goodwill among both union and non-union
355   members which its messages have not lived up to. Given the high correlation between character and dynamism, and the marginal significance of the difference between the union and its messages with respect to dynamism, it could be inferred that increasing the dynamism of the communication attempts might also increase the character per-
360   ception of unions' messages. Unfortunately, even sizable increases in perceived dynamism of unions' messages will not necessarily increase

the perceived character of many union messages, which all too frequently are perceived as expensive campaign literature with each message (i.e., newspapers, bulletins, etc.) centered around a grinning picture and headline dedicated to the President, or whomever else is in charge politically. Future studies will need to assess more specifically the problems labor unions have constructing messages which live up to their accepted character image.

These differences between perceptions of the labor union and its messages suggest that communication within organizations may sometimes lag behind other aspects of the organization. Such a lag could be the case if communication within the organization is seen merely as a means to an end rather than as vital in and of itself. Such a view could appear to run counter to Hawes' conception of organization emerging from communication.[43] If unions and other organizations fail to understand that organization in part grows from communication, they may tend to use communication only as a means to an end, thereby contributing to their messages being seen as significantly less trustworthy than the organization itself. This may, in turn, imply that unions, and possibly other organizations, have a more limited potential for influencing their members through oral and written communication than has been thought to be the case. A good example of this was the virtually unanimous organizational support on the part of labor union leadership for Jimmy Carter in the 1980 presidential election, in spite of which 42 percent of union households voted for Ronald Reagan, and another seven percent voted for John Anderson.[44]

The findings reported above suggest that organizational communication researchers cannot necessarily generalize about subjects' attitudes toward an organization itself solely on the basis of their attitudes toward an organization's messages, and vice versa. While there is probably a strong link between perceptions of organizations and perceptions of organizations' messages—which appears to hold true for any specific demographic variable this study investigated (given the lack of significance for any two-way interactions involving questionnaire)—these two perceptual referents seem to differ significantly when summed over workers' demographic characteristics.

While there exist significant differences between workers' trust in the character dimension of the union and its messages, both levels of trust occur within the same general range, given the parameters of the instrument. It is important for organizational communication researchers to know whether perceptions of organizations and percep-

[43]Hawes.

[44]*New York Times*, 4 Jan. 1981, sec. 3, p. 1.

tions of their communication attempts always fall in the same general range for trust, and other relevant organizational perceptions, as they did in this study. If this is the case, it may suggest that organizations cannot significantly alter perceptions of themselves without also addressing the need to alter perceptions of their message attempts, thereby reinforcing Hawes' position.[45]

With respect to affiliation behavior, union members trusted the union and its messages to a significantly greater degree than did non-union members on all relevant dimensions of trust. These differences are not startling; nevertheless, they do confirm the prediction advanced for this study. What is surprising, however, is the fact that all scores on all dimensions of the trust instrument for both the union and its messages achieved only medium levels of trust. The finding of only medium levels of trust for the union and its messages for *both members and non-union members* may attract the most attention from unionists and industrial relations personnel alike. Union officers frequently decry the "apathy" or disinterest of union members. It may well be the case that workers are communicating to union leaders that an organization and its messages which earn only lukewarm levels of trust for their character, expertness, and dynamism earn only lukewarm participation and support. If later research establishes a link between trust and support for, or participation in, labor unions, the above reported medium levels of trust may prove to be one cause for the decline in labor union membership and support over the last quarter century.

It is also important for organizational communication researchers to investigate whether the medium levels of trust which were demonstrated in this study toward the union and its messages, on all dimensions of the trust instrument, generalize to other organizations and their communication attempts. The findings from this study suggest that the labor union has much room to improve perceptions of its messages. Is this the case with other types of organizations, or is the finding a specific artifact of the labor union context?

Of the demographic variables which cut across organizational contexts, three out of the four (race, age, and seniority) demonstrated significant effects.

With respect to race, the findings confirm previously held beliefs that blacks hold higher evaluations of the union than do whites.[46] In this study, the union leadership is primarily black while nationally

---

[45]Hawes.

[46]See Farber and Saks; and Kochan.

blacks are underrepresented in leadership positions;[47] yet blacks demonstrate higher evaluations of the union than did whites. Future research might potentially explain this seeming paradox by ascertain-
445 ing whether the observed racial differences are due to different needs which white and black workers have, including communication needs, and their perceptions of the union's ability (expertness) and willing-ness (character) to meet such needs.

Both age and seniority were found to be positively correlated
450 with trust in the union and its messages. These findings are best understood, however, in light of the subsequent regression analyses in which age alone carried significant weight. The findings from this study indicate that trust in the labor union and its messages is a function of age and not necessarily a function of length of service with
455 the employer.

With respect to gender, no significant differences were found. However, in light of the indication that female union members' com-munication needs are not being adequately met and the increasing role of females in the labor force and labor unions, further research is
460 needed before generalizable conclusions can be drawn.

The fact that three of the four demographic variables chosen demonstrated significant effects lends validity to the generalizability of these variables across organizational contexts. In addition, the re-gression analyses demonstrated that these variables function as differ-
465 ent predictor variables when affiliation behavior is partialled out. Hence, future communication research within the labor union, partic-ularly that research directed at understanding affiliation behavior, will need to take these variables into account, if only as salient second-ary factors. However, the two demographic variables embedded
470 within the labor union context did not demonstrate any significant effects. Future research will need to determine more clearly what types of variables specific to the labor union context influence workers' perceptions of their labor union and its messages.

This exploratory study has been an initial attempt to understand
475 how labor unions and their messages are perceived by workers within the labor force. The findings suggest a number of profitable direc-tions for future research with respect to the study of communication within the labor union context. First, it is important to employ a causal model to investigate more fully the relationship between workers'

[47]See William Kornhauser, "The Negro Union Official: A Study of Sponsorship and Control," in *Black Workers and Organized Labor,* ed. John H. Bracey, Jr., August Meier, and Elliott Rudwick (Belmont, CA: Wadsworth Publishing Company, 1971), pp. 185–98.

480   perceptions of the messages they receive from their labor union and
      union affiliation and participation. For example, workers' perceptions
      of the types of compliance-gaining strategies used by labor unions in
      certification and decertification elections might be studied and the
      success rate for these messages directly assessed. Second, we need to
485   understand how other specific receiver characteristics influence
      workers' perceptions of the messages they receive from their labor
      union, and the relationship between these perceptions and other rele-
      vant variables. For example, it might be important to know if workers'
      preferred amounts of information, or perceived ability to communi-
490   cate upwards to the union leadership, are related to such things as
      perceived accuracy of messages, subsequent distortions of the mes-
      sages received, job satisfaction, worker morale, and commitment.

          In many regards, this study raises more questions with respect to
      the role of communication within the labor union context than it
495   answers. If this study provides impetus for other researchers within
      the speech communication discipline and labor relations to begin ad-
      dressing these and other concerns in this massive, and almost unex-
      plored field, then it has served an important purpose.

COMMENTS ON THE STUDY

Introduction

The article's introduction helps readers see why the research question is
worth asking, the general assumptions or theory behind it, and thus, the
value of conducting the study. Botan and Frey maintain that the economic
and social importance of unions warrant academic study (6–12). They
adopt a *receiver orientation*—being interested in how receivers, in this case
union and non-union members, view their labor union (29–38). Further,
they argue that organizational communication can be studied both as product and process, and that a labor union is a good context for studying
organizational communication in these two ways (13–28). The three goals
of the study then are explained (39–52).

    The authors might have done more to explain their theoretical per-
spective and its implications for this study. They also focus only on labor
unions, so it is not clear how readers can use these results to better understand trust in other kinds of organizations.

Review of the Literature, Research Question,
and Hypotheses

The literature review reports previous research related to the topic being
investigated, in this case communication within unions and other organiza-

tional communication issues. Their review of the scant literature leads them to conclude that, "The communication needs of workers are not being adequately met by labor unions" (80–81). The independent variables (94–113), and the dependent variable (114–150) are then explained.

The review of the literature justifies the research question (153–154). The principal hypothesis for this study (155–156) is extrapolated from the research question. In this case, a formal theory was not used to generate the hypotheses; rather, they were derived from the review of literature. The research, therefore, tests an "informal" theory. Four subsidiary hypotheses related to demographic variables such as age, sex, and race are also generated from the literature and tested (208–219). Researchers sometimes tend to "throw in" several hypotheses based on such demographic variables. However, only variables indicated as relevant by the review of the literature should be included, and they should be phrased as hypotheses. The tendency to throw in extraneous, often demographic, variables comes, we think, from one of two factors.

First, researchers sometimes do not do a good enough review of the literature to know which variables are likely to be important, so they collect information on every variable they can think of so as not to miss anything. This can be costly because it usually makes the survey longer and may offend or bore respondents, thereby reducing response rate and validity.

Second, researchers sometimes conduct **variable analytic studies,** which involve collecting information on many variables and testing them all to see what might turn out to be significant. The variable analytic approach does not take its direction from a theory or body of literature, so it is more of a "fishing expedition" than systematic research and contributes little to theory development. Naive consumers are often fooled when the variable analytic approach yields significant findings. But the laws of chance say that if enough statistical tests are run on enough variables something will turn out statistically significant, so these results are less meaningful than the results generated by theory-driven research.

Botan and Frey use the relevant literature to justify the variables studied. Nevertheless, the fourth hypothesis (212–216) is worded poorly because it really contains two testable statements, which is confusing. They should be phrased as two separate hypotheses; one contrasting workers who have and have not previously been labor union members, and one contrasting workers who have and do not have a labor union member in their families.

Method

The authors begin the methods section by explaining that the sampling frame of an *open shop* (required by law for federal employees) was particularly appropriate for studying the role of trust in organizational communication (222–228). In an open shop employees may choose to avoid paying union dues while the union is required by law to extend its protection to them, as well as the benefits and pay scale gained in negotiations. Therefore, trust in the union and its messages is not confounded by material interests. An open shop also allows comparisons between perceptions of members and nonmembers of the same union, thereby eliminating differences in workplace or union as a potentially confounding factor.

The population of interest was the 4,225 employees of a metropolitan postal district (229–232). In many communication studies a random sample is drawn from the available sampling frame, but in this study the researchers mailed a questionnaire to all members, thus attempting to conduct a *census*. This decision was based on two reasons. First, the researchers realized that if they only surveyed a small sample they might have a low response rate due to the nature of the questionnaire, to possible negative attitudes toward participation in research, or to possible concern that respondents' answers, if revealed, might get them in some difficulties with either their union leadership or management. Second, given the number of variables and their levels, or conditions (such as the two levels or conditions of gender—male and female), a large number of respondents was needed to conduct the statistical procedures involved. The decision to mail questionnaires to all employees seems, therefore, to have been a good one.

Of course, this union is only one among the many unions and millions of organizations that exist. So while the generalizability of the study's findings to *this* union is strong, the generalizability to all unions or all organizations is questionable. Using this union as an example was desirable because only a limited number of contexts exist in which possibly confounding variables, such as personal economic incentive, could be controlled. This study enhanced internal validity by controlling for such confounding variables, but, as often happens, a trade-off with external validity (generalizability) was necessary.

The literature review indicates that 8 independent variables—a fairly large number—might influence how workers view unions (234–240). Most communication studies use fewer independent variables because that requires fewer respondents for the statistical analyses to be meaningful. Six of this study's eight independent variables (referent [labor union versus labor union's messages; called "questionnaire" as a shorthand way to indicate how it was operationalized], affiliation, gender, race, previous union membership, and presence of a union member in the family) each have two levels (such as male/female or member/nonmember). Each level of each variable, when crossed with the other variables, creates a cell, each of which must have enough responses, usually about 20 per cell, for the statistical procedure used. But this study used a maximum of five independent variables at one time (270–274), so $2 \times 2 \times 2 \times 2 \times 2 = 32$ cells $\times$ 20 subjects per cell = 640 subjects needed. An adequate number of subjects (710) were used (262–263). Also, most independent variables were defined precisely or *operationalized* (except the third, seventh, and eighth). The authors assumed readers would know that gender is measured as male or female, and that age and seniority are measured in years.

The goal of this study was to find out what brings about changes in the dependent variable, trust, so how it is measured is central to establishing internal validity. To measure trust, a well known scale was used. The basic characteristics of this scale are explained and the reader is given several published citations which explain it (242–250; footnotes 37 and 38).

Researchers' responsibility does not end when an existing scale is adopted. They still have to take their specific situations and respondents into account. The trust scale used in this study was developed and tested with college students, but college students and industrial workers may not interpret this scale in the same way. To assure that the scale was comprehensible to this group, a pilot test was conducted. The test showed that several industrial workers had difficulty understanding one of the words (footnote 39), so the scale was modified slightly. If the modified scale was too different from the original, everything known about the original might not apply. So a statistical test was run to make sure that the modified scale was clear to the respondents while still yielding the same information as the original. This was found to be the case.

Because they wanted to learn the opinions of an entire organization, which made personal contact with every respondent outside of work prohibitively time-consuming, the researchers used a questionnaire (252–261). Using a mail questionnaire rather than conducting interviews seems appropriate because the questionnaire used closed questions, was less costly than training interviewers to administer it over the phone, and better assured respondents' anonymity. Because all respondents had passed various written exams to become postal workers, to qualify for specialized jobs, and to handle written mail, the researchers also assumed the written format would not exclude anyone.

The researchers also chose to mail the questionnaires to respondents, which posed other potential problems. For example, only employees with a current mailing address on file could be sent mail. Postal workers, however, probably have valid mailing addresses, so the researchers did not think these potential problems affected their study.

A cover letter was included in the mailing to explain the purpose of the study and to provide instructions (253–254). A cover letter usually generates a higher return rate when it is on a university's letterhead because respondents know the study is legitimate and will not result in a sales call. (These authors failed to report that their cover sheet was on university letterhead.) They included a postage-paid return envelope (255–256), which also has been shown to improve response rate. Without a postage-paid return envelope, only respondents highly committed to the research study usually return a questionnaire. These authors also failed to report that they sent a follow-up mailing, or reminder notice, two weeks after the initial mailing.

These researchers chose to operationalize one of their main independent variables—referent (the labor union versus the labor union's *messages*)—by having two versions of the questionnaire, one referring to "the union" and the other referring to the "written and spoken messages I have received from the union" (256–261). This allowed them to compare how the workers respond to their union as an entity versus how they respond to its messages. These two referents thus served to operationalize this independent variable.

While 866 questionnaires were returned, only 710 could be used (262–263). Incomplete questionnaires are a thorny problem, particularly when the scoring requires totaling responses to all the individual items, called **summative scales.** A missing answer to one item, therefore, makes a respondent's score not comparable with the scores of other respondents. Summative scales are widely used so this is a common problem. When calculating the response rate, only complete questionnaires can be counted.

A data treatment section is provided to explain how the statistical calculations were done and why (267–279). **Multivariate procedures** are used whenever there are two or more dependent variables. In this case, a *Multivariate Analysis of Variance* procedure, called *MANOVA,* was used because the three parts of the dependent variable (character, expertness, and dynamism) were highly correlated. (Incidentally, the original submission to the journal did not use a MANOVA analysis, but a "blind" reviewer of the article suggested this as the appropriate technique.)

Results

This is a quantitative hypothesis-testing study, so the findings take the form of statistical results. The statistical analyses indicate which variables have a *significant* effect on the outcome. Specifically, each statistical test reveals the probability that the scores would be obtained by chance if the independent variable being studied really had no effect. Remember that the default probability level in the social sciences is usually $p = .05$, or a 95% probability that the effect reported did not occur by chance. (Other levels, such as $p = .01$ [99%], however, are often adopted by researchers.) The little "p" stands for probability and the number after it indicates the degree of assurance that the results are not due to chance. Most readers first look for this "p" figure because whether it is smaller or larger than .05 tells whether to adopt or reject a **null hypothesis** (which argues that there are no differences between groups or no relationships between variables). Keep in mind, however, that a finding might be statistically significant yet not meaningful, so researchers have to interpret what the results mean.

The first set of results explain the effects of each independent variable that is measured on a nominal scale (such as gender) on perceptions of trust (281–314). The MANOVA analyses demonstrate that many of the independent variables affected the interrelated components of trust (expertness, character, and dynamism). **Univariate tests** were then used to see how each independent variable affected each of the dependent variables of expertness, character, and dynamism. The authors report F-values, so you know ANOVA was used (see Chapter 2) and the eta^2 scores report the proportion of variance in the dependent variable that is explained. The researchers also clarify these effects by providing the relevant means and **standard deviations** (which show how much scores vary from the mean "on the average") for each of the significant findings.

Note that the findings indicate that gender (H_2) and previous union membership and union member in the family (H_4) did not significantly affect trust in either the union or its messages (311–314). Specific results (such as means and standard deviations) are not given for these findings because nonsignificant findings usually require no elaboration.

The second set of results examine the relationships between the two independent variables that were measured with a continuous scale (age and seniority [number of years]) and the three dimensions of trust (315–325). A correlational procedure yields a **correlation coefficient**—a numerical summary of the type and strength of a relationship between two variables. A correlation coefficient ranges from +1.00 (a perfect positive relationship) to .00 (no relationship) to −1.00 (a perfect negative relationship). For example, age was found to correlate positively ($r = .20$) with the character dimension of trust. The correlation coefficient tells researchers how much one variable changes as another one changes, so this positive correlation means that as age goes up trust in the character of the union and the union's messages goes up.

A correlation coefficient that has less than a .05 chance of error is significant, but squaring the correlation coefficient yields an even more useful figure, the *coefficient of determination.* A **coefficient of determination** tells researchers what percentage of the change in one variable is explained by changes in the other. The results, show, for example, that even though age is positively correlated with character perceptions, only 4% of character is explained by age, a relatively low level, as the authors acknowledge (320–325).

The final set of results examine the extent to which a set of independent variables can predict scores on a dependent variable (or even a set of dependent variables), called **regression analyses** (326–339). A regression analysis yields a **beta score** that indicates whether each independent variable significantly affects the dependent variable, and also yields a correlation coefficient and a coefficient of determination for each independent variable. In this study, a regression analysis demonstrated that labor union affiliation and age were the two best predictors of trust in the union and its messages. Additional regression analyses also showed that there were some differences between which variables predict labor union and non-union members' trust in the union and its messages. Only age was a significant predictor for union members, while age, race, gender, and previous union membership were all significant predictors for non-union members. It should be pointed out, however, that the referent variable (the union versus the union's messages) was not included in the regression analyses, and conclusions based on analyses that exclude variables may be suspect. Additionally, if there is a significant difference between perceptions of the labor union and its messages, as the MANOVA results showed, then perhaps separate regression analyses should have been run for each referent.

Discussion

The discussion starts with a brief summary of the findings and the authors then draw some conclusions. For example, they argue that increasing the dynamism of union messages increases character perceptions of those messages because these two variables are related strongly to each other (350–360). This is not a "fact," but an opinion based on the results. The authors also tie the results back to their original theory discussion and use an example from politics to support their conclusion (369–387).

The conclusions from this study are also related to other situations. Based on their results the authors warn that, "Organizational communication researchers cannot necessarily generalize about subjects' attitudes toward an organization itself solely on the basis of their attitudes toward an organization's messages, and vice versa" (388–391). This may be important because organizational communication researchers and practitioners sometimes fail to distinguish between workers' attitudes toward messages and their attitudes toward the entity sending the messages. However, this conclusion needs to be investigated further. The two levels of the referent variable (the union versus the union's messages), for example, were probably not equivalent. Using a scale to rate the expertness, character, or dynamism of an organization makes sense to most people, but rating message behavior is difficult to do. The researchers also did not assess workers' perceptions of the different types of messages they have received from the union (such as verbal comments from labor union representatives or newsletters).

Research often produces results that both support and contradict the starting point of a study. In this case, the authors point out that Hawes' position, which they referred to earlier in the article, is *both* contradicted and supported (369–408).

The findings are put into perspective for the reader by pointing out that *all* scores were only in the *middle* range of possible scores (398–401). This is important because sometimes researchers report only statistically significant results and neglect to discuss how meaningful these results are. In this case, the range of scores sheds some light on a major social trend. Clearly, if all scores for trust in the union and its messages had been very high, the results would have meant something different. The union, for example, would not need to change any of its messages.

The article concludes by pointing out that this study is exploratory (474–476). This means the study addresses a new area and, although not giving definitive answers, points to other useful research (476–492). Labeling one's work as exploratory is sometimes done to prevent being held to the same high standards as more definitive or less exploratory research should be. Some research is exploratory, but the term is often used to minimize critical standards, and that may have been the case here. Finally, the authors point out two specific issues that need further study and conclude with a call for other research on communication in labor unions (493–498).

CONCLUSION

In conclusion, Botan and Frey's research gives us an opportunity to examine closely the strengths and limitations of conducting survey questionnaire research. When used effectively, questionnaires are an important means of collecting information from a population or from a sample and then generalizing the results back to its population.

QUESTIONS AND ACTIVITIES TO CONSIDER

1. Was a mail questionnaire the best way to gather the data for this study? What are its relative advantages and disadvantages compared to other research methodologies possible for these authors' particular research objectives?
2. What can you conclude about communication in labor unions after reading the results from this survey? What can you conclude about communication in other kinds of organizations?
3. Develop a survey questionnaire to find out something about communication behavior. For example, write four or five questions you could use to assess why people lie and what they lie about. Exchange these with a classmate and then explain why you worded each question as you did. Does each question get at lying behavior in a valid manner? Will potential respondents understand each question as you intended? Now hand this questionnaire out to ten of your friends, have them complete it, and then ask them to give you feedback about the question-

naire. What problems, if any, did they have completing it? What changes do you need to make in the wording?

4. Evaluate the questions asked in this survey according to the criteria given earlier in the chapter. Would you have reworded any?

5. Suppose the authors had personally contacted nonrespondents to the survey and asked them to complete the questionnaire. How would that have helped or hindered the quality of their findings?

FURTHER READINGS ON SURVEY QUESTIONNAIRE RESEARCH

Babbie, E. R. (1973). *Survey research methods.* Belmont, CA: Wadsworth.

Belson, W. R. (1981). *The design and understanding of survey questions.* Aldershot, England: Gower.

Berdi, D. R., & Anderson, J. F. (1974). *Questionnaire design and use.* Metuchen, NJ: Scarecrow.

Converse, J. M., & Presser, S. (1986). *Survey questions: Handcrafting the standard questionnaire.* Beverly Hills, CA: Sage.

Fink, A., & Kosecoff, J. (1985). *How to conduct surveys: A step-by-step guide.* Beverly Hills, CA: Sage.

Labrow, P. (1980). *Advanced questionnaire design.* Cambridge, MA: Abt Associates.

Sudman, S., & Bradburn, N. (1982). *Asking questions: A practical guide to questionnaire design.* San Francisco: Jossey-Bass.

EXAMPLES OF SURVEY QUESTIONNAIRE RESEARCH

Cline, R. J. W., Freeman, K. E., & Johnson, S. J. (1990). Talk among sexual partners about AIDS: Factors differentiating those who talk from those who do not. *Communication Research, 17,* 792–808.

This study investigated differences among four groups relative to talking about acquired immune deficiency syndrome (AIDS) with a sexual partner: safe-sex talkers, general AIDS talkers, nontalkers, and want-to-be talkers. A questionnaire assessing respondents' knowledge, attitudes, and behaviors with regard to AIDS and communication about AIDS, homophobia, and reactions to people with AIDS was mailed to 1,300 randomly selected undergraduate students at a southeastern university. The results from 588 questionnaires demonstrated that the differences between the groups concerned relational issues rather than health issues, as those who did not talk with their sexual partners about AIDS were more concerned about interpersonal relationships than about their long-term health. A sad irony, however was the finding that these groups failed to differ in most attitudes about condom use and AIDS talk and in their sexual and preventive behavior.

Gladney, G. A. (1990). Newspaper excellence: How editors of small & large papers judge quality. *Newspaper Research Journal, 11,* 58–72.

Four hundred questionnaires were mailed to senior-level editors at large (140,000+), medium (30,000–139,999), and small daily (<30,000) newspapers, and a sample of 100 was drawn from each group. The questionnaire asked respondents to rank the importance of nine organizational standards (such as integrity and editorial coverage) and nine content standards (including lack of sensationalism and good writing). Results from 247 respondents showed that editors of smaller papers evaluate newspaper excellence differently than do their big-paper counterparts.

Greenhalgh, L., & Jick, T. D. (1989). Survivor sense making and reactions to organizational decline: Effects of individual differences. *Management Communication Quarterly, 2,* 305–327.

This study investigated differences in employees' reactions to major organizational upheavals, such as mergers or restructuring of declining organizations. Questionnaires were distributed randomly to 200 employees at a hospital who were experiencing great uncertainty regarding an announced merger with another hospital. The questionnaires measured employees' ambiguity about the organization's future and tasks, two personality factors (tolerance of ambiguity and need for security), and hypothesized reactions (health problems, emotional strain, job satisfaction, job involvement, and propensity to leave). Responses from 163 employees demonstrated that personality explained the differences in employees' reactions to the situation. Employees who had a low tolerance for ambiguity and a high need for security saw a rosier picture regarding the cloudy future of their jobs and the organization, remained more satisfied with their jobs, and reported less likelihood of leaving the organization. This counter-intuitive finding occurred because these employees responded to potentially threatening communication by maintaining a defense mechanism that denied the validity of the information.

Lamude, K. G., Lamude, D., & Scudder, J. (1989). The relationship between physicians' use of power strategies and type A orientation in physician-patient communication. *Communication Research Reports, 6,* 106–110.

This study investigated the relationship between physicians' personality and their use of behavior alteration techniques (BATs) with patients. A nonrandom sample of 107 patients and 96 physicians completed questionnaires that assessed whether the physicians had a "type-A" orientation (individuals who have a constant sense of time urgency, an unrelenting drive, and an aggressive manner) and their use of 22 different BATs, such as punishments and rewards for behavior. The results demonstrated that both physicians and patients positively associated type-A physicians with use of antisocial BATs and negatively associated type-A physicians with use of positive BATs.

Manev, O. (1991). The disagreeing audience: Change in criteria for evaluating mass media effectiveness with the democratization of the Soviet society. *Communication Research, 18,* 25–52.

Survey questionnaires measuring respondents' use of the media and agreement with and trust in the assessments expressed in media reports were obtained from a representative sample of 2,000 Byelorussians, ages 16 to 30, in five social class categories (collective farmers, workers, technical employees, secondary and professional school students, and university students) between 1985 and 1987. Survey results were compared to a content analysis of reports of problems on Soviet radio and television and in youth newspapers. The results showed that those who disagreed with and did not trust the mass media in the Soviet Union, as compared with the agreeing audience, demonstrated more self-consciousness and social activity—behaviors that indicate greater preparedness for the restructuring of Soviet society. The author suggests that disagreement with the mass media is an important positive force for the democratization of society.

Chapter 5

Survey Interview Research

INTRODUCTION TO THE METHOD

Have you ever been stopped in a mall and asked questions by a market researcher, or been called on the telephone and questioned by a political polling firm? If so, you are one of the growing number of respondents who have been asked to complete a marketing survey or political poll interview. Survey Sampling, Inc. (1990), a survey research firm, estimates that 26% of people in the United States have been contacted by telephone and asked to complete a survey. Interviews, however, are not just used by market researchers; they also are an important methodological procedure used by communication researchers and other social scientists.

An interview involves the presentation of oral questions by one person (an interviewer) to another (the respondent). Kahn and Cannell (1958) describe an interview as a "conversation with a purpose." Researchers conducting *survey interviews* pose questions orally to a sample of respondents for the purpose of drawing inferences about the population the respondents represent. In communication research, survey interviews are used to describe, explain, and predict the communication behavior of a population of interest.

Advantages and Disadvantages of Survey Interviews

The primary difference between a survey interview and a survey questionnaire is the method used to elicit the self-reports: oral versus written, respectively. This difference produces some relative advantages and disadvantages which survey researchers take into account when choosing between these two procedures.

Interviews are particularly useful when respondents do not have proficient reading skills, or when researchers ask complex and difficult questions that need explanation. Interviews also provide opportunities to establish **rapport** between the interviewer and respondents, which can encourage respondents to share more information than they would when completing a questionnaire. Tucker, Weaver, and Berryman-Fink (1983) point out that some researchers prefer to conduct interviews when asking sensitive or embarrassing questions, because people are more likely to answer these questions when they have developed rapport with an interviewer. Another important advantage of interviews is that researchers can *probe* for more detailed and complete answers. A **probe** is defined by Babbie (1989) as, "a neutral, nondirective question designed to elicit an elaboration on an incomplete or ambiguous response, given in an interview in response to an open-ended question. Examples would include: 'Anything else?' 'How is that?' 'In what ways?'" (p. 258). Interviews, therefore, produce more complete answers than questionnaires because respondents cannot skip questions and interviewers can probe for more detailed answers. Finally, interviews typically produce a higher response rate than questionnaires—effective interviews should achieve a completion rate of at least 80 to 85%.

There are, however, some important limitations of interviews. First, interview data may be made unreliable by the interviewer. A number of researchers have found, for example, that interviewers tend to skip questions, vary the way they ask questions, and engage in discussions with respondents that depart from the interview format (Cannell & Kahn, 1968; Hansen, Hurwitz, Marks, & Maudlin, 1951; Hyman, 1954; Kish & Slater, 1960). Interviewers also potentially may bias respondents' answers (the researcher effects discussed in experimental research). For example, the way interviewers look, dress, and interact with respondents may influence the answers given. If multiple interviewers are used, these effects may be compounded. Interviewers, therefore, have to be trained carefully and supervised. Finally, interviews conducted in person typically are more costly and can demand a longer time frame for completion than questionnaires.

Types of Interviews

There are different types of interviews, which range along a continuum from highly structured to unstructured. **Highly structured** (or **scheduled**) **interviews** are ones in which interviews ask respondents the same questions using the same wording, in a predetermined order, and respond in a consistent way to respondents' questions and answers. A highly structured interview minimizes any researcher effects by *standardizing* the interview process. Standardization is usually achieved by using primarily closed questions and by insisting on conformity in the order of the questions, the manner in which they are asked, the response categories provided to respondents, the way the interviewer probes for follow-up responses, and the way the interviewer records respondents' answers. Note that highly structured interview procedures can be quite similar to the researcher-administered questionnaires discussed in the last chapter. In both cases, the researcher is present to explain and encourage completion of the questionnaire and to answer questions.

Moderately structured interviews are ones in which researchers adhere to a standard set of questions in a predetermined order but also are allowed the freedom to probe for additional information in a more spontaneous manner than is allowed under a highly structured interview.

Unstructured interviews are ones in which interviewers are given a set of general questions to ask, but are allowed maximum freedom in phrasing and ordering the questions and probing for additional information. An unstructured interview takes the form of a spontaneous conversation in which interviewers and respondents adjust to the moment. While this undoubtedly produces some interviewer bias and inconsistency between interviews, unstructured interviews sometimes are used in the exploratory stages of survey research when researchers are trying to find out which questions to ask and how respondents are likely to answer for more structured interviews, to analyze case studies of particular individuals or organizations, or when researchers prefer to ask open rather than closed questions (Fowler & Mangione, 1990). (For further explanation of minimally structured interviews, see Chapter 10.)

Interview survey research requires that interviewers be trained and/or experienced. Generally, the less structured the interview and the more sensitive the questions being asked, the greater the training or experience required. This is particularly true when multiple interviewers conduct less structured interviews. All interviewers should receive some training, however, to help assure consistency and combat interviewer bias.

A researcher's intent determines which type of interview is most appropriate. Generally, if the intent is to generalize about many people, then closed questions and highly structured interviews are conducted. On the other hand, if the intent is to describe more fully the communication behavior of particular individuals, then less structured interviews are used.

Interview Administration

Survey researchers make at least two decisions after choosing to conduct interviews. First, they decide whether to interview respondents over the telephone or face-to-face. Second, if they choose the face-to-face method, they decide whether to interview respondents individually or in a group

setting. There are many similarities between these administration procedures, but each has advantages and disadvantages.

Telephone interviewing is generally less costly than face-to-face interviews. Groves and Kahn (1979) and Hochstim (1967) both found that a
telephone survey costs about half as much as a face-to-face survey. The
telephone also is more effective for reaching respondents in distant geo-
graphical locations. Telephone interviews, therefore, are more convenient
and less time-consuming than face-to-face interviews. Telephone interviews
also provide respondents with more anonymity than face-to-face interviews, which may lead respondents to provide more honest and detailed
answers. Wimmer and Dominick (1991) point out, however, that many
people are wary of telephone surveys because many companies disguise
their telephone sales pitches as surveys. This unethical selling often leads
people to hang up the phone quickly, even in response to a legitimate
survey, which then may produce a biased sample.

Some researchers also have questioned whether telephone surveys
generate a biased sample because of the potential unavailability of some
people. Babbie (1982) argues, however, that some of this concern is unwar-
ranted. As evidence, he cites the U.S. Bureau of the Census which esti-
mated that 97% of all households had telephones in 1978. Researchers also
can get around the problem of unlisted phone numbers by using a
random-digit dialing (RDD) technique, in which telephone numbers are
called at random, to obtain a representative sample of respondents. Busy
people are often not at home, however, when telephone surveyors are most
likely to call, thereby possibly excluding them from the respondent pool.

Finally, researchers also have started using **computer-assisted telephone interviewing (CATI),** a computerized program that shows interviewers on a monitor the questions to be asked and enables them to enter
responses to questions as they are being given. This procedure helps stan-
dardize telephone interviews and allows the data to be recorded and analyzed in a quick and efficient manner.

Face-to-face interviews may be more costly and time-consuming than
telephone interviews, but they also provide some unique advantages. First,
they allow interviewers to note respondents' physical characteristics (without having to ask potentially embarrassing questions over the phone) as well
as nonverbal responses to the questions asked (which may contradict verbal
responses and be more accurate indicators of respondents' attitudes). Face-
to-face interviews also allow researchers to ask questions about visual stim-
uli, such as pictures. Finally, face-to-face interviews provide greater opportunities to establish rapport between interviewers and respondents and to
question respondents in greater detail, which may lead to more complete
and honest answers. Of course, face-to-face interviews also provide more
opportunities than telephone interviews to introduce interviewer bias due
to the behavior and appearance of the interviewer.

If a researcher decides that face-to-face interviews are most appropriate, the next decision is whether to interview respondents individually or in a group setting. For the most part, survey researchers interview respondents individually. This allows them to spend a significant portion of time with each respondent and mitigates the possible detrimental effects of *intersubject bias*—when the people being studied influence each others' answers, such as by suppressing minority positions in a group setting.

Some researchers choose, however, to conduct interviews in a group setting, which can save time and money. They often use a procedure called a **focus group interview** in which a facilitator leads a group of about 5 to 7 people in a relatively unstructured discussion about a specific topic. The facilitator introduces topics, probes for additional answers, and encourages people to "piggyback" on others' ideas. While this procedure is primarily used by market researchers to understand consumer preferences and decision making, it is becoming more popular with applied survey researchers. Krueger (1988) points out that applied researchers often use focus groups to generate information for questionnaires, assess organizational needs, test new programs, and recruit new members to organizations.

QUESTIONS FOR EXAMINING SURVEY INTERVIEW RESEARCH

In addition to the general questions posed about research, the questions concerning the selection of respondents in survey research, and many of the questions from the preceding chapter on survey questionnaire research, several criteria apply specifically to reading and evaluating survey interview research. Keep these questions in mind when reading the following article, or any survey study that employs the interview method:

A. Use of an Interview

1. Was the *choice of an interview* appropriate for answering the research questions posed? Did interviews provide specific advantages over the use of questionnaires in this study? Did the interviews lead to more valid and detailed responses than could be obtained easily by using questionnaires?

2. Were the interviews highly structured, moderately structured, or unstructured? What specific benefits were gained by the particular *type of interview* conducted?

3. Were the *questions* posed, such as closed and/or open questions, appropriate to the type of interview conducted? Should different or additional questions have been asked?

B. Interview Administration

1. Were the interviews conducted over the *telephone* or *face-to-face?* Was this an effective choice? What advantages did this method provide? What were the limitations of using this method?

2. Were the interviews conducted *individually* or in a *group* setting? What were the advantages and limitations of this procedure? If the interviews were conducted in a group setting, did the respondents influence each others' responses, for example?

C. Interviewer Conduct

1. Was there a *single interviewer* or *multiple interviewers?* If multiple interviewers were employed, were they matched with interviewees on important characteristics, such as gender or race, in order to decrease potential interviewer effects? What other procedures were used to minimize the *confounding effects* of the interviewers on respondents, such as from inconsistent interviewing techniques?

2. Did the interviewers receive sufficient *training?* Were the interviewers supervised and their interviews checked for accuracy by the researcher?

3. Did the interviewers appear to have established *rapport* with the interviewees which led to more valid and in-depth responses?

4. Did the interviewers *probe* effectively? Did the probing produce more detailed responses?

THE ILLUSTRATIVE STUDY

Many communication researchers are interested in how people use the mass media to meet particular needs, such as acquiring information about the environment or escaping from the day-to-day pressures of the workplace. Babrow (1989), for example, surveyed college undergraduates and found they watched daytime television soap operas primarily to meet entertainment and social interaction needs.

Researchers are also interested in how people respond to and compensate for the loss of a favorite mass medium. What do you do, for example, when your favorite weekly television show is on hiatus or when the daily newspaper you read is on strike? Do you substitute another television show or newspaper in its place?

In the following study Rosenberg and Elliott set out to compare how reporters and the general public cope with a newspaper strike. They saw a unique opportunity to compare media use and coping behavior when the Philadelphia newspapers went on strike.

Comparison of Media Use by Reporters And Public During Newspaper Strike

William L. Rosenberg

William R. Elliott

Media use during strike similar for both groups, but reporters spent more time reading other newspapers.

1   In the fall of 1985 Philadelphia's daily newspaper service stopped when the employees of the Philadelphia *Inquirer* and the Philadelphia *Daily News* went on strike. The strike inconvenienced the city's newspaper readers (*Inquirer* daily subscription of 519,000 and Sunday edi-
5   tion 1 million and the afternoon weekday *Daily News* subscription of 284,000) and advertisers, reduced Knight-Ridder's (the parent company of both papers) income, and deprived the striking workers of their jobs. Striking reporters lost their opportunity to report the news and, like other newspaper readers, they lost access to the information
10   from their own striking newspapers.
        The newspaper strike gave us the opportunity to apply two theoretical models to the media behavior of journalists and members of the public when the local daily newspapers were on strike. Based on the uses and gratifications model, we expect that newspaper readers
15   would attempt to substitute media providing similar gratifications for the missing newspapers. And, according to media dependency theory, this substitution should be highest for those thought to be most dependent on the newspapers, the journalists. Comparisons between gratifications sought by the general public and journalists should also
20   reveal differences in the way both of these groups compensated for the missing newspapers.

PAST STUDIES

Uses and gratifications research assumes that individuals are purposive in their media use, that they select media for gratifications associ-

Source: Rosenberg, W. L., & Elliot, W. R. (1989). Comparison of media use by reporters and public during newspaper strike. *Journalism Quarterly, 66,* 18–60. Reprinted by permission of the Association for Educational Journalism and Mass Communication.

William L. Rosenberg is director of the Drexel University Survey Research Center. William R. Elliott is director of journalism graduate studies at Southern Illinois University.

25   ated with maintaining ties between themselves and society, surveying
events in the environment, and satisfaction of the desire for "self
indulgence" or escape.[1] Recently, Becker[2] found that media gratifications fell into political and non-political clusters. Within the political
cluster, McLeod and McDonald[3] identified two gratification factors,
30   "surveillance" and "communications utility." Other studies have
shown that newspaper readership is associated with community identification and community ties[4] and with the use of media for surveillance reasons.[5]

While media uses and gratifications studies of the public are
35   common in the research literature, few uses and gratifications studies
of journalists exist. The study closest to a uses and gratifications study
of journalists is one by Burgoon, Bernstein and Burgoon.[6] They
found no major differences between the public and journalists on
four factors describing reasons given for reading newspapers: imme-
40   diacy and thoroughness, local awareness, redundancy and entertainment, and social extension. Journalists were more likely than the public to describe newspaper functions in terms of the "watchdog" role,
the explanation of events, and the uncovering of wrongs in society.
The public was more likely than journalists to read the newspaper to
45   monitor local events.

Media dependency theory, as developed by DeFleur and Ball-
Rokeach,[7] proposes that media influence is determined by the inter-

---

[1]Elihu Katz, Michael Gurevitch and Hadassah Haas. "On the Use of Mass Media
for Important Things," *American Sociological Review,* 38:164–181 (1973).

[2]Lee B. Becker, "Measurement of Gratifications." *Communication Research,* 6:54–
73 (1979).

[3]Jack M. McLeod and Daniel G. McDonald, "Beyond Simple Exposure Media
Orientations and Their Impact on Political Processes." *Communication Research,* 12:3–33
(1985).

[4]The research on newspaper use and community ties is reviewed and tied together theoretically by Keith R. Stamm in *Newspaper Use and Community Ties: Toward a
Dynamic Theory* (Norwood, NJ: Ablex, 1985).

[5]The literature on television and newspapers as reviewed by David H. Weaver
and Judith M. Buddenbaum. "Newspapers and Television: A Review of Research on
Uses and Effects." *ANPA News Research Report* 19 (April 20, 1979). A review is also
available by Philip Palmgreen, Lawrence A. Wenner and Karl Erik Rosengren. "Uses
and Gratifications Research: The Past Ten Years," in Karl Erik Rosengren, Lawrence A.
Wenner and Philip Palmgreen, eds., *Media Gratifications Research: Current Perspectives.*
(Beverly Hills, CA: Sage, 1985).

[6]Judee K. Burgoon, James M. Bernstein and Michael Burgoon, "Public and
Journalist Perceptions of Newspaper Functions," *Newspaper Research Journal,* Autumn,
1983, pp. 77–89.

relations between the media, its audience, and society. The individual's desire for information from the media is the key variable in
50   explaining why media messages have cognitive, affective, or behavioral effects. Media dependency is high when an individual's goal
satisfaction relies on information from the media system.[8] This dependency is increased in situations where there is a high degree of
social stress resulting from conflict or change.

55   Rubin and Windahl[9] have extended the dependency model to
include the gratifications sought by the audience as an interactive
component with media dependency. For Rubin and Windahl, media
use is also heavily influenced by the psychological and social characteristics of individual audience members. The combination of grati-
60   fications sought and societally determined dependency determines
media effects. Dependency on a medium or a message results when
individuals either purposely seek out information or ritualistically use
specific communication media, channels, or messages. Newspaper reporters, because of the demands of their profession, are placed in a
65   newspaper dependent situation. Other research has supported this
idea of dependency by noting that reporters value explaining events
to the public[10] and, as information sources, are more likely to rely on
newspapers than on television for information.[11]

Newspaper strikes create environments where normal media
70   use is suddenly disrupted. Newspaper readers may elect other activities to replace the missing newspaper or they may attempt to "compensate" for the striking newspaper by seeking another medium that
satisfies similar gratifications.[12] In a situation where a suitable replacement medium exists, the more important the gratification

---

[7]Melvin L. DeFleur and Sandra Ball-Rokeach. *Theories of Mass Communication.*
4th Edition (New York: Longman, 1982).

[8]S. J. Ball-Rokeach. "The Origins of Individual Media-System Dependency: A
Sociological Framework," *Communication Research,* 12:485–510 (1985).

[9]Alan M. Rubin and Sven Windahl. "The Uses and Dependency Model of Mass
Communications," *Critical Studies in Mass Communication,* 3:184–199 (1986).

[10]Burgoon *et al., op cit.*

[11]Verling C. Trodahl and Robert Van Dam. "Face-to-face Communication About
Major Topics in the News," *Public Opinion Quarterly,* 29:626–634 (1965).

[12]"Compensation" is the term used by William R. Elliott and William L. Rosenberg to describe "the substitution of media serving functions similar to the missing
medium" in "Gratifications Lost: the 1985 Philadelphia Newspaper Strike and Media
Use," paper presented to the Communication Theory and Methodology Division of the
Association for Education in Journalism and Mass Communication, Norman, OK, August, 1986. This is similar to Rubin and Windahl's idea of "functional alternative."

75 sought and the higher the media dependency, the more likely it would be that individuals will substitute a medium to compensate for the lost newspaper. Across several cultures, the surveillance activities served by newspapers can also be met by television; social contact gratifications can also be satisfied by radio and magazines; and entertainment

80 gratifications may also be served by other print media.[13] The likelihood of compensatory media use to replace a striking newspaper, depending on the gratification sought, should be directly tied to an individual's newspaper dependency.

The possibility that individuals use compensatory media during

85 a newspaper strike has been documented in several studies. Berelson examined the public's media behavior during the 1945 strike of eight major New York City daily papers.[14] He found that newspaper readers during the strike relied on reading non-news publications as replacements (compensatory media use) for their missed newspapers.

90 Kimball[15] replicated Berelson's study during the 1958 New York City newspaper strike and found that 50% of the subjects indicated that they were reading more books and magazines.

More recently, deBock[16] studied the effects of newspaper and television strikes in the Netherlands in 1977. Using a panel study,

95 deBock found that during the strike heavy newspaper readers paid unusually high attention to radio and television news. Elliott and Rosenberg[17] used some of the data reported in this study to investigate the public's media uses and gratifications sought from newspaper readership during and after the 1985 Philadelphia newspaper strike.

100 They found that the missing local papers were most often replaced by national newspapers.

The newspaper strike gave us the opportunity to investigate the differences in gratifications associated with media use between individuals more dependent on the local newspaper (reporters) and those

[13]In Israel, Katz, Gurevitch and Hass, *op. cit.;* in the United States, William R. Elliott and Cynthia Quattlebaum, "Similarities in Patterns of Media Use: a Cluster Analysis of Media Gratifications," *Western Journal of Speech Communication.* 43:61–72 (1979); in Australia, Susan Kippax and John P. Murray, "Using Mass Media: Need Gratification and Perceived Utility," *Communication Research,* 7:335–360 (1980).

[14]Bernard Berelson, "What Missing the Newspaper Means," in Paul F. Lazarsfeld and Frank N. Stanton eds., *Communications Research: 1948–1949,* (New York: Harper, 1949).

[15]Penn Kimball. "People Without Papers," *Public Opinion Quarterly,* 23:389–398 (1959).

[16]Harold de Bock, "Gratification Frustration During a Newspaper Strike and a TV Blackout," *Journalism Quarterly,* 57:61–66, 68 (1980).

[17]William R. Elliott and William L. Rosenberg, "The 1985 Philadelphia Newspaper Strike: A Uses and Gratifications Study, *Journalism Quarterly,* 64:679–87 (1987).

105 less newspaper dependent (the majority of the public). Higher newspaper dependency should be reflected by higher newspaper and
other news consumption by reporters than by the public. In addition,
it has been suggested that media dependency is associated with media
use for surveillance and social contact reasons.[18] For this study, re-
110 porters who rely on local papers for their story ideas, confirmation of
their own work, reviews of competitive papers, and as examples of
their own success as professionals should show higher surveillance
and social contact newspaper gratifications than the general readership. In addition, individuals seeking surveillance and social contact
115 information from the local newspapers should be expected to substitute media that provide the lost gratifications connected with the
missing papers. This substitution should be highest for those individuals most dependent on the newspaper (reporters) to gratify their
information desires.
120   Based on our review of the theory and research findings, we
advance two general hypotheses.

*H1: Dependency on a medium is positively related to use of the medium and to grat-
ifications sought from that use.*

Associated with this hypothesis are two specific sub-hypotheses.

125 *H1a: The higher the dependency on a medium, the higher the use of that medium.*
          *H1b: The higher the dependency on a medium, the higher the surveillance
and social contact gratifications sought from that medium.*

          Our second general hypothesis relates to compensatory media
use.

130 *H2: Dependency on a medium will be positively associated with substitute media use
in the event that medium is suddenly removed from circulation.*

The sub-hypotheses associated with H2 are:

*H2a: The higher the dependency on a medium, the greater the increase in the use of
substitute media to compensate for the loss of that medium.*
135   *H2b: The higher the dependency on a medium, the greater the reliance on
similar media to serve as substitutes for the lost medium.*

          To test these hypotheses, interviews were conducted with strik-
ing reporters to determine their media use, backgrounds, informa-

[18]Rubin and Windahl, *op. cit.*

tion sources and the gratifications they sought from newspaper read-
140 ing. We were particularly interested in how reporters might compensate for the missing newspapers. The reporters' survey was compared
with a survey of the public's media use during and after the strike so
that comparisons on strike related behaviors could be made between
reporters and the general public.

145 **METHOD**

In order to undertake an evaluation of reporters' newspaper uses and
gratifications during a strike in which the reporters were participants,
their knowledge and cooperation of the study was essential. We contacted representatives of the Newspaper Guild of Greater Phila-
150 delphia, Local 10, to inform them of the research project and seek
their cooperation. The Guild cooperated fully and published an an-
nouncement of our study in their daily strike paper. In addition,
several members of the Guild were already aware of our past research
activities. An anonymous self-administered survey was distributed to
155 reporters on the strike line and at the Guild offices by trained interviewers over a two day period. This procedure resulted in 54 usable
reporter interviews. This opportunity sample yielded a sample with
no known cases of a reporter refusing to participate.

During the same time period (October, 1985) we interviewed a
160 sample of 215 members of the general public about their media use
before and during the strike and about the gratifications they sought
from newspaper reading. We used random digit dialing techniques to
select this sample of the public. The completion rate for the public
sample was 55.5%.

165 We used a variety of media use measures as our dependent
variables. To measure media use during the strike, we first asked the
public and the reporters which newspapers they read yesterday and
the amount of time they spent reading each. We also asked both
groups about yesterday's viewing of local television news, national
170 television news, entertainment television, radio news listening and
which magazines they had read in the last week. The responses to the
newspaper use question were categorized into national newspapers
(*USA Today, Wall Street Journal,* etc.), out-of-state newspapers (*New York
Times,* etc.) and suburban and community papers. Responses to the
175 question on magazine use were categorized as news magazines (*Time,
Newsweek,* etc.) or other magazines. All questions related to the time
spent using the various media were coded in minutes.

Toward the end of the questionnaire the subjects were asked to
provide us with estimates of their media use on a typical weekday
180 before the strike. This allowed us to evaluate changes in media use

that could be expected to result as people attempted to compensate for the missing local newspapers.

We also gave the public and the reporters a list of possible information sources that could be used as replacements for the missing
185   *Inquirer* and *Daily News*. The list included friends or relatives, co-
workers, radio, television, suburban newspapers, out-of-state newspapers, news magazines, and other sources. The subjects were requested to indicate which of the possible information sources they
used most frequently as a replacement for the *Inquirer* and/or *Daily*
190   *News* and which source they used second most frequently. Unnamed
sources were left unranked.

Finally, we collected data on two dimensions of media gratifications. The first of these dimensions, surveillance, is defined as "the
use of the mass media to obtain information about what is going on in
195   the world."[19] Each subject was presented the following statement:

*"Many people have given the following statement as reasons why they read a daily
newspaper. Would you please tell me whether these reasons sound a lot like you, a
little like you, or not at all like you?"*

Of the 11 gratification statements given, three composed our sur-
200   veillance measures.

*1) To determine what is important in the country and in the world (Impor-
tant).*
2) To keep up with the way government does its job. (Govt Job).
3) To get to know the quality of our leaders (Quality).

205   Our second gratification dimension, social contact, is defined as
the use of the newspaper for information that can be used to
strengthen relations with other people and with society. Social contact
can be improved by gathering information about daily life, information for use in arguments and interpersonal discussion, and informa-
210   tion that will make one feel involved in the events of the day. Subjects
indicated how much each of the following three statements was a lot
like them, a little like them, or not at all like them.

1) To obtain information about daily life (Information).
2) To gather information which will strengthen my argument (Argue).
215   *3) To feel I'm involved in important events (Events).*

---

[19]Daniel G. McDonald and Caroll J. Glynn, "Conceptualization and Measurement of Media Orientations," paper presented to the Communication Theory and
Methodology Division of the Association for Education in Journalism and Mass Communication, Norman, Oklahoma, August, 1986.

The influence of media gratifications and public or reporter group membership on strike related media use was tested using hierarchical least-squares regression techniques. Since we anticipated that the strongest influence on news media use would come from the
220   surveillance measures,[20] the three surveillance variables were entered as a block first. We next entered the social contact variables, and finally the public or reporter measure was added as a dummy variable. The standardized partial regression coefficients (Betas) provided a way to evaluate the relative contribution of each gratification
225   measure after controlling for all other variables in the regression equation. The incremental R^2s provided measures of the contribution of each variable group to the total variation explained by the full regression model.

RESULTS

230   *Dependency Differences Between Reporters and the Public.* Reporters who depend on the newspaper for their income, many of their ideas and for self-esteem, are situationally more dependent on the local newspapers than the public. Based on this, we advanced the hypothesis that dependency would be positively related to media use and to
235   gratifications sought from a specific media channel (H1). To test this general hypothesis, we advanced two sub-hypotheses. First, we hypothesized (H1a) that reporters would have higher newspaper news consumption than the public. Second, (H1b) reporters should have higher newspaper surveillance and social contact gratification scores
240   than the public. The test of H1a is presented in Table 1. The test of H1b is presented in Table 2.

When comparing newspaper use differences between reporters and the public before and during the strike, the findings follow our hypothesized expectations. Reporters, situationally more dependent
245   on local newspapers than the public, consistently show higher use of print news media than the public. In terms of the reported numbers of newspapers read before the strike, reporters read significantly more national, out-of-state and suburban and community papers than the public. Reporters showed significantly higher readership of the
250   *Inquirer* and *Daily News* before the strike than the public. The total number of papers read by reporters was also significantly higher than the number read by the public.

Reporters indicated they spent significantly more time than the

---

[20]Palmgreen *et al.*, *op. cit.* review the literature on gratifications and find support for the hypothesis that the use of media to satisfy information related needs is associated with the choice of newspapers or television for local or national news.

TABLE 1

Mean Scores and Mean Score Differences Media Use and Gratification Measures Before and During the Newspaper Strike for the Public and Reporters

	Mean Scores Before Strike			Mean Scores During Strike		
	Reporters	*Public*	*Difference*	*Reporters*	*Public*	*Difference*
Number of Newspapers						
National	0.31	0.07	0.25*	0.33	0.16	0.17
Out of State	0.85	0.08	0.77*	0.80	0.15	0.65***
Suburban	0.31	0.06	0.26**	0.41	0.13	0.28**
Tot. Nat. Oss. Sub	1.48	0.20	1.28*	1.54	0.44	1.10***
Inq. & Daily News	1.72	1.12	0.60*			
All Papers	3.20	1.32	1.88*	1.54	0.46	1.10***
Minutes Reading Newspapers						
National	6.46	4.51	1.95	8.00	6.98	1.02
Out of State	16.06	4.88	11.18*	27.30	7.57	19.73***
Suburban	5.46	2.53	2.93	12.04	4.69	7.35*
Total Nat. OOS. Sub	27.98	11.93	16.05***	47.33	19.24	28.09***
Inq. & Daily News	64.74	69.76	-5.02			
All Papers	92.72	81.69	11.03	47.33	19.24	28.09***
Number of News Magazines	0.91	0.26	0.65*	0.87	0.25	0.62***
Minutes TV and Radio						
Local TV News	30.38	64.42	-34.04*	40.04	60.91	-20.87*
Network TV News	19.06	36.49	-17.43*	23.06	32.22	-9.16*
Radio News	45.65	68.94	-23.29***	46.11	59.48	-13.37

*p < .05.   **p < .01   ***p < .001 (all two tailed tests).

Public Ns ranged from 198 to 215 while reporter Ns ranged from 52 to 54.

TABLE 2

Mean Scores for Gratification Sought Measures During the Newspaper Strike
for the Public and Reporters[1]

Newspaper Gratifications	Reporters	Public
Surveillance		
Important	2.91**	2.59**
Gov't Job	2.65***	2.37***
Quality	2.50	2.35
Social Contact		
Information	2.81***	2.41***
Argue	2.04	2.26
Events	2.07	2.11

*p < .05   **p < .01   ***p < .001 (all two tailed t tests).

Public Ns ranged from 198 to 215 while reporter Ns ranged from 52 to 54.

public before the strike reading out-of-state papers and reporters'
total time spent with national, out-of-state and suburban and community papers was significantly higher than for the public. However,
the total time spent with all papers before the strike did not differ
significantly between reporters and the public, largely because members of the public reported spending more time before the strike
with the *Inquirer* and the *Daily News* than reporters, an unanticipated
finding.

Newspaper use differences during the strike show parallel findings. Reporters read significantly more national newspapers and community papers ($\Delta = .28$) with a resultant higher total number of
papers read than the public. Reporters also spent significantly more
daily time reading out-of-state papers, more time reading suburban
and community papers and more total daily time with all papers.

Significant differences between the use of non-newspaper news
media by the public and reporters were also found. Reporters read
more news magazines before and during the strike than the public.
However, reporters watched significantly less daily local television
news before the strike and during the strike than the public. They
also watched less daily network television news before and during the
strike than the public. Reporters also listened daily to less radio news
before the strike than the public but no significant difference was
found between reporters and the readers during the strike.

To test H1b, that reporters would have higher surveillance and
social contact gratifications sought than the public, we evaluated the
differences between reporters and the public on our newspaper gratifications sought measures using t-tests. The differences between re-

porters and the public were as predicted and statistically significant for two of our three newspaper surveillance gratification measures. Reporters were significantly more likely than the public to indicate they used newspapers "to determine what is important in the country and in the world" and "to keep up with the way government does its job."

285

The evidence for hypothesized differences between reporters and the public on the social contact gratification measures is less clear. Reporters were significantly more likely than the public to indicate that they used the newspaper to serve the social contact gratification of obtaining "information about daily life." However, the differences on the other social contact gratifications sought measures were not statistically significant and were in the opposite direction to that hypothesized (reporters had lower mean scores on the measure "to gather information which will strengthen my arguments" and "to feel I'm involved in important events").

290

295

Compensatory Media Use. Our general compensatory media use hypothesis (H2), that individuals will substitute another medium to replace the missing local newspaper, is tested in Tables 3 and 4. The first sub-hypothesis (H2a), that individuals will increase their use of substitute media to compensate for the missing medium, is tested for reporters and the public in Table 3.

300

The public was likely to compensate for the missing *Inquirer* and *Daily News* by increasing their readership of other newspapers. They read significantly more national, out-of-state papers, and suburban and community papers each day during the strike than they recalled reading before the strike. When the readership scores for national, out-of-state, and suburban and community papers are summed, the reported compensatory newspaper use is indicated by an increase from a mean sum of .20 papers before the strike to the sum of .44 papers during the strike. The total number of newspapers read each day during the strike and the number read before the strike for the public understandably decreases reflecting the readership before the strike of the *Inquirer* and the *Daily News*.

305

310

However, similar compensatory behavior is not shown by the reporters. The differences between their newspaper use before and during the newspaper strike is slight for all newspaper readership categories except for the total number of papers read yesterday where the decline in the number of newspapers read during and before the strike is due almost entirely to reporters' readership of the *Inquirer* and *Daily News* before the strike.

315

320

The measures of the time subjects spent reading the newspapers provides additional evidence for compensatory newspaper use by the public. For them, significantly more daily time was reported reading

TABLE 3
Mean Scores and Mean Score Differences (Δ) Media Use Measures Before and During the Newspaper Strike for the Public and Reporters[1]

	Mean Scores Reporters		Mean Scores Public		Mean Scores Differences (During-Before)	
	Before Strike	During Strike	Before Strike	During Public	Public	Reporter
Number of Newspapers						
National	0.31	0.33	0.07	0.16	0.09***	0.02
Out of State	0.85	0.80	0.08	0.15	0.07**	−0.06
Suburban	0.31	0.41	0.06	0.13	0.07***	0.09
Tot. Nat. OOS. Sub	1.48	1.54	0.20	0.44	0.24***	0.06
Inq. & Daily News	1.72		1.12			
All Papers	3.20	1.54	1.32	0.46	−0.86***	−1.67***
Minutes Reading Newspapers						
National	6.46	8.00	4.51	6.98	2.47	1.54
Out of State	16.06	27.30	4.88	7.57	2.69	11.24**
Suburban	5.46	12.04	2.53	4.69	2.16*	6.57
Total Nat. OOS. Sub	27.98	47.33	11.93	19.24	7.31*	19.35**
Inq. & Daily News	64.74		69.76			
All Papers	92.72	47.33	81.69	19.24	−62.45***	−15.39***
Number of News Magazines	0.91	0.87	0.26	0.25	−0.01	−0.04
Minutes TV and Radio						
Local TV News	30.38	40.04	64.42	60.91	−3.47	10.42*
Network TV News	19.06	23.06	36.49	32.22	−4.27	4.00*
Radio News	45.65	46.11	68.94	59.48	−9.63	0.46

*p < .05   **p < .01   ***p < .001 (all two tailed t tests).

Public Ns ranged from 198 to 215. Reporter Ns ranged from 52 to 54.

[1]Difference between changes in public use before and during the strike and changes in reporters' use before and during the strike significant at .05 level by two-tailed t test.

TABLE 4
Rankings for Newspaper Replacement Sources for the Public and Reporters

Newspaper Replacements	Reporters			Public		
	Ranked First	Ranked Second	Not Ranked	Ranked First	Ranked Second	Not Ranked
Friends or Relatives***	0.0%	0.0%	100.0%	10.4%	13.4%	76.1%
Coworkers	6.1%	8.2%	85.7%	4.0%	5.0%	91.0%
Radio	24.5%	26.5%	49.0%	13.9%	23.9%	62.2%
Television*	22.4%	30.6%	46.9%	42.8%	19.9%	37.3%
Suburban Newspapers	6.1%	16.3%	77.6%	9.5%	9.0%	81.6%
Out of Town News-papers***	32.7%	20.4%	46.9%	13.9%	11.9%	74.1%
News Magazines	2.0%	8.2%	89.8%	3.0%	8.0%	89.1%
Other Sources	0.0%	0.0%	100.0%	2.5%	2.5%	95.0%
		N = 49			N = 201	

$*p < .05$ $**p < .01$ $***p < .001$ (χ^2 test)

325 suburban and community papers during the strike than before the
strike and the total time reading all papers expect the *Inquirer* and
Daily News increased significantly during the strike. The decrease in
the total daily time reading newspapers during the strike reflects the
time lost in readership of the *Inquirer* and *Daily News* before the strike.
330 The evidence indicates that reporters practiced substitute newspaper
use. Reporters had significantly higher daily reading times for out-of-
state newspapers during the strike than before the strike.[21] The total
time given to national, out-of-state, and suburban and community
papers was also significantly higher during the strike than before the
335 strike. For reporters, the decrease in reading time during the strike
compared to time before the strike was about 45 minutes, accounted
for largely by the missed daily time spent reading the *Inquirer* and
Daily News.
       A further test of the compensatory media use hypothesis in-
340 volves comparing changes in non-newspaper news media use before
and during the newspaper strike. To test for these changes, differences between media use before and during the newspaper strike for
news magazines, local television news, network television news and
radio news were analyzed (Table 3). The results do not support the
345 compensatory media use hypothesis. There is virtually no difference
between the number of news magazines read before the strike compared to news magazine reading during the strike for the public or

       [21]The majority of reporters' reading of out of state newspapers came from
reading the New York Times. Thirty of the 54 reporters (55.6%) reported reading the
New York Times while only 11 (20.4%) reported reading other out-of-state papers.

for reporters. None of the differences in the time spent with local
television news, network television news, or radio news reached statis-
350   tically significant levels for the public or reporters.

Direct comparisons between the changes in media use between
the public and reporters provides slight support that high newspaper
dependency is associated with high compensatory media use. Reporters did show significantly higher differences in compensatory
355   media use than the public for the time spent reading out-of-state
newspapers, and watching local and network television news.

Table 4 presents a test of our second sub-hypothesis relating to
compensatory media use (H2b), that high medium or channel dependency would be associated with the substitution of similar media or
360   channels as substitutes for the missing medium or channel. Subjects
were asked to provide their most important and second most important substitute for the missing *Inquirer* and *Daily News*. The entries in
Table 4 are the percentages of respondents ranking each substitute
source first or second. We expected reporters would be more likely to
365   name out-of-town newspapers, suburban and community newspapers, and news magazines as newspaper substitutes than the public.
The differences were statistically significant only for out-of-town
newspapers. Here 53.1% of the reporters named out-of-state newspapers as their first or second replacement choice compared with only
370   25.8% for the public. However, the differences in naming suburban
papers or news magazines as first or second choices between reporters
and the public was slight and nonsignificant.

The public was significantly more likely to rank friends or relatives as newspaper replacements than reporters. And, although both
375   ranked television as an important replacement medium, the public
was significantly more likely to list TV as their first or second replacement choice compared with reporters.

These findings provide some support for the hypothesized relationship between media dependency and compensatory media use,
380   but that support is limited to the medium most like the missing medium of channel. In this case, that was usually the New York *Times*. It
is not surprising that suburban newspapers were not used as a substitute for the striking papers, but the finding that news magazine use
was not influenced, as indicated in the results presented in Tables 3
385   and 4, is surprising.

It appears that when a normally used source of information is
suddenly removed, as in a newspaper strike, compensation is accomplished through the substitution of a similar medium serving a similar
habitual role. Structurally different media, in this case non-
390   newspaper media, apparently do not serve the same habitual pat-

terns. This supports the idea that much media use may be habitual and not based entirely on some form of internal need satisfaction.

395   Our findings suggest that the media compensation that did take place for the striking newspapers was primarily limited to the use of other newspapers and did not extend, as hypothesized, to other news media. This finding was more consistent for the public than for journalists. This suggests to us the possibility that media use patterns result as much from habit as from a need to satisfy some internalized state. Such a need state, if it exists, should have lead to the substitution
400   of news media serving similar functions for the missing newspaper. In general, that did not seem to occur.

Hierarchical Least-Squares Regression Models. Table 5 presents the results of a number of hierarchical least squares linear regression models of our independent measures on the media use dependent
405   variables for newspaper use. Because our two samples differed demographically in terms of the sex of the subjects (65.6% female in the public sample, 27.8% female in the reporter sample), sex was added as an independent variable in our regression model. We elected to follow the logic suggested by Cohen and Cohen[22] in entering the
410   independent variables in the regression equation. Because we knew to expect differences in media use based on the sex of the respondent,[23] it was the first independent variable entered in the equation. Since sex serves as a control and not as a source of hypothesized differences, its influence on the dependent variables is not discussed in the text.

415   Based on the work of McLeod and McDonald[24] who found the surveillance dimension the strongest overall predictor of political knowledge and behavior, our three surveillance measures were added as the second variable set. The three measures of social contact gratifications sought were entered as the third set of variables while mem-
420   bership in the public or reporter groups was entered last. The figures in the tables are the standardized regression coefficients for the entire model (Betas), incremental R^2s (the additional variation explained after each block of variables has been added to the equation), and the total R^2 for the regression model.

425   The evidence for the influence of newspaper gratifications

---

[22]The logic of hierarchical regression models is explained in Jacob Cohen and Patricia Cohen, *Applied Multiple Regression/Correlation Analysis for Behavioral Sciences* (Hillsdale, N.J.: Lawrence Erlbaum Associates, 1975).

[23]Elliott and Rosenberg, *op cit.*

[24]The importance of the surveillance dimension has been demonstrated by McLeod and McDonald, *op. cit.* and by Wayne M. Towers, "Weekday and Sunday Readership Seen Through Uses and Gratifications." *Newspaper Research Journal* Spring 1985, pp. 20–32.

TABLE 5
Linear Regression Analysis—Newspaper Use Before and During the Strike with Gender, Gratifications and Public/Reporter Measures
(N = 197 for the Public, N = 50 for Reporters)

Independent Variables	Number of Papers				Time Reading Papers			
	Total[a] (–IDN) Before	Inq/DN Before	Total Before	Total During	Total[a] (–IDN) Before	Inq/DN Before	Total Before	Total During
Female/Male								
Beta	-0.02	-0.04	-0.04	-0.08	-0.11	0.01	-0.05	-0.14*
Incremental R^2	0.041***	0.023*	0.055***	0.047***	0.027**	0.001	0.005	0.046***
Surveillance								
Betas: Important	0.03	0.02	0.03	-0.06	0.06	0.01	0.04	-0.01
Govt Job	0.07	0.09	0.10	0.08	0.09	0.08	0.12	0.06
Quality	0.00	-0.09	-0.05	-0.03	0.04	-0.03	0.00	-0.05
Incremental R^2	0.028	0.057**	0.064***	0.024	0.029	0.042*	0.068***	0.029
Social Contact								
Betas: Information	-0.01	0.10	0.04	0.01	-0.09	0.13	0.06	0.05
Argue	0.07	0.12	0.12*	0.11	0.18**	0.09	0.17*	0.16*
Events	-0.08	0.11	0.00	-0.05	0.13	0.14	0.05	0.07
Incremental R^2	0.025	0.038*	0.029*	0.013	0.031*	0.044**	0.029	0.021
Public/Reporter								
Beta	0.60***	0.38***	0.66***	0.47***	0.14*	-0.07	0.02	0.24***
Incremental R^2	0.293***	0.118***	0.355***	0.181***	0.016*	0.003	0.000	0.047***
Total R^2	0.387*	0.235***	0.504***	0.266***	0.102***	0.090**	0.102***	0.115***

*p < .05.   **p < .01   ***p < .001.

Sex was dummy variable coded (female = 0, male = 1). This sample was 58.3% female. Public/Reporter was dummy variable coded (public = 0, reporter = 1).

[a] Sum of all papers (state, suburban and community) excluding readership of *Inquirer* and *Daily News*.

sought, and public or reporter membership on newspaper use (number and time) is presented in Table 5.

The contributions to variation explained by the surveillance gratification measures are statistically significant for two of the four
430   newspaper use measures (readership of the *Inquirer* and *Daily News* before the strike, the total number of papers before the strike) where 5.7% and 6.4% of the total variation explained is accounted for by surveillance gratifications sought.

The same pattern is shown for the social contact newspaper
435   gratifications sought. Higher percentages of variation explained by social contact gratifications exist for readership of the *Inquirer* and *Daily News* before the strike (3.8%) and for the total number of papers read before the strike (2.9%).

The remaining predictor variable in the hierarchical model,
440   identification as a member of the public or as a reporter, is the strongest predictor across each of the four number of newspaper read measures. The incremental R^2 associated with being part of the public or a reporter, after the other three variable sets have been entered into the equation, ranges from 11.8% for reading the *Inquirer* and *Daily News*
445   before the strike to 35.5% for the total number of papers read before the strike. All these measures were statistically significant. The total variation accounted for in the number of newspapers read for the full regression models ranged from 23.5% for readership of the *Inquirer* and *Daily News* before the strike to 50.4% of the variation in all papers
450   before the strike.

Table 5 provides the finding of the regression analyses for media use measures of the time spent reading the newspapers. The pattern presented parallels that of the number of newspapers read although the results are not quite as striking. The newspaper surveillance grati-
455   fications sought measures add to the incremental proportions of the variation explained for each of the newspaper reading time measures. They account for 4.2% of the variation in time spent with the *Inquirer* and *Daily News* before the strike and 6.8% of the variation in the total time spent reading newspapers before the strike.

460   The use of the newspaper "to gather information which will strengthen my arguments" was positively related to the total time reading newspapers excluding the *Inquirer* and *Daily News* before the strike (Beta = .18), with the total time spent reading the newspaper before the strike (Beta = .17), and with the total time spent reading
465   the newspaper during the strike (Beta = .16). This social contact use of the newspapers had the strongest and most consistent set of relationships with media use of all our gratification measures.

Newspaper social contact gratifications account for significant incremental R^2s for the total time spent reading newspapers exclud-

470   ing the *Inquirer* and *Daily News* before the strike (3.1%) and for time
spent reading the *Inquirer* and *Daily News* before the strike (4.4%).
Unlike previous research that has suggested greater importance associated with surveillance measures, our findings tentatively suggest
giving new consideration to the use of newspapers as sources of infor-
475   mation for interpersonal discussion.

Identification as a reporter or a member of the public had statistically significant incremental R^2s for two of the four time readership
measures, the total time reading all papers except the *Inquirer* and
Daily News before the strike (1.6%) and the time spent reading papers
480   during the strike (4.7%). For the total regression model, each proportion of variation explained was significant, ranging from 9.0% for
readership of the *Inquirer* and *Daily News* before the strike to 11.5% of
the variation explained for the total time reading newspapers during
the strike.

485   The hierarchical least squares linear regression analyses of other
news media use before and during the newspaper strike showed the
incremental variation in news magazine reading before the strike by
surveillance gratifications (4.8%) and by being a member of the public
or reporter (7.1%) are each statistically significant. During the strike
490   the newspaper surveillance gratifications and public or reporter
membership have statistically significant incremental R^2's of 4.4% and
7.8% respectively. The total variation for the before strike model explained 19.9% of the variation while the during strike model accounted for 17.3% of the variation explained. Radio news listening is
495   apparently uninfluenced by any of the independent variables we used
in this study.

The pattern for local television news is not much different than
the radio results. Here one measure, public or a reporter, adds a
significant incremental R^2 to the time spent viewing local television
500   news before the strike. The public spent more time with local television news (Beta = $-.27$) than reporters. The overall R^2 of 9.8% is
statistically significant for viewing local television news during the
strike.

More of a pattern is evident for the time spent viewing network
505   television news. Before the strike, the incremental R^2 for newspaper
surveillance gratifications was 5.9%, equal to the highest incremental
contribution of any of the independent variable blocks. Being either a
member of the public or a reporter accounted for an additional 3.4%.
The total regression model accounted for 10.5% of the variation ex-
510   plained in the reported time viewing network television news before
the strike. During the strike, only the newspaper surveillance gratifications block had a significant R^2 increment (4.9%). The total model

accounted for a statistically significant 7.3% of the variation in network news viewing.

515   In general, these results suggest that news magazines and network television news are related to newspaper surveillance gratifications. In terms of media dependency, being a journalist is strongly associated before and during the strike with news magazine use where the standardized partial regression coefficients are significant and
520   positive while being a journalist is negatively related to local television news viewing before and during the strike and to network television news viewing before the strike. The social contact newspaper gratification measures do not show statistically significant relationships with any of the non-newspaper use measures. For newspaper sur-
525   veillance functions, individuals partially compensated for the missing newspapers by using news magazines or watching network television news.

Discussion

In this investigation we were interested in examining the effect of a
530   daily newspaper strike on the uses and gratifications of reporters and the general public. In particular, we were interested in people's dependency on the daily newspapers, the strike, and people's use of substitute media to compensate for missing newspapers. In addressing these issues we developed two general hypotheses which struc-
535   tured our inquiry.

First, we hypothesized that dependency would be positively related to media use and gratifications sought from media use. To test this we compared reporters' newspaper news consumption with the general public's. Our analysis indicates that reporters before and dur-
540   ing the strike read more newspapers.

We hypothesized (H1b) that reporters should have higher newspaper surveillance and social gratification scores than the general public. Reporters were more likely than the public to use newspapers for some surveillance activities. The hypothesized differences were
545   not clear for social contact gratifications.

Second, (H2) we hypothesized that dependency would be positively associated with the use of substitute media to compensate for the loss of a missing media source. In this case, (H2a) newspaper dependent individuals would substitute another medium to replace
550   the local daily newspaper. We found this to be the case when the substitute medium was another newspaper.

This hypothesis (H2a) was not upheld when analyzing the results for non-newspaper sources. Neither the public nor reporters

showed a significant increase during the strike in readership of news
555   magazines, local television news viewing, network television news
viewing, or radio news listening.

In examining the reporters' and public's rankings of newspaper
replacement sources (H2b), reporters were more likely to identify out-
of-town newspapers while the public ranked television, and friends or
560   relatives higher as replacement sources than the journalists.

We also used linear regression techniques to examine the multivariate pattern of influence of our measures of surveillance, social
contact, and public or reporter group membership on each of our
dependent variables. The surveillance and social contact activities as-
565   sociated with the daily newspaper seemed to play independent roles.
Each influenced the number of newspapers read and the time spent
reading newspapers before but not during the strike. Similarly, for
most of these measures, being a reporter or a member of the public
also explained significant proportions of the variance in the news-
570   paper use measures in both the before and during measures.

It appears that using the daily newspaper is positively associated
with some social contact and surveillance activities for both the public
and reporters. When the paper is missing, individuals may compensate for lost surveillance activities by using news magazines and net-
575   work television news broadcasts but not by using radio news or local
television news. During the newspaper strike, neither surveillance nor
social contact gratifications were associated with substitute newspaper
use. This strongly suggests the possibility that gratifications sought
can reflect rationalizations for habitual media use in non-strike situa-
580   tions. If gratifications sought measured underlying needs, then we
would have expected these measures to be positively associated with
substitute newspaper use. This was not the case.

Our results indicate that for both the public and reporters a
similar pattern of use existed as a result of the strike. Neither group
585   compensated for the loss of the daily newspaper through the use of
televised local or network news or news magazines. If compensatory
media use was taking place, it was likely to be a medium which was
similar to the one displaced. For the reporters, it was generally the
New York *Times.* The public tended to depend more on their friends
590   and relatives for information which they would normally receive in
the newspaper.

Our overall conclusion from this research is that most media use
is not a need based process, but rather a habitual one. For some the
habit may be more highly structured, and when access to this informa-
595   tion is removed they will seek a similar alternative source of information. Future research should extend the concept of "dependency" to

include opinion leaders, investigating how they use the media to enhance their position in the social and political system.

COMMENTS ON THE STUDY

Introduction and Review of the Literature

The researchers do a good job of explaining the background concerning the union strike (1–10) and showing how this situation allowed them to test in one study predictions derived from two contemporary theories that purport to explain mass media usage: uses and gratifications, and media dependency (11–21). *Uses and gratifications theory* suggests that people purposely use and choose media to meet particular needs, such as keeping current with political events (23–33). One implication of this theory is that people should choose other media which provide similar gratifications when a favorite mass medium, newspapers in this case, is not available (13–16). The second theory, *media dependency*, argues that the ability of the media to influence cognitions, affect, and behavior is based on individuals' need for information from the media. Further, this dependency is maximized when people are denied access to a preferred medium and have to change their reading, viewing, or listening habits (46–54). Rosenberg and Elliott hypothesize, therefore, that those most dependent on newspapers— the striking journalists themselves—would substitute the most (16–18).

The researchers review some studies based on uses and gratifications theory, and identify some of the categories into which uses have been grouped (23–33). Differences between journalists and the general public in terms of media use is also established (34–45). The authors then review briefly the literature on dependency theory (46–54), and show that this theory has been used to study newspaper reporters (65–68). They also show that the two theories have been linked together by other researchers, and that they are relevant to newspaper reporters (55–65).

The first four paragraphs of the review of the literature thus give the reader a good, basic understanding of these two theories and how they have been applied in related research. Note that the authors do *not* give a laundry list of all the studies based on uses and gratifications theory and media dependency theory. Instead, they provide a sufficient background relevant for their research purposes and then move on to discuss the effects of newspaper strikes on the information environment and how media consumers respond (69–101). While the discussion of these theories could have been longer, this section does its job in a *parsimonious*, or economical, manner.

Hypotheses

The conclusions drawn from the research literature (102–119) led the researchers to propose specific, testable hypotheses (120–136). There are, however, two problems in how these hypotheses are phrased: the construction of compound hypotheses and arguments being made within a formal hypothesis. First, H1 and H1b both use the word "and" in them, which usually is not advisable. It is possible, for example, that the first part of H1 could be confirmed (dependency on a medium could be related positively to the amount of use), but the second part might not be confirmed (gratifications might not be related to use). If this were the case, what would the authors conclude? Similarly, in H1b, suppose surveillance gratification increases and social contact gratification decreases with higher dependence. Should the hypothesis be accepted or rejected? Even though these two ideas are tied together so tightly in this study that they can be tested together, they should, for the sake of clarity, be expressed as separate hypotheses. A hypothesis, therefore, should make only one prediction in order to eliminate the possibility of obtaining two conflicting answers to the same hypothesis.

Second, the researchers state their predictions in H2a and H2b, but then, in the phrases following "to," provide reasons for their predictions. It is inappropriate to insert this argumentative reasoning into hypotheses because it is possible that the results will support the hypotheses but for reasons different from the one argued. Many paths, after all, may lead to the same outcome. While it is helpful to know the reasoning for a prediction, it should be explained in the text and should not be part of a formal hypothesis.

Finally, the hypotheses may be inconsistent with respect to the relationships between the variables being investigated. H1, H2, and the subhypotheses predict that the two variables will co-vary, not that one causes the other, so this is a *correlational* study, one that investigates non-causal relationships between variables. The researchers, however, later report *differences* between groups (reporters and the public) and times (before and after the strike). This appears to make the groups and times the causal, independent variables that influence the differences in the dependent variables of media usage. The researchers probably should have articulated two clear hypotheses regarding these differences. (They actually reword the hypotheses later to reflect these differences [236–241], and address the relationships between the variables using regression analyses later in the results section.)

On the whole, this review of the literature is well written and explains clearly the theories being studied and some of the findings from the relevant past research. The hypotheses emerge logically from the previous findings and the terms used in the hypotheses are already familiar to the reader. The final paragraph in this section (137–144), however, describes the procedures used in this study, so it could go in the next section on methods.

Methods

The methods section begins by explaining the two subsamples studied (146–164). To gain access to a sample of striking reporters, these researchers contacted the office of the striking union to request cooperation. They could have simply interviewed reporters on the picket line, but the decision to make an official contact first was probably wise. Many respondents become suspicious when approached as members of an organization during a time of controversy and high emotion. Official sanction of some kind is often necessary in research conducted inside places of employment. But the approval which enables a researcher to contact respondents may also influence the responses obtained. If respondents think the research has been approved by their employers or organizational leaders, they might answer in ways they think are appropriate politically, rather than as they really feel. For example, striking reporters might underreport their dependency on the media and their substitution behavior because they do not want to appear weakened by the strike.

The first subsample consisted of interviews with 54 striking reporters (156–157). It is not clear, however, whether the reporters were actually interviewed because they were handed "an anonymous self-administered survey" (154–156). This phrasing suggests that the reporters completed a self-administered questionnaire, and we are left wondering what the "trained interviewers" did. The unclear reporting of this procedure leads us to suspect that interviews were not conducted, but that the "interviewers" merely distributed and collected questionnaires from respondents.

The researchers acknowledge that this subsample of striking reporters constitutes an opportunity, or *convenience,* sample (157–158), one composed of whatever members of the population happened to be available. Sometimes convenience samples are necessary and appropriate, but they always raise the question about whether the respondents accurately *represent* the population from which they are drawn. The respondents in this study were active union members on a picket line. Do their responses represent the feelings of other union members who chose not to be on the picket line? Would they give the same responses while involved emotionally on a picket line, surrounded by their "comrades in arms," as they would if interviewed in the privacy of their own homes? Since the guild office was being supportive, the researchers could have used a random procedure to select reporters. The result would have been a much more representative subsample, and we would be more confident about being able to generalize the findings to the population of striking reporters.

The second subsample was composed of 215 members of the general public who were selected by the *random digit dialing* (RDD) method (159–163). Random samples, as we know, assure researchers the best chance of obtaining a representative sample. The random digit dialing method, however, does have a potential bias. In spite of the high percentage of people with phones, those who do not have one are excluded from the study as well as those not home when called, unless an effective call-back procedure is used. If the people who are excluded are different in some important ways from the people included in a random sample, the sample may be biased. That is why survey researchers strive to maximize response rate. The completion rate in this study, however, was 55.5%, so some potential bias may exist in this subsample.

The data from these two subsamples were compared, which raises two potential problems. First, one of the subsamples is much larger than the other. Differences in group sizes can be a problem in extreme cases (comparing 1,000 men and 10 women, for example, might yield distorted results), and this difference could be a potential problem in this study (54 reporters versus 215 members of the general public). Second, since one subsample is a random sample while the other is a nonrandom sample, the results have only the strength of the nonrandom convenience sample because that sample may be biasing the results. The strength of the random sample is, in a statistical sense, "wasted" because the nonrandom sample limits the generalizability of the results.

The researchers do not specify the independent variables. Differences (in mean scores) between reporters and the public, as well as differences before and after the strike started, are compared in Tables 1–3. These different groups and times thus function as the independent variables, while the various measures of media use function as the dependent variables. This study, therefore, appears to be a series of factorial designs with independent variables being tested for their impact on several dependent variables, but the authors do not make this clear.

The researchers explain in some detail the numerous dependent variables and how they were *operationalized*, or measured (165–215). They seem to have done a thorough job of assessing people's use of the media. Not only do they assess different types of media (newspapers, magazines, television, and radio), but they also assess differences within a particular medium (such as the amount of time people spent reading national, out-of-state, and suburban and community papers).

Two issues are raised by how some of these variables were measured. First, to obtain a measure of media use prior to the strike, people were asked to estimate their media use on a typical weekday before the strike (178–180). This estimate was then compared with their media use during the strike. While this procedure is undoubtedly the only way to obtain a prestrike measure of media use, since it is difficult to anticipate a newspaper strike, these estimates may not be accurate. People simply may not be able to recall accurately the extent to which they used all of these media prior to the strike. (Can you remember how many newspapers and magazines you read, television news shows you watched, and radio news shows you listened to last week?) It is also possible that the striking reporters figured out the purpose of the research and purposely gave answers that showed they were not caving in during the strike.

Second, the two "dimensions" of media gratifications (192–215) asked people to indicate the extent to which gratification statements were either a lot like them, a little like them, or not at all like them. The researchers then treated these items as *interval* measurements with equal distances between the points (as evidenced in Table 2). Not all researchers would agree, arguing instead that these types of items are only *ordinal,* or rank-ordered, measurements. It is, however, common practice in the social sciences to treat scales constructed with such items (called **Likert-type scales**) as interval measurements. It also is not clear why these researchers used a 3-point format instead of the traditional 5-point format, or why these items were not combined into two subscales.

In all, then, these researchers conducted highly structured interviews, at least with the general public, to obtain the needed information. They asked closed questions that demanded numerical answers (such as the number of minutes spent reading newspapers) or fixed-response answers (such as a lot, a little, or not at all). There is no evidence that the interviewers asked any open questions or probed for additional information from people, although they might have. The interviews thus were highly standardized, which means that we can be reasonably confident that there probably weren't many variations between the interviews. Of course, the mere presence or characteristics of the interviewers still may have affected respondents' answers. Hence, while interviewing may have saved some time, we are left wondering whether, given the use of apparently highly structured interviews, mailed questionnaires might have worked as well.

Results

The results section is fairly long (229–527), for several reasons. First, each dependent variable is treated as if it were separate, or independent, from all the others. This brings up two concerns. First, the variables may not be distinct. The amount of time people spend watching local TV news and network TV news, for example, are probably related; that is, they probably vary together, either high or low. The same relationship is likely for the number of national and out-of-state newspapers people read. Note that we pointed out that two of the authors of this text made the same mistake in handling interrelated variables in the article analyzed in Chapter 4 (see lines 268–274 of that article). The more appropriate way to analyze data based on interrelated dependent variables is called *multivariate analysis.*

The second, and more serious, issue concerns the number of statistical tests conducted. In the social sciences the accepted probability level is p = .05, or a 5% probability that the results are due to chance. Tables 1 and 3 each report the results of 30 separate statistical tests. Error adds up, so with almost 30 tests, each having a 5% chance of error, there is a high probability (but obviously not 150%) that at least one of the significant findings in each table is due to chance. Who knows which ones they might be?! If the researchers wished to avoid this potential problem, they could either have used a more stringent confidence level, such as the .01 level (in which case only 1 out of 100 statistical tests would likely be significant by chance alone), or, better yet, used a multivariate procedure.

The researchers also use the four subhypotheses to test the two general hypotheses (230–241, 297–392), but this is questionable. Each hypothesis should be tested separately. If the "general" hypotheses could not be tested directly, it would be better to present them as research questions which the four testable hypotheses were intended to answer. These authors do a good job, however, of explaining how the four subhypotheses actually do answer the "general" questions, so this criticism really is more about labeling than about the actual procedures employed.

Finally, the researchers used *regression analyses* to build predictive models about which variables seem to explain media use most (402–527; Table 5). These regression analyses should be linked back to the specific hypotheses advanced, as are the other results. The number of regression analyses performed also raises the issue of additive error again. The researchers do point out, however, how their results differ from past findings (472–475).

Discussion

The researchers report the results for each hypothesis in the Discussion section. These results lead them to conclude that, "For both the public and reporters a similar pattern of use existed as a result of the strike" (583–584). They suggest that, "If compensatory media use was taking place it was likely to be a medium which was similar to the one displaced" (586–588). They then give examples of similar media substitutes; for reporters it was other newspapers, while for the general public it was friends and relatives (588–591). Yet the actual results showed that, "The public was likely to compensate for the missing *Inquirer* and *Daily News* by increasing their readership of other newspapers. They read significantly more national, out-of-state papers, and suburban and community papers each day during the strike than they recalled reading before the strike" (303–307). The researchers thus appear to give two opposing answers to the same question. This is why great care is needed when specifying hypotheses, why there should be only *one* testable statement per hypothesis, and why the Results and Discussion sections should focus on specific answers to these hypotheses.

The researchers also argue that they examined "the multivariate pattern of influence of our measures of surveillance, social contact, and public or reporter group membership on each of our dependent variables" (561–564). This is not, however, the most common use of the term "multivariate," which typically describes statistical procedures that study the effects of independent variables on a set of *related* dependent variables, not their effects on *each* dependent variable.

The authors conclude this study by pointing out what the results mean with regard to mass media usage (592–598). They claim that people probably use the media more out of habit than out of need, but the difference between a need and a habit is not very clear. Finally, the authors urge future researchers to test other aspects of mass media dependency theory, such as how opinion leaders use the media to enhance their political aspirations. Thus they do a good job of tying their study back to its starting point, testing two theories of mass media use, and suggesting a specific direction for future theory-driven research.

CONCLUSION

The survey interview method is one of the most popular methodologies employed in the social sciences. Rosenberg and Elliott's study demonstrates one way in which interviews are used in survey research to acquire information about people's communication behavior.

QUESTIONS AND ACTIVITIES TO CONSIDER

1. What were the advantages of using interviews rather than questionnaires to assess the general public's use of the media in this study? What were the disadvantages?

2. These researchers used a highly structured interview composed of closed questions. What were the advantages and limitations of using this procedure? Can you think of any open questions they could have asked about people's use of the media and their substitution behavior during the newspaper strike?

3. The third activity at the end of Chapter 4 asked you to construct some questions to assess why people lie and what they lie about. Put these questions on a questionnaire and pass them out to 10 people. Now ask 10 other people the same questions, only this time ask them orally. Were there any differences between these procedures? Was it difficult to

maintain consistency from interview to interview? Did these two methods yield similar answers?

4. Take a topic you want to investigate and conduct two types of interview surveys, one that is highly structured and one that is more unstructured. In the highly structured interviews, ask closed questions and try to make sure that each interview is standardized by being conducted in exactly the same way. In the unstructured interviews, ask the same closed questions, but then ask some open questions and probe for more information. Tape record all interviews so that responses can be compared. What were the key differences between these interviews? What were the advantages and limitations of each type of interview? Which type of interview produced the most valid data, given the purposes of your research? Why?

5. Finally, conduct two other types of interviews, some face-to-face and some over the telephone. Ask some nonthreatening questions and one or two questions about controversial topics. What were the differences in these methods? Was it easier to establish rapport in the face-to-face situation than over the telephone? Which type of interview administration procedure was most effective for assessing people's responses to the controversial topics?

FURTHER READINGS ON SURVEY INTERVIEW RESEARCH

Beed, T. W., & Stimson, R. J. (Eds.). (1985). *Survey interviewing: Theory and techniques.* Boston: George Allen & Unwin.

Fowler, F. J., Jr., & Mangione, T. W. (1990). *Standardized survey interviewing: Minimizing interviewer-related error.* Newbury Park, CA: Sage.

Frey, J. H. (1989). *Survey research by telephone* (2nd ed.). Newbury Park, CA: Sage.

Guenzeel, P. J., Berkmans, T. R., & Cannell, C. F. (1983). *General interviewing techniques.* Ann Arbor, MI: Institute for Social Research.

Steward, D. W., & Shamdasani, P. N. (1990). *Focus groups: Theory and practice.* Newbury Park, CA: Sage.

EXAMPLES OF SURVEY INTERVIEW RESEARCH

Babrow, A. S., Black, D. R., & Tiffany, S. T. (1990). Beliefs, attitudes, intentions, and a smoking-cessation program: A planned behavior analysis of communication campaign development. *Health Communication, 2,* 123–143.

This research sought to develop a communication campaign urging people to quit smoking based on a study of smokers' beliefs, attitudes, and intentions toward participating in a smoking-cessation program. College smokers were contacted over the telephone and asked in highly structured interviews how much they smoked, and to indicate on rating scales: their attitudes toward, interest in, and intention to participate in a stepped smoking-cessation program; their beliefs about the consequences of participation; the subjective norms influencing them to participate; and the factors that might prevent them from participating. The results showed that intention to participate was most related to beliefs about positively evaluated outcomes, suggesting that communication campaigns must use promotional messages that address both the perceived likelihood and evaluation of the positive consequences of participating in a smoking-cessation program.

Kramer, M. W. (1989). Communication during intraorganization job transfers. *Management Communication Quarterly, 3*, 219–248.

This study investigated the communication behavior of people who are transferred within an organization from one city to another and those who stay behind. A convenience sample of 18 transferees and 18 "stayers" from nine organizations were asked in relatively open, unstructured interviews to recall their typical communication patterns within the organization three months before the transfer, during the last days before the transfer, during the first two weeks the transferee was on the new job, and currently. The results showed that a three-stage model explains communication related to intra-organizational job transfers: (1) a loosening stage (in which the transferee passes on important information and stayers anticipate his or her loss); (2) a transition stage (in which stayers increase in-group communication to cope with the loss, and the transferee develops new work-group relationships); and (3) a tightening stage (in which the transferee develops normal work relationships and network links beyond the immediate work group, and communication between the transferee and stayers is reduced.

Pease, T., & Stempell, G. H., III (1990). Surviving to the top: Views of minority newspaper executives. *Newspaper Research Journal, 11*(3), 64–79.

This study assessed the extent to which racism remains in America's newsrooms. Forty-two minority newspaper executives (including African-Americans, Latino/Hispanics, and Asian-Americans who were assistant managing editors or higher) were interviewed over the phone about how they got started in their newspaper careers, what their experiences had been as minorities in the newsroom, and what suggestions they had for improving the population of minority newsroom executives. The interviewers asked primarily open questions and probed respondents to elaborate on their answers about how race figured into hiring, job assignments, and advancement. The findings showed that racism still exists in most newsrooms; that it reflects the attitudes of the communities and society in which those newsrooms are located; and that retaining talented minority journalists and developing them into positions of responsibility depend on good communication with white managers.

Ritchie, L. D., & Fitzpatrick, M. A. (1990). Family communication patterns: Measuring intrapersonal perceptions of interpersonal relationships. *Communication Research, 17*, 523–544.

This study investigated whether researchers' common assumption that family communication norms are shared by all family members is valid. A random sample of children and parents from Madison, Wisconsin were contacted by telephone and asked in structured interviews to complete an instrument that used a rating scale to measure family communication norms. These norms emphasized either an orientation toward maintaining a harmonious relationship with the parents (socio-orientation), or an orientation toward the open expression of ideas and active engagement in debate (concept-orientation). The results showed differences across age groups, as 7th-grade children shared their mothers' views on concept-orientation and their fathers' views on socio-orientation, but by 11th grade the opposite pattern held. Patterns of mother-child communication also were shown to be distinct from patterns of father-child communication. The findings suggest that communication researchers cannot treat the family as a single unit but must view it as a set of complex interactions among individuals whose perspectives are distinct but not independent.

Wright, J. W., II. & Hosman, L. A. (1990). Deregulation and public perceptions of television: A longitudinal study. *Communication Studies, 41,* 266–277.

In 1984, the Federal Communications Commission (FCC) deregulated television programming, leaving it up to broadcasters to decide on the number and length of commercials, the percentage of time to devote to news and public affairs, and ways to meet community needs. This study assessed changes in public perceptions of television programming and commercials since deregulation. Three groups were chosen randomly from Gainesville, Florida, and interviewed over the phone (one in 1984 before deregulation took effect, one in 1986, and one in 1988). Respondents were read statements referring to particular policy or programming issues and asked to indicate their agreement with these statements on 5-point scales. The results from these structured interviews showed significant differences between pre- and post-deregulation perceptions, such as the perceived increase in the number of commercials shown since deregulation (even though broadcasters contend that the total number of commercials aired has not increased substantially). The results also revealed strong public support for requiring broadcasters to cover alternative sides of controversial issues. Perceptions of the amount of news broadcasted, coverage of local issues, and the extent to which programming met local needs, however, showed no change since deregulation.

TEXTUAL ANALYSIS

How much violence are children exposed to in "Teenage Mutant Ninja Turtles" cartoons? What strategies do lawyers use when cross-examining crime witnesses? How did persuasive appeals used by George Bush and Michael Dukakis in the 1988 presidential campaign debates differ? Communication researchers answer questions like these by studying a recorded or visual message, or what is called a *text*. Recorded or visual texts take the form of spoken, written, artistic, and electronic documents or products of communication. Examples of texts include written transcripts of speeches and conversations, written documents (such as letters, personnel records, newspapers, and magazines), electronic documents (such as audiotapes, films, videotapes, and computer files), and visual texts (such as paintings, photographs, and architecture). *Textual analysis* is the method researchers use to describe, interpret, and/or evaluate the characteristics of a recorded or visual message.

Textual analysis serves three purposes. First, researchers often try to *ascribe meaning* to the messages contained within a text. The meaning of a text can be inferred by determining what the producer of the text probably intended and/or by learning how receivers, either naive or expert, interpreted the text. Second, researchers often attempt to understand *the influence* of input variables, factors that pre-existed the text (such as elements in the historical and social contexts in which the text was produced), on the text's messages, and/or *the effects* of those messages on outcomes (such as the effects of politicians' campaign literature on voting behavior). Finally, researchers often apply standards to *critique* or evaluate textual messages.

TYPES OF TEXTUAL ANALYSIS

Textual analysis encompasses several different approaches to communication inquiry. Specific textual analytic research techniques include *rhetorical criticism* (the critical analysis of persuasive messages), *content analysis* (the identification and measurement of message units and patterns in texts), and *interaction analysis* (the empirical examination of functional and structural components in transcripts and recordings of dyadic and small group interactions). An example of each type of analysis will be presented and examined in this section of the book.

Textual analysis holds an honored place in the history of communication inquiry, since the earliest printed works dealing with human communication were commentaries on rhetorical public discourse. Rhetorical criticism was first practiced in the fifth century B.C. during the *classical period* of communication inquiry. Classical rhetoricians, such as Plato and Aristotle, examined the speaking strategies of ancient Greek orators. Later rhetoricians, such as Cicero and Quintillian, analyzed the functions of public discourse within the Roman Empire. Content analysis developed formally in the twentieth century, was first used to study written media, such as newspapers and books, and was later applied to the electronic media, such as television and film. Today, content analysis is a mainstay of media research. Indeed, by 1975, Comstock (1975) reported that more than 225 content analyses had already been conducted on television programming alone. Finally, interaction analysis has received considerable attention by communication researchers within the last two to three decades.

SELECTING TEXTS

The first step in any textual analysis is identifying and acquiring the texts most relevant for answering the specific research questions posed. Researchers must decide what *type* of texts they will study. Texts fall into two general categories: transcripts or outputs of communication. **Transcripts of communication** are verbatim written versions of what people actually say, such as reports of court proceedings, scripts of television shows, and dialogue typed from audiotapes. Transcripts are particularly difficult to obtain, since most discourse is not recorded, and it is very tedious to type accurately what is recorded. **Outputs of communication** are texts produced by the communicators themselves, such as letters, photographs, and even graffiti. Outputs such as books, magazines, art works, films, and television programs are easier to obtain since most are created for public consumption, are available for sale, or can be borrowed from libraries or viewed at archives.

Second, researchers must *select* texts carefully. The best procedure, of course, is to conduct a *census* of all the relevant texts. If a researcher is interested, for example, in analyzing President Bush's public statements about Saddam Hussein, it may be possible to obtain all public statements made by Bush. In other cases, however, it simply is not possible to conduct a census. A researcher interested in analyzing violence in children's television cartoons, for example, could not obtain a copy of every cartoon ever made. In such cases, the researcher has to select a *sample* of texts to analyze. In survey research we saw how important it is for researchers to sample respondents carefully so that they represent the population being studied. The same standard applies to textual analysis. Researchers must select a sample of texts that represents the universe of texts being studied. Likewise, to generalize findings from a sample of texts, researchers should use a *random* sampling procedure because it provides the best guarantee that the sample is representative of the universe of texts being studied. In many cases, however, random selection will not be possible or feasible. It is not possible, for example, for a researcher to select a random sample of all fan letters written by teenagers to celebrities. In such cases, a *nonrandom* sample of texts will be selected, but the researcher must be careful of the conclusions drawn from these nonrepresentative samples. In the final analysis, the sampling strategy used to gather texts determines the *generalizability* of the findings.

Finally, researchers must strive to select texts that are *complete* and *accurate*. Written transcripts, for example, are usually produced from notes taken, perhaps by a journalist or stenographer, or from audiotape or videotape recordings. Written transcripts are not always complete or accurate, however, because the transcriber may not have recorded everything said. Audiotape recordings are inherently incomplete because they fail to account for nonverbal elements (such as gestures, postures, and facial expressions of the speakers) or elements in the physical environment that may influence what was said (such as the room decor, the time of the event, or the seating arrangement). Even videotape recordings of an interaction may produce an incomplete and inaccurate text because of the limited point of view afforded by the camera positions chosen. Outputs of communication may also not be complete and accurate, because they are susceptible to the problems of "selective deposit" and "selective survival"—there may be some bias in which ones were saved. Researchers must thus take care to authenticate that the texts selected have not been altered, embellished, or edited after the original act of communication. If the text has been altered, the textual analyst must note and consider this when drawing conclusions from the data.

Because the selection of texts is crucial to evaluating the results of any study that employs a form of textual analysis, keep the following questions in mind when reading textual analytic research studies:

1. Were the most *appropriate texts* selected for analysis? Were the texts selected for analysis the most relevant available for answering the research questions posed, or might other texts have been more appropriate?

2. Did the *method used to produce the text* pose a threat to the validity of the data? For example, did a recording device, such as audiotape or videotape, bias which textual messages were available for analysis?

3. Is the researcher sure that the texts selected are *complete* and *accurate*? What might be left out of these texts, and how might any omissions affect the results?

4. Was a *census* of communication texts on this topic analyzed, or was a *sample* selected? If a sample was selected, was a *random* procedure used to assure that the texts are *representative* of the universe of texts being studied? If a *nonrandom* sample was used, does the selection appear representative of the whole corpus of material?

DISTINCTIVE CHARACTERISTICS OF TEXTUAL ANALYSIS

Textual analysis has several attributes that distinguish it from experimental, survey, and ethnographic research methods. First, textual analysis is *message-centered*—the data being analyzed are the actual words and non-discursive symbols (such as pictures, gestures, and props) speakers used. Second, the texts are usually taken from communication acts that occur *naturally*, rather than being structured or prompted by researchers, so they preserve the integrity of the original communication. Third, because researchers study texts rather than the people who produced them, textual analysis is considered a *nonreactive* research technique (Webb, Campbell, Schwartz, & Sechrest, 1973). This means that the methodology itself does not usually influence the data or texts that are produced. For example, the researcher does not usually interact with the people whose messages are recorded, so the researcher effects examined in Chapter 2 are not a concern in textual analysis. Interaction analysts recognize, however, that they can influence the data because they create the text from audio or video recordings. That is why transcriptions are so important and so tedious to do. Many researchers work in teams to better capture the nuances of talk.

There are, however, some constraints involved in textual analysis. Because researchers study texts rather than the people who produced them, they usually don't assess directly the intentions of the producers by asking them questions. Instead, researchers must infer communication motives from the discourse itself. Communicators, however, sometimes construct messages so as to mask their true meanings, and even when they attempt to disclose their true intentions, their ideas may be misinterpreted. Textual analysts, therefore, must take care to qualify conclusions reached about the intentions of communicators. Textual analysis also is primarily descriptive or evaluative—seeking to understand the characteristics embedded in a text or to evaluate the text according to a set of standards. Textual analysis thus does not usually meet the scientific criteria for establishing causality or making accurate predictions. Precise and insightful descriptions of communication events, however, help increase our understanding of communication practices and subsequently increase our ability to interpret and predict future events.

Chapter 6

Rhetorical Criticism

INTRODUCTION TO THE METHOD

The term "rhetoric" is used in many contexts. Some people apply it to the teaching of grammar and composition in freshman English courses, others to the bombastic and verbose discourse of politicians and marketers, such as when we say that a manipulative debator is "engaging in rhetoric." *Rhetoric*, however, was originally defined by Aristotle as "the available means of persuasion." For communication scholars, the available means are the symbols persuaders (rhetors) use to influence people's thoughts and actions.

The term "criticism," while often viewed negatively as tearing down what someone has to say, in this context means making a substantiated judgment. For scholars, criticism involves "the systematic process of illuminating and evaluating products of human activity" (Andrews, 1983, p. 4). **Rhetorical criticism** thus is the "description, analysis, interpretation, and evaluation of persuasive uses" of human communication (Campbell, 1972, p. 12).

Early rhetorical theory and criticism developed by the ancient Greeks and Romans, referred to as *classical rhetoric*, examined the characteristics and effects of persuasive public speaking, such as how political speeches enlisted public support for a specific leader or helped establish and maintain social order. Today, *contemporary rhetorical criticism* incorporates a wide range of theoretical and methodological perspectives to study the persuasive impact of many different oral, written, and mediated messages.

Andrews (1983) explains that rhetorical criticism can accomplish five goals. First, rhetorical criticism sheds light on the *purposes* of a persuasive message, or its intended effects on an audience. Second rhetorical criticism seeks to understand the effects of the historical, social, and cultural *contexts* on the creation of rhetors' persuasive messages, thereby informing us about the relationship between one's environment and communication. Third, rhetorical criticism is often used to evaluate contemporary society and its practices. Rhetorical criticism functions as *social criticism* when it "evaluates the ways in which issues are formulated and policies justified, and the effects of both on society at a particular historical moment" (Campbell, 1974, pp. 10–11). Fourth, rhetorical criticism contributes to *theory-building* by offering generalizations about the process of persuasion. Finally, rhetorical criticism serves a *pedagogical* function by helping students learn what constitutes effective and ineffective persuasion.

Conducting Rhetorical Criticism

Rhetorical criticism is a systematic method for describing, analyzing, interpreting, and evaluating the persuasive force of messages embedded within texts. According to Foss (1989), this systematic method involves four steps: (1) choosing a text to study; (2) choosing a specific type of rhetorical criticism; (3) analyzing the text according to the method chosen; and (4) writing the critical essay.

Rhetorical critics first identify what they will analyze. Some critics formulate a research question about the process of persuasion and then choose rhetorical texts to answer the question; others first choose an interesting, significant rhetorical text and then pose research questions about it.

The second step involves choosing an appropriate type of rhetorical criticism with which to analyze the text. All rhetorical critics view texts through a method, or "lens," that is used to illuminate the meaning of the text. A critic may choose a method that already exists, modify an existing method, combine elements from different methods, or create an entirely new method.

The third step is the systematic application of the method to illuminate the meaning of the text. If, for example, the method calls for analyzing the fantasy themes contained in the text (see the explanation following), then the critic looks for these fantasy themes, describes them, and evaluates their persuasive effectiveness.

The final step involves writing the critical essay. Foss (1989) claims that a critical study should address seven major topics: "(1) introduction; (2) description of the artifact [text]; (3) description of the critical method; (4) report of the findings of the analysis; (5) interpretation of the findings; (6) evaluation of the artifact; and (7) contribution of the study to rhetorical theory" (p. 20).

Types of Rhetorical Criticism

Three general types of research questions are asked by rhetorical critics (Foss, 1989), and several different types of rhetorical criticism may be used to answer each question.

The first question is: *What is the relationship between the rhetorical text and its context?* Critics who ask this question analyze how elements of a social context (such as the time, place or occasion) influence the production of a persuasive communication. Four methods are used to answer this question: historical criticism, Neo-Aristotelian criticism, generic criticism, and feminist criticism.

Historical criticism studies how important past events shape and are shaped by rhetorical messages. Historical critics analyze the relationship between a text and its context by conducting four types of studies. First, *oral histories* examine spoken accounts of personal experiences to understand more fully what happened in the past. Terkel (1970), for example, interviewed people who had lived through the Great Depression and analyzed their stories. Second, *case studies* analyze an important historical event. Rowland and Rademacher (1990), for example, analyzed the rhetorical strategies Ronald Reagan used to avoid losing support during his handling of the Superfund controversy when the Environmental Protection Agency's enforcement of toxic waste control legislation was accused of corruption. Third, *biographical studies* interpret the public and private communication of important persons. Sauceda (1991), for example, studied James Joyce's work from a performance-centered perspective. He documented virtually every performance James Joyce gave of his work and defined a "Joycean performance style" as preserved on recordings and from the critiques provided by his audience. Fourth, *social movement studies* examine the historical development and persuasive strategies used to influence specific campaigns and causes. Brock and Howell (1988), for example, analyzed how the Palestinian national consciousness has been institutionalized as a social movement into the Palestinian Liberation Organization (PLO). They assessed the historical reasons for, and the effectiveness of, the PLO's use of terrorism as a strategy by applying rhetorical concepts derived from studying American New Left rhetoric from the 1960s.

Neo-Aristotelian criticism evaluates whether the most appropriate and effective means were used to create the rhetorical text(s) intended to influence a particular audience. The effectiveness of a persuasive message is evaluated according to Aristotle's five "canons of classical rhetoric": (1) *invention*, the development of persuasive arguments through *ethos* (appeals based on the character of speakers), *pathos* (appeals based on emotion), and *logos* (appeals based on logic); (2) *disposition*, the organization of persuasive messages; (3) *elocution*, speakers' use of language; (4) *delivery*, the nonverbal characteristics of speakers; and (5) *memory*, the strategies speakers use to recall information for their speeches.

Generic criticism rejects using a single set of criteria to evaluate all persuasive messages, arguing instead that standards vary according to the particular type, or genre, of text being studied. Critics, for example, would use different criteria to evaluate a state-of-the-union speech to Congress delivered by President Bush than they would for a stand-up comedy routine presented by Eddie Murphy. Rhetorical acts are classified and evaluated according to the type of situation that gives rise to them. For example, texts have been classified as *forensic* (concerning the past and covering issues of legality and justice); *deliberative* (dealing with the future and involving political oratory); *epideictic* (ceremonial communication concerning the present event); *apologic* (presenting a public defense of character); *inaugural* (accepting induction into political office); *eulogistic* (honoring a deceased individual); *campaign* (urging an audience to support or reject a political candidate or public policy); and *jeremiad* (blaming a group for current problems and urging them to change their behavior).

Feminist criticism analyzes how conceptions of gender are produced and maintained in persuasive messages. Feminist critics argue that societal members' conception of the characteristics of men and women are influenced by rhetoric describing men and women. Feminist critics also argue that a masculine view of the world has traditionally dominated rhetorical criticism and that females' thinking differs fundamentally from males', providing a distinct and valuable perspective from which to understand and evaluate persuasive messages.

The second question rhetorical critics ask is: *How does the message construct a particular reality for the audience and the rhetor?* Critics who ask this question analyze how the characteristics of persuasive messages influence audiences' conception of reality. Two methods are used to answer this question: metaphoric criticism and narrative criticism.

Metaphoric criticism assumes that we can never know reality directly. Rhetors' language represents reality, functioning as a metaphor, likening one thing to another. Metaphors used in persuasive messages, therefore, create visions of reality for receivers. Critics identify how rhetors create metaphors and evaluate how well the metaphors influence a shared reality for the audience.

Narrative criticism assumes that many (or all) persuasive messages function as narratives—stories, accounts, or tales. Stories embedded in texts provide descriptions of situations, central characters, and action sequences, and often carry implicit or explicit "lessons" that lead an audience to make sense of, or account for, important events. Narrative criticism, therefore, involves analyzing the stories rhetors tell and evaluating how effective they are at shaping an audience's perception of reality.

The third question rhetorical critics ask is: *What does the text suggest about the rhetor?* Critics who ask this question analyze how the characteristics, perspectives, and motives of a rhetor influenced the construction of a persuasive message. Two methods are used to answer this question: dramatistic criticism and fantasy theme analysis.

Dramatistic criticism primarily analyzes texts according to Kenneth Burke's (1945, 1950, 1960) view that all communication can be seen in terms of elements in a dramatic event. The nature of the event is captured, in part, by a *pentadic analysis,* which consists of five elements: an *act* (a particular message produced by a communicator); *purpose* (the reason for the communicative act); *agent* (the person who performs the symbolic act); *agency* (the medium used for the communicative act); and *scene* (the context in which the communicative act occurs). Dramatistic criticism examines the *ratios* (relationships) between the elements of this pentad to explain rhetors' motives and the characteristics of their messages. Burke and his interpreters also suggest additional concepts and methods to aid dramatistic criticism.

Fantasy theme analysis, based on the work of Ernest Bormann (1972, 1973, 1982), examines the common images used to portray narrative elements of situations described in a text. Critics reveal the motives of rhetors and how they shape the ways people create social reality by analyzing *fantasy themes* (archetypal or mythic stories superimposed on events), *fantasy types* (patterns of fantasy themes that recur within a text), *rhetorical visions* (interpretive schemes shared by groups of people), and *rhetorical communities* (the nature of the groups of people who share rhetorical visions).

QUESTIONS FOR EXAMINING RHETORICAL CRITICISM

In addition to the general criteria used to evaluate all research and the questions about the selection of texts, several criteria are of particular relevance to rhetorical criticism. Keep them in mind when you read the following study, or any study that employs rhetorical criticism.

A. Choice of Method

1. Was the *purpose* of the study explained clearly? Was the purpose to analyze the effects of the *context* on the message, the specific characteristics of the *message,* or how the characteristics of the *rhetor* influenced the production of the message? Did this purpose fit this particular message especially well?

2. Did the critic choose an existing method *intact, modify* an existing method, *combine* elements from various methods, or create an entirely new method? Was this choice optimal for answering the research question?

3. If an existing method was chosen, what *type of rhetorical criticism* was it:

historical, Neo-Aristotelian, generic, feminist, metaphoric, narrative, dramatistic, fantasy theme analysis, or some combination of these? Did this choice illuminate the messages analyzed particularly well, or did you see elements in the messages that suggest that an alternative method would have been more appropriate and effective?

4. Was the *specific method chosen* explained sufficiently? Do you now understand the requirements for conducting rhetorical criticism according to this method?

B. Analyzing the Text

1. Did the critic follow the *guidelines for the specific* method chosen in a systematic and comprehensive manner? Were all the necessary steps performed? Any omitted or shortchanged?

2. Did the critic *analyze* the text thoroughly? Were any significant aspects of the rhetorical text left unexplained?

3. Did the critic fulfill all the *functions of rhetorical criticism*—the description, analysis, interpretation, and evaluation of the text—or did any seem inadequate?

4. Did the critic produce a *compelling argument* about the meaning of the text? What *evidence* was used to support the argument? Did the critic, for example, use actual quotations from the text or provide detailed descriptions of the messages in the text? Were counterarguments ever considered?

5. Was the *subjectivity of the critic* acknowledged? Was the critique presented as a claim about reality or as one way of analyzing and evaluating the text? What personal or professional rationale lay behind the choice made?

6. Did the critic recommend how the analysis functions as *social criticism,* contributes to *rhetorical theory,* or serves a *pedagogical function?* What are the larger implications of the study? Do they seem justified?

7. In the final analysis, did the essay produce a *richer understanding of human persuasion?*

THE ILLUSTRATIVE STUDY

The essay you will read studies coverage by print media of the Chrysler Corporation and its chief executive officer, Lee Iacocca, from 1977 to 1985. Its purpose is to examine the print media's role in shaping public perceptions of Lee Iacocca as a popular cultural hero.

   This study provides an example of *historical rhetorical criticism,* which analyzes the relationship between a particular context and the creation of rhetors' persuasive messages. When reading this article, note how Dionisopoulos explains the specific ways in which the print media portrayed Iacocca in the context of specific social and economic events and established him as a folk hero of mythic proportions.

This study also provides an example of a historical *case study*. Case studies in rhetorical criticism, and other forms of communication research, provide in-depth descriptions of specific social situations from which insights are gleaned into communication strategies and processes that were used or could have been used in those situations (Kreps & Lederman, 1985). This case is chosen as an example of the *mythopoetic* function of the media—the ability of the media to create and disseminate public myths. Evaluate the strengths of the rhetorical evidence Dionisopoulos provides to explain the persuasive role of mass communication in creating Lee Iacocca as a popular folk hero.

A Case Study in Print Media and Heroic Myth: Lee Iacocca 1978–1985

George N. Dionisopoulos

Previous literature concerning the hero myth has not addressed how someone becomes a contemporary folk hero. This essay suggests that an answer can be found within the mythopoetic role of the media. The mediated "Chrysler drama" and subsequent popular proclamation of Lee Iacocca as a national folk hero is examined as a case study to determine the rhetorical strategies that present mediated actions and actors as "heroic."

1   By 1984–85, media proclamations that Lee Iacocca had become a "national folk hero" were commonplace. He was called a "real world 'Rocky'" (Alpern, 1984) and compared favorably to Indiana Jones (Andersen & Witteman, 1985). He was a "miracle man" (Ser Vaas,
5   1984, p. 42), one of the country's most admired figures ("We're a

Source: Dionispoulos, G. N. (1988). A case study in print media and heroic myth: Lee Iacocca 1978–1985. *The Southern Speech Communication Journal, 53,* 227–243. Reprinted by permission of the Southern States Speech Association.

George N. Dionisopoulos is Assistant Professor of Speech Communication at San Diego State University, San Diego, CA 92182. A version of this paper was presented at the Western Speech Communication Association Convention. Tucson, AZ, 1986. The author would like to thank Paul C. Gaske and Al Weitzel for their insightful comments on previous drafts of this paper.

Colony Again," 1984), and a "symbol of an America that's finally regained its confidence" (Stuller, 1984, p. 46). "Lessons" were culled from his life and offered as models to the American public.

Affirmation of Iacocca's status as a cultural hero extended be-
10   yond pronouncements by the media. The American public behaved toward him in a manner symptomatic of what Klapp (1972) called the unorganized, naive, and spontaneous behavior that is hero worship. By 1985 Iacocca was receiving 5,000 letters a month and 3,000 speaking invitations a year (Fotheringham, 1985). He was touted as presi-
15   dential and vice-presidential timber and his autobiography was the best selling nonfiction hardcover book in history. Even Chrysler workers, whose wages he froze, "cheered wildly" during his factory visits (Stuller, 1984, p. 106).

However, for several reasons, Iacocca's status as a cultural folk
20   hero presents an interesting problem for the study of the hero myth. First, Iacocca was only one of a collection of "significant persons" who paraded through the media environment from 1978 to 1985. Indeed, much of the culture industry is dependent upon the creation and subsequent exploitation of "celebrities." But public reaction to Iacocca
25   went beyond his recognition as "another media celebrity," to that of a cultural hero.[1]

Second, Iacocca was identified with "big business," a segment of our culture which had not produced cultural heroes in the past. Stuller (1984) observed that as a nation we were fascinated with
30   Howard Hughes, and we respected or feared industrial giants like John D. Rockefeller and Andrew Carnegie. But Iacocca became a cultural folk hero, "a corporate capitalist with a populist appeal" (Andersen & Witteman, 1985, p. 30). That "average Americans" reacted in this manner to a businessman was unprecedented.

35   Finally, understanding the public's reaction toward Iacocca is complicated further by the realization that, as "symbolic speech," the Chrysler bailout in the form of federal loan guarantees "communicated to Americans the inequity and injustice inherent in American politics and economics" (Foss, 1984, p. 87). In fact, as late as 1979,
40   public opinion polls indicated that three out of five Americans opposed federal loan guarantees to Chrysler (Nicholson & Jones, 1979).

Initially, one would be tempted to agree with Rollin (1983) that when members of the pubic bestow the status of "hero," they seem to do so for reasons of their own, "in violation of all definitions of terms,
45   consensus and even common sense" (p. 19). This temptation would be prompted further by the realization that the cultural hero myth has an amorphous quality that precludes the drawing of a definitive portrait of the American hero (Fisher, 1982).

Two communication studies have focused upon the Chrysler

50   "drama." Foss (1984) wrote that the Chrysler bailout symbolized three
      important failures for the Chrysler Corporation; that the company
      had (1) produced cars that failed to meet the public's standards for
      quality, (2) failed to respond to the demand for small cars, and
      (3) failed to run its operations profitably. She observed further that
55   Chrysler's advertisements illustrated how the company accepted and
      atoned for the public guilt symbolized by the bailout. Seeger (1986)
      employed Mintzberg's role system to analyze Iacocca's C. E. O. perfor-
      mance at Chrysler. However, neither of these works can account for
      Iacocca's status as a folk hero. In fact, Seeger observed that "Iacocca's
60   performances at Chrysler were not unique. . . . [and clearly] followed
      the individual roles described by Mintzberg" (p. 66).
          Nor can an adequate answer be found in previous communica-
      tion research concerning the archetypal hero. This corpus of work
      (e.g. Rushing, 1983; Fisher, 1982; Hankins, 1983; Bass & Cherwitz,
65   1978) has focused upon the suasory characteristics associated with the
      hero myth, but has not yet addressed *how* it is that periodically a
      "celebrity" becomes a cultural folk hero.
          I suggest that an answer can be found by considering the print
      media's role in the creation of popular heroes; that is to say, its mytho-
70   poetic function. Since publicity is the *sine qua non* of contemporary
      heroism (Barber, 1980), insight into public ascription of the status of
      "cultural hero" may be offered through an examination of the pat-
      terns of contemporary media coverage that *present* action and actors as
      "heroic."
75   I examined coverage in 1977–1985 print media stories concern-
      ing Chrysler, Iacocca, and the bailout guarantee from newspapers
      (*New York Times; Washington Post*), news periodicals (*Times, Newsweek,
      U. S. News & World Report*), business periodicals (*Business Week, For-
      tune*), and "popular" magazines (*Saturday Evening Post, Nation, People,
80   Harpers, Macleans, New Republic*). From 1977 to 1985, the mediated
      Chrysler "drama" and Iacocca's role in it "unfolded in the press al-
      most like a weekly serial" (Andersen & Witteman, 1985, p. 32). How-
      ever, the amount of exposure cannot account for Iacocca's hero status
      since exposure alone "cannot make a celebrity a hero" (Rollin, 1983,
85   p. 19). Instead, we must explore the form of the exposure.
          Toward that end, this essay first examines the rhetorical patterns
      underlying media coverage concerning the Chrysler bailout and sub-
      sequent recovery. I coded the articles in these periodicals and news-
      papers according to content themes about Chrysler, the bailout, and
90   Iacocca. From this coding, I sorted the themes into the four major
      ones discussed in the media. The first two concerned how the media
      portrayed the act of "saving Chrysler" as a "heroic task." A third
      pattern highlighted Iacocca's role in the successful accomplishment of

this task. Coverage during Chrysler's recovery evidenced a fourth
95   pattern which presented the mediated persona of Iacocca as a condensation symbol for American cultural values. The suggestion here
is that these patterns generated rhetorical forces as engaged publics
were compelled to identify with the action as "heroic" and with
Iacocca as a contemporary cultural hero. Finally, this essay offers
100   some conclusions—drawn from the case study—concerning the
mythopoetic role of the contemporary media in society.

PATTERNS OF HEROIC MYTHOPOEIA

Saving Chrysler as a "Herculean Task"

The first identifiable pattern within the media concerned the descrip-
105   tion of the difficult task facing Iacocca. In the fall of 1978, Iacocca
came out of his "retirement" from Ford, to accept an offer from
Chrysler Chairman John Riccardo. On November 2, Chrysler re-
leased two public announcements. The first was that the company had
just posted a record $158.5 million loss in the third quarter; the
110   second was that Lee Iacocca would become the president of Chrysler
(Iacocca & Novak, 1984).
In the media's accounts of Iacocca's job appointment, Chrysler's
problems were portrayed as "bigger than one man's ability to solve
them" (Nicholson, Jones & Friendly, 1978, p. 101), especially a man
115   whose reputation was built "more on product development and marketing savvy than on management and financial skills" ("Could Bankruptcy Save Chrysler?" 1979, p. 72). Iacocca was described as "walking
into an automotive disaster area" (Nicholson, Jones & Friendly, 1978,
p. 99). Even while Ford and General Motors enjoyed "robust sales and
120   profits," Chrysler was in its "worst years since 1975" ("Chrysler Gets,"
1978, p. 94). Pronouncements concerning Chrysler's future suggested
that the company needed "a lot of fixing" ("It Won't Be Easy," 1978, p.
130), or a complete change of direction ("Chrysler Gets," 1978, p. 94).
Media descriptions concerning the near hopeless nature of
125   Chrysler's predicament continued for the next two years. *Business
Week* observed that "some auto executives think Chrysler cannot be
saved" (Norman, 1980, p. 23), and *Fortune* entitled its feature story
about the auto company "Chrysler's Pie-in-the-Sky Plan for Survival"
(Bohr, 1979). Others, even while praising Iacocca, stated simply that
130   his ability was irrelevant because his company was "beyond salvation"
(Miller, 1980, p. 23). Chrysler's chances of survival were described as
"bleak" (Ross, 1981), with "odds" running from "one-in-four" (Miller,
1980, p. 38) to "a chance in a million" ("Ford's Mr. Mustang", 1979,

p. 42). Congress, the investment community, and the American people were all "increasingly skeptical" about the survival of Chrysler,
and Iacocca was "likely to become a General Custer" ("Could Bankruptcy," 1979, p. 72). By the winter of 1980 the "odds on Chrysler's
survival grew longer" (Nicholson, Marbach, Thomas & Dentzer, 1980,
p. 54). "[B]umper to bumper with bankruptcy" (Taylor, Bolte, & Seaman, 1980, p. 53), the company's deadline was "now measured in
weeks, not months"; failure seemed "inevitable" (Nicholson, Marbach,
Thomas & Dentzer, 1980).

Thus, the first identifiable media pattern emphasized the difficulty of Iacocca's task. A second important pattern emphasized that
the successful accomplishment of this task would benefit the weak and
helpless of society.

Saving Chrysler Will Benefit Others

The mediated drama cast the bailout "debate" in mythic terms,
grounded primarily in the "important symbolic meaning of the automobile industry [as a central value] for Americans: 'What's good for
GM is good for the USA.'" (Broms & Gahmberg, 1982, p. 24).

The automobile has assumed a central place in our culture and
become one of the defining characteristics of our standard of living.
This fact is not lost on advertisers who invite American consumers to
improve self-image through the purchase of a "high-status" automobile. Post-WWII changes in American culture, such as the growth
of suburbs, were possible in large part because of the role of the
automobile. According to a 1979 study by the Hertz Corporation,
Americans spend more than one-fourth of national personal income,
approximately $445 billion a year, on automobiles. As a nation, we
own almost half of the automobiles in the world and consume fifteen
percent of the world's annual production of petroleum in our cars
(McCarthy, 1980, p. 13).

But the symbolism of the automobile industry in America is
deeper than our post-war love affair with the car. The sheer size of
the American automobile industry means that it represents a major
element in the United States' role as a "manufacturing nation." This
point was emphasized by Kraft in the *Washington Post* in an editorial
entitled "The Chrysler Warning" (1979):

. . . *the United States cannot afford to become a pure service economy. On the contrary, if this country is to maintain industrial jobs, save its major cities and sustain
its traditional role in high technology and international security, it needs to formulate over the next few years an explicit policy for the re-industrialization of America.
(p. A19)*

175 Media reports emphasized the magnitude of the corporation and its role in the economy of the United States. References to Chrysler portrayed it as the nation's "tenth largest manufacturer" ("Chrysler's Cry," 1979, p. 33) or the "tenth largest industrial corporation" (Cameron, 1979, p. 30). During the summer of 1979, President Carter

180 disclosed that his administration viewed Chrysler as "a very important part of our national economy" ("A Collapse of Chrysler Corp," 1979, p. A8; Cowan, 1979). A shutdown of this "vital component of America's economic and industrial might" (Stuart, 1979a, p. A27) would have "far-reaching consequences" ("Chrysler's Cry," 1979, p. 33).

185 These consequences would include a "devastating impact on the Midwest" (Weisman, 1979, p. D4), an increase in the nation's trade deficit of $2.1 billion ("New Report," 1979, p. A33), and a lessening of competition by robbing "America of a major producer of fuel-efficient cars" (Blanchard, 1979, p. A19).

190   No one disputed the claim that Chrysler's management had made serious mistakes. Chrysler (1979b) admitted as much in their full-page advertisement, "Does Chrysler Want to Stay in Business Just to Build Gas Guzzlers?" (p. D3). However, Chrysler was also portrayed as having suffered from "a remarkable string of bad timing and worse

195 luck." These were events beyond the control of the corporation's management, including two gas shortages and Federal regulations that hit Chrysler harder than Ford or General Motors (Cameron, 1979; Stuart, 1979b). The Chrysler corporation was not the only company suffering. The "general climate for all American industry [had]

200 changed for the worse" (Kraft, 1979, p. A19). Even Iacocca felt that Chrysler was a "classic microcosm of everything that is wrong with the U. S." ("Lee Iacocca's Hard Sell," 1979, p. 74). Thus, as Chrysler evolved symbolically into "simply the prototype of a more general problem" (Samuelson, 1979, p. D6), the future of the company was

205 transformed symbolically within the media into a test of our national value system.

          This mythic symbolism attached to the task of saving Chrysler was enhanced further by media reports specifying that a failure of this important part of our economy would result in hardship for the

210 "little people" who worked for Chrysler. These were the everyday Americans who were weak and helpless before the unfolding of events over which they had no control and which they could not even understand.

          A failure of the Chrysler Corporation would throw hundreds of

215 thousands of Americans out of work. Samuelson (1979) observed in the *Washington Post* that there was little dispute over the fact if Chrysler failed "somewhere between 150,000 and 500,000 workers would probably lose their jobs immediately, and only the most reckless forecaster can say how easily they could be re-employed" (p. D6). A

220   Chrysler failure would mean a "permanent loss of 200,000 to 300,000 jobs" (1979) ("A Collapse of Chrysler," 1979, p. A8; "New Report," 1979). A large percentage of these were "blue collar" jobs. Further, the company itself had a strong identification with the "working class" in America. Chrysler's "prosaic but well-engineered cars appealed

225   mostly to lower-income blue collar workers, who were particularly vulnerable to recession or depression" (McDowell, 1979, p. A12).

Many of the jobs that would be lost if Chrysler failed were held by minorities: "One third of the company's blue-collar work force and one-tenth of its white collar employees are members of minority

230   groups, mostly blacks." In fact, Chrysler's black employees received $800 million a year from the corporation, approximately one percent "of all the personal income of blacks in this country" (Morgan, 1979, p. A2). Certain areas would be especially hard hit if Chrysler failed. Detroit, already hit hard economically, could see its unemployment

235   jump from 8.7% to over 19%, and over a million people would have to go on welfare (Luther, 1979).

The media offered several personae who seemed to clarion this point succinctly (D8). The *Washington Post* quoted a congressional aide as saying, "The nation has a moral obligation to support this plan. . . .

240   Families are at stake" (Morgan, 1979, p. A2). Michigan's Democratic Congressman, James Blanchard, maintained that if America let Chrysler fail, it would be because, as a nation, we had succumbed to what he termed, "'disaster as a spectator sport': that is, we are so used to observing serious human and social tragedies on television and at

245   the movies that we are too numb to act when faced with a real disaster—a disaster we have the power to prevent" (Blanchard, 1979, A19).[2] Tip O'Neill warned his colleagues in the House that failure to help Chrysler could result in the "laying off of 700,000 people. . . . I speak to you as Tip O'Neill, as an American" (Miller, 1979, p. A1).

250   During this time rhetoric attributed to both the Chrysler corporation and Iacocca emphasized the consequences of a corporate failure in humanistic terms. In a full-page advertisement entitled "Would America Be Better Off Without Chrysler," the company asserted:

255   *. . . to turn our back on 140 thousand of our own employees would be irresponsibility. To close the doors in 52 American communities in which Chrysler is a major factor of the local economy would be irresponsibility. To deny employment to the 150 thousand people who work for the dealers who sell Chrysler products would be irresponsibility (Chrysler, 1979a, p. A22).*

260   Similarly the media carried accounts of Iacocca's own rhetoric concerning the bailout. These accounts suggested that Iacocca's biggest concern was the human cost of a Chrysler failure. To him, the

"most important part of [the bailout]" was "not products but people" ("Lee Iacocca Speaks Up," 1979, p. 64; Ser Vass, 1984).

265   Thus, the media cast the drama of the "bailout debate" in mythic terms. Much more was at stake than the success or failure of an American conglomerate. The size and symbolic importance of Chrysler transformed the crisis into a public metaphor for a crisis in American self-image. The media highlighted the people who would

270 be most affected by the collapse of Chrysler. These were "everyday Americans" who had been placed in their precarious situation through no fault of their own, and who were being victimized by events beyond their control or comprehension.

Indeed, against such a mediated backdrop the persona under-

275 taking the task of saving Chrysler would be performing a deed of "heroic" proportions. This person would be acting against seemingly insurmountable odds to bring a triumphant resolution to the value challenge posed by the impending failure of Chrysler, and would in the process, help the weak and powerless in society.

280   These first two patterns are important when considering the mythopoetic role of the media in Iacocca's proclamation as a hero. The mediated picture of the task suggested that "saving Chrysler" would be a "great deed" requiring Herculean effort. As Wecter (1966) noted, no American hero "has lacked a touch lent by the struggle

285 against odds" (16). But equally important, this task was portrayed as being performed for the benefit of the weak and helpless in society. It seems obvious that a Herculean effort perceived as having been performed to increase the power or social standing of the actor him/herself, or to benefit dominant members of society, could not inspire the

290 accolades of hero worship from the American public. The next identifiable media pattern highlighted Iacocca as instrumental in the saving of Chrysler.

Iacocca Saves Chrysler

Coverage of Chrysler's "recovery" left little doubt that this was the

295 personal triumph of Lee Iacocca. Iacocca was the man who had "sav[ed] and then rebuil[t] Chrysler Corp. against all odds" (Andersen & Witteman, 1985, p. 30). Stuller (1984), who acknowledged that Iacocca "had help," asserted that it is "doubtful that anyone else could have led [Chrysler] out of harm's way" (p. 106). That observation is

300 echoed throughout the media. Iacocca was a "miracle man" (Ser Vass, 1984, p. 42), who "led Chrysler from the Temple of Doom" (Stuller, 1984, p. 106). Chrysler's recovery was "largely Iacocca's doing, a triumph of brains, bluster, and bravado" (Taylor, Moritz, Witteman & Seaman, 1983, p. 50). *Business Week* maintained that Iacocca's "value to

305   Chrysler may be impossible to quantify," and quoted an automobile "industry analyst" as saying, "If [Iacocca] wasn't there, Chrysler wouldn't be there" ("Chrysler's Iacocca," 1984, p. 90).

Media accounts of the Chrysler comeback featured *Iacocca* as the savior of the company, and thereby, the jobs of thousands of powerless
310   in society. He was the man who had "saved Chrysler Corp. from bankruptcy" (Hampton, 1984, p. 12), and "600,000 American jobs" (Alpern, 1984, p. 50). While "Congress had fussed [and] the White House had postured," *Iacocca* had acted. He had whipped "a sprawling company into shape, and saved American autoworkers' jobs by the
315   tens of thousands" (Andersen & Witteman, 1985, p. 32). He was the agent that had made things work.

Burke wrote that the contemporary hero is "first of all a [person] who does heroic things;" and thus, heroism resides in the person's acts (1969, p. 42). The patterns identified herein suggest how Americans
320   could identify with the portrayed task as a "heroic" undertaking— requiring a Herculean effort and undertaken to help the weak and powerless of society. These patterns generated rhetorical force as they constructed for the engaged audience a drama of significant symbolic importance. Clearly, much more had been at stake here than the
325   survival of an American corporation. This was a dramatic enactment of basic American values, and its successful completion was presented as the personal accomplishment of Lee Iacocca. Media coverage during the "recovery phase" of the Chrysler drama evidenced a fourth underlying pattern that is important when considering Iacocca's
330   "hero" status; the persona of Lee Iacocca took on its own symbolic importance as it was portrayed as a type of cultural condensation symbol.

Iacocca as a Condensation Symbol

A symbol functions as an interpretation of a situation (Burke, 1968,
335   p. 154). A condensation symbol is an emotive interpretation within a situation (Eldeman, 1964, p. 6), stirring "vivid impressions involving the listener's most basic values" (Graber, 1976, p. 289). During the "recovery" phase of the Chrysler drama the media evidenced a pattern which offered the persona of Iacocca as the representation of
340   American cultural values.

Although it is not possible to isolate the exact point at which this media pattern emerged, it is clear that by 1984 the persona of Lee Iacocca had attained a symbolic importance that transcended his achievements as the "savior" of Chrysler. He became a heroic "myth-
345   ical figure, a character of a [public] fairytale people believe in" (Broms & Gahmberg, 1982, p. 24). He was, in essence, presented as a cor-

poreal condensation symbol, an emotive symbolic interpretation of the American value system during the economic recovery of 1982–85. As a condensation symbol Iacocca's own rhetoric—detailed in inter-
350 views, his autobiography, and his speeches—took on importance as his words reflected back upon shared cultural values.

The media's Iacocca was a "symbol of an America that's finally regained its confidence" (Stuller, 1984, p. 46), and America's "fore-most symbol for 'hanging tough,' for 'toughing it out' under high-
355 pressure nerve-wearing situations" (Furlong, 1982, p. 72). Stuller (1984) observed that at the beginning of this decade America was "simply, a nation in despair. But then there was this pugnacious Iacocca fellow, briskly striding through Chrysler commercials as if . . . he were on his way to the radiator department to show the
360 workers how to bolt 'em in so they wouldn't rattle" (p. 46). President Reagan, who had opposed the original Chrysler bailout package touted Iacocca as "example Number One of a recovering economy" (Nicholson & Jones, 1983, p. 64).

Even during the darkest days of the Chrysler drama, Iacocca
365 had stood "absolutely resolute and tough." He had "talked directly to the American people," "tapped into America's frustrations," and told Americans, "It doesn't have to be this way. You can create your own destiny" (Anderson & Witteman, 1985, p. 32).

Iacocca's life and career offered Americans "some significant
370 lessons on how to act and react in a world that offers unending pres-sure" (Furlong, 1982, p. 72). These lessons included the "necessity of weighing right from wrong on a regular basis" (Iacocca & Novak, 1984, p. 8), the importance of maintaining "the highest possible value system" (Furlong, 1982, p. 74), and warnings that "only hard work
375 succeeds" (Alpern, 1984, p. 51). Iacocca argued for the importance of teamwork and emphasized that the key for a successful America was for everyone to pull together (Iacocca & Novak, 1984, pp. 54–59).

Iacocca's success demonstrated "what can be achieved with talent and tenacity." He proudly told of letters from troubled Americans
380 who had identified with his accomplishments at Chrysler and resolved to "stick it out, work a little harder and claw [their] way back up" ("We're a Colony Again," 1984, p. 64). Sean Fitspatrick, an advertising executive who works for Chevrolet, a Chrysler competitor, felt that Iacocca captured the essence of Faulkner's Nobel Prize address: "he
385 showed us that man—and Chrysler—will not merely endure, he will prevail" (Glassman, 1984, p. 21).

The Iacocca persona was a "family man"; an "immigrant's son," with "directness, humor and salty language that appeal[ed] to the public" ("Chrysler's Iacocca," 1984, p. 91). He had a knack for "plain
390 talk that [struck] the most responsive note" among Americans

(Hampton, 1984, p. 12). He "proudly admit[ted]" to being "an old fashioned man at heart," an "unabashed patriot" who got "choked up" when touring the Ellis Island entry hall (Ser Vaas, 1984; Andersen & Witteman, 1985), and he worked on the restoration of
395   the Statue of Liberty as a "labor of love for my parents and freedom and liberty" (Ser Vaas, 1984, p. 86). His rhetoric reminded us "more than ever just what [the Statue of Liberty and Ellis Island] stand for." And he challenged us not "to take that trust too lightly" (Iacocca, 1985, p. 346).
400   In sum, during the recovery phase of the Chrysler drama Iacocca was presented as a condensation symbol around which Americans were elevated through the therapeutic process of identification with Iacocca, as his deeds were presented—in true heroic form— as the corporal embodiment of our potential as a people (Fisher,
405   1982). He was presented as a reflection of our cultural values and the promise of our greatness. To paraphrase Wecter (1966), Iacocca's story—as presented in the media—was the "mirror of the folk soul" (p. 488).

CONCLUSION

410   Societies obviously produced cultural heroes before the media became as pervasive and influential as they are today. However, popular proclamation of heroism has always rested upon publicity in some form or another. In earlier societies bards or storytellers offered narratives proclaiming the exploits of the hero. In contemporary society
415   the media helped organize the chaos of our experiences by functioning as storytellers—"our composite Homer." In so doing, the media provide engaged publics with the possibilities and meanings that comprise the modern cultural hero myth (Barber, 1980).
           I have suggested that insight into the mythopoetic role of the
420   contemporary media can be provided by focusing upon the patterns that present action and actors as heroic. Four such patterns, identified in the 1978–1985 coverage of the "Chrysler drama," suggest how the media engendered a sense of collective cultural identification with Lee Iacocca and prompted his proclamation as the first contemporary
425   cultural hero drawn from the ranks of businessmen. Although it is not realistic to offer the precise formulation of these patterns in a "recipe" fashion ("a hero equals one part Herculean endeavor mixed with two cups of personal achievement"), the following conclusions are suggested from this study.
430   First, it appears that the description of the action involved is a primary element of the media's mythopoetic role. Previous research

about the hero myth suggests that a hero is one who is perceived as having accomplished something against long odds (Boorstin, 1962; Klapp, 1954; Wecter, 1966). In a very real sense these "odds" are set by the storyteller—the media in contemporary society. In portraying a task as "almost impossible" the media suggest that only a figure of heroic stature could possibly accomplish it.

Second, mass media descriptions of the hero must be consonant with basic cultural values. In America, that means the mediated persona of the hero must be presented as "essentially a champion of the little man, a righter of wrongs, a protagonist of democracy" (Klapp, 1954, p. 30). Interestingly, this also suggests that the hero's own rhetoric should discount his/her accomplishments and highlight the contributions made by the "unheralded little people" in the drama.

Finally, this study also suggests that if all of these patterns adhere in the media the rhetorical force generated may take on a momentum which transcends concerns for the accuracy of mediated perceptions. For example, a great many factors contributed to the recovery of the Chrysler Corporation, not the least of which were the 1981 "loosening" of credit by the Federal Reserve Board and the Japanese voluntary limit upon the number of automobiles shipped to this country (Reich, 1985).

Although concern for the heroic is an inherent part of human history, America has been described as obsessed with heroes (Blyth and Sweet, 1983). As Boorstin (1962) observed, even in our "twentieth-century of doubt . . . [Americans] have desperately held on to our belief in human greatness" and with it our "need" to believe in, and identify with, the heroic (p. 48). In short, American hero worship has taken on dimensions of a secular religion (Wecter, 1966). This essay has attempted to provide some insight into that religion by detailing the patterns used to depict the "heroic" within a mass mediated framework.

NOTES

1. Previous work on "heroes" has illustrated the difference between the "hero" and the "celebrity." The "celebrity," in essence, is merely a media phenomenon exhibiting popularity. That is, the "celebrity" is a "tautology" in that s/he is "well known for his well knownness." Thus, while all heroes are celebrities, not all celebrities are heroes (Boorstin, 1962; Rollin, 1983). However, previous work has not offered a perspective concerning *why* some celebrities attain hero status, while others do not.

2. Senator Eugene McCarthy, who voted against the Chrysler aid package, stated that congressional debate concerning the bailout "never got much beyond consideration of the narrow and immediate issue of loss of jobs,

and of effects on communities, especially Detroit, which have Chrysler installations" (McCarthy, 1980, p. 14).

REFERENCES

Alpern, D. M. (1984, October 8). Behind the wheels. *Newsweek*, pp. 50–51.

Andersen, K., & Witteman, P. A. (1985, April 1). A spunky tycoon turned superstar. *Time*, pp. 30–35, 38–39.

Barber, J. D. (1980). *The pulse of politics: Electing presidents in the media age*. New York: W. W. Norton.

Bass, J. D., & Cherwitz, R. (1978). Imperial mission and manifest destiny: A case study of political myth in rhetorical discourse. *Southern Speech Communication Journal, 43*, 213–232.

Blanchard, J. J. (1979, December 18). Saving Chrysler: The why. *Washington Post*, p. A19.

Blyth, H. & Sweet, C. (1983). Superhero: The six step progression. In R. B. Browne & M. W. Fishwick (Eds.), *The hero in transition*. Bowling Green, OH: Bowling Green University Press.

Bohr, P. (1979, October 22). Chrysler's pie-in-the-sky plan for survival. *Fortune*, pp. 46–48, 50, 52.

Boorstin, D. J. (1962). *The image: A guide to psuedo-events in America*. New York: Harper Colophon.

Broms, H. & Gahmberg, H. (1982). *Mythology in management culture*. Helsinki: School of Economics and Business Administration.

Burke, K. (1968). *Counter-statement*. Berkeley: University of California Press (Originally published, 1931).

Burke, K. (1969). *A grammar of motives*. Berkeley: University of California Press. (Originally published, 1945).

Cameron, J. (1979, August 27). Chrysler's quest for federal welfare. *Fortune*, pp. 30–31.

Chrysler Corporation (1979a, August 20). Would America be better off without Chrysler? *New York Times*, p. A22.

Chrysler Corporation. (1979b, September 10). Does Chrysler want to stay in business just to build gas guzzlers? *New York Times*, p. D3.

Chrysler gets some firepower. (1978, November 13). *Time*, p. 94.

Chrysler's Cry. (1979, August 13). *Time*, p. 33.

Chrysler's Iacocca: The most bang for the corporation buck. (1984, May 7). *Business Week*, pp. 90–91.

A collapse of Chrysler Corp. seen costing U. S. 200,000 jobs. (1979, August 12). *Washington Post*, p. A8.

Cowan, E. (1979, August 1). Administration worried about Chrysler finances. *New York Times*, p. D4.

Could bankruptcy save Chrysler. (1979, December 24). *Business Week*, pp. 70–72.

Edelman, M. (1964). *The symbolic uses of politics*. Urbana, Il.: University of Illinois Press.

Fisher, W. R. (1982). Romantic democracy, Ronald Reagan, and presidential heroes. *Western Journal of Speech Communication, 46*, 299–310.

Ford's Mr. Mustang takes the wheel at Chrysler and tries to steer it away from bankruptcy. (1979, December 24). *People*, pp. 42–43.

Foss, S. L. (1984). Retooling an image: Chrysler Corporation's rhetoric of redemption. *Western Journal of Speech Communication 48*, 75–91.

Fotheringham, A. (1985, April 15). Experience not required. *Macleans*, p. 60.

Furlong, W. B. (1982, March). Chrysler's Lee Iacocca. *Saturday Evening Post*, pp. 72–75, 88, 91, 116.

Glassman, J. K. (1984, July 16 & 23). The Iacocca mystique. *New Republic*, pp. 20–23.

Graber, D. A. (1976). *Verbal behavior and politics*. Urbana, Il.: University of Illinois Press.

Hampton, W. J. (1984, November 5). Blunt talk from the hero of Detroit. *Business Week*, pp. 12, 16.

Hankins, S. R. (1983). Archetypal alloy: Reagan's rhetorical image. *Central States Speech Journal, 34*, 33–43.

Iacocca, L. A. (1985, March 15). We're taxing our own kids: Are we becoming a colony again. *Vital Speeches of the Day*, p. 342–346.

Iacocca, L. A. & Novak, W. (1984). *Iacocca: An autobiography*. New York: Bantam Books.

It won't be easy. (1978, November 27). *Forbes*, p. 130.

Klapp, O. E. (1954). The clever hero. *Journal of American Folklore 67*, 21–34.

Klapp, O. E. (1972). *Heroes, villains and fools: Reflections of the American character*. San Diego: Aeges Publishing.

Kraft, J. (1979, August 9). The Chrysler warning. *Washington Post*, p. A19.

Lee Iacocca's hard sell for help. (1979, October 8). *Time*, p. 74.

Lee Iacocca speaks up: Why bailout Chrysler. (1979, December 17). *U. S. News & World Report*, pp. 63–64.

Luther, J. (1979, September 12). Big job loss seen if Chrysler closes. *Washington Post*, p. C5.

McCarthy, E. (1980, January 5 & 12). Chrysler and country. *New Republic*, pp. 13–14.

McDowell, E. (1979, August 17). Behind Chrysler's long decline: Its management and competition. *New York Times*, pp. A1, A12.

Miller, J. (1979, December 19). Chrysler aid plan approved in House by vote of 271–136. *New York Times*, pp. A1, D5.

Miller, J. (1980, January 6). Detroit's battle for survival. *New York Times Magazine,* pp. 22–24, 26, 38, 40, 42.

Morgan, D. (1979, November 7). Free enterprise is fine. Chrysler supporters agree, but . . . *Washington Post,* p. A2.

New report describes some possible effects of a Chrysler collapse. (1979, August 12) *New York Times,* p. 33.

Nicholson, T. & Jones, J. (1979, October 1). Chrysler changes its drivers. *Newsweek,* p. 55.

Nicholson, T. & Jones, J. (1983, February 14). Iacocca shifts into high. *Newsweek,* pp. 64.

Nicholson, T., Jones, J., & Friendly, D. T. (1978, November 13). Iacocca to the rescue. *Newsweek,* p. 99, 101.

Nicholson, T., Marbach, W. D., Thomas, R., & Dentzer, S. (1980, December 29). Chrysler's last battle plan. *Newsweek,* pp. 54–55.

Norman, J. R. (1980, March 3). Chrysler's credibility is on the line. *Business Week,* p. 23.

Reich, R. B. (1985, May 13). The executive's new clothes. *New Republic,* pp. 23–28.

Rollin, R. R. (1983). The Lone Ranger and Lenny Skutnik: The hero as popular culture. In Browne, R. B. & Fishwick, M. W. (Eds.), *The hero in transition* (pp. 14–45). Bowling Green, OH.: Bowling Green University Press.

Ross, I. (1981, February 9). Chrysler on the brink. *Fortune,* pp. 38–42.

Rushing, J. H. (1983). The rhetoric of the American western myth. *Communication Monographs 520,* 14–32.

Samuelson, R. J. (1979, November 6). Chrysler aid quest: Theater of absurd? *Washington Post,* pp. D6, D8.

Seeger, M. W. (1986). C. E. O. performances: Lee Iacocca and the case of Chrysler. *Southern Speech Communication Journal 52,* 52–68.

Ser Vaas, C. (1984, October). The miracle of Detroit. *Saturday Evening Post,* pp. 42–45, 84–86.

Stuart, R. (1979a, August 11). Six governors join in plea to Carter for Chrysler help. *New York Times,* pp. A1, A27.

Stuart, R. (1979b, August 14). Loan-guarantee plan apparently upset Chrysler's campaign for tax aid. *New York Times,* p. D3.

Stuller, J. (1984, October). Lee Iacocca and an America that's back on its feet. *Saturday Evening Post,* pp. 46–47, 104, 106, 110.

Taylor, A., Bolte, G., & Seaman, B. (1980, December 29). Chrysler goes back to the well. *Time,* p. 53.

Taylor, A. L., Moritz, M., Witteman, P. A., & Seaman, B. Iacocca's tightrope act. (1983, March 21). *Time,* pp. 50–54, 57–58, 60–61.

Wecter, D. (1966). *The hero in America: A chronicle of hero-worship*. Ann Arbor: University of Michigan Press.

Weisman, S. (1979, November 1). Financial and political urging called impetus to Chrysler aid. *New York Times*, p. D4.

We're a colony again: This time of Japan. (1984, April 16). *U. S. News & World Report*, pp. 63–64.

COMMENTS ON THE STUDY

Introduction, Review of the Literature, and Research Question

Dionisopoulos begins by establishing Iacocca's heroic status (1–18) and the significance of understanding how he attained it (19–74). As evidence he cites pronouncements by the media of Iacocca as a national folk hero, as well as the enthusiastic public response to Iacocca (such as attempts to recruit him to run for President of the United States and his autobiography becoming the best selling nonfiction hardcover book in history). Dionisopoulos claims that this elevation of Iacocca into a cultural hero was significant for three reasons: (a) the media could have focused on many other significant persons from 1978 to 1985; (b) no other representative of "big business" had ever achieved equivalent popular appeal; and (c) Iacocca became a hero in spite of the public's generally negative response to the federal loan guarantees to Chrysler which he solicited (19–41). Dionisopoulos thus established the uniqueness and significance of this particular case.

Dionisopoulos also justifies this study by pointing out that little communication research examines the development of folk heroes or explains the rhetorical factors that produce cultural heroes in general, or the Iacocca phenomenon in particular (42–67). He suggests that the rhetorical messages in the print media's coverage of Iacocca and the Chrysler bailout drama strongly influenced Iacocca's unprecedented popularity and the public's view of him as a mythic hero (68–74). Dionisopoulos thus justifies studying the rhetorical features of this case study as a step toward developing a broader theory about the ways heroes are generally created.

Method

To examine the effects of the print media on this social phenomenon, Dionisopoulos analyzed stories about Chrysler, Lee Iacocca, and the Chrysler bailout program in selected newspapers, news periodicals, business periodicals, and popular magazines between the years 1977 and 1985 (75–80). He provides readers with little information, however, about the sampling strategy used for selecting the publications and the specific stories; we merely know that they do represent major print media (such as the *New York Times, Newsweek,* and *People*). Evidence about circulation rates and importance of these print media would be useful for evaluating the impact and representativeness of the sample selected. Dionisopoulos probably conducted a census by examining the total universe of stories in these publications over the years studied, but we do not know for certain. Dionisopoulos also does not explain the rationale for studying only stories published between 1977 and 1985. We are left to assume a historical rationale for the salience of this particular period of time. It also would be helpful to know which sections of the newspapers the stories came from to distinguish "news stories" from "editorials," for example.

The lack of detail about the sampling procedures makes it difficult to assess how much confidence to place in the representativeness of the texts selected and the subsequent conclusions. While choosing a sample of texts is a decision reached by an individual researcher, regardless of the specific type of textual analysis employed, explaining and justifying that sampling procedure is just as important in rhetorical criticism as it is in any other form of communication research.

Results and Discussion

Dionisopoulos coded the stories into three content themes: Chrysler; the bailout; and Iacocca (88–90). He then sorted these themes into four major topical patterns of media coverage: (1) the act of saving Chrysler; (2) saving Chrysler as a heroic task; (3) Iacocca's role in saving Chrysler; and (4) Iacocca as a *condensation symbol,* an exemplar of basic American values that transformed him into a cultural hero (90–96). Dionisopoulos coded these stories himself, as opposed to employing assistants, or **coders,** and he does not describe the specific criteria used to identify these content themes and topical patterns. (Rhetorical criticism differs from content analysis and interaction analysis, which assess mathematically the level of agreement of coders' categorizing to determine the reliability of the coding scheme.) Since the reliability of the codings was not assessed in this particular case study, the reader must decide how well Dionisopoulos operationalized and coded these content themes and patterns. Obviously, more information about the codings would increase our confidence in the validity of the data presented.

Dionisopoulos then examines each of these content categories in some depth and provides some data to support these categories (102–408). The evidence presented in this study, and most rhetorical criticism, is *qualitative* as opposed to *quantitative.* That is, Dionisopoulos presents sample messages from print media stories as evidence to support his positions on the role of rhetoric in establishing Lee Iacocca as a cultural hero. He does not enumerate messages or message characteristics, and no statistical tables report the relative number of stories or content themes in the print media. (Contrast this approach with the media content analytic study discussed in the next chapter.) This qualitative analysis provides symbolic evidence to support his conclusions about the texts studied. Note, for example, how artfully he weaves examples of print media headlines and story quotes into his own text (for example, *Fortune*'s title, "Chrysler's Pie-in-the-Sky Plan for Survival") to illustrate how the media portrayed Chrysler's financial problems (124–129). Qualitative data describe communication events in rich detail to enable readers to understand and put themselves into the context of the rhetorical acts being examined.

Dionisopoulos draws upon Kenneth Burke's dramatistic theory and Edelman's (1964) concept of the condensation symbol to explain Iacocca's heroic public image (333–408). He does not explain these perspectives in much depth, but they do serve to illuminate the persuasive role of the media in this particular case study. He claims that the thematic patterns in the material he read describe an engaging symbolic drama of mythic proportions. By enacting the basic American values of hard work ("Herculean effort"), confidence, and concern for the powerless in society, Iacocca appeared to do much more than save Chrysler; he validated the American dream and public faith in American values.

Dionisopoulos concludes this essay with the larger claim that all heroes are produced through publicity and that the media now control this process (410–418). He then offers some tentative generalizations about the role of the media in contemporary society (419–452). He suggests that the media perform a mythopoetic function by helping the public organize social events into dramatic narratives. To do so, he claims that the media portray a hero accomplishing something against long odds, that compelling narratives must accord with basic cultural values, and that, once cultural hero status is established, the accuracy of mediated perceptions hardly matters. Thus, Dionisopoulos' study of the Iacocca phenomenon contributes to rhetorical theory about the role of the media in contemporary society. And, as a tantalizing parting thought, Dionisopoulos claims that the American public has a need to believe in and identify with heroes—a need that takes on the dimensions of a secular religion (458–459). Do you agree?

CONCLUSION

Dionisopoulos' analysis of this particular case study shows the importance of rhetorical criticism for communication researchers, and illustrates one way in which this methodology is conducted. When employed effectively, rhetorical criticism offers a rich methodology for describing, analyzing, interpreting, and evaluating persuasive, symbolic behavior.

QUESTIONS AND ACTIVITIES TO CONSIDER

1. What is the primary purpose of this study? Was rhetorical criticism an apt means for accomplishing this purpose, or would another approach have been more effective?

2. Identify one apparent strength and one weakness of using rhetorical criticism to study persuasive public communication in general, and print media stories about Lee Iacocca in particular.

3. How could Dionisopoulos have overcome the concerns mentioned in this critique about the sampling strategies used in this study?

4. How compelling to you was the specific evidence Dionisopoulos provides to explain the persuasive influence of the print media in establishing Iacocca's public image? Can you think of additional evidence that Dionisopoulos could have provided to make a more compelling case?

5. Think of additional illustrations of Dionisopoulos' view of the mythopoetic functions of the media. What other people or events have been raised to mythic status by the media? Which media do you think are most effective at creating public myths?

6. How do historical and dramatistic criticism used by Dionisopoulos differ from other approaches to rhetorical criticism, such as Neo-Aristotelian or generic criticism? Do some reading about an alternative method and apply it to the media's coverage of Iacocca. Did you reach the same conclusions?

7. How would some of the previous methodologies discussed in this text be applied to studying the effects of the media on creating public heroes? How might Dionisopoulos' findings be phrased as one or more hypotheses that could be tested in an experimental research study? How would survey researchers design a questionnaire to study these effects?

FURTHER READINGS ON RHETORICAL CRITICISM

Andrews, J. R. (1990). *The practice of rhetorical criticism* (2nd ed.). New York: Macmillan.

Black, E. (1978). *Rhetorical criticism: A study in method*. Madison, WI: University of Wisconsin Press.

Brock, B. L., Scott, R. L., & Chesebro, J. W. (Eds.). (1989). *Methods of rhetorical criticism: A twentieth-century perspective* (3rd ed.). Detroit: Wayne State University Press.

Campbell, K. K., & Jamison, K. H. (Eds.). (1978). *Form and genre*. Falls Church, VA: Speech Communication Association.

Foss, S. K. (1989). *Rhetorical criticism: Exploration & practice*. Prospect Heights, IL: Waveland.

EXAMPLES OF RHETORICAL CRITICISM

Bormann, E. G. (1982). A fantasy theme analysis of the television coverage of the hostage release and the Reagan inaugural. *Quarterly Journal of Speech, 68,* 133–145.

    Bormann uses fantasy theme analysis to explain the simultaneous television coverage of the hostage release by Iran and President Reagan's inaugural address of January 20, 1981. Bormann shows how Reagan used a powerful fantasy theme of "restoration," a call for a return to basic values and standards established by the founders of America, to meet the needs of a conservative political movement in the 1980s, and how this theme was reinforced by television's coverage of the hostage release.

Carpenter, R. H. (1990). America's tragic metaphor: Our twentieth-century combatants as frontiersman. *Quarterly Journal of Speech, 76,* 1–22.

    Carpenter explores how Americans and the mass media tend to think about war metaphorically as an extension of the Western frontier experience that shaped the United States. Using statements made by politicians and army personnel, as well as books, films, and television shows, Carpenter shows how the frontier metaphor explains discourse about World War II, the Cold War, and the Vietnam War. Carpenter concludes by engaging in social criticism, arguing that using the frontier metaphor in the context of war is tragic and that there are ethically more responsible uses for frontier metaphors.

Hill, F. I. (1972). Conventional wisdom-traditional form: The President's message of November 3, 1969. *Quarterly Journal of Speech, 58,* 373–386.

    Hill uses Neo-Aristotelian criticism to evaluate President Richard Nixon's address to the nation on November 3, 1969 asking for support of his position on the Vietnam War. This analysis shows how Nixon and his advisors made choices among the available means of persuasion for this particular situation, how their arguments were structured, and how their rhetorical choices helped to reinforce the audience's perception of Nixon's ethos (credibility).

Johannesen, R. L. (1986). Ronald Reagan's economic jeremiad. *Central States Speech Journal, 37,* 79–89.

    Johannesen uses generic criticism to show how President Reagan's speech on February 5, 1981 about the state of the American economy functioned as a jeremiad, a type of speech that castigates a specific group. Johannesen shows how Reagan skillfully utilized the elements of this genre of speech to castigate the general public for being easily swayed by bad leadership and for living in easy lifestyles, and to urge a return to the Puritan values of hard work and competition.

Rushing, J. H. (1989). Evolution of "the new frontier" in *Alien* and *Aliens:* Patriarchal co-optation of the feminine archetype. *Quarterly Journal of Speech, 75,* 1–24.

    Rushing argues that, although the metaphor of the Western frontier inspired much of American literature, it continually portrays women as being dominated by men. This analysis of the frontier metaphor in the films *Alien* and *Aliens* shows how these films portray a lost and vengeful female who is killed by a patriarchalized heroine. Rushing argues that the domination of males in heroic myths is dangerous because it neglects myths informed by feminine consciousness. As Rushing concludes, "The new myth for humankind needs to be *quest,* not a conquest; its purpose, to *search* rather than to search and destroy" (p. 21).

Chapter 7

Content Analysis

INTRODUCTION TO THE METHOD

Consider these questions: How much violence is there in children's television cartoon shows? Do rock music videos treat women as sex objects? Do the stories in recent children's books promote equality between boys and girls? Do newspapers today sensationalize the news? Does most advertising rely on emotional or informational appeals to sell products?

We probably all have opinions on these questions based on our own informal observations of the messages these media contain. Our opinions differ based on what we happen to see or watch. Researchers, in contrast, seek answers to these questions by engaging in systematic inquiry. They employ the method of *content analysis* to identify, enumerate, and analyze occurrences of specific messages and message characteristics embedded in communication *texts*. Notice how each of the questions posed above can be answered by selecting relevant texts, defining the central terms, and then counting their occurrences.

Content analysis was developed and is used primarily to study the messages embedded in mass-mediated and public texts, such as public speeches. Dovring (1954–1955) reports that content analysis was used as early as the eighteenth century by Swedish scholars when they counted the number of religious symbols contained in a collection of hymns to see whether they were preaching against the church. Modern content analysis can be traced back to the study of American newspaper content in the early part of the twentieth century. During the 1930s, content analysis was applied to radio and public speeches. Content analysis proved to be an invaluable tool during World War II as researchers were able to detect changes in Nazi troop concentrations by content-analyzing and comparing songs played on German radio stations with songs played on other radio stations in occupied Europe (Wimmer & Dominick, 1991). Today, content analysis is a popular methodology for studying the nature of mass-mediated and public messages. Moffett and Dominick (1987), for example, reported that 21% of the studies published in the *Journal of Broadcasting and Electronic Media* from 1977 to 1985 used content analysis.

Goals of Content Analysis

A primary goal of content analysis is to *describe* characteristics of the content of the messages in mass-mediated and public texts. Berelson (1952), for example, defined content analysis as "a research technique for the objective, systematic, and quantitative description of the manifest content of communication" (p. 18). The term "manifest" in this definition refers to "the apparent content, which means that content must be coded as it appears rather than as the content analyst feels it is intended" (Stempel, 1989, p. 126). Berelson encouraged researchers to study both the *substance* of the manifest content (what is said) and its *form* (how it is said). Bogart (1985), for example, studied substance by conducting a longitudinal content analysis of the topics covered in U.S. newspaper articles in 1963, 1974, 1979, and 1983 to show changes over time. Flesch (1949), on the other hand, studied form by developing a readability formula to assess whether the writing style of articles submitted by journalists could be understood by a person with an eighth-grade education.

Bowers (1970) argues, however, that mere counting isn't enough:

This [Berelson's] definition excludes the inferential leaps analysts make from their descriptions of messages to the antecedents and consequences of those messages. Descriptions of messages are useful to students of communication only insofar as they lead to helpful inferences about the process of communication, and the process goes beyond the messages. (p. 291)

Hence, many scholars believe that content analysis needn't be restricted to studying the manifest content of messages. Krippendorf (1980), for example, defines content analysis as a "research technique for making replicable and valid inferences from data to their context" (p. 21). According to this view, content analysts can draw valid *inferences* about the characteristics of producers and receivers of messages and of the context in which a message is produced. For example, if a content analysis reveals that a communicator uses tentative phrases throughout a public speech (for instance, beginning statements with qualifications such as "could" or "might"), a researcher might infer that the communicator lacks confidence or self-esteem. Similarly, identifying specific, recurring metaphors used by successful politicians in campaign speeches might tell us something about their audience's receptivity to particular symbols.

Conducting Content Analysis

Once researchers decide that content analysis is the most useful methodology for answering the research questions posed, they, like all textual analysts, must select appropriate texts to analyze. In some cases, it may be possible for researchers to conduct a *census* of all relevant texts. For example, it might be possible to study all the scripts of a weekly television show that ran for thirteen episodes. In other cases, it is not possible to conduct a census, so researchers must select a *sample* of texts from the *universe* of relevant texts. As with all sampling procedures, researchers must strive to select a *representative* sample. As we know from survey research, the most representative sample is one chosen *randomly.* Researchers who wish to choose a random sample of texts must first obtain a complete list of all the texts in that universe and then use a procedure that guarantees each text an equal chance of being selected. When random sampling procedures are not possible, researchers will use a nonrandom sample.

Once a set of texts has been selected, researchers identify the *units of analysis,* or the message elements, they will study. The process of identifying appropriate units of analysis is called **unitizing.** Krippendorf (1980) identifies five units of analysis often studied in content analysis: (1) *physical units* (kinds of texts, such as books, television shows, or speeches); (2) *syntactical units* (individual symbols, such as words, metaphors, or diagrams); (3) *referential units* (what the text is about, such as positive or negative accounts of a certain individual); (4) *propositional units* (specific positions taken, such as the kinds of appeals used to support a specific candidate or issue); and (5) *thematic units* (specific topics, like the use of racist or sexist themes).

Content analysis sometimes involves simply counting the relevant units in the selected texts, such as the number of times "democracy" is mentioned in a political speech. Usually, however, researchers construct relevant **content categories** into which the units will be placed (such as references to forms of government like democracy or monarchy). Any content category system must meet three criteria: the categories must be mutually exclusive, equivalent, and exhaustive. For example, television shows might be classified into the following five categories: news, comedy, action, sports, and all other shows. This five-part classification of television shows is *mutually exclusive* if every program fits into only one of the five categories. If a particular show fits into more than one category, the researcher will have to select the most appropriate category for it or refine the category scheme. The five categories are *equivalent* if each describes television programs of the same type and if general and specific categories are not mixed. For example, sports shows could be categorized into football, baseball, basketball, and so on. Finally, this classification scheme is *exhaustive* if every television show fits into one of the categories. The inclusion of the "all other shows" category in the first example assures that all television program types are covered. Wimmer and Dominick (1990) contend, however, that if 10% or more of the units fall into the "other" category, the content category scheme probably needs to be revised.

The content categories chosen obviously are important when evaluating content analytic research. Berelson (1952) points out that, "Content analysis stands or falls by its categories. Particular studies have been productive to the extent that the categories were clearly formulated and well-adapted to the problem and content" (p. 147). Hence, researchers must pay careful attention to constructing *valid* content categories. There are, however, different ways to validate a content category scheme, or any measurement technique or procedure. First, **face validity,** the weakest form of validity, is established when a researcher simply claims (perhaps based on previous research or widely shared public beliefs) that the content categories reflect the attributes or content of the concept being investigated; in other words, the sorting procedure "appears" right to one's "common sense." Second, **semantic validity** "exists when persons familiar with the language and texts examine lists of words (or other units) placed in the same category and agree that these words have similar meanings or connotations" (Weber, 1990, p. 21); that is, when a panel of informed judges agree on a sorting procedure. Third, **criterion-related validity** is established when a content category scheme is shown to relate to a valid outcome. The content category scheme used to analyze the German radio broadcasts during World War II, for example, was valid to the extent that it allowed researchers to predict troop movements. Finally, **construct validity** is established when the content categories are derived from theoretical propositions and predictions. For example, Chesebro (1991) used Northrup Frye's critical framework and Kenneth Burke's dramatistic theory to analyze central characters on 903 prime-time network television shows from the 1974–1975 season through the 1990–1991 season. These theories led Chesebro to classify central characters as either: (1) ironic (both intellectually inferior and less able to control circumstances than is the audience); (2) mimetic (equally intelligent and equally able to control circumstances as those surrounding and viewing the central character); (3) leader-centered (superior in intelligence to others but only in degree by virtue of special training, personality conditioning, and so on); (4) romantic (superior in kind to members of the audience in degree, both in terms of intelligence and the ability to control circumstances); or (5) mythical (superior in kind to others both in terms of intelligence and in terms of his or her ability to control circumstances).

Once the units and categories have been determined and defined operationally, the units can be placed, or **coded,** into the categories. Researchers themselves seldom code the units into categories. Instead, they use two or more trained assistants who have no stake in the research (and are usually unaware of the research questions or hypotheses), called *coders,* to work independently, identifying the relevant units and classifying each into its appropriate content category. (In some cases, the text can be entered into a computer and a program can be used to identify and code the units). Researchers then assess the *reliability* of the codings, or the degree of consistency between coders in identifying the units and classifying them into the categories. The correlation between the coders' sorting decisions measures the degree of agreement among them. In other words, the higher their agreement in coding the units, the higher the level of **intercoder** (or **interobserver**) **reliability**, as calculated by a statistical formula that produces a *correlation coefficient.* (Some formulas even account for chance agreement.) This correlation coefficient ranges from .00 (no agreement) to 1.00 (perfect agreement). While the higher the correlation the better, a correlation coefficient of at least .70 is required before concluding that a coding procedure is reliable (Bowers & Courtright, 1984). Once reliability is established, the coders may be asked to discuss and reach agreement on the units they disagreed about, or the researcher may cast the deciding vote.

Finally, researchers use statistical procedures to analyze the data. *Descriptive statistics* can be used to summarize and construct simple generalizations about the data. Researchers may, for example, count the number of units or ascertain the percentages for each category and determine the **mode,** the most frequently occurring category. *Inferential statistics* might also be used to generalize from a random sample of texts to its parent universe, or to test for significant differences and relationships between categories. Researchers might, for example, test whether certain categories are used significantly more than others (such as politicians' positive versus negative public statements about the state of the economy), or whether there are significant differences between groups (such as Democrats and Republicans) in their use of the categories.

In conclusion, content analysis is an objective, systematic, and quantitative approach to analyzing texts. The key words in this sentence, as we have seen, are "objective," "systematic," and "quantitative." Stempel (1989) explains that, "Objective to begin with means the opposite of subjective or impressionistic. Objectivity is achieved by having the categories of analysis defined so precisely that different persons can apply them to the same content and get the same results" (p. 125). Systematic means, "first, that a set procedure is applied in the same way to all the content being analyzed. Second, it means that categories are set up so that all relevant content is analyzed. Finally, it means that the analyses are designed to secure data relevant to a research question or hypothesis" (Stempel, 1989, p. 125).

Third, content analysis yields quantitative data by measuring the presence and frequency of symbols in a text.

QUESTIONS FOR EXAMINING CONTENT ANALYSIS

In addition to the general criteria used to evaluate all communication research and the questions about the selection of texts, several criteria are of particular relevance to content analytic studies. Keep these criteria in mind when you read the following study, or any study that uses content analysis.

A. Units and Content Categories

1. What was the *unit(s) of analysis* in the study? Did the unit of analysis reflect the substance of content (what is said) or its form (how it is said)? Was it appropriate for answering the research questions in the study? Should any other(s) have been added?

2. Were the units classified into *mutually exclusive* content categories?

3. Were the units classified into *equivalent* content categories?

4. Were the units classified into *exhaustive* content categories?

5. Were the content categories *valid*? What justification or argument did the researcher give for the validity of the content category scheme? What type of validity is asserted: face, semantic, concurrent, or construct?

B. Coding Units into Content Categories

1. Was the *coding* done by a *person not invested* in the research? If it was done by more than one person, did the coders operate independently?

2. Was the coding done on the *entire text* or on a *portion* of the text? If done on a portion of the text, was this sample adequate for the research purposes? Was this sample drawn randomly?

3. Was *intercoder reliability* reported in this study? Was it sufficient, at least .70 or higher?

THE ILLUSTRATIVE STUDY

The content analytic study you will read examines how often messages concerning sex, contraception, and sexually transmitted diseases (STDs)—the content categories—are presented on afternoon television soap operas. The study replicates an earlier content analysis of the sexual behavior portrayed on television soap operas (Lowry, Love, & Kirby, 1981). Replications examine the same variables with different subjects, different periods of time, and/or incorporate additional variables, different operationalizations, and new measurements. Replications help to assess the *external validity* of previous research by showing whether the new results validate those found in earlier studies. If substantially similar results are obtained, the replication confirms our confidence in the earlier findings. Replications that contradict previous findings call into question the validity and reliability of the previous studies and lead us to rethink the original conclusions. Thus, replications are important for evaluating the validity of conclusions drawn from research. Indeed, Tukey (1969) argues that no single study can establish a generalization; only when findings from numerous studies are consistent can a generalization be advanced. After all, we would not want the medical profession to release a new drug based solely on the findings from one study.

The study you will read in this chapter is almost a *literal replication* of Lowry, Love, and Kirby's 1981 study because it duplicates the methodology, variables, operationalizations, and measurements used in the previous study as closely as possible. Lowry and Towles, however, extend the earlier study by examining several additional related topics, including how soap operas portray issues concerning contraception, sexually transmitted diseases, and pregnancy. They also include a new measure of the duration of sexual behaviors that was not part of the previous study. As you read this study, think about how the changes from the original study, such as examining the portrayals of STDs, provide the researcher with new and relevant information and expand our understanding of this research topic.

Soap Opera Portrayals of Sex, Contraception, and Sexually Transmitted Diseases

Dennis T. Lowry
David E. Towles

A replication of a 1979 study of sexual behaviors on the soaps finds a substantial increase in sex between unmarried persons and a norm of promiscuous sex, with few attendant consequences.

1   In 1986, a full-page newspaper advertisement for the Planned Parenthood Federation of America (11) carried the headline, "They did
it 9,000 times on television last year." The ad went on to state that
television "is a major influence on teenagers about sexuality and re-
5   sponsibility. It may now be a more important influence than school,
parents, or even peers. The problem is that television is putting out an
unbalanced view [about sex] which is causing *more* problems for teenagers and society." A second ad stated, "Today's TV message is this:
'GO FOR IT *NOW*. GO FOR IT AGAIN. DON'T WORRY ABOUT
10   ANYTHING.' But there is *plenty* to worry about" (12).
        Asking the question, "Is TV sex getting bolder?" in an article in
TV Guide, Hill states: "network censors . . . agree that television is
indeed on an upward curve of permissibility that has steadily increased the amount and types of sexual behavior that can be shown"
15   (6, p. 3).
        In a survey of 1,400 Cleveland parents, television was con-
sidered to be the highest ranked source (after the parents themselves)
of sexual learning for their children and, in particular, a source of
inaccurate information about sex (13). Other studies have indicated
20   that the majority of married men and women believe that there is too
much sex on TV (7) and that adults are uneasy about children being
exposed to televised sex (17).
        For more than a decade, beginning with Franzblau, Sprafkin,
and Rubinstein's (2) study of 1975–1976 prime-time programs, com-
25   munication scholars have been analyzing the sexual behaviors por-

Source: Lowry, D. T., & Towles, D. E. (1989). Soap opera portrayals of sex, contraception, and sexually transmitted diseases. *Journal of Communication, 39*(2), 76–83. Copyright © 1989, *Journal of Communication.* Used with permission.

Dennis T. Lowry is Professor in the Department of Communication at the University of Southwestern Louisiana. David E. Towles is Associate Professor in the School of Communications at Liberty University.

trayed in network TV programs (1, 5, 15). In a 1981 study, Sprafkin and Silverman found a sharp increase in the amount of sexual content in 1978–1979 prime-time network TV programs:

30
Specifically, contextually implied intercourse increased from no weekly occurrences in 1975 to 15 in 1977 and 24 in 1978; sexual innuendos increased in frequency from about one reference per hour in 1975 to 7 in 1977 and to almost 11 in 1978. Most dramatically, direct verbal references to intercourse increased from 2 occurrences per week in 1975 to 6 references in 1977 and 53 in 1978 (16, p. 37).

35
Focusing specifically on afternoon soap operas, Greenberg, Abelman, and Neuendorf concluded, "Soap operas have more sexual content than do prime-time programs, but the types of intimacies portrayed differ" (3, p. 88). Lowry, Love, and Kirby's study (10) of soap operas from the 1979 season found an average of more than six sexual behaviors (e.g., erotic touching, implied intercourse, prostitu-
40
tion) per hour. And, like several earlier studies, they found more than three instances of sexual behaviors involving unmarried partners for every instance involving married partners.

The subject of contraception was almost totally ignored by these studies. Only Sprafkin and Silverman had a category labeled "sex
45
education and romance, comprised of verbal references to issues such as contraception, pregnancy, and going steady" (16, pp. 35–36), but one cannot determine whether any of the average of 9.5 references per hour were to contraception per se. The subject of contraception has become much more important in the 1980s in light of the greatly
50
increased public health concern about sexually transmitted diseases (STDs) in general and AIDS in particular.

The study reported in this article had three major purposes. The first was to replicate the Lowry, Love, and Kirby (10) study of 1979 soap operas to determine whether the networks' alleged "up-
55
ward curve of permissibility" could be seen to have manifested itself in the amount of sexual content in 1987 soap operas.

The second purpose was to analyze how soap operas portray issues relating to the prevention of STDs and pregnancy. More than one million teenagers get pregnant in the United States every year,
60
costing taxpayers $16 billion (11), and every day 33,000 Americans become infected with a sexually transmitted disease (9, p. 57). Given the relatively high rates of sexual behaviors between unmarried partners found in past studies of TV and given the estimates of soap opera audiences that range as high as 60 million viewers (8, p. 4), it is
65
important to evaluate what sexual messages the network soap operas are communicating to their viewers, especially the public health implications of those messages.

The third purpose of this study was methodological. Greenberg,
Abelman, and Neuendorf (3) had suggested that future content anal-
70   yses of sex on TV should measure the *duration* of the sexual behaviors
as well as their *frequency*. Therefore we compare selected behavioral
frequency data with duration data to determine whether they present
similar information about the sexual content of soap operas. Is the
extra work of measuring both types of data justified?

75   **We sampled from all ABC, CBS, and NBC afternoon soap operas
broadcast from May 1 through August 11, 1987.** ABC carried five
different programs in its four-hour segment, CBS four programs
over three-and-a-half hours, and NBC three one-hour programs. A
simple random sample of five different afternoons was drawn for
80   each network, and all of the soap operas for each sampled afternoon
were videotaped, for a total sample of 52.5 hours of programming
(including the time taken up by commercials, which were not coded).

Our coding system followed that used by Lowry, Love, and Kirby
(10), which in turn had been based upon Silverman, Sprafkin, and
85   Rubinstein's (15) classification of sexual behavior in terms of physical
acts, implied acts, and verbal references. We also followed the example
of Fernandez-Collado et al. (1), who analyzed the sexual behaviors
between married and unmarried partners separately.

Erotic touching was defined as interpersonal touching that had
90   clear sexual overtones, demonstrated or intended to demonstrate sexual love, or aroused or expressed sexual desire. If there was doubt as
to whether the touching was sufficiently erotic to be counted, the
coders did not include it. Although not every behavior that has romantic overtones has sexual overtones, the category included "heavy"
95   kissing, sexually romantic embraces and hugs, sexual caressing or
touching of any part of someone else's body, and other similar touching behaviors. It excluded casual hand-holding, an arm casually
around someone's waist or shoulder, a casual "peck" type of kiss,
nonsexual greeting and farewell kisses, parent-child kissing and hug-
100 ging (unless incest was implied), and other nonsexual touching. Brief
"peck" types of kisses were counted, however, when they were part of
an implied intercourse scene. When the context was ambiguous,
coders used a "three-second rule"—i.e., kisses three seconds or longer
were coded as erotic but shorter kisses were not. An erotic kiss that
105 also involved an embrace counted as two instances of erotic touching
if both acts met the above requirements.

Heterosexual intercourse was classified as verbal, implied, or physically depicted. "Verbal" references to the act of heterosexual intercourse included "an affair," "cheat on me," "roll in the hay," "shack up
110 with her," "unfaithful," and "make love." "Implied" heterosexual in-

tercourse was coded when a scene depicted the start or end of lovemaking but did not show the physical act itself. The most common
example of implied intercourse in soap operas occurs when two lovers
are in bed kissing and embracing, and then the cameras cut to a
115   commercial break or a different scene. Another common variant occurs when the scene opens on the two lovers in bed "the morning
after" a night of implied lovemaking. A lovemaking scene of this type
was coded each time the scene appeared. For example, a single lovemaking scene interrupted by a commercial break was counted twice.
120   Following the example of Greenberg and D'Alessio (4, pp. 311–312),
visual behaviors of this type were coded at the level of the scene; for
verbal behaviors, sexual phrases within sentences were used as the
units of analysis. The "physical" category was reserved for actual
physical portrayals of intercourse.
125   The remaining categories were *prostitution, aggressive sexual con-*
tact (including rape), *homosexuality, incest, pedophilia, exhibitionism, fetish-*
ism, masturbation, transvestism and transsexualism, voyeurism, and *other*
unnatural sexual behaviors. All of the above categories were subdivided
into verbal, implied, and physical.

130   **A number of categories concerning pregnancy prevention and sex-**
ually transmitted diseases were coded for the first time in this study.
These categories, which had not been used by Lowry, Love, and Kirby
(10), were *pregnancy prevention* (talking about, implying, or practicing
any form of birth control), *sexually transmitted disease prevention* (talking
135   about "safe sex" or implying or actually takings steps to prevent
STDs), and *sexually transmitted diseases contracted* (verbal, implied, or
physical depictions of someone who has contracted gonorrhea, syph-
ilis, herpes, AIDS, or other STDs).
         All of the programs in the sample were coded independently by
140   both authors. The overall proportion of intercoder agreement was
.79. The proportion of agreement on the most-used categories was
.78 for erotic touching, .76 for heterosexual intercourse, .77 for prostitution, and .90 for aggressive sexual contact. Where the coders disagreed in their frequency scores for a given scene, the mean of the
145   two scores was used for data analysis purposes.
         It is important to note that the coding system used by Lowry,
Love, and Kirby (10) and in the present study was generally more
conservative than that used by Silverman, Sprafkin, and Rubinstein
(14, as reported in 15). In their study, if a man and woman kissed one
150   time it was counted *twice*—once for the man and once for the
woman—whereas in the present study it was counted as *one* act of
kissing. Likewise, in their study an implied intercourse scene was
counted *twice*—once for the man and once for the woman—whereas

in the present study it was counted as *one* act of implied intercourse.
155 In one type of situation, though, we used a more liberal approach to tabulating behavior. Silverman, Sprafkin, and Rubinstein counted implied intercourse scenes interrupted by a commercial break or by other scenes only once; we coded the implied behavior each time the scene appeared.

160 Table 1 presents the 1979 and 1987 frequencies for different types of sexual behaviors. We found a total of 387 codable sexual behaviors, or an overall rate per hour of 7.4. This compares with 6.6 per hour in Lowry, Love, and Kirby's (10) analysis of 1979 programs.

Several major conclusions can be drawn from Table 1. First, the

TABLE 1

Frequency and Rate of Sexual Behaviors in 1979 and 1987 Soap Operas

	1979 Frequency	1979 Rate per Hour	1987 Frequency	1987 Rate per Hour
Erotic touching				
Married	26	.5	9	.2
Unmarried	115	2.3	205	3.9
Unclear marital status	2	.0	0	0
Subtotal	143	2.9	214	4.1
Heterosexual intercourse				
Married/verbal	29	.6	3	.1
Married/implied	3	.1	0	0
Unmarried/verbal	63	1.3	64.5	1.2
Unmarried/implied	5	.1	15	.3
Unclear marital status/verbal	1	.0	0	0
Subtotal	101	2.0	82.5	1.6
Other sexual behaviors				
Prostitution/verbal	11	.2	58.5	1.1
Prostitution/implied	0	0	1	.0
Aggressive sexual contact/verbal	68	1.4	19	.4
Aggressive sexual contact/implied	5	.1	8	.2
Other unnatural sexual behavior/verbal	1	.0	4	.1
Subtotal	85	1.7	89.5	1.7
Pregnancy prevention	n.a.	n.a.	0	0
STD prevention	n.a.	n.a.	0	0
Total, all behaviors	329	6.6	387	7.4

All hourly rates are rounded to one decimal point.

165 overall amount of sex on network soap operas has indeed increased, but the amount of increase was only .8 instance per hour.

Erotic touching between unmarried persons increased from 2.3 to 3.9 codable acts per hour. Verbal references to prostitution increased from .2 to 1.1 instances per hour, an increase that is probably 170 attributable to two separate programs that had story lines involving former prostitutes who were discussing their past lives with their husbands, parents, and others. Verbal references to aggressive sexual contact decreased from 1.4 to .4 instances per hour, probably because the 1979 study had included the widely publicized Luke and Laura 175 rape story line on "General Hospital." Not surprisingly for network television, neither the 1979 programs nor the 1987 programs contained any physical depictions of intercourse or rape.

In terms of who is engaged in the various forms of sexual behavior, there was a major increase in the ratio of sexual behaviors 180 between unmarried and married partners from 1979 to 1987. In 1979 there were 183 codable acts involving unmarried partners and 58 involving married partners, or a ratio of 3.2 to 1. In 1987 there were 285 codable sexual acts involving unmarried partners and 12 involving husbands and wives, a ratio of 23.7 to 1. This ratio of almost 185 24 to 1 would jump to 31 to 1 if aggressive sexual contact, prostitution, and other forms of sexual behavior were included.

"Days of Our Lives" had by far the highest rate of sexual behaviors, 20.7 per hour. Among the 1979 programs "General Hospital" had ranked highest, with 16.0 per hour, but it dropped to the 190 ninth position in the present study. "The Guiding Light" ranked lowest, with only .2 codable behaviors per hour. The hourly rates for the individual networks were 4.2 on ABC, 7.0 on CBS, and 12.0 on NBC. Thus NBC presented almost three times the number of codable sexual behaviors per hour as ABC.

195 In addition to measuring the duration of the on-screen sexual behaviors themselves, we also measured the duration of the scenes in which the behaviors occurred. The frequency scores and duration of behaviors correlated at .78, frequency scores and duration of scenes at .87, and duration of behaviors and duration of scenes at .94.

200 **Although there may be an increased amount of sexual behavior on prime-time TV, there does not seem to be a major increase within soap operas, at least as measured for 1979 and 1987 programs.** The overall rates of codable sexual behaviors per hour in the 1979 and 1987 programs were generally similar, with only a slight increase in 205 1987. It is important to emphasize that the coding system used in this study produces generally conservative statistics. Several other studies have coded sexual innuendos as references to intercourse; we coded

rather direct euphemisms (e.g., "make love") but not innuendos per se. Nonetheless, although the finding of 387 codable sexual behaviors (7.4 per hour) may not seem high, if projected for an entire year of viewing the result would be 20,124 codable sexual behaviors (387 × 52 weeks).

The best example of a change in an individual program between 1979 and 1987 was "General Hospital," which declined from first to ninth in terms of number of sexual behaviors. This change could be due to the particular plots being used during the study period, changes in the program's writers and directors, changes in network policies, or other reasons.

In general, the value of measuring both the frequency and duration of behaviors appears to be limited, since they were so highly correlated. There is no doubt, however, that in particular instances the differences in results would be striking. For example, one episode of "Another World" contained an implied rape scene that was divided into six segments, interspersed with other scenes and commercials. The program thus received a score of 6 on "aggressive sexual contact," but the total time amounted to 463 seconds, a very long stretch for a specific behavior to continue in a program.

There was no treatment—verbal, implied, or physical—of pregnancy prevention or STD prevention in the 1987 sample, and it seems safe to assume that this would have been the case as well in the 1979 sample. The transcending message on soap operas concerning sex is that it is primarily for unmarried partners. Yet, though contraception is seldom mentioned, pregnancy is rare. Even though life on most of the soap operas takes place in the sexually fast lane, no one ever catches a sexually transmitted disease.

One could argue, with Planned Parenthood, that the soap operas are engaging in a national sex disinformation campaign. The results of this study suggest that such charges may in fact be understated.

Of course, one cannot demonstrate audience effects (especially long-term effects, the most important kind) with content analysis studies alone. What are the cumulative effects, for example, upon a teenage girl or boy who has watched soap operas for three or four years? To what extent does the transcending message about worry-free, promiscuous sex influence that teenager's own perceptions of sex and sexual practice? Such questions highlight the need for large-scale public health surveys and field studies.

It is possible that in the summer of 1987, when the data for this study were collected, network TV soap operas were in a transition period, moving toward greater social and public health responsibility. In addition to the 15 afternoons of programming analyzed in detail, we also videotaped another randomly selected sample of 15 after-noons for general screening. In one instance in this supplemental sample, an uncle, after catching his unmarried nephew about to take a 255 girlfriend upstairs to bed, sat the nephew down for a talk to stress the importance of not rushing into sex without a serious commitment and, especially without one of the partners using some form of birth control. In a second instance in the supplemental sample, on an epi-sode of NBC's "Santa Barbara" (Aug. 11, 1987), a woman about to 260 trade sexual intercourse for information insisted that it be "safe sex." Even this scene, though, treated "safe sex" as a laughing matter:

JANE: All right. One more thing.

KEITH: What?

JANE: Safe sex.

265 KEITH: OK. I'm buckled up if you're buckled up.

JANE: I *mean* it, Keith. [Jane reaches into the pocket of her jeans and takes out a small, flat package.]

KEITH: Sounds a little kinky, but what the heck. [He takes the pack-age from her, takes her by the arm to lead her to the sofa or 270 bedroom. Scene ends.]

One other incident suggests that the soap operas were just beginning to deal with AIDS. About a week after the videotaping for this study ended, one of the soap operas introduced a story line about a major character who decided to get an AIDS test because he had formerly 275 shared needles with other intravenous drug users.

A replication of our study in the near future could determine to what extent these three incidents might represent a trend of more accurate and socially responsible portrayals of sexual behavior. Re-gardless, the results of the present study suggest that in the summer 280 of 1987 network TV soap operas were offering a view of sex as a spur-of-the-moment activity pursued primarily by unmarried partners with little concern about either birth control or disease prevention.

REFERENCES

1. Fernandez-Collado, C. and B. S. Greenberg with F. Korzenny and C. K. Atkin. "Sexual Intimacy and Drug Use in TV Series." *Journal of Com-munication* 28(3), Summer 1978, pp. 30–37.

2. Franzblau, S., J. N. Sprafkin, and E. A. Rubinstein. "Sex on TV: A Con-tent Analysis." *Journal of Communication* 27(2), Spring 1977, pp. 164–170.

3. Greenberg, B. S., R. Abelman, and K. Neuendorf. "Sex on the Soap Operas: Aftern)on Delight." *Journal of Communication* 31(3), Summer 1981, pp. 83–89.

4. Greenberg, B. S. and D. D'Alessio. "Quantity and Quality of Sex in the Soaps." *Journal of Broadcasting & Electronic Media* 29, 1985, pp. 309–321.

5. Greenberg, B. S., D. Graef, C. Fernandez-Collado, F. Korzenny, and C. K. Atkin. "Sexual Intimacy on Commercial TV During Prime Time." *Journalism Quarterly* 57, Summer 1980, pp. 211–215.

6. Hill, D. "Is TV Sex Getting Bolder?" *TV Guide*, August 8, 1987, pp. 2–5.

7. Johnson, D. K. and K. Satow. "Getting Down to Specifics about Sex on Television." *Broadcasting*, May 22, 1978, p. 24.

8. Lawlor, J. "Passionate about Soaps." *USA Weekend*, June 26–28, 1987, pp. 4–5.

9. Lord, L. J. "Sex, with Care." *U.S. News and World Report*, June 2, 1986, pp. 53–57.

10. Lowry, D. T., G. Love, and M. Kirby. "Sex on the Soap Operas: Patterns of Intimacy." *Journal of Communication* 31(3), Summer 1981, pp. 90–96.

11. Planned Parenthood Federation of America. "They Did It 9,000 Times on Television Last Year." Advertisement in the *Washington Post*, November 25, 1986, p. A18.

12. Planned Parenthood Federation of America. "Sex Education for Parents." Advertisement in *USA Today*, December 15, 1986, p. 11A.

13. Roberts, E., D. Kline, and J. Gagnon. *Family Life and Sexual Learning: A Study of the Role of Parents in the Sexual Learning of Children.* N.p.: Population Education, 1978.

14. Silverman, L. T., J. N. Sprafkin, and E. A. Rubinstein. *Sex on Television: A Content Analysis of the 1977–78 Prime-Time Programs.* Stony Brook, N.Y.: Brookdale International Institute, 1978.

15. Silverman, L. T., J. N. Sprafkin, and E. A. Rubinstein. "Physical Contact and Sexual Behavior on Prime-Time TV." *Journal of Communication* 29(1), Winter 1979, pp. 33–43.

16. Sprafkin, J. N. and L. T. Silverman. "Update: Physically Intimate and Sexual Behavior on Prime-Time Television, 1978–79." *Journal of Communication* 31(1), Winter 1981, pp. 34–40.

17. Sprafkin, J. N., L. T. Silverman, and E. A. Rubinstein. "Reactions to Sex on Television: An Exploratory Study." *Public Opinion Quarterly* 44, Fall 1980, pp. 303–315.

COMMENTS ON THE STUDY

Introduction, Review of the Literature, and Research Questions

Lowry and Towles begin this research study by describing several reports in the popular press that claim that: (1) the portrayal of sexual permissiveness on television is increasing over time and is on an upward curve; and (2) that these current portrayals of sex on television are inaccurate and irresponsible (1–15). If these statements are true, then the portrayals of sexual behavior on television are potentially dangerous for public health, especially for children who often learn about sex from what they see on television. Lowry and Towles also cite several surveys of the beliefs and attitudes of the American public that indicate serious and widespread concern about the way sexual behavior is portrayed on television (16–22). This introduction establishes the importance of this research topic and provides pragmatic justification for conducting the study.

The authors go on to review the relevant research literature, explaining the findings from previous communication research studies concerning the coverage of sex on television (23–51). The studies they cite provide strong support for their contention that over the past decade there has been a sharp increase in the sexual behavior portrayed on television. By citing this literature, they demonstrate that their study builds upon and will contribute to an established area of communication research. They also maintain that soap operas, in particular, broadcast more sexual content than other programs on television (34–42), justifying the need to examine soap operas as the central unit in this study.

Lowry and Towles list three major purposes of their study: (1) to determine if, in fact, there are more portrayals of sex on the soap operas at the point in time when these data were gathered (1987) than when the previous data were collected (1981); (2) to describe how soap operas portray prevention of sexually transmitted diseases and pregnancy; and (3) to determine whether it is useful methodologically to measure both the frequency and the duration of portrayals of sex on television (52–74). To meet the first goal, they compare the results of this content analysis with the findings from the previous study. To meet the second goal, they content analyze all messages on soap operas that refer to STDs and pregnancy. By examining the way these topics are portrayed, the researchers can determine whether soap operas are promoting "safe sex" behavior (those practices that help people avoid STDs and unwanted pregnancies) or promoting unsafe sexual practices. To meet the third goal, the researchers gather selected frequency and duration data about the portrayals of sex on television and compare those data to determine whether they present similar (redundant) or dissimilar (unique) information. If they provide similar information, there is no need to gather both types of data, but if they provide unique information, it is useful to gather both types of content analytic information.

Method

In conducting this study, Lowry and Towles analyzed a sample of afternoon soap operas broadcast on the three major television networks (ABC, NBC, and CBS) from May 1 through August 11, 1987 (75–76). They used a *random* sampling strategy to select five different afternoons for each network and videotaped *all* soap operas shown on those afternoons, generating a total sample of 52.5 hours of programming for analysis (78–82). Using a random selection procedure is the best assurance that the sample programs are similar in all relevant characteristics to all soap opera programs broadcast within the time frame.

It is important to ask whether the time frame from which the sample was selected (May 1 through August 11) is adequate for this study. Are the soap operas shown during this period different from the soap operas shown at other times of the year? For example, does this study account for changes in the content of soap opera broadcasts during the "sweeps weeks" when data are gathered about program popularity? We must wonder why they did not sample randomly from all 52 weeks in the year being studied. Lowry and Towles provide no rationale for the time frame chosen in this study (probably *assuming* their program data are "typical"), so we cannot be sure whether their sampling frame is optimal for this study.

We also might ask whether the authors selected a large enough sample (52.5 hours from 5 days of programming) from the sampling frame they used to provide them with a representative sample. Generally, the larger a random sample is, the more likely it will reflect its parent universe. Five days of programming out of a total of the 113 possible days of programs in their time frame (May 1–August 11) appears to be a relatively small sample—less than 5% of the sampling frame. In the earlier study (Lowry, Love, & Kirby, 1981), the sample was also 5 days of programming from the three television networks. But the sampling frame for that study was only 40 days of programming from October 22 through November 30, 1979, so their 5-day sample was more than 12% of the sampling frame.

Using a random sample allows researchers to measure the level of probability that any statistical conclusion about a sample (such as the sample mean) is actually representative of the population or universe from which it was drawn. They do so by calculating a confidence level (such as a .05 or 95% confidence level, or a .01 or 99% *confidence level*) which provides an indication of the amount of error the sample statistics contains, called the *confidence interval*. For example, researchers might find that a sample mean for time spent watching television is 24 hours per week. At a confidence level of 95%, the confidence interval might be plus or minus 2 hours. Therefore, they can be 95% sure that people spent somewhere between 22 and 26 hours per week watching television. The significance of a random sample is that researchers can tell the degree to which it is representative of the larger population or universe from which it was drawn. The authors of this study, however, do not report their confidence level or confidence interval for their random sample, so we cannot be sure how representative their sample is.

Lowry and Towles used a content-analytic coding system that had proved effective in previous studies. They coded sexual behaviors in terms of physical acts, implied acts, and verbal references (83–86). They also distinguished between sexual behaviors of married and unmarried partners (86–88). Note that the authors also provide clear operational definitions for coding portrayals of sexual behavior into a number of content categories, such as erotic touching and heterosexual intercourse (89–129).

We should evaluate whether these content categories are exhaustive of all sexual behaviors, whether they are mutually exclusive, and whether they are equivalent. Several new content categories were included in this content analysis, such as pregnancy prevention, STD prevention, and STDs contracted (130–138). These additions make the list appear comprehensive, giving it "face" validity (at least to unadventurous academics like us!), and since there is an "other" category in the classification, we might assume exhaustiveness. More problematic, however, appears to be the criterion of mutual exclusivity. We suspect some overlap among categories. For example, a behavior coded as erotic touching could also be categorized as aggressive sexual contact or masturbation. Due to such overlaps, the authors may have coded some of the sexual behaviors into multiple categories, rather than into one exclusive content category as a precise analysis requires. Or, the overlap between categories may have resulted in some categories being underrepresented. The final criterion, equivalence, is hard to judge. If we were to content analyze flowers, roses and tulips would be equivalent categories. But are masturbation and pedophilia equivalent? We leave you to judge that! On the whole, however, we would rate these content categories as adequately exhaustive, mutually exclusive, and equivalent.

The two authors independently coded the entire sample of programs in the study into the appropriate categories (139–140). We must question why the authors did not employ trained coders who were not invested in the research. It is possible that the authors' involvement with the project may have biased their determination of the units of sexual behavior portrayed and how these units were coded into the categories.

To establish the reliability of the coding scheme, the level of agreement between the codings of the two authors was computed (140–145). Remember that the higher the agreement in coding the data (as indicated by the calculated correlation coefficient of intercoder reliability), the more reliable a content-analytic procedure is assumed to be, but generally, a coefficient of at least .70 is the acceptable reliability level for a coding procedure. In this study, the overall rating of intercoder reliability was .79—not an outstanding, but acceptable, level. Probably, our earlier concerns about the content categories explain why the reliability was not higher. However, when we went back and read the the earlier study (Lowry, Love, & Kirby, 1981), the coefficient of intercoder reliability was .72, so the reliability of the coding scheme was higher in this replication than in the original study.

Results

The results of the study are presented with respect to each of the research goals (160–199). To achieve the first goal of the study, the researchers give comparative data about the relative number of times the earlier study found sexual behaviors presented in the 1979 soap operas and the number of instances found in 1987 (160–166; Table 1). The most important comparison between the 1979 and 1987 data is the summary statistic of 6.6 codable sexual behaviors per hour in 1979 compared to the 7.4 per hour rate in 1987, indicating that more sexual references were present in soap operas in 1987 than in 1979. This finding provides empirical evidence that sexual permissiveness on television has increased over time and appears to be on an upward trend. The significance of this finding is questionable, however, since the total increase in codable sexual behaviors between these two measurement points is less than 1 instance per hour (.8). A statistical test of whether this difference is significant (that is, not due to chance or error) could have been conducted by these researchers. Such a test would have helped us interpret the importance of this increase.

Next, the authors compare different categories of sexual behavior between the two measurement points (167–177; Table 1). The largest increases in codable sexual behaviors per hour were in unmarried erotic touching (2.3 in 1979 compared to 3.9 in 1987), and in verbal references to prostitution (.2 in 1979 compared to 1.1 in 1987). But there also were some relatively large decreases in codable sexual behaviors per hour, such as in verbal references to aggressive sexual contact (1.4 in 1979 compared to .4 in 1987), verbal references to intercourse between married couples (.6 in 1979 compared to .1 in 1987), and in verbal aggressive sexual contact (1.4 in 1979 compared to .4 in 1987).

The authors then tally and compare the number of sexual behaviors portrayed between married partners and unmarried partners (178–186). The 1987 data show a ratio of unmarried to married sexual behaviors more than 7 times larger than in the 1979 results. The differences between these two time periods would almost certainly be statistically significant if such a difference test had been conducted. Next the authors compare the relative rates of portrayals of sexual behaviors between the different soap operas examined (187–194)—a finding helpful for deciding which soap operas to watch (if sex discomforts you, avoid "Days of Our Lives"!), but irrelevant to the three research questions posed in the study.

The second goal of the study was met by analyzing the number of references to STD prevention, pregnancy prevention, and STDs contracted in the 1987 sample of programs. The data presented in Table 1 show that there were no portrayals of STD prevention or pregnancy prevention in the programs analyzed. The STDs contracted category was dropped from the presentation of the results without explanation, so we have to assume that there were also no portrayals of STDs contracted in this sample. According to these data, we can conclude that the soap operas of 1987 were not a source of public information about STDs, STD prevention, or pregnancy prevention.

The third goal of this study was to determine whether it is useful methodologically to measure *both* the frequency and the duration of portrayals of sex on television. To meet this goal, Lowry and Towles calculated correlation coefficients between the frequency scores and duration of behaviors (.78), between frequency scores and duration of scenes (.87), and between the duration of behaviors and duration of scenes (.94) (195–199). These correlations are all quite high, indicating that researchers can assume that frequency and duration of sexual behavior increase or decrease simultaneously. These results suggest, therefore, that it is not necessary to measure both the frequency and duration of these messages. Either measure should be adequate alone; the second measure does not appear to provide additional insights into television portrayals.

Discussion

Lowry and Towles examine the main implications of their findings (200–275). They explain that, although the observed increases from 1979 to 1987 in portrayals of sexual behaviors on soap operas were relatively small, the fact remains that the overall amount of sexual content on these shows is quite high (200–212). After all, the projection based on their data shows that there would be 20,124 sexual behaviors portrayed for the entire year (209–212)!

Perhaps the most striking finding in this study, according to the authors, is the lack of coverage of STD prevention and pregnancy prevention in these programs, given the relatively frequent coverage of sexual content on the soap operas (228–235). These empirical data support the contention that television soap operas are irresponsible in their portrayals of sexual behavior. The authors rightly point out that their content-analytic study does not demonstrate the effects of television on the audience, although they do pose some important and thought-provoking questions about such effects (240–247). The authors also provide a caveat concerning the lack of coverage of safe sex in the soap operas studied, explaining that there were portrayals of pregnancy and STD prevention in another random sample of 15 afternoons examined (248–275). The authors also provide an extended example, including actual dialogue, from an episode of "Santa Barbara" in 1987 to illustrate the growing concern with portraying safe sex practices (258–270). This caveat, however, reflects the concerns we mentioned earlier about the sampling procedures used in this study.

Lowry and Towles conclude this article by urging future researchers to replicate their research in the near future (276–278). After all, given that the content of television changes over time, as some of their research findings demonstrate, then future research should reveal that television in general, and soap operas in particular, have responded to the need to be more accurate and socially responsible in their portrayals of sexual behavior.

CONCLUSION

Lowry and Towles' study demonstrates the purposes, methods, and important conclusions of a content analysis of communication behavior. When used effectively, content analysis is an objective, systematic, and quantitative method for studying the messages embedded in mass-mediated and public texts.

QUESTIONS AND ACTIVITIES TO CONSIDER

1. What concerns do you have about the content categories used in this study? Can you think of any additional categories that Lowry and Towles could have used to describe the portrayals of sexual behaviors on soap operas? Is their category system exhaustive?
2. What concerns, if any, do you have about the sample selection procedures used in this study? What kinds of information about sample selection criteria would be useful to know about this study?
3. We indicated that the intercoder reliability in this study (.79) wasn't as high as it might have been. How might this intercoder reliability rating be improved?
4. Do you think the incidence of portrayals of sexual behavior on other types of television shows, such as sitcoms, is higher or lower than that portrayed on soap operas? Conduct your own content analysis by choosing a sample of such shows, analyzing the sexual behavior portrayed using the content categories explained in Lowry and Towles' study, and comparing your results with theirs.
5. Why is it important to conduct replications of previous studies, such as this study? How does this replication increase our understanding of the issues examined in Lowry, Love, and Kirby's 1981 study?
6. What were the advantages of using content analysis in this study as opposed to using rhetorical criticism? What are the disadvantages, if any, of using content analysis?

FURTHER READINGS ON CONTENT ANALYSIS

Berelson, B. (1952). *Content analysis in communication research.* New York: The Free Press.

Budd, R. W., Thorp, R. K., & Donohew, L. (1967). *Content analysis of communication.* New York: Macmillan.

Holsti, O. (1969). *Content analysis for the social sciences and humanities.* Reading, MA: Addison-Wesley.

Kaid, L. L., & Wadsworth, A. J. (1989). Content analysis. In P. Emmert & L. L. Barker (Eds.), *Measurement of communication behavior* (pp. 197–217). White Plains, NY: Longman.

Krippendorf, K. (1980). *Content analysis: An introduction to its methodology.* Newbury Park, CA: Sage.

Stempel, G. H., III (1989). Content analysis. In G. H. Stempel III and B. H. Westly (Eds.), *Research methods in mass communication* (2nd ed, pp. 124–129). Englewood Cliffs, NJ: Prentice Hall.

Weber, R. P. (1990). *Basic content analysis* (2nd ed.). Newbury Park, CA: Sage.

EXAMPLES OF CONTENT ANALYSIS

Basil, M. D., Schooler, C., Altman, D. G., Slater, M., Albright, C. L., & Maccoby, N. (1991). How cigarettes are advertised in magazines: Special messages for special markets. *Health Communication, 3,* 75–91.

This study assessed how tobacco companies practice *segmentation*—providing audiences with ads appropriate to their behavior and to their demographic and psychological characteristics when advertising in specialty magazines. Tobacco advertisements in ten specialty magazines (including *Ebony, Ladies Home Journal, Rolling Stone,* and *TV Guide*) from 1924—the year of the first tobacco ad found—through July, 1989 were sampled randomly. These ads were content analyzed with regard to the number of cigarette ads, the characteristics of the models used, the focus of the ads (on the product or the models), and the themes portrayed. The findings revealed significant content differences in magazines read by different market segments. For example, women, blacks, youths, and less affluent readers were targeted with more overtly sexual appeals than men or general audiences.

Larson, S. G. (1991). Television's mixed messages: Sexual content on "All My Children." *Communication Quarterly, 39,* 156–163.

Larson's study focused on the portrayals of sexual relationships between unmarried persons on a particular television daytime soap opera. He argued that previous studies had focused only on sexual *behavior* between unmarried persons, while ignoring the degree of *commitment* between the partners. Hence, one-night stands were treated the same way as relations between people who had lived together for years. Two hundred and seventy episodes of "All My Children" were content analyzed for romantic kissing (lip-on-lip kissing between members of the opposite sex). The participants of each kiss were coded with regard to their race, gender, age, and social status. Each kiss was coded as forced (accompanied by a physical struggle which demonstrated resistance) or not forced. Each couple's marital status, relationship commitment (determined by the exclusiveness of the relationship during the year, the legal and living arrangements, and conversations that revealed character intentions and feelings), and sexual activity during the year were also coded. Kisses were coded as to whether they involved couples who were: married; committed and would marry during the year; committed but would not marry during the year; in transition toward commitment; uncommitted; or other. The findings showed that while most kissing occurred between unmarried couples, it was typically part of a committed relationship. The findings also showed, however, that forceful kissing was an effective strategy for developing and maintaining relationships. Larson argues that the "wrong messages" given on daytime dramas are not about the frequency of sexual interaction between unmarried consenting couples, but about the glorification of sexual aggression.

Martindale, C. (1990). Coverage of black Americans in four major newspapers, 1950–1989. *Newspaper Research Journal, 11*(3), 96–112.

To assess the newspaper coverage of black Americans, 120 issues during the 1980s were drawn randomly from four newspapers. The unit of analysis was any newspaper item—news or feature story, editorial or opinion column, letter to the editor, photo or cartoon—that concerned black Americans or events involving or directly affecting blacks (a total of 1,174 items). The researcher coded the coverage into 15 subcategories that were grouped into three main content categories: (1) stereotypic coverage—accounts of crimes committed by blacks and items about entertainment and sports figures; (2) everyday life coverage—items that showed African-Americans as part of the normal life of the community (including community activities, individual achievements and political activities); and (3) civil rights coverage—items about black protest, riots, whites' resistance to integration, and problems facing black Americans. Intercoder reliability (.89) was assessed by having several persons not involved in the study code various sample issues that included 39 pertinent items. The content analysis showed that although newspaper coverage of black Americans has increased, the content remains highly stereotypical, with little attempt to get at the underlying causes of the situations and forces still obstructing equality for African-Americans.

Sherman, B. L., & Dominick, J. R. (1986). Violence and sex in music videos: TV and rock' n' roll. *Journal of Communication, 36*(1), 79–93.

This study assessed the extent of violence and sexual content in rock music videos. One hundred and sixty-six concept rock music videos (those in which more than 50% of screen time was devoted to a story, dramatization, or narrative and not to performance) shown on MTV and WTBS's "Night Tracks" were sampled for seven consecutive weeks from April 6 to May 18, 1984. The visuals in these videos were categorized by three independent coders with regard to: (a) physical or sexual intimacy and (b) violent acts. The content categories for intimacy covered flirting, nonintimate touching, intimate touching, embracing, and kissing; and each act was coded into eight categories of sexuality (heterosexuality, homosexuality, transvestitism, prostitution, exhibitionism, voyeurism, bondage, and indeterminate). Violent acts were categorized using Gerbner et al.'s (1979) definition: "the overt expression of physical force with or without a weapon, against self or other, compelling action against one's will on pain of being hurt or killed or actually killing or hurting" (p. 178). The findings showed that rock music videos generally are violent (with women, older adults, and nonwhites more likely to be the aggressors than the victims), male-oriented (with women dressed provocatively), and laden with sexual imagery.

Wanta, W., & Leggett, D. (1988). "Hitting paydirt": Capacity theory and sports announcers' use of cliches. *Journal of Communication, 38*(4), 82–89.

This study assessed the effects of stress on the processing and communication of information by examining whether college football telecasters use more clichés (worn-out phrases that lack interest or originality) under stressful situations, such as when a game deviates from its expected outcome, when the teams are ranked nationally, and when the final outcome is close. A list of 209 clichés that could be used in various sports were identified from lists of overused and trite terms in Harold Evan's *Newsman's English*, from guidelines of the *Dallas Times Herald, Arizona Daily Star*, and *Albuquerque Journal*, and from terms suggested by reporters and journalism instructors. The fourth quarter of 34 regular-season college football games, chosen by convenience, from the fall of 1986 were coded for the frequency of these clichés (intercoder reliability was .94). The findings demonstrated support for "capacity theory"—that changes in environmental stimulation can alter the relative efficiency of different processes—as announcers under stress relied on clichés in order to maximize their attention to the game.

Interaction Analysis

INTRODUCTION TO THE METHOD

We engage in conversation every day to socialize, conduct business, and resolve conflicts, but usually do not think much about it. Some people, however, pay more attention than others to what they say and how they say it. Snyder (1974) differentiates "high self-monitoring" communicators from "low self-monitors" based on the degree to which they pay attention to their verbal and nonverbal behaviors and adapt them to the requirements of social situations. In some situations people monitor their conversations more than they normally do, such as when students discuss their academic work with teachers, when job candidates interview for a position, or when travelers meet speakers of a different language. Most of the time, however, people generally take for granted how they produce ordinary, everyday conversation.

However, it is more difficult than it appears to maintain a conversation that flows smoothly enough for participants to focus on *what* they are saying rather than on *how* they are interacting. In fact, many researchers try to identify the implicit guidelines we use to conduct conversations and find them hard to pin down. These researchers now see conversation as a complex process that is difficult to analyze. Their common research question is: How do individuals coordinate their respective intentions and interpretations of the world when conversing? Coordination is particularly difficult when participants have different goals, such as when one relational partner attempts to break off a relationship and the other person wishes to maintain it. But even the simplest conversation requires much implicit ability to coordinate actions.

Interaction may be viewed as an intricate dance between people. Conversational partners may take the lead and initiate their own moves, yet must also respond to and coordinate their messages with the other person's if both are to be satisfied by the exchange. When coordination is successful, conversation flows onward like partners involved in a social dance. When coordination falters, a conversation feels awkward and people tend to withdraw or feel annoyed with one another.

Directions for the Study of Conversation

The study of conversation represents a fruitful area of research for communication scholars. Its overall goal is to examine messages exchanged in dyadic or small group interactions to discover the "systematic and orderly processes which are meaningful to conversants" (Heritage, 1989, p. 23). Identifying conversational conventions allows researchers to understand, explain, and even predict interactions.

One focus of conversational analysis is the specific *topics* covered. Several researchers study the topics interactants discuss and how these topics are influenced by the context and the relationship between interactants. Deakins, Osterink, and Hoey (1987), for example, found that male dyads and female dyads talked about different topics. Male dyads talked most frequently about money or business and amusement while female dyads talked most frequently about women, clothing, interior decoration, and men. Furthermore, women were found to adapt more to men within mixed-gender dyads by talking about the topics that interested men. The nature of the interactants' relationship also influences the type and range of their conversational topics. Marital partners discuss a wider range of topics than do teachers and students or supervisors and subordinates.

A second direction is identifying the *purposes* of individuals' utterances. Conversations involve coordinating interactants' intentions or purposes—utterances may be seen as moves or strategies people employ to accomplish their individual and relational goals. Some researchers seek to understand what functions particular conversational messages serve. For example, they study the kinds of messages intended to increase how much people like each other (called affinity-seeking strategies) (Bell & Daly, 1984), what messages provide emotional support and help (comforting strategies) (Samter & Burleson, 1984), what messages get others to comply with requests (compliance-gaining strategies) (Marwell & Schmitt, 1967), and what messages are used to manage relational disagreements (conflict management strategies) (Sillars, Coletti, Parry, & Rogers, 1982).

A third direction involves studying the *structure* of conversation, or the relationship between conversants' moves. A structural approach examines conversation from an interactional perspective. In conversation participants take turns constructing and exchanging messages. Therefore, what each person says subsequently affects what the other person is likely to say. In an argument, for example, what one person says influences how the other will respond—an attack often prompts a counterattack—so it takes two to argue. The interactional nature of conversation presumes that all verbal exchanges are based on shared "rules," or implicit agreements, among people in a culture about what conversational moves "ought" to follow each other. If you say "hello" to someone, the rule is that the other person should also respond with a greeting; "thank you" is coupled with "you're welcome"; "I'm sorry," with "that's all right"; and "excuse me" with "go ahead." These are the simplest of conversational rules. Communication researchers often seek to identify the more subtle rules that underlie the structure of conversation.

A fourth direction is understanding how properties of conversation affect important *outcomes,* regardless of the parties' intentions. Choices made in terms of the topics discussed, the functional messages exchanged, and the structural properties of conversation affect a wide range of outcomes, including how well the partners wind up liking, persuading, or helping one another.

Selecting Samples of Conversation

Once researchers choose a focus for their research, they must select samples of conversation to study. Researchers must make a number of important decisions when selecting samples of conversation.

First, they must determine a *source* for samples of conversation. Grimshaw (1974) explains that researchers can choose, for example, between listening in on everyday conversations (such as those that occur between customers and clerks in a store), requesting samples of conversation directly from participants (for example, by asking marital partners to discuss a problem in their home and tape-record it), or by bringing people into a laboratory—a setting created by a researcher—and creating a reason to converse. These context differences affect the nature of the conversational samples gathered.

A second decision is whether to select *general* or *specific* conversations. Some researchers, for example, study how people generally use rules to organize talk sequences by analyzing a wide range of conversational episodes. Others may obtain samples of one particular type, such as marital arguments, or dialogues in which supervisors attempt to influence their subordinates.

A third decision is whether to select conversations that are *unprompted* or *prompted* ("natural" or "structured"). Natural or unprompted conversations (obtained by tape-recording, for example, a city council meeting or a family dinner) are useful for studying how people coordinate turn-taking, no matter what the topic might be. More focused research usually requires prompting people to have a particular kind of conversation. Socha (1988), for instance, wanted to study how marital partners communicate and manage power during conversations about decision topics which they had never previously discussed but were of equal importance to both spouses. He asked (prompted) his subjects to select a topic from a list for discussion which met these two criteria.

A fourth decision is whether to analyze *real* or *hypothetical* conversations. The conversations mentioned in the preceding paragraph are all "real." They record what people actually say about matters that come up in the normal conduct of their lives. Some researchers create hypothetical situations, by asking people, for example, to imagine themselves serving as a jury (called a mock jury) that must reach a decision about a hypothetical (or even an actual) case. Other researchers use dialogue from cultural sources, such as novels and films, to examine properties of conversation. Many researchers construct examples of conversation by using messages we all would agree people *could* say, comments that appear typical of everyday interaction.

Recording Conversations

Once researchers decide on the type of conversational sample desired, they must choose the means by which conversations will be observed and recorded. Some researchers, for example, simply listen in on everyday conversations and take notes that then serve as the basis for their analysis. Other researchers audiotape conversations and then transcribe the tapes into written form for analysis. They must make sure the transcriptions are accurate and complete since people often do not talk fluently or in complete sentences. Other researchers videotape conversations, which allows them to study interactants' nonverbal behaviors as well.

Qualitative and Quantitative Approaches to Analyzing Conversation

Researchers who study conversation demonstrate many philosophical, theoretical, and methodological differences. In particular, researchers often disagree about whether qualitative or quantitative methods should be used to study conversation.

One qualitative approach to studying conversation is called **conversation analysis.** The goal of conversation analysis is to explicate the "methods that members of a culture use in accomplishing everyday activities" (Pomerantz, 1990, p. 231). Tracy (1991) explains that conversation analysts first tape record a naturally occurring conversation and then carefully transcribe it to preserve the vocal and prosodic features of the interaction. They then study the transcription inductively, not using pre-determined schemes, to identify interesting, everyday conversational practices. The written research report presents and discusses an example or a series of examples to "account for interactional patterns (practices, techniques, devices) in a manner that is understandable to readers, including those not familiar with the analytic method or the detailed features of the phenomenon being investigated" (Beach, 1989, p. 86). Jacobs (1990) contends that the especially nice fit between qualitative methods and the organization of natural conversation enables researchers to "sensitively study the meaningfulness and flexibility of patterning in discourse" (p. 248).

The quantitative analysis of conversation is usually called **interaction analysis.** Capella (1989) explains that the two goals of interaction analysis are to empirically identify the regular sequences of events that occur in interaction and to identify what functions an event and event sequences serve in conversation. Researchers usually achieve these goals by employing **structured observational schemes,** pre-determined, interpretive schemes that are used to categorize conversational units into categories. Observed event sequences are then compared to hypothetical sequences that could occur by chance alone.

The qualitative study of conversation is an important and growing area of research. The remainder of this chapter, however, examines how researchers use structured observational schemes to study interaction.

Analyzing Interaction Using Structured Observational Schemes

When making structured observations, researchers follow many of the systematic procedures used to conduct content analysis. First, they determine the specific message unit to note and record. Possible units of analysis include, for example, the *topics* discussed, the particular *messages* designed to obtain compliance, or the *sequences* that constitute an argument. They then ask at least two (and preferably more) *coders* to work independently, identifying the units in the discourse, a process known as *unitizing.*

The coders are then asked to *sort* each unit into the different and mutually exclusive categories predetermined by the researcher. Bales (1950), for example, developed a structured observational scheme that called for coding each message uttered by members of a decision-making group into one of twelve functional categories. (These were: seems friendly, dramatizes, agrees, gives information, gives opinions, gives suggestions, asks for suggestions, asks for opinions, asks for information, disagrees, shows tension, or seems unfriendly.) Sometimes they provide coders with a list of conversational units that are phrased in technical jargon or just subtly different from each other, like the types of questions used in interviews, so coders must be trained beforehand as to what precisely each category entails.

After coders identify and categorize each unit independently, the researcher compares their codings to see whether they agree about the identification and meaning of each unit. As in content analysis, if coders agree at least 70% of the time about the individual units, their observations are typically assumed to be *reliable*. If the codings are not sufficiently reliable, the observational scheme probably needs to be made more precise, or coders need better training in its use.

Once all codings are complete and reliable, these data are analyzed, usually with statistical techniques. The analysis may involve counting and ranking different topics discussed within a conversation, analyzing differences among the functional messages each participant used, determining which message sequences occur consistently to understand structural aspects of a conversation, or assessing how predictably certain conversational processes lead to particular outcomes.

QUESTIONS FOR EXAMINING INTERACTION ANALYSIS

In addition to the general criteria that are used to judge the quality of any research study and the questions posed about the selection of texts, several criteria apply specifically to interaction analysis. Keep these questions in mind when reading the following study, or any article that uses structured observational schemes to study conversation:

A. Recording the Conversation

1. Did the particular procedure used for *recording the conversation* capture all the relevant conversational data without influencing it?

2. Did conversants react to the *recording device* and, therefore, distort what they said (such as being apprehensive about communicating because they knew they were being recorded by a video camera)?

3. Did the recording procedure accurately *capture all conversational processes* relevant to the research questions? Were any important features of the conversation, such as nonverbal behaviors, not included in the recordings?

B. Using Structured Observational Schemes

1. Did the researcher build a *cogent argument* (based on theory and previous research) for the conversational variables selected?

2. Did the *structured observational scheme* include all important units of conversation related to those variables? Were any relevant elements of the conversation omitted?

3. Did the *units* or *categories* of the observational scheme seem precise and mutually exclusive, or do they appear to be ambiguous or overlapping categories?

4. Were the categories *valid?* What argument did the researcher make for their validity?

5. Did the researcher use a *sufficient number* of coders (at least 2)?

6. Were *coders who had no stake in the research* employed?

7. Was the *coding done independently* (without consulting each other until the coding was completed)?

8. Are the codings *reliable?* Were reliability findings presented for coder agreement in identifying message units? Have the coders demonstrated sufficient agreement about categorizing each unit?

THE ILLUSTRATIVE STUDY

This study deals with conversation in decision-making groups. The authors investigated what happens when a group of people, after conversing about a decision, makes a more extreme decision than they were initially predisposed to make. Individual jurors, for example, may be predisposed toward awarding a plaintiff a certain amount of money immediately after listening to testimony, but after deliberating, award far more (or less) than any of them had previously considered. A shift to a more extreme decision after engaging in conversation is known as *polarization* (or a "choice shift").

Polarization often occurs as people talk together and try to reach a collective decision. Sometimes, an extreme position that emerges out of conversation has negative effects. Janis (1982), for example, showed how members of President John F. Kennedy's cabinet reached a polarized decision, in spite of serious reservations they had individually, to sanction an attack on Cuba at the Bay of Pigs—an invasion that failed miserably.

A question some communication researchers study is: What conversational processes lead groups to polarize? Understanding features of conversation associated with group polarization may well prevent future groups from engaging in faulty decision making. In this article, the authors focus on *argumentation* within groups that polarize. Their purpose is to discover whether group polarization is explained better by the *type of arguments* uttered or by the *reactions* that follow these arguments.

Effects of Reactions to Arguments on Group Outcome: The Case of Group Polarization

Steven M. Alderton
Lawrence R. Frey

1   **THE PROBLEM**

When we refer to the tendency for a group of young, liberal lawyers to be even more committed to egalitarianism after a discussion about civil rights than at the outset, we are talking about a concept called
5   *group polarization.* Group polarization is defined operationally as the tendency for average post-discussion positions to favor in a significantly more extreme way the group's average prediscussion decision.[1] This rather simplistic-sounding phenomenon draws attention to most of the variables which interest group performance researchers. Spe-
10   cifically, polarization is a product of group member predispositions plus group member interaction plus decision-making output. Of those variable clusters, the one which emerges as most ripe for exploring the notion of group process, and yet remains far from understood, is the study of how communication is used to influence the group mem-
15   ber shift toward a more extreme final decision.

Leading the way in research-based views of how this communicative influence functions is Vinokur and Burnstein's persuasive arguments explanation.[2] According to their model, group decisional shifting is the result of argumentation which is effective if it has the
20   following characteristics: direction (arguments favor the generally preferred trend in decision-making); persuasiveness (arguments are seen as nontrivial and relevant); and novelty (arguments include new

Source: Alderton, S. M., & Frey, L. R. (1983). Effects of arguments on group outcomes: The case of group polarization. *Central States Speech Journal, 34,* 88–95. Reprinted by permission of the Central States Communication Association.

Steven M. Alderton is Assistant Professor of Speech Communication at Howard University. Lawrence R. Frey is Assistant Professor of Communication at Loyola University of Chicago.

[1]The concept of polarization, as used here and in the literature upon which this study is based, is distinct from the related notions of extremization and risky shift. Polarization is the general tendency to shift decisionally in a direction initially preferred by the group. The study of extremization, however, only focuses on shifts away from neutrality, regardless of the direction, while analyses of risky shift center only on the degree of risk represented in the decision.

[2]Amiram Vinokur and Eugene Burnstein, "Effects of Partially Shared Persuasive Arguments on Group-Induced Shifts: A Group-Problem-Solving Approach," *Journal of Personality and Social Psychology,* 29 (1974), 305–15.

information). Alderton found significant positive correlations between each of these characteristics of reasoning and the tendency to
decisionally shift in discussions about attribution of responsibility.[3]
The best singular predictor of the degree and direction of polarization, however, seems to be the quantity of arguments supporting a
position.[4]

As an explanation of polarization, these findings have told us
little. An analogy would be to simply say that group leaders are the
people who talk most. A more sensitive analysis would, it seems, focus
upon how group members respond to bases of reasoning as signs of
acceptable and unacceptable argumentation. The worth of investigating the role of reactions to arguments in polarizing groups seems
apparent. Indeed, reactions to arguments seem to serve to establish
the standards for acceptable and unacceptable arguments, and by
suggesting what is acceptable, these behaviors probably guide communication of arguments throughout the discussion process.

Consistent with this focus is a conceptualization of argumentation which suggests a processual rather than a static speech view. To
date, treating an argument or a basis of reasoning as an act separate
from its context was relatively easy and could answer certain simplistic
questions. This view of argumentation is what O'Keefe calls *making an
argument,* or *argument$_1$.*[5] Ignoring how group members respond to
formulated arguments$_1$, however, reveals little about the effects of
interaction on argument development and argument impact. As
Willard explains, "The danger [of extracting arguments from their
context] rests specifically with dealing with argument as a 'unit of
proof' or a 'unit of reasoning.' At the very least this view must be
integrated into a broader conceptual structure viewing argument as a
form of interaction."[6]

An alternative view is O'Keefe's notion of *argument$_2$,* or what he
calls *having an argument.*[7] As he explains:

*Crudely put, an argument$_1$ is something one person makes (or gives or presents or
utters), while an argument$_2$ is something two or more persons have (or engage in).*

[3]Steven M. Alderton, "Locus of Control-based Argumentation as a Predictor of
Group Polarization," *Communication Quarterly,* 39 (1982), 381–87.

[4]See George D. Bishop and David G. Myers, "Informational Influence in Group
Discussion," *Organizational Behavior and Human Performance,* 12 (1974), 92–104.

[5]Daniel J. O'Keefe, "Two Concepts of Argument." *Journal of the American Forensic
Association,* 13 (1977), 121–28.

[6]Charles A. Willard, "A Reformation of the Concept of Argument: The Con-
structivist/Interactionist Foundations of a Sociology of Argument," *Journal of the American Forensic Association,* 14 (1978), 124.

[7]O'Keefe.

Arguments₁ are thus on a par with promises, commands, apologies, warnings, invitations, orders, and the like. Arguments₂ are classifiable with other species of interactions such as bull sessions, heart-to-heart talks, quarrels, discussions, and so forth.[8]

Brockriede has further clarified this distinction between making an argument (argument₁) and having an argument (argument₂) as the difference between product and process.[9] He suggested that, "[O'Keefe's] argument₁, making or advancing arguments, may be represented by the noun 'argument' since a *thing* has been produced. His [O'Keefe's] argument₂ may be referenced better by 'arguing' since persons are *doing* something. Argument₁ focuses on a *product* made, argument₂ on a *process* engaged in."[10]

The processual analysis of argumentation is a more dynamic approach but, unfortunately, the unit of analysis would, in many conflict-filled small groups, constitute the whole discussion. A middle position might be one in which the focus is upon process, and yet the unit of analysis is small enough to provide comparisons. To this end, the notion of the *adjacency pair* (e.g., question-answer, request-grant/refusal, etc.) as a basic unit for the analysis of conversation seems appropriate. As Jackson and Jacobs explain, "The first pair part (FPP) of an adjacency pair establishes a 'next turn position' which is expected to be filled by an appropriate second pair part (SPP). The interpretive frame established by issuance of a FPP makes the SPP conditionally relevant on the occurrence of that FPP."[11] Having an argument, then, may occur as a result of unexpected, and hence undesired, SPP reactions to FPP issuances.

The present study concentrated upon the nature of communicative influence in group polarization. Components which seem critical for study are the effects of the positive and negative quality of reactions to majority and minority positions on the polarization process. The first pair part (FPP) of the adjacency pair under consideration in this study, then, consists of the basis of reasoning provided by a group member (arguments₁) while the second pair part (SPP) consists of the initial reaction (positive or negative) to those arguments₁. Hence, our focus is upon explicating how arguments₁ are treated by group members in the process of having an argument₂.

---

[8]O'Keefe, p. 121.

[9]Wayne Brockriede, "Characteristics of Arguments and Arguing," *Journal of the American Forensic Association*, 13 (1977), 129–32.

[10]Brockriede, p. 129.

[11]Sally Jackson and Scott Jacobs, "Structure of Conversational Argument: Pragmatic Bases for the Enthymeme," *Quarterly Journal of Speech*, 66 (1980), 252.

RESEARCH HYPOTHESES

Reactions to Majority Arguments and Polarization

95

100

105

Using the notion of the adjacency pair as discussed above, it seems reasonable to infer that the expected response (SPP) to an initial argument$_1$ (FPP) is some sense of agreement with or approval of either the content of the position or the right of the person to assert that position;[12] otherwise, a lack of agreement or approval would result in the participants having an argument$_2$. This would be true especially in those cases where the arguments$_1$ advanced support the generally preferred direction held by the participants. Consequently, if the initial SPP reaction to a preferred argument$_1$ within a group setting is a positive reaction, we might expect that this reaction would tend to encourage group members to be more committed to the preferred direction; that is, to polarize in the expected direction. Concurrently, a negative SPP reaction to a FPP preferred argument$_1$ might tend to encourage group members not to be committed to the preferred direction; hence, not to decisionally shift in the expected direction. In line with this reasoning, the following hypotheses were advanced:

110

H_1: *The greater the use of positive reactions to majority arguments, the greater the degree of group polarization.*

H_2: *The greater the use of negative reactions to majority arguments, the less the degree of group polarization.*

Reactions to Minority Arguments and Polarization

115

120

Consider next the effects of alternative reactions to arguments$_1$ which are not in the preferred direction, i.e., minority arguments$_1$. First, negative reactions to minority arguments might tend to encourage group members to abandon minority positions and be more committed to the expected position, that is, to polarize in the expected direction. Second, positive reactions to minority arguments might tend to

---

[12]The study of the right of a person to assert a position seems most closely related to the study of confirmation/disconfirmation. See Evelyn Sieburg, "Interpersonal Confirmation: Conceptualization and Measurement," paper presented to the International Communication Association Convention, Montreal, Canada, 1973; Evelyn Sieburg, "Confirming and Disconfirming Organizational Communication," in *Communication in Organizations*, eds. James L. Owen, Paul A. Page, and Gordon I. Zimmerman (St. Paul, MN.: West, 1976), pp. 129–49; and Kenneth N. Leone Cissna and Sr. Suzanne Keating, "Speech Communication Antecedants of Perceived Confirmation," *Western Journal of Speech Communication*, 43 (1979), 48–60. The responses in which we were interested correspond primarily to comments upon the content of the position/argument being advanced.

decrease the likelihood of group polarization. In addition, reactions
to minority arguments might influence the number of minority positions advocated by group members. Hence, negative reactions to minority arguments should decrease the likelihood of minority argu-
125   ments being advanced, while positive reactions should increase the
likelihood of minority arguments being advanced. In line with this
reasoning, the following hypotheses were advanced:

H_3: *The greater the use of positive reactions to minority arguments, the less the degree of group polarization.*

130   H_4: *The greater the use of negative reactions to minority arguments, the greater the
degree of group polarization.*

H_5: *The greater the use of positive reactions to minority arguments, the greater the
number of minority arguments advanced.*

H_6: *The greater the use of negative reactions to minority arguments, the less the*

135   *number of minority arguments advanced.*

METHODOLOGY

Experimental Procedures

Participants were sixty-four randomly selected subjects attending a
large, urban university. At the outset of the study, in line with the
140   typical group polarization research format, subjects individually completed questions about two case studies. The cases included information about an individual who was either predominantly responsible
for the outcome of a low course evaluation or was not predominantly
responsible for the outcome.[13] Subjects completed questions about
145   the degree of personal responsibility (1–7 scale), the degree of imper-

---

[13]The cases used in this study were as follows:
A. Case Including Evidence Favoring a Person's Innocence
   George is a junior majoring in theatre. The program in which he was enrolled
included a large number of performance courses. In addition to getting practice at
acting and technical work, however, George was also interested in getting good grades
(he stated) because he was planning to go on for a Master's degree.
   The grade which is being disputed is for a course in directing. The course
required that each student direct six 20-minute videotaped plays during the semester.
Each of the directed scenes was critiqued by the instructor. The instructor, however, did
not give the students any grades after the critiques. Since George, who has a 3.3 GPA,
got favorable oral critiques from the instructor, he assumed that he would do well in the
course.
   The final grade given to George in the class was a D−. George went to the
instructor and asked for a justification of the grade. The instructor told George that,
even though he might have received a B or an A from any other instructor in the
department, this work did not meet his own high standards. George took the tapes to
another instructor, who testified that it was at least B− to A− range work.
   George is appealing the D− because he felt that the instructor was too subjective

sonal responsibility (1–7 scale), and assigned an appropriate grade (a range of grades from E to A). After completion of the questions, subjects were placed in groups of four and advised to discuss the questions and reach a consensus in each case. Subjects then completed
150   the questions again, individually, after they reached consensus. Discussions of the cases were approximately thirty to forty minutes in total length.

     Results of a 2×3 analysis of variance (incriminating/exonerating cases by the three time periods of prediscussion, consensus, and post-
155   discussion) demonstrated that decisional shifts on the attribution-of-responsibility scales were in the predicted direction (shifting on the grade scale did not occur at a significant level for either case). Specifically, discussions of the case which predominantly included incriminating evidence led to increased attributions of responsibility to the person
160   ($F[1, 58] = 5.74, p < .05$) and decreased attributions of responsibility to the situation ($F[1, 58] = 5.98, p < .05$). Discussions of the case in which the person was primarily portrayed as innocent resulted in increased attributions of responsibility to circumstance ($F[1, 58] = 4.34, p < .05$), but a significant shift on the degree of personal responsibility scale did
165   not emerge. Overall, subjects demonstrated evidence of polarization after group discussion.

Communication Analysis

To test the research hypotheses, methods were developed to content analyze arguments, determine whether or not they represented a

---

and unfair in grading. This was the third complaint of this sort leveled against the instructor.

B. Case Including Evidence Designed to Characterize a Person as Guilty:

     Bill was an undergraduate business major. He recently completed his final semester. His GPA is 3.00. He is in the process of interviewing for a number of different marketing jobs. The interviewer for the job Bill wants is concerned about a D+ which Bill received in a marketing class last semester. Bill has brought the situation before the Academic Fairness Committee because he feels that the low grade was unfairly given and is preventing him from getting a desired position. A grade change to a B, he argued, is justified and would help him get the job.

     The course required one major final project. The instructor, however, asked the students to turn in two drafts of the project so that he could react to the drafts and tell the students what changes to make. Bill did not turn in the drafts because he felt that the project was so simple that anyone could do it well, even without taking the class.

     Bill argued that everyone else probably got an A or a B in the class even though many probably did not turn in drafts for a reaction, and that he didn't get a good grade because the instructor didn't like him. The instructor stated that he had no reason for disliking Bill. In reviewing the paper, however, the instructor stated that it was of such poor quality that an E would be the more appropriate grade. A colleague of the professor agreed that the project was of very poor quality. This is the second time that Bill has brought a complaint to the committee for unfair grading practices.

170   majority or minority viewpoint, and determine whether the initial
reactions to arguments were supportive or negative. For the purposes
of testing the coding scheme, the taped recordings of twelve group
discussions were transcribed. Two independent raters isolated behaviors identified as arguments ($\emptyset$ = .95, df = 1, p < .001). This
175   included all communicative acts in which there were data leading to a
stated or unstated claim. Using this procedure, thirty percent (444) of
the total number of acts constituted arguments. The raters then
categorized the arguments, in line with information provided in the
case studies, as either supportive of personal responsibility or imper-
180   sonal responsibility ($\emptyset$ = .27, df = 1, p < .001). A third category in
this analysis, simply referred to as "all other arguments" (i.e., procedural arguments), accounted for twelve percent of the categoriza-
tions. This content analytic technique thus allowed for determination
of whether an argument represented the majority view (personal at-
185   tributions in the incriminating case discussions or impersonal attributions in the exonerating case discussions) or was an example of a
minority viewpoint (personal responsibility in the exonerating case
discussions or impersonal attributions in the incriminating case discussions).
190   Content analytic categories also were developed to identify
various types of reactions to arguments (positive, negative, and neutral) which group participants may use in responding to a basis of
reasoning (see Table 1). The major sources for determining types of
argument reactions were texts on argumentation and debate[14] and
195   intuition. Two independent raters coded the first response to each
argument as one of nine positive reactions ($\emptyset$ = .81, df = 1, p < .001),
one of nine negative reactions ($\emptyset$ = .72, df = 1, p < .001), or one of
two neutral reactions ($\emptyset$ = .87, df = 1, p < .001). Of the total number
of reactions, sixty-one percent were positive, twenty-eight percent
200   were negative, and eleven percent fell into neutral categories. A closer
inspection of the data revealed a significant difference between positive and negative reactions with respect to the number of categories
used (X^2 = 119.2, df = 8, p < .001). Specifically, the vast majority
of positive reactions employed fell into three categories (catego-
205   ries 1 [14.9%], 2 [32.8%], and 9 [49.5%]), while the total number of
negative reactions were more equally distributed across six categories
(categories 1 [23.6%], 2 [26.8%], 4 [7.3%], 6 [13.8%], 8 [7.3%], and 9
[10.6%]).
        In all cases of disagreement about a coding decision, the raters

[14]For example, see Austin Freeley, *Argumentation and Debate*, 5th ed. (Belmont,
Ca.: Wadsworth, 1981); and George E. Ziegelmueller and Charles A. Dause, *Argumentation: Inquiry and Advocacy* (Englewood Cliffs, N.J.: Prentice-Hall, 1975).

TABLE 1
Types of Reactions to Arguments

Positive Reactions	Negative Reactions
1) Respond with a paraphrasing of the previously stated argument	1) Respond with an argument which is the opposite of the one previously forwarded
2) Respond with a new argument, but one that generally argues for the same position	2) Respond with a new argument which takes a position that is generally opposite that of the one previously stated
3) Respond with a statement which enhances the source credibility of the previous speaker	3) Respond with a statement designed to denigrate the source credibility of the previous speaker
4) Respond with a statement which implies that the facts were correctly interpreted by the previous speaker	4) Respond with a statement which implies that the facts given by the previous speaker are wrong
5) Respond with a statement which implies that the conclusion reached by the previous speaker is plausible	5) Respond with a statement which implies that the conclusion reached by the previous speaker is wrong
6) Respond with a statement which implies that the line of reasoning forwarded by the previous speaker is important and should be pursued	6) Respond with a statement which argues that the topic issued by the previous speaker is unimportant and should be changed
7) Respond with a statement which implies that the previous speaker's argument is consistent with what has been argued previously	7) Respond with a statement which implies that the previous argument is inconsistent with what has been argued earlier on in the discussion
8) Respond with a statement which implies that the previous speaker's argument is relevant to the discussion	8) Respond with an argument which states that the previous speaker's argument is irrelevant to the discussion
9) Respond with a simple affirmation of the previous speaker's position	9) Respond with a simple negation of the previous speaker's position

Neutral and Other Categories

1) Respond with an asking for clarification
2) Respond in a way that does not fit into one of the positive or negative categories

210   returned after the analysis to discuss the case and coded it when
      possible. This procedure allowed for use of most of the data in the
      final analysis.

Data Treatment

      For the first four hypotheses, Pearson Product Moment correlations
215   were performed between the variables of argument reactions to ma-
      jority and minority arguments (using proportions) and degree of
      group polarization (as measured by the combined polarization change
      scores, from prediscussion to consensus, on the two numerical
      scales).[15] The data were derived from six group discussions which
220   included the most apparent shifts on two out of the three polarization
      measures. In addition, to understand the significance of types of reac-
      tions to majority and minority arguments as explainers of polarization
      over and above the sheer forwarding of majority and minority argu-
      ments, correlations between majority and minority arguments (using
225   proportions) and degree of polarization were performed. For hypoth-
      eses five and six, correlations were performed between argument
      reactions to minority arguments (using proportions) and the number
      of minority arguments advanced (using proportions).

RESULTS

230   **Reactions to Majority Arguments and Polarization**

      With respect to Hypothesis$_1$, there was no significant correlation be-
      tween the use of positive reactions to majority arguments and the
      degree of group polarization, although the correlation was in the
      predicted direction ($r = .32$). With respect to Hypothesis$_2$, no signifi-
235   cant correlation between the use of negative reactions to majority
      arguments and the degree of group polarization was found. Indeed,
      the correlation was not even in the predicted direction ($r = .44$).
      Finally, no significant correlation existed between the advancement of
      majority arguments per se and the degree of group polarization ($r =
240   .10$). The results do not show support for the belief that either the

----

[15]For example, in an incriminating case discussion, if the change score on the
attribution of personal responsibility scale, from prediscussion to consensus, was $+.20$
and the change score on the attribution of impersonal responsibility scale, from prediscussion to consensus, was $-.20$, the combined polarization change score was .40.
Note that the $-.20$ change score on the attribution of impersonal responsibility scale is
in the expected direction; hence this results in a positive combined polarization change
score. If the change score on the attribution of impersonal responsibility scale had been
$+.20$, the combined polarization change score would be .00.

advancement of majority arguments or reactions to majority arguments were directly related to the degree of group polarization.

Reactions to Minority Arguments and Polarization

With respect to Hypothesis$_3$, there was, as predicted, a significant
245 negative correlation between the use of positive reactions to minority arguments and the degree of group polarization ($r = -.85$, $r^2 = .72$, t $= 3.21$, df $= 4$, $p < .05$). With respect to Hypothesis$_4$, the results indicate that there was a nearly significant positive correlation between the use of negative reactions to minority arguments and the
250 degree of group polarization ($r = .80$, $r^2 = .64$, t $= 2.69$, df $= 4$, $p \cong$ .06). Of importance, no significant correlation between the advancement of minority arguments per se and the degree of group polarization ($r = -.13$) was found. If the sheer number of minority arguments were significantly related to the degree of group polarization, it
255 would be difficult to assess the degree to which reactions actually influenced the decisional-shifting process. The results thus indicate direct support for the belief that reactions to minority arguments, but not the advancement of minority arguments, were significantly related to the degree of group polarization.
260　　　With respect to Hypothesis$_5$, the results revealed no significant correlation between the use of positive reactions to minority arguments and the number of minority arguments advanced ($r = .10$). In addition, the results with respect to Hypothesis$_6$, demonstrated no significant correlation between the use of negative reactions to minority
265 ity arguments and the number of minority arguments advanced ($r = .05$). There does not appear to be a basis for the belief that reactions to minority arguments significantly influence the number of minority arguments advocated within a group discussion.

DISCUSSION

270 This study attempted to grapple with the problem of how to analyze processually group member arguments to help illuminate group outcome. For this study, an argument first was defined as data leading to a stated or unstated claim. The actual unit of analysis, however, included both the argument and the immediate reaction to the argu-
275 ment. To detail supportive and nonsupportive types of reactions occurring after arguments, a twenty-category scheme was developed. In this manner, we sought to go beyond a static view of argument and look at how group members react processually to arguments so as to better understand why a group achieves a particular level of outcome
280 following discussion.

The processual character of this analysis was used to offer insight into one type of group outcome, group polarization. Polarizing groups shift decisionally in a direction initially preferred by the participants. Of course, to convince those group members who are less
285   committed to the majority mode of thinking, or simply to bolster the predominant decisional preferences, argument construction plays an important role in group polarization. Indeed, the persuasive arguments hypothesis and supporting research has found that the sheer number of majority arguments forwarded correlates positively with
290   the degree of the outcome.

The results from the present study, however, indicate that reactions to arguments may be more important than argument construction in explaining the degree of group polarization. Specifically, neither the sheer number of majority arguments nor the number of
295   minority arguments were significantly related to the degree of group polarization. While the reactions to majority arguments were not significantly correlated with degree of group polarization, the correlations were significantly higher than the correlations for majority or minority arguments initially advanced. Most important, however, the
300   findings from this study demonstrate that the proportion of reactions to minority arguments relate directly to the degree of group polarization. When groups positively reward minority arguments, they tend to polarize less; when they negatively respond to minority arguments, they tend to polarize more.

305   One implication of such a finding is that the adage of assigning a "devil's advocate" to balance a group discussion may not be sufficient in and of itself. As Janis has explained, groups which demonstrate symptoms of "groupthink" develop norms in favor of a particular course of action, norms which lead to "Direct pressure on any mem-
310   ber who expresses strong arguments against any of the group's stereotypes, illusions, or commitments, making clear that this type of dissent is contrary to what is expected of all loyal members."[16] What is most important is to develop a climate within a group which encourages positive consideration of minority arguments.[17] While the tactics
315   which encourage such a climate remain unspecified, the results from

[16]Irving L. Janis, *Victims of Groupthink*, 2nd ed. (Boston: Houghton Mifflin, 1982), p. 175.

[17]As evidence of the possible impact which an overly supportive environment may have on group decision-making, Janis makes reference to an unpublished content analysis by William Wong-McCarthy in which the transcripts of the "Watergate team" from June 1972 to March 1973 were found to include "relatively few instances of disagreement and very little debate about what is the best thing to do" (ibid., pp. 218–9). Curiously, once President Nixon in the spring of 1973 started suggesting to Haldeman and Erlichman that they resign, the percentage of disagreement seemed to climb.

the present study indicate that this may be one way a group can vigilantly guard against extreme polarization.

320   It also was hypothesized that positive reactions to minority arguments would tend to increase the sheer number of minority positions advocated, while negative reactions would tend to decrease the number advanced. The results do not support this hypothesis. The lack of significant findings suggest that the advancement of minority arguments is not a simple function of the response which the argument generates. Rather, the advancement of minority arguments is proba-
325   bly a function of numerous intervening variables, including a possible confounding interaction effect with the type of individual who advances such positions. Future research efforts will need to investigate in more detail the make-up of the group and whether reactions to minority arguments interact with other important research variables
330   to influence the number of minority arguments groups consider.

The results from this study lend validity to using a processual analysis to offer insight into how the group discussion process is related to particular group outcomes. Methodological refinements may help to advance this research area. For instance, the characteristics
335   of the argument reactions need additional attention. Certain types of reactions (a simple "no" versus an attack on the source credibility of the speaker) may have different levels of impact on suppression of arguments and arguers, for example. We need to start thinking about the intensity of valence of the positive or negative reactions and its
340   relation to the functioning of arguments. Moreover, we need to continue thinking about how best to processually analyze argumentation in the group discussion process. Discussant argumentation and its impact does not neatly stop at the point of an initial reaction. Establishment of adequate parameters for studying the progression of
345   group member arguments is the next step.

COMMENTS ON THE STUDY

Introduction, Review of the Literature, and Hypotheses

The article begins with a clear explanation of, and rationale for studying, group polarization (1–15). The authors point out the drawbacks of focusing group polarization research only on the *function* an argument serves (for example, whether an argument advances a majority or minority opinion) and advocate a *structural* approach, one that focuses on interaction (16–38). Their rationale shifts the research orientation away from viewing argumentation as something that one person does to another person (a one-way approach) and towards argumentation as an interaction between people (a two-way approach) (39–66)—a perspective more harmonious with behavior in conversations.

To unitize the argumentation process, the authors examined *adjacency pairs*, two interrelated message acts (called an "interact"). In this case, the interact consists of an argument advanced and the initial reaction it generates from another group member (67–90). The study's hypotheses predict that the second half of the interact, participants' *reactions* to opinions, will influence polarization (91–135).

Method

The conversations were elicited from "sixty-four randomly selected subjects attending a large, urban university" (138–139). Not enough information is provided to explain how research participants were selected "randomly." Did the researchers use a complete list of all students at this university and select 64 randomly, assuring each person an equal chance of being selected? Did everyone selected agree to participate in the study? If they did not follow these random selection procedures, the authors should be more specific about the pool from which subjects were selected and how they were selected, so that readers can judge for themselves the extent to which the findings can be generalized.

The researchers used a traditional procedure to test for polarization (139–152). Subjects were first given two written case studies involving an issue likely to interest them: student-faculty disputes about low course grades. Next, they privately answered questions about each case as to what grade they would award and who was responsible for that grade. These 64 subjects were then placed in groups of four (in a setting chosen by the researchers) and asked to discuss the same cases until they reached consensus on their answers. Then the subjects answered the same questions for a third time, individually. We are not told (although we *should* be) whether the discussion was held immediately after they read the two cases, whether the subjects were placed in groups of four randomly, or whether the setting for the discussion was a classroom.

Presenting both case studies verbatim is helpful for understanding the procedures (Footnote #13). It is not clear, however, why *two* attribution of responsibility cases were employed in this study. Perhaps the researchers wanted to generalize their findings to situations in which a person is primarily responsible for an outcome *and* to those in which he or she is not. Using two cases, however, might have created a sensitization, or testing, bias. That is, judging the first case might influence subjects' responses to the second case, which would call into question the validity of the data obtained. To control for this potential bias, the researchers should have varied the order of the cases; that is, half the subjects should have gotten the personal responsibility case first and the other half should have gotten the impersonal responsibility case first. We do not know whether this was done or not. Further, while the cases appear on the surface to be valid examples of personal and impersonal responsibility, we do not know whether they were interpreted by subjects the way they were intended. While subjects' perceptions about the degree of personal and impersonal responsibility represented in these cases were assessed, mean scores are not presented to validate the cases.

A statistical analysis of the difference between subjects' first opinion (called the pretest) and their second opinion (called the posttest) shows that polarization did indeed occur (153–166). The experimental procedure (discussion of two grade arbitration cases) seems appropriate, given that the phenomenon of interest, polarization, was produced, and, therefore, could be studied.

The researchers audiotape-recorded and then transcribed the group conversations. They selected 12 transcripts for analysis (171–173). Using audiotape captured the verbal argumentation in the group, but not members' nonverbal behavior. Since the researchers were studying *reactions* to arguments, it seems inappropriate to omit nonverbal reactions. Group members may well signal agreement or disagreement with an argument by nodding their heads, and this nonverbal cue might occur prior to someone expressing verbal agreement or disagreement. It would have been more effective to have videotaped the group interactions.

We are also left wondering why only 12 of the 16 group conversations were analyzed. Did the other 4 conversations not demonstrate group polarization? If so, why didn't the researchers analyze the differences between groups that polarized and those that didn't? Or perhaps these four conversations were not recorded fully and accurately. In any case, the researchers simply dropped these cases from their analysis, and the reader is left wondering why, as well as whether this omission biased the findings.

We are also not told of any procedures for verifying the accuracy of the verbal transcripts. Capturing oral language on paper is difficult, and errors can easily be made. Transcripts ought to be checked, but we do not know whether this was done.

The researchers employed two independent observers to code the group conversations (173–212). We do not know whether the coders were blind to the research hypotheses. (Ideally, they should be). The coders' first task was to determine whether a communicative act was or was not an argument, defined as, "data leading to a stated or unstated claim" (175–176). They had little difficulty completing this task (given the high reliability figure of .95). Thirty percent of the conversational units were coded as arguments. Given this broad definition of an argument, one wonders what the other communication acts were. If we assume that an additional 30% of the communication acts constituted reactions to arguments (agreement or disagreement), that still leaves 40% of the group conversations unexplained or unaccounted for. This remaining 40% is a large portion of the conversations to exclude from the analysis. Some description of these uncoded comments in the transcripts would be helpful for judging the validity of this observational coding scheme. Perhaps some of the untallied statements explain group polarization better than the coded arguments and/or reactions.

The coders next categorized the argument units as either representing a majority or minority opinion, given the direction of the case (177–189). They seem to have had some difficulty completing this task, as the reliability figure of .27, although statistically significant (not due to chance), is extremely low. The coders discussed their disagreements and reached a decision in each case (209–212), but the researchers should have provided some explanation of why this was necessary, and why the codings did not achieve the generally accepted level of reliability (.70). The coders agreed much more often when categorizing the first response to each argument as being either positive, negative, or neutral (190–208).

We can also raise several questions concerning the *validity* of this observational coding scheme (the degree to which it accurately captures the concepts being studied). First, as mentioned previously, we do not know how nonverbal behaviors function as reactions to arguments, since they were not included in the scheme. Second, the researchers only studied the first reaction that an argument generated. This could be too limited given that, in a group setting, the first reaction might well be negated by subsequent comments from other group members. Adjacency pairs are used mostly in research on dyadic interaction in which one person acts and only one other person responds. Using adjacency pairs treats interaction in this study more as a series of two-person exchanges than as a four-person group interaction. Applying concepts from one domain (interpersonal) to another (the small group setting) compromises the study's validity. Third, there is no attempt to capture the valence, or strength, of a reaction to an argument. There is a big difference between saying, "I don't think so," in a soft voice and screaming "No!," but with this coding scheme both would be rated uniformly as "negative." The researchers identify these last two limitations in the final paragraph to the article, and suggest that future observational schemes should account for the valence of reactions and expand beyond the study of interacts (333–345). Thus, while the observational coding scheme used in this study is better than previous schemes because of its focus on interaction, it has some important limitations. A more comprehensive analysis of small group argumentation would be desirable.

Results

In spite of some questions about the methods employed, this research study produced some fresh and important findings (229–268). In contrast to previous findings, this study revealed that the degree of group polarization is associated more with *reactions* to minority arguments than with the advancement of minority arguments per se. When minority arguments are responded to positively, group polarization decreases, but when minority arguments are responded to negatively, group polarization increases (244–259). Further, in contrast to previous research, this study found that the advancement of majority arguments is unrelated to changes in group polarization (238–240). In addition, neither positive nor negative reactions to majority arguments were associated with group polarization (231–237).

Discussion

The authors argue that the findings from this research have implications regarding how interaction analysis should be conducted: a processual approach is preferable (270–290). To understand group polarization, it is not actions or reactions themselves that influence the result. It is the combination of an action (forwarding a minority argument) with a reaction (a positive or negative response).

The study also has practical implications. The authors suggest that assigning a "devil's advocate" to forward minority opinions (a practice commonly taught in small group communication classes) may not be enough to decrease group polarization, since negating his or her arguments will increase polarization. Instead, the entire group must develop a climate within which minority arguments are respected, encouraged, and discussed (305–317). Unfortunately, the authors do not provide any suggestions for developing such a group climate. Can you think of any?

Finally, to evaluate the conclusions from this research we must consider the statistical analyses used. This study employed *correlational procedures*, which only show the extent to which variables are related, not whether one variable causes changes in another. Thus, we only know that reactions to minority arguments are *associated* with increases and decreases in group polarization, not that they *cause* such changes. Future researchers might employ the experimental method to manipulate arguments and reactions to determine whether a causal relationship exists. Also, only groups that polarized were studied. To assess the conclusions drawn from this study, future researchers will need to study whether the conversational differences found (and others) exist between groups that polarize and those that don't.

CONCLUSION

Interaction analysis is an important method used to study communication behavior. The study reviewed in this chapter illustrates some of the principles, values, and difficulties in conducting interaction analysis using a structured observational scheme.

QUESTIONS AND ACTIVITIES TO CONSIDER

1. Identify one apparent strength and one weakness in using structured observational schemes to study interaction.

2. Try inventing a structured observational scheme of your own to study an aspect of conversation that interests you (such as what topics couples discuss on a first date, or what messages employees use to ask for a raise). Compare your category scheme with someone else's. What similarities and differences did you find?

3. Think about the variety of phenomena that can affect conversation. What characteristics of a group's discussion, other than the arguments forwarded and reactions to them, might influence group polarization? Would a high status group member make a difference (such as a teacher among a group of students)? How about having only a short time period to make the decision? What else might account for group polarization?

4. The subjects in this study had little at stake, since they were only participating in an academic study. How might a comparable study be conducted in the "field," with a naturally occurring group discussion? Where might you find group polarization in the "real world?" What challenges would you face in recording and analyzing that interaction?

5. How might reading this study influence what you say the next time you are involved in a decision-making group task? Write precisely what you might say to the group, if anything, about this study. What specific procedures might you propose that the group use to avoid group polarization?

6. How could a researcher study the causal effects of reactions to arguments on group polarization? Design a full laboratory experiment.

FURTHER READINGS ON THE STUDY OF CONVERSATION

Heritage, J. (1989). Current developments in conversation analysis. In D. Roger & P. Bull (Eds.), *Conversation: An interdisciplinary perspective* (pp. 21–47). Clevedon, England: Multilingual Matters Ltd.

McLaughlin, M. L. (1984). *Conversation: How talk is organized.* Beverly Hills, CA: Sage.

Nofsinger, R. E. (1991). *Everyday conversation.* Newbury Park: CA: Sage.

Poole, M. S., Folger, J. P., & Hewes, D. E. (1987). Analyzing interpersonal interaction. In M. E. Roloff & G. R. Miller (Eds.), *Interpersonal processes: New directions in communication research* (pp. 220–256). Beverly Hills, CA: Sage.

Rogers, L. E., & Farace, R. V. (1975). Relational communication analysis: New measurement techniques. *Human Communication research, 1,* 222–239.

Tracy, K. (1991). Discourse. In B. M. Montgomery & S. Duck (Eds.), *Studying interpersonal interaction* (pp. 179–196). New York: Guilford.

EXAMPLES OF INTERACTION ANALYSIS

Meyers, R. E., Seibold, D. R., & Brashers, D. (1991). Argument in initial group decision-making discussions: Refinement of a coding scheme and a descriptive quantitative analysis. *Western Journal of Speech Communication, 55,* 47–68. This study refined an argument coding scheme and applied it to group polarization discussions. Subjects were randomly assigned to 5-member groups and they reached consensus about three problem tasks. Two independent coders identified the unit of analysis—any statement that functioned as a complete thought or change of thought. Two pairs of two coders then coded the group discussions into five content categories: (1) *arguables*—ranging from potential arguables (assertions and propositions), reason-using arguables (elaborations and responses), and reason-giving arguables (amplifications and justifications); (2) *reinforcers*—divided into agreement and "agreement-plus" (that is, when a person agrees and then states an additional argument); (3) *promptors*—divided into objection, "objection-plus," and challenge; (4) *delimitors*—including frames (providing a context for arguables), forestall/secure (forestalling refutation by securing common ground), and forestall/remove (forestalling refutation by removing possible objections); and (5) *nonarguables*—including process (orienting the group to its task), unrelated (statements unrelated to group's argument or process), and incomplete statements. The results revealed that group arguments consisted mainly of assertions, elaborations, and agreement, while explicit support for claims (justifications and amplifications) as well as statements of disagreement (objections and challenges) were infrequent.

Samter, W., & Burleson, B. R. (1984). Cognitive and motivational influences on spontaneous comforting behavior. *Human Communication Research, 11,* 231–260.
This study examined the influence of several input variables (cognitive and motivational characteristics) on the conversational behavior used to comfort another person. Female subjects were first measured for their cognitive complexity (the degree to which people possess differentiated and abstract systems of interpersonal constructs), emotional empathy, communication apprehension, and locus of control (whether or not they hold people responsible for their actions). While signing up for an additional experiment, they were videotaped interacting with a female confederate who mentioned that she was distressed about having been dropped by her long-term boyfriend the prior evening. Two independent coders placed each of the subjects' conversational turns into one of six content categories: (1) acknowledgement; (2) information-seeking, (3) disclosure (4) advice; (5) comfort (empathizing with the confederate, providing an explanation for another's actions, offering sincere sympathy and support; or suggesting a broader perspective from which the confederate could view the breakup situation); and (6) other. The results showed that cognitive characteristics affect comforting behavior, as highly complex subjects sought to alleviate the confederate's distress, and did so by employing more comforting strategies or more sophisticated strategies, and by asking more relevant questions about the breakup.

Sillars, A. L., Weisberg, J., Bruggraf, C. S., & Wilson, E. A. (1987). Content themes in marital conversations. *Human Communication Research, 13,* 495–528.

This study examined whether different ways of looking at marriage are related to the content themes evidenced in marital conversations. Married couples were defined as either traditional (couples who maintain conventional beliefs about marriage), separate (couples who emphasize autonomy), or independent (couples who balance togetherness and autonomy). They were asked to audiotape-record conversations in their homes about ten topics, each representing a common marital conflict. Individuals who had little knowledge of the goals of the study first read the transcripts and summarized the core propositions stated by each person on each topic. Two of the authors, through a process of discussing and re-sorting, arrived at an agreed-upon set of three categories of outlooks: (1) communal—marriage seen as a product of joint qualities of the couple; (2) individual—marriage seen as the product of separate identities or roles; or (3) impersonal—marriage seen as the product of factors beyond the direct, personal control of the couples. As expected, traditional couples emphasized communal themes, separate couples emphasized individualistic themes, and independent couples fell between these extremes. Finally, marital satisfaction was positively associated with communal and impersonal themes and negatively associated with individual themes.

Vangelisti, A. L., Knapp, M. L., & Daly, J. A. (1990). Conversational narcissism. *Communication Monographs, 57,* 251–274.

This article reports the results of six studies on conversational narcissism, the tendency to focus a conversation on self to the exclusion of the other. The first two studies coded conversational narcissism behaviors into four categories: (1) self-importance (such as "one-upping" the other's disclosure); (2) exploitation (such as interrupting another); (3) exhibitionism (such as loud laughter); and (4) impersonal relationship (such as lack of response). The third and fourth studies coded the behaviors people use to cope with conversational narcissism into two strategies: (a) active—such as confronting and maintaining the floor; and (b) passive—such as demonstrating disinterest and leaving. Finally, the last two studies asked people to evaluate conversational narcissists and coded people's perceptions of when conversational narcissism was considered appropriate into four categories: (1) when one person wants to show his or her superior knowledge and the other wants or needs that expertise; (2) when one person expresses himself or herself to the exclusion of the other and wants the other to help or understand; (3) when one person wants control and the other is willing to comply; and (4) when both persons are willing to operate according to a norm which focuses attention on the conversational narcissist.

Von Friederichs-Fitzwater, M. M., Callahan, E. J., Flynn, N., & William, J. (1991). Relational control in physician-patient encounters. *Health Communication, 3,* 17–36.

This study described the relational control patterns evidenced in conversations between physicians and patients. Paired, sequential messages from 30 natural conversations between physicians and patients were audiotape-recorded and transcribed. Two coders categorized each individual's utterances using a three-digit code. The first digit represented the speaker, the second digit represented the message format (assertion, question, talk-over, noncomplete, or other), and the third digit represented the response mode of the message (support, nonsupport, extension, answer, instruction, order, disconfirmation, topic change, initiation-termination, or other). These three-digit codes were then translated into one of three control patterns: (1) one up—movements toward gaining control of the interaction; (2) one down—movements toward accepting control; or (3) one across—movements toward neutralizing control of the interaction. The results suggest that patients often use domineering behavior and that physicians typically exercise control by questioning patients and changing topics.

ETHNOGRAPHY

OVERVIEW OF ETHNOGRAPHY

More than the other methods covered in this book, ethnography is akin to the kind of "research" we do naturally in our own lives every day. Whenever we enter a new situation (say a new school, workplace, social event, or public institution), we look around to familiarize ourselves with the setting and with what the people there appear to be doing. We talk to those we encounter first, or know already, to get a sense of how people interact and to learn what will be expected of us. We go through this "orientation" period because we know accepted behavior and styles of relating differ from place to place. We don't interact in a classroom the way we do with our family at home, with our friends at a ballgame, or with a salesperson in a store. We must determine in each new situation what is appropriate and what we must do to achieve our goals. When doing this, we practice a "common sense" form of ethnographic research.

Ethnography has the same ultimate goals as other methods for investigating communication, but its particular aims differ in three essential ways. First, ethnographers attempt to *describe how* communication occurs, rather than making "if-then" predictions about communication behavior or critiquing messages. Second, ethnographers seek to discover or *infer* patterns in their subjects' communication and to build theories from the ground up, rather than approaching their work already armed with a theory and studying how well the extrapolated hypotheses hold up. Finally, ethnography usually involves **fieldwork,** studying communication as it occurs naturally in an ongoing social *context,* such as a home, business, or institution, rather than creating and controlling a laboratory task or examining texts in a library. To summarize, the aim of *ethnographic communication research* is to describe and infer people's patterns of communication in particular social contexts.

Ethnography complements other research methods, and its unique characteristics make it the preferred approach in some circumstances. It is especially applicable when researchers want to study how people interact in a particular setting. Examples include learning how urban high school teachers lead discussions, how managers in firms seeking to avoid unionization deal with employees, how Japanese mothers influence their children's education, and how unmarried couples talk about birth control. It is also especially useful for studying contemporary (versus historical or hypothetical) social phenomena which would be inaccessible to most other people, such as the functioning of urban gangs or corporate boards of directors. Ethnographers can study the kinds of private events researchers cannot control in laboratory conditions, such as children's upbringing or romantic relationships.

ETHNOGRAPHERS' ORIENTATION

Ethnographers tend to subscribe to a **symbolic interactionist** approach to human behavior. They believe what people do is influenced primarily by their *interpretation* of (or the meaning they ascribe to) themselves, others, and the situations they are in. This is in contrast to a positivist or behaviorist orientation that leads experimental and other communication researchers to search for universal laws regarding human behavior. Symbolic interactionism emphasizes that individuals perceive situations differently, that what's "really" happening in a social situation depends upon participants' perspectives at a given time and the interpretative concepts they apply to what they perceive. For example, students and teachers, bosses and workers, or parents and children are likely to perceive the same interaction (such as a critique by one of the other's performance) quite differently, and each party's interpretation of that interaction is, in part, "correct." Symbolic interactionist explanations of communication phenomena are consequently complex, multiple, and context-dependent, not expressed in the short simple generalizations other researchers try to discover. Ethnographic findings, therefore, might include descriptions of the people involved, how they view past encounters they have had, how they and their culture define the situation they are in, and the influence of the physical environment in which they are operating, as well as explicating what the people say and do as they interact.

This is a culturally relative perspective, one that believes universal statements are not likely to explain much that is significant about human behavior, and, in fact, are more likely to reveal their proponents' ethnocentrism. In other words, ethnographers assume that each culture proscribes and influences what its members do; they reject the assumption that behavioral constraints are inherent or "hard-wired" into the body and mind of those individuals.

AIMS OF ETHNOGRAPHIC RESEARCH

It is especially relevant to our field that ethnographers believe that all we perceive and do is influenced by communication. Our thoughts and behaviors are neither random (they usually fit what is going on around us), nor fully programmed (we have choices). We are constrained in our speaking and listening, however, by "customs" or implicit patterns—sometimes called norms, rules, or scripts—that our culture deems appropriate. At an early age these constraints are communicated to us, and from then on we tend to communicate within their limits. Ethnographers seek to identify those culturally imposed constraints, the patterns which continue to be learned and to influence our communication throughout our lives.

Communication patterns can be strong. Saville-Troike (1989) cites as an example the opening of a telephone conversation. The ring is a summons, and the person who answers must speak first, even though the caller knows the receiver has been picked up. If you try *not* speaking first the next few times you answer the phone, you will learn from your callers that you have violated a key step in a taken-for-granted communication pattern. Innumerable patterns are equally entrenched, and many have greater social significance, such as how teenagers in some communities respond when dared to use drugs, or how some parents respond when their children refuse to obey an order.

Once we identify such patterns, we can understand, appreciate, evaluate, change, or copy them. If the subjects of an ethnography are different from us, we can use the findings to understand them better; if they seem strange, we can appreciate better the underlying logic of how they communicate. If the group being studied is experiencing problems, we can evaluate how their communication patterns contribute to those problems and advocate changes for them (or for others who wish to avoid the same problems); or, if the group is unusually successful, we can emulate their behavior.

Ethnographers investigate a wide range of communication patterns that exist at societal, group, and individual levels. For example, they may study how people in *particular roles* interact differently, such as staff and residents in a nursing home, doctors talking with their patients, or salespeople calling on their customers. They may study how members of *particular racial or ethnic groups* interact, to identify, for example, interaction patterns among black men socializing in an urban ghetto or interaction patterns between Native American students and their Anglo-American teachers. They may focus on *messages* of a particular type, such as customary greetings, requests for assistance, compliments, excuses, or storytelling. They may be interested in how a particular communication pattern influences *social structure,* such as how teenagers provoke police (and vice versa), how certain rules of etiquette define social class, or how insulated groups use "shunning" to control their members' behavior. They may study what message forms are deemed *appropriate* or "competent" in particular speech communities, such as how people are expected to talk to those of different statuses and roles in a hospital, or what communication behaviors adolescent girls in a suburban community expect from their friends. This list could go on and on, since communication varies so much among contexts, people, and interaction purposes.

CONDUCTING ETHNOGRAPHIC RESEARCH

To describe such interactions and to identify patterns that underlie them, ethnographers may take one (or a combination) of two approaches: a) an **external** or **etic approach,** or b) an **internal** or **emic approach.** Taking the etic approach, they might study the *environmental or cultural forces* that influence their subjects' messages and social behavior. They would focus primarily on *observable* communication phenomena in a particular context and then infer a pattern from their data—the pattern being articulated by the researchers. Or, when taking the emic approach, researchers would seek to learn how their subjects think about their communication, what *cognitive categories, assumptions,* and *rules* guide how they encode and decode messages exchanged in that context. To do so, they usually *interview* their subjects in order to make explicit (and often report verbatim) their tacit concepts relevant to communication. In most ethnographies, researchers use a combination of etic and emic approaches because their concern is to capture all the salient elements in the particular social episodes they are studying. They prefer holistic, inclusive descriptions, rather than confining their investigation to just a few variables as most other researchers do. In the next two chapters, however, we will read studies using etic (observation) and emic (interview) methods exclusively to permit scrutiny of each in turn.

Ethnographers usually seek opportunities for extended, first-hand contact with their subjects. Unlike many experiments which last for just a few minutes, most ethnographers spend hours, days, weeks, months, or longer with the people they are studying. And they usually spend that time in contexts in which the subjects normally operate: their home, work, or community settings (Rose, 1990). To observe them communicating as they do normally, ethnographers try to observe subjects interacting in situations that matter more to them than the fact that they are being studied, whereas experimental research is usually done with people called together primarily for the purpose of participating in a study.

Although other researchers are often unseen by their subjects, ethnographers usually have direct contact with the people they study. This means they must somehow "gain entry" to the social setting in which communication is being studied. They must have sufficient social skills to elicit desired information from people or the trust needed to observe events inaccessible to most other people. In effect, ethnographers are their own major "research tools," rather than relying on questionnaires or texts (Smith & Kornblum, 1989).

Because they gather and analyze their own data, and because their goal is to discover previously unidentified patterns (rather than test *a priori* hypotheses), ethnographers must be very careful not to impose their own preconceptions on their subjects or their communication behavior. Their stance toward the phenomena they study has been likened to that of a child, a stranger, or a second language learner. They must, in a way, return to square one and view what they are studying as if they had never seen it before. They must break free of existing conceptual categories and perceive communication events as the participants themselves do. To do so, they often record beforehand what they know about the topic and mentally "bracket" it off from what they observe and hear from their subjects.

Of course, ethnographers first review the extant literature relevant to their research topic to discover what has been learned about it before. Doing so provides some guidance about what to look for and to ask in their own investigations. It also alerts them to which of their own findings might contradict previous assumptions and, therefore, be especially "newsworthy." But unlike other researchers, they take pains *not* to predict what they might find and to consciously detach from or "defamiliarize" themselves with what they have learned so their own research procedures will not be tainted (Agar, 1986).

Moreover, once "in the field," ethnographers often seize unexpected opportunities to make inquiries and to record what they learn in

fieldnotes, which means their methods of gathering data are not standardized and the reliability of their findings cannot easily be checked by others. Nevertheless, the length of their contact with subjects and the variety of data available to them enable them to check the validity of their findings. To do so, ethnographers may ask several people for comparable information, compare different modes of inquiry (such as comparing people's statements in interviews with their observed actions), and compare their findings with reports by others studying similar phenomena. The process of checking the validity of preliminary results with other findings to assess their consistency is called **triangulation** (the three points of the "triangle" being the phenomenon and the two different points from which it is measured).

Ethnographers do not take the same pains other researchers do to study a large and random sample of subjects from the population they are investigating. They feel freer to study a **purposive sample,** to interview the people most likely to give optimum useful information and to observe only the interactions most appropriate to their research objectives (Johnson, 1990). They tend to discontinue gathering data when their findings merely repeat what previous inquiries already have revealed.

The process of gathering, checking, and analyzing data is ongoing and recursive for ethnographers. Other researchers collect and analyze data, then draw their conclusions in a single, relatively linear sequence. In contrast, as ethnographers observe and interview people, they are constantly on the alert for insights about communication patterns. They record in their fieldnotes what they perceive and the inferences they draw from those data. Periodically, sometimes every evening, they write *memoranda* to themselves that encapsulate what they have learned to date. Doing so enables them to identify contradictions in their existing data, which they can resolve through further inquiries; to draw tentative conclusions, which they can check out in subsequent analyses; and to spot gaps in their knowledge, which they can fill in as they go along (Gubrium, 1988).

ANALYZING AND PRESENTING ETHNOGRAPHIC DATA

A consequence of having extensive contacts with subjects and taking prolific fieldnotes (or taping numerous conversations) is having an abundance of data to analyze. Ethnographers, therefore, must take great pains to reduce, analyze, and display their data in order to be manageable and meaningful to them and to the recipients of their research reports. First, they usually sort their data using a kind of coding system, such as those used in content analysis (see chapter 7). Then they give some order to the data within each category by displaying them in a list, or on a diagram, chart, or matrix. These data configurations help illuminate underlying patterns (Hammersley, 1989).

The concern of ethnographers is to move gradually and cautiously from their raw data to develop categories of data, then relationships within and between those categories before developing *working hypotheses* and, ultimately, theories about communication phenomena to offer for follow-up research that uses more controlled methods. (This sequence reverses the order most researchers follow—they start with theory and hypotheses and then seek data to test them.) In other words, ethnographers seek to develop *grounded theory*, or theory that emerges from data, rather than speculating about theory and then applying it to data (Strauss & Corbin, 1990). Consequently, ethnographers interpret their data more creatively than other kinds of researchers since, to a greater extent, they select the data they will record and their modes of analysis *after* they start their investigation. In this way, they operate more like investigative reporters (Fetterman, 1990) than technicians simply carrying out a detailed, preordained research plan.

Ethnographers also usually do not report their findings in the same dry, quantitative, terse format found in most other studies. They function as intermediaries, or translators, between their subjects and their readers, and often use a variety of reporting strategies to provide vivid portraits of what they learned. Ethnographers must be both scientists and storytellers. Their results are usually expressed as *thick descriptions* of the phenomena studied. They often include information about what *individuals* said or did in specific situations, rather than aggregating the behavior of all the subjects, as other researchers do. They may describe in vivid detail the *setting* in which the interactions occurred and provide *verbatim examples* to illustrate the *communication patterns* being reported, if that enables the readers to perceive the communication phenomena being described as the participants perceive it (Wolcott, 1990).

Ethnographers also often express the patterns they discover using literary figures of speech, such as metaphors. Miles and Huberman (1984), for example, describe the interactions in a remedial learning room of a school they studied as an "oasis" for the pupils sent there for part of each day. This metaphor communicates, more vividly than paragraphs of academic jargon that, for these students, the larger school is a dry, harsh environment (like a desert) and in that room they obtain rest and sustenance (caring and learning).

Ethnographic reports that convey the full sense of what is being described are what Van Maanen (1988) calls "realist tales." Sometimes ethnographers violate a norm that prevails in most other research by describing in the first person their own data-gathering experiences. Van Maanen calls these personal accounts of the research process "confessional tales."

In conclusion, ethnography is a distinct methodology for studying communication. Practitioners and lay readers can use ethnographic research reports to gain vivid and insightful accounts of communication in the contexts that interest them, and researchers can look to them for explanations of their previous findings and for hypotheses to test later on in more controlled investigations.

Chapter 9

Ethnographic Observational Research

INTRODUCTION TO THE METHOD

Observing, then recording and analyzing, people's communication behavior is a common research procedure. Ethnographic observation is the
primary tool some researchers use when the communication behavior they
wish to study is embedded in a particular social context. For example, if the
interaction of interest is among children at play, workers in a factory, or
governmental bodies making decisions, researchers go to those settings and
observe what takes place there. Craig and Metze (1986) explain that in
ethnographic observation, "Research participants are observed as they behave in real-life situations. The researcher does not actively interfere (that
is, manipulate independent variables), but rather observes the behaviors as
they occur and records observations as unobtrusively as possible" (p. 164).
Because the research is conducted on-site, this work is called **field research.**

The most common goal of ethnographic observers is to describe
situation-specific conventions of conduct—learning what people commonly
do in particular settings. An example might be how politicians answer
questions during press conferences. They cannot learn from such observations how politicians talk in other settings; they obviously are not as formal
or guarded when speaking with their friends and family. But from these
limited data they can infer norms for "press conference talk."

Researchers also may use ethnographic observation as a primary research tool to infer from a specific context something more *universal* about
communication behavior. For example, they may choose to observe how

children in a playground argue while playing games to discover the kinds of moral principles children use to reason about all kinds of events. The researchers, in this case, are seeking general information about how children justify their actions, not about their situation-specific ("playground talk") patterns of behavior. They use the playground as an observational setting because they are likely to overhear children arguing there—more likely than they would in the classroom or other settings.

Strengths and Limitations of Ethnographic Observation

The main strength of ethnographic observational research lies in its "realism." Communication events are recorded as naturally as possible—as they would occur if no researcher were present. Subjects are either unaware of the observers' presence, or are so attentive to what they themselves are doing that they ignore the researchers' activities. Ideally the data analyzed are unblemished "slices of life."

Ethnographic observers can gather data unavailable to interviewers. They can use observations to study communication processes people *cannot* talk about, usually because the subjects perform those behaviors unconsciously or can't remember everything they did during a particular situation. Observation is also preferable when dealing with behavior people *will not* talk about, such as communication processes that might be embarrassing or socially unacceptable to the people being observed. For example, Miller (1987) wanted to study what family therapists do during their treatment sessions with clients. He observed more than 300 therapy sessions through a one-way mirror over the course of a year. From these observations, he learned some things the therapists said that they themselves were not aware of, some they did not remember saying, and some they probably would have hesitated to reveal in an interview.

The realism that gives ethnographic observation an advantage over other forms of research also accounts for its limitations. The difficulties of conducting detailed observations require that researchers work in only a few settings. Therefore, ethnographic observational studies lack the generalizability that survey research affords. Also, since observations are usually conducted in the field, where many factors influence whatever occurs, the control provided by experimental research is lost. One does not know, for example, whether conclusions based on observations of bank managers in a small town are explained by variables not observed by the researcher (such as bank policies reached in private meetings, past experiences with particular customers, or federal regulations). It is also uncertain whether they are equally applicable to bankers in large cities or to other managers in small town businesses—or, for that matter, to people anywhere else or in any business other than the one observed. External validity or generalizability to other settings—called "transferability" by Lincoln and Guba (1985)—is provided by readers familiar with those other settings.

The Observer's Role

Ethnographers must decide the position from which they can best observe the communication behavior they are studying. Their role can range from being a **complete observer,** a detached and uninvolved onlooker, to being an active or **complete participant** in the process they are observing (Gold, 1970). For example, Babrow (1990) chose to be a complete observer in studying how people react to television soap operas. As part of his investigation, he spent 20 hours over the course of an academic year in two bars observing students as they watched soap operas together between the hours of noon and two P.M. (mostly "All My Children" and "One Life to Live"). From noticing their behavior and overhearing their conversations, he learned how they view soap operas and their characters. Rose (1987), on the other hand, became a complete participant to study social relations in an urban ghetto. He lived for two years in a south Philadelphia neighborhood, took a job at an automobile repair shop, rented an apartment, and tried to become part of that community. Most ethnographers, however, fulfill both roles by being **participant observers.** Smith (1990), for example, studied organizational change by being a participant observer in two week-long training seminars for bank employees. She participated in seminar activities and mingled with the managers involved while she observed and took notes on their reactions to the changes being advocated.

A controversial aspect of ethnographic observation is how researchers relate to the subjects of their study. Some approach subjects *overtly* and are frank and informative about their research intentions. Others are *covert*— the subjects are unaware of the observers' research activities. In the studies just mentioned, Smith conducted **overt observations**—the trainers and the participants at the seminars she attended knew that she was on the staff of the University of California and studying the response of middle managers to corporate change. Babrow and Rose, however, conducted **covert observations.** They did not inform the people they observed of their academic endeavors or affiliations. The latter approach raises ethical questions, since ideally people should not be studied without their knowledge or agreement. However, these researchers thought that announcing their purposes would have caused their subjects to alter their behavior.

Observational Settings

Ethnographic observational research is often used to learn about behavior in important contexts to which most people have no access. Examples might be how Russian and American representatives negotiate during disarmament talks, how drug dealers talk children into using narcotics, or how ghostwriters collaborate with political candidates to prepare their speeches. Observers act as our emissaries, bringing back reports of important social interactions we wish to understand better, but would have difficulty observing firsthand.

Some researchers, on the other hand, observe everyday events to which we all have access. Their contribution is analyzing what they observe more carefully than we usually do to detect subtle behavioral patterns that are not readily apparent. We can watch people do something for a long time and still find it difficult to infer the "rules" that guide their behavior. People may hear countless speeches or read newspapers for years, for example, and still not be able to describe basic strategies for public speaking or writing newspaper articles. Even the people carrying out those behaviors—the public speakers and reporters themselves—would be hard-pressed to put into words the guidelines they follow. So observers often record readily observed events, subject their data to careful scrutiny, and then infer otherwise unnoticed consistencies that underlie most of those events.

Coding Ethnographic Observations

Ethnographic researchers, like survey interviewers, usually proceed from the general to the specific. They begin with what Werner and Schoepfle (1987) call *descriptive observation,* which involves impressionistic scanning or a "shotgun approach" to the situation and its components: the physical setting, the key people involved, the events in which they participate, and the ways they divide themselves into subgroups. They then move on to *focused observation,* in which they note the specific communication activities of the people, and they conclude with *selective observation,* in which they note particular attributes or characteristics of those activities. They often attempt to identify connections between the general and specific elements of situations, such as how particular communication behaviors influence the nature and outcomes of significant social phenomena.

For example, Yount (1991) studied how female coal miners deal with sexual harassment and how their responses influence their success in that traditionally male role. She lived for five months in mining communities and observed work procedures and interactions in mines and in informal social gatherings. First she generally described these milieus and then the types of harassment episodes she observed. She focused in further on the women's responses to them, and identified three types of female miners: "ladies" (who sought to cast men into roles as "gentlemen" and withdrew socially when they encountered offensive behavior); "flirts" (who acted seductively and interpreted come-ons as flattery); and "tomboys" (who emphasized their identity as miners, interpreted sexual razzing as friendly, inclusionary treatment, and reciprocated in kind). She connected these response patterns to the women's (and their male cohorts') attitudes, career tenure, and advancement in that work setting.

Like Yount, ethnographers sort what they observe into categories, so they can analyze and explain what occurred. Sometimes, they develop categories *inductively,* as she did. When observing, they simply record what is said and done. Only later do they divide those observations into categories and then use their category system to infer patterns regarding how people communicate in that setting. They also consider what those people could have said, but did not—that is, they identify categories of communication behavior that were avoided.

We all use this "research method" intuitively in our own everyday lives when we enter a social context for the first time, such as a new store, a formal dinner party, or a different house of worship. We look around at what everyone else is doing to learn what people are "supposed to do" in that setting, as well as what seems "out of place." We gradually pick up the implicit conventions ("scripts," "rules," or "codes of conduct" as communication patterns are sometimes called) that insiders apply when dealing with each other.

In other studies, observers *deductively* sort what people say into an *already established* set of categories. Say they want to study whether managers in for-profit organizations conduct decision-making meetings differently than managers in nonprofit organizations. They might hypothesize in advance what those differences are likely to be, create categories for coding comments made in such meetings, observe a sample of meetings in both kinds of organizations, tally their data, and then compare the organizations in terms of how often each type of statement is made. Or, if researchers want to compare the content of television programs on cable and free channels, they also might create, in advance, categories to guide their observations.

Sometimes, simply categorizing and describing the phenomena they study are the ultimate objectives of ethnographic observers. Often, however, they go further and *interpret* their data, suggesting new perspectives with which to view them. For example, Turner and Saunders (1990) conducted a one-year participant observer study of two Gamblers Anonymous groups. Over the course of their regular attendance at these groups, they noticed how forcefully the group imposed a "medical model" on members' thinking about gambling—how the group convinced them to accept a "gambling disease" diagnosis and pressured them to achieve a "new self"— a different view of the group than it publicly acknowledges.

To be sure their descriptions and interpretations are correct, ethnographic observers often operate in teams, thereby allowing them to confer about and/or measure interobserver reliability. To improve validity, they also compare what they learn from observation with data gathered by other means, such as documents and interviews. Wharton (1991), for instance, studied how adult women volunteers defined their role in a program that pairs them with teenage mothers to provide child-care guidance. She gathered most of her data by acting as a complete participant, that is, she was matched with a pregnant teenager for a year. But she also interviewed a number of the other volunteers in the program to compare her observations with theirs. Finally, she directed independent study projects for three students, each of whom spent six months as a volunteer in the program and kept detailed journals of their experiences. She incorporated data from these journals in reaching and checking out her own conclusions.

Finally, ethnographic observers occasionally check their findings with the people they observe. In fact, Werner and Schoepfle (1987) state emphatically that, "All ethnographers' observations *must* be submitted to comments by the natives [or subjects]" (p. 260). Sometimes researchers test their inferences with members of the groups they study other than their own particular subjects. Williams (1989), for example, studied gender differences at work by observing (among other groups) male nurses interacting with their female co-workers. In reporting her research to a chapter of the AAMN (American Assembly of Men in Nursing) she stated, "I got further insight into many issues from the thoughtful comments of those who attended my presentation" (p. 147).

QUESTIONS FOR EXAMINING ETHNOGRAPHIC OBSERVATIONAL RESEARCH

Clearly, ethnographic observational research involves many choices and opens up many possibilities. Therefore, readers must keep a number of issues in mind when they read and judge the quality of particular studies. In addition to the general questions about research, keep these questions in mind when reading the following study, or any other ethnography based on observational research:

A. *The Method*

1. What justified observation as an *appropriate method* to use? Would an experiment, survey, or textual analysis have been better suited to answering the research questions?

2. Were the observations conducted *on-site,* where people are communicating *naturally,* as they would if they weren't involved in a research project? Could a more naturalistic context have been observed?

3. Was the site observed a good *example of its general type*? Would more sites have been preferable? If several were observed, did they represent a good mix of the type being studied?

4. Was sufficient *time* spent observing? Were a sufficient *variety of events* observed during that time? Did the events observed include all that were relevant to the communication process being studied, or should other events have been observed, too?

B. *The Observer's Role*

1. Was the ethnographer's choice to be an *onlooker* or a *participant* in the situation during the observational period appropriate? What was gained or lost by that choice?

2. Were the subjects *aware* they were being observed, or was the observation done *covertly*? If the researcher was *overt,* do you think that awareness influenced the subjects' behavior? If *covert,* do you believe that stretching of research ethics was justified?

3. Was the *observer(s)* qualified (by training or experience) to notice all the salient elements in the phenomenon being investigated?

4. Was *reactivity* minimized? Was the observer's behavior obtrusive; did the process of observing influence what the subjects did?

C. *Observational Coding*

1. Was the observation guided by *pre-established categories,* or was the category system created *inductively* by the observer as the study progressed? Do you believe the categories fit the data and the system as a whole was comprehensive?

2. Were the *categories* used *defined* precisely, so there was minimal ambiguity regarding whether a behavior belonged in one category or another?

3. Did the observers *exhaustively record* all the communication behavior related to the research questions, not omitting an important type of message, such as nonverbal actions?

4. Did the observers record the target communication behavior in *sufficient detail* so important distinctions were not glossed over?

5. Did the observers record the behavior of *all the key players* in the social situation, not omitting anyone who was influential?

6. Did the observers record *what occurred before and what occurred after* the target behaviors, so behaviors linked together were not separated artificially?

7. Did the observers record the communication behavior *impartially,* instead of bringing assumptions to bear that distorted the phenomena in terms of their own preconceptions?

D. Drawing Conclusions

1. Were the observational data "reduced" or *synthesized* and *reported* appropriately, so you believe the conclusions reflect what actually occurred?

2. Were the observations *reliable?* Would observations made at another time show similar patterns of behavior? If an observation team was used, were the observers' reports sufficiently consistent with each other? If differences exist, were they resolved in a way that increases observational accuracy? If there was only one observer, did that individual report efforts to check the reliability of his or her findings through multiple observations over a period of time?

3. Are the observations *valid?* Do you believe the data reflect accurately the communication that occurred? What procedures were used to assess and increase validity? For example, were two or more means for measuring the phenomena compared (triangulation), and were their outcomes consistent?

4. Were any *interpretations* made based upon the observational data? Are they compelling—do they appear to fully contain and explain the data? Or do they seem imposed upon the data to justify a conclusion reached beforehand? Are any of them surprising or counterintuitive? Do they present a new way of looking at a familiar problem?

5. Are *working hypotheses* or *grounded theory* proposed that explain concisely underlying patterns of communication behavior in this setting and that may be tested in subsequent research?

6. Are the findings described in *sufficiently rich and vivid detail* (a "thick description") so the reader may visualize the communication behavior observed and the context in which it occurred?

THE ILLUSTRATIVE STUDY

The authors of the study you will read observed the arguments made by plaintiffs and defendants in a small claims court, a setting much like the one depicted on the television show "People's Court," presided over by Judge Wapner.

The law court is a setting with distinctive rules for argumentation. Lawyers' statements are constrained by long-established customs and legal requirements. (Violations of these rules usually generate an immediate and vociferous, "Your honor, I object!") Yet even courtrooms may be subdivided further into several discrete contexts, from the Supreme Court to small claims court, in which different kinds of legal arguments are appropriate.

The litigants in small claims court do not have lawyers. They plead their own cases, and most are unfamiliar with the formal "rules" of legal conduct. Their behavior is guided, instead, by a combination of two ingredients: 1) the kinds of argument they are accustomed to using in everyday conversation, as influenced by 2) their rudimentary knowledge of courtroom communication procedures (probably gained from watching television shows, reading mystery novels, or prior participation in a trial as a juror, witness, or litigant).

In small claims court, therefore, litigants do not talk as they do at home, nor do they talk like lawyers. Instead, they combine these two forms of discourse. This combination produces a unique form of "conversational" or "quasi-legal" argument in the small claims court that the authors observed and attempt to describe in this article.

Arguing for Justice: An Analysis of Arguing in Small Claims Court

Thomas A. Hollihan

Patricia Riley

Keith Freadhoff

1   In an attempt to account for differences in the "form and merit" of
    successful arguments, Toulmin (1958, p. 15) suggests that scholars
    focus on "fields" of argument. Although exactly what constitutes a
    field, or how this principle should be utilized is a source of some
5   dispute, the notion of fields is relatively simple and compelling: uni-
    versal standards cannot explain all successful argumentation or argu-
    ment types because certain concepts are field-dependent (Toulmin,
    1958; Toulmin, 1972; Willard, 1981). In describing the development
    of "concepts," Toulmin (1972) relates the notion of field to that of
10 "rational enterprise." From this perspective, a field is "a community

Source: Hollihan, T. A., Riley, P., & Freadhoff, K. (1986). Arguing for justice: An analysis of arguing in small claims court. *Journal of the American Forensic Association, 22,* 187–195. Reprinted by permission of the American Forensic Association.

Mr. Hollihan and Ms. Riley are Assistant Professors, and Mr. Freadhoff is a doctoral candidate, in the Department of Communication Arts and Sciences, University of Southern California. An earlier version of this paper was presented at the meeting of the Speech Communication Association in Chicago, November 1984.

united by concept-use, by the creation, use, testing, modification, and abandonment of concepts, which are the products of human understanding" (Miller, 1983, p. 148).

Although disagreements regarding the specific nature of fields are numerous (e.g. Rowland, 1982; Wenzel, 1982; Zarefsky, 1981), the "collective concept-use" perspective defined above is important because it represents enacted social rules and contextual sense-making. From this vantage point, fields are conceptualized as institutions that are created and recreated through the application of their members' social knowledge. Willard (1982, p. 28), for instance, refers to fields as "a constellation of practices organized around one or a few dominant assumptions." He further notes that fields can be considered "special understandings created for particular interactions" (Willard, 1982, p. 30). This description of fields is similar to Kuhn's notion of paradigms (disciplinary matrices), where the use of particular scientific concepts marks the scientist as a member of a specific community, and the community is determined concurrently by the sharing and practice of these concepts (Kuhn, 1962).

Religion, science, art, and politics have been suggested as fields, but the most confident designation has been bestowed on law, perhaps because it is one of the most highly rule-oriented human endeavors (Sheppard & Rieke, 1983). The legal field also interests scholars because it is "value-laden, socially adaptive, and heavily reliant on rhetoric" (Makau, 1984, p. 380). The law, however, is not a singular argument field. In fact, many different settings for the generation of legal arguments exist, including quasi-legal negotiation settings, civil hearings, criminal proceedings, appellate proceedings, and small claims court actions. On closer examination, one might discover an "underlying thread that holds together the field of legal reasoning, but they must all be examined before that can be found" (Rieke, 1981, p. 154).

Most argumentation research in legal settings has centered on the development of such rules as, "What may be disputed by whom, when, how, where, and to what end" (Gronbeck, 1981, p. 15). These rules are determined partially by formal declaration, via statutes or precedents, and they are also determined by the practices of the participants in the legal dialogue. In this sense, the rules are shaped by the social knowledge of the participants—by their conceptions of the symbolic relationships among problems, persons, interests, and actions, which imply certain notions of preferable public behavior (Farrell, 1976). This social knowledge is assumed to be shared by the participants in the legal field; presumably, these persons will regularly respond to problems in a similar fashion (Farrell, 1976). The social knowledge generated within the legal field embodies long established customs, traditions, and requirements for the arguers who wish to use

55   these forums to resolve their problems, and it implies a set of decision making tools developed for use in this field (Goodnight, 1982).

The relationship between social knowledge and the rules of the legal system can be effectively explicated by the theory of structuration. From this perspective, systems of deeply-layered structures form

60   the framework—the institution—of the legal field. Concurrently, people draw on stores of knowledge to create and recreate the patterns of interaction that constitute the institution (Giddens, 1979).

Structures are the rules and resources people use in interaction, and they are analyzed as dualities: they are both the medium and the outcome of interaction. They are

65   *the medium, because structures provide the rules and resources individuals must draw on to interact meaningfully. They are its outcome because rules and resources exist only through being applied and acknowledged in interaction—they have no reality independent of the social practices they constitute (Riley, 1983, p. 415).*

Thus legal concepts and practices are institutionalized structures

70   that are continually being recreated and legitimized by their use (Giddens, 1979).

The "speech community" of the legal field is constituted by those individuals who carry and create the structures that recursively organize the social system of law. The structurationist perspective has pre-

75   viously been used to study arguments in small group settings, and the authors concluded that "arguments [are] reexpressed and transformed through the stream of interaction in the service of interpersonal influence and group decisioning" (Siebold, McPhee, Poole, Tanita, and Canary, 1981, p. 684).

80   The legal field, as a social system, does not exist in isolation. In a number of circumstances, members of the legal field interact with individuals (laypersons) whose communication is not generated by the same rules. According to structuration theory, the structuring processes interpenetrate to create new patterns of interaction and new

85   institutional patterns (Poole, Siebold & McPhee, 1985).

The litigants who enter the small claims courtroom are given little or no real guidance by the court, and they must rely upon their own wits and judgment regarding the kind of appeals which will likely produce a ruling in their behalf (Purdum, 1981). Lacking training in

90   the law, they enter the highly formalized legal argument field with only their social knowledge of the function, purpose, and traditions of the legal field to guide them in constructing their arguments. Structuration thus allows researchers to focus on a unique feature of the small claims format—an arena where the legal profession meets the

95   untrained advocate. The resulting interactions become a form of

"conversational argument" that is mediated by its context and transformed into "quasi-legal" argument."

THE SMALL CLAIMS COURT AS AN ARGUMENT FIELD

The small claims court was established in response to the need for the
100 speedy, inexpensive and informal disposal of cases involving small
dollar amounts. The earliest forum of this type was in London in
1606, but the small claims concept was not tried in the United States
until 1913 (Stauber, 1980). While small claims courts were intended to
provide a forum where ordinary citizens could have access to the
105 courts for settling their disputes, studies consistently demonstrate that
more than half of small claims filers are not individuals but government entities or companies. Indeed, some have claimed that the small
claims process has become a "judicial collection agency" (Stauber,
1980, p. 130; Goodrich, 1983).
110   The assumption behind the small claims process is that individuals do not need attorneys and can plead their own cases. Thus the
limits for claims are intentionally set quite low to discourage attorneys
from taking cases and to protect litigants from themselves. A number
of states forbid litigants from being represented by attorneys (includ-
115 ing California where this research was conducted) unless the other
party in the suit is an attorney (Spurrier, 1970).
The small claims court is intended to be a citizen's forum, and as
a result it is a much less formal courtroom setting. The very infor-
mality of the small claims court process, and the relative inexperience
120 of the litigants, places the judge in a quite different role. The judge is
not a mere umpire in the small claims court, but must actively participate in the hearing process in the pursuit of "truth." The judge thus
represents both parties, and the law (Purdum, 1981).
Despite the unique nature of the small claims court process, it
125 has received little attention from researchers. Several studies have
investigated the degree to which income and educational factors
hamper litigants—particularly when they are called upon to defend
themselves against businesses—and have concluded that the low income litigant is indeed at a great disadvantage (Pagter, McCloskey and
130 Reinis, 1964; Moulton, 1969; Kronheim, 1951). Still other research
concludes that an experienced plaintiff (someone who has argued a
case in small claims before) has a much better probability of winning a
claim against an inexperienced defendant (Hollingsworth, Feldman
and Clark, 1973). There is a distinct lack of research in small claims
135 court advocacy, however, and what exists is criticized for relying on
court records as opposed to actual observations of the procedures
(Yngvesson and Hennesey, 1975).

Despite the unique nature of the small claims court as a setting where natural argument users are thrust into a formalized rule-governed setting, past research has not systematically examined either the arguments produced by these litigants, or the small claims courtroom as an argument setting. The theory of structuration allows researchers to analyze actual arguments and investigate both the transformation of social knowledge via its interpenetration with institutional structures and the effectiveness of strategies in this setting.

Since the small claims court litigants are untrained advocates, discourse is generated by the rules that underlie conversational argument and simultaneously constrained by the rules that produce more formal arguments in the legal field. In the production of quasi-legal arguments, individuals likely will rely on strategies utilized in less formal conversational discourse since structuration theory posits a bias for "what has come before." Examples of such conversational strategies include: excuses, justification, refusals, etc. (McLaughlin, Cody & O'Hair, 1983). These discourse practices are the enactment of stores of knowledge strategically drawn upon by individuals to achieve their goals.

Argumentation theory holds that better decisions are reached once advocates learn to argue in accordance with the rules of a given field (Toulmin, 1958; 1972). Likewise, a major principle of our judicial system is that the best arguments win adherence and that legal disputes are resolved by engaging in forensic disputations. The criteria for weighing arguments include an evaluation of an advocate's analysis, use of evidence, refutation, etc. While these elements of effective argument have been analyzed in other fields, the nature of arguments in the unique context of the small claims court is unknown.

In order to gain further insight into small claims court as a field, the following research questions were developed:

1. What features characterize the arguments used by small claims advocates?

2. What rules are drawn upon by litigants in creating their strategies?

3. What strategies/arguments are the most successful?

4. What is the influence of prior small claims court experience on the choice of arguments?

METHOD

Three observers were permitted to view small claims court trials from the jury box of a suburban Los Angeles County courtroom. Court

cases were scheduled Monday through Thursday with the majority of
the week's cases scheduled on Mondays. Each day was observed twice
except Thursday (no cases were scheduled the second Thursday). A
180   total of eighty-one cases were tried before three different judges.
Thirty-six of those cases were contested. Since only the contested
cases involved arguments from both plaintiffs and defendants, they
became the sample for this study.

The researchers were permitted to make audio-tapes of the
185   trials but were instructed to be as non-obtrusive as possible. Because
the observations took place from inside the bar, the researchers were
able to hear the arguments being made and to see the expressions on
the faces of the litigants. The researchers took comprehensive written
notes on both the discourse and the major nonverbal behaviors (e.g.,
190   questions that were answered by head movements, extreme facial expressions, and extreme paralinguistic cues). The nonverbal observations were gross measures intended to aid in the categorization of
arguments, and were not considered as separate data. Later the
audio-tapes were used to reconcile the notes of the three observers
195   and to develop argument transcripts (pauses, stutters, vocal fluctua-
tions, etc. were not included). Because these were naturalistic recordings, the audio-tapes were scattered with mumbles, incomplete and
incoherent phrasings, and unintelligible expressions that could not be
transcribed. The researchers operated under the rule that any state-
200   ment they could not agree upon would not be included in the analysis.
The types of evidence introduced into the proceedings were also
noted. Thus, the use of documents, photographs, witnesses, or material objects was recorded.

The researchers were permitted to examine the court records
205   following the disposition of the cases in order to discover the outcome
of the cases which were "taken under submission" with judges notify-
ing the litigants by mail at a later date.

Following the development of argument transcripts, both a
quantitative and a qualitative analysis of the transcripts were con-
210   ducted (preliminary results of the quantitative analysis were reported
in Hollihan, Riley & Freadhoff, 1984). This study reports the results
of the qualitative analysis.

Structuration theory posits that analyzing communication requires an understanding of the context and suggests that interaction
215   research should focus on language-in-use (Giddens, 1979; Riley
1983). Familiarity with small claims court procedures, and actual observation is necessary in such an investigation. This study is analogous
to a "mini-ethnography" (Knapp, 1979) of communication in context
of use.

220 **RESULTS AND DISCUSSION**

Our analysis divides the results into three separate issues. First, we delineate the appeals to "fairness" or "justice," which are common to the argument strategies of both plaintiffs and defendants. Second, we discuss the fact that the dominant mode of argument in the court-
225 room was storytelling. And third, we consider the outcomes of the cases that we observed, relate the judges' decisions, differences in the amount of evidence presented, and make comparisons with the find-ings of past research in the small claims courtroom.

Fairness Themes

230 One of the most interesting findings of this study was that appeals for "fairness" were found in more than half the cases analyzed and were utilized by both plaintiffs and defendants. Most frequently this theme was found in arguments directed to the judge which asked him or her to make a decision which would be "just." The most salient aspect of
235 this theme is that it illustrates the intersection of social knowledge and the legal forum—the litigants were often asking for a ruling that was apart from the law, an area in which they had little knowledge—they wanted justice, which they felt transcended the law.

The appeals to fairness were of several distinct and identifiable
240 types. First, there were appeals for a decision that was fair in an egali-tarian sense. Plaintiffs often declared that they had been wronged by the defendant and that the court should afford them some remedy. They used the small claims court to achieve what they believed was rightfully due them. Defendants also made egalitarian fairness ap-
245 peals, often recalling past associations with the plaintiff which justi-fied their own claim of having been violated. An illustration of this was an electrician who had mistakenly been sent a check for work done by another man with the same name. The defendant cashed the check and refused to return the money to the management company
250 representing the apartment complex. His argument was that the pre-vious management company for the same apartment complex had not paid him full value for past work that he had performed. That this check was for another electrician was irrelevant. He was owed the money, and he was only acting in the interest of what was fair. The
255 electrician was very unhappy when the judge explained that just be-cause someone else owed him money, that was not a valid reason for him to keep *this* plaintiff's money. This example demonstrates that the social sense of fairness was guiding the arguments presented, not the rules governing the legal forum.
260 A second strategy for appealing for a fair decision was to argue

that a determination of their opponent's "motive" was crucial to the just dispensation of the case. Defendants often used this strategy to establish that the plaintiffs brought their cases to court merely to seek revenge for past small claims court judgments which were decided
265   against them, or for malicious reasons. Arguments attacking the plaintiff's motives were frequently part of long diatribes which sought to undermine the credibility of the plaintiff. Plaintiffs primarily used this strategy to build up their own credibility and establish positive motives of their own, not to attack the motives of their opponents.
270   Judges usually were not very interested in hearing about motives and sometimes cut off litigants' arguments on this theme by stating that such suspicions or statements were not relevant to the facts of the case. Many citizens persisted with this strategy. They protested that such information *was* crucial to their case. An obvious explanation for
275   the litigants drawing on this strategy is a rule that motives and witness credibility are key aspects of trials—a "Perry Mason" view of the law held by those possessing social knowledge, but lacking understanding of the legal field.

A third, and somewhat different, type of appeal to fairness was
280   noted in the arguments developed by several of the plaintiffs who seemed to be familiar with the small claims court process, and who used the system fairly often (one landlord was observed in court on three different occasions). These plaintiffs avoided saying anything even vaguely negative about the defendants; in fact, they often tried
285   to say something positive. In these instances their social knowledge apparently incorporated as a "rule" the experience that positive arguments are the most successful and that plaintiffs, particularly when suing poor, uneducated, or minority defendants (as was often the case) had nothing to gain by being hostile or vindictive. This strategy
290   also may be future oriented—they may overemphasize positive issues (in comparison to other plaintiffs) in order not to "wear out their welcome" with a particular judge. In addition, judges may have a bias for structures that have previously been utilized.

A fourth strategy used to argue fairness was produced by defen-
295   dants who offered no real defense. They frequently admitted their responsibility for the plaintiff's claim, and indicated that they had offered to fix or remedy what went wrong, and/or made an excuse about why they had not resolved the dispute without going to court. Defendants thought they should have the right to "fix" the problem
300   via means of their choice and that court action should not be necessary. That this interpretation of "what was fair" was not the law proved disconcerting to numerous defendants.

The fifth, and final, strategy for appealing to fairness was used by defendants who simply threw themselves on the mercy of the

305   court. These defendants usually acknowledged that they should have
      to pay a settlement to the plaintiff, but offered excuses about their
      limited financial status which prevented them from making restitu-
      tion. The judge always found for the plaintiffs in these cases and
      instructed the parties in the lawsuit to work out a payment plan.
310   Several of the observed cases were back in court because the defen-
      dant had not kept up with the payment schedule or because the
      litigants could not negotiate how much the payment should be. An
      implicit rule seemed to be operating in the social knowledge of these
      defendants that circumstances beyond their control should mitigate
315   some or all of their responsibility. From this perspective, this social
      norm legitimated their inaction.
           Although the litigants seemed to understand that judges would
      apply the rules of the legal system in adjudicating their cases, their
      social knowledge that judges are "reasonable" people who can reject
320   "unjust" applications of the law seemed to guide them. This concep-
      tion of the legal field as ultimately grounded in justice reproduces
      arguments of fairness and legitimates their "justified" behaviors. Such
      arguments ask the judge to use his or her authority to mitigate the
      rules of the system; the power (domination) of the court should not
325   apply to their particular circumstances.

Storytelling

      Another interesting finding that emerged from our observation of
      these proceedings was that the small claims courtroom was a setting
      for storytelling. Both plaintiffs and defendants described their cases
330   by "telling their story." In almost every instance, the litigants pro-
      ceeded through their stories chronologically, and often provided a
      great deal of background information which may not have been ger-
      mane to their specific case but which helped make their stories more
      vivid or understandable.
335   The judge was a willing participant in this storytelling process.
      In fact, judges would often turn to either the plaintiff or the defen-
      dant and say, "tell me your story." In addition, the judges seldom
      interrupted the litigant's stories, instead, they listened patiently and
      sometimes permitted the litigants to embellish their stories with extra
340   details. While many of these stories appeared quite disjointed and
      confusing to the observers, the judges followed them without diffi-
      culty. While this can partially be accounted for by the fact that the
      judges had prior access to the written documents regarding the case,
      they apparently are accustomed to listening to rambling stories. The
345   judges seem to have developed trained capacities for sorting through
      the confusing details and providing their own structure to the argu-

ments. Thus the interpenetration of natural argument—the narrative—and the legal forum transforms the act of relating facts to the process of telling and listening to stories as a means of reconstructing
350 the legal forum. This method of argument is particularly crucial given the advocates' lack of formal training. In this manner, they can draw on a mode of signification, a natural conversational tool, as a resource in explaining their case while simultaneously reproducing the structure of storytelling as a legitimate form of explana-
355 tion/argument in the legal field.

The dominance of storytelling in the courtroom confirmed the findings of Bennett and Feldman (1981), who have argued that stories are very important to the legal process and that "adjudicators judge the plausibility of a story according to certain structural relations
360 among symbols in the story. . . . Stories are judged in terms of a combination of the documentary or 'empirical' warrants for symbols and the internal structural relations among the collections of symbols presented in the stories" (p. 33). Since few plaintiffs use evidence to support their claims—and virtually no defendants use evidence—the
365 stories have to stand on their own merits. Also, given that these arguments occurred in a legal arena, the fact that very few references are made to laws or legal procedures confirms a social knowledge construction of the field by the participants.

The preponderance of storytelling in the courtroom is also con-
370 sistent with Fisher's (1984) conclusion that "good reasons are the stuff of stories, the means by which humans realize their nature as reasoning-valuing animals" (p. 8).

Outcomes

An examination of court documents revealed that all but two of the
375 thirty-six contested cases in our sample were won by the plaintiff. As a consequence, an extensive discussion of the differences in argument strategies employed by winning and losing plaintiffs or defendants is not warranted. The outcomes of these trials are not totally surprising, however, as it was previously mentioned that plaintiffs tend to do
380 much better in small claims courts than do defendants. This is consistent with other research into small claims courts (Yngvesson & Hennessey, 1975).

The preponderance of plaintiff victories may be at least partially accounted for by the differences in the rate of evidence usage, with
385 plaintiffs using seven times as much evidence (pictures, documents, legal precedents, etc.) as the defendants. While there was no appreciable difference in the number of witnesses brought to court, or the number of questions asked, the disparity in the use of evidence clearly

390 favored the plaintiff's cases and enhanced the credibility of their stories.

While the high rate of plaintiff victories might be understandable, however, what was truly remarkable in our sample was that out of thirty-six contested cases, the only two which the defendants won were cases where the plaintiffs appeared emotionally unbalanced.
395 (The researchers are not psychologists; this is a lay impression.) In one of the two cases, a woman in her eighties sued her next door neighbors for damage to a fence around her property. Once the judge began to ask her questions about her claims he discovered that the woman had been living in a nursing home for the past year, only
400 visited her home once a month, and had become deeply distressed about the condition of her home when she had last visited it. Still more probing questions revealed that the fence she claimed these neighbors had damaged had been damaged years earlier when a gardener she had hired cut a tree down and allowed it to fall on her
405 fence. The woman, apparently, was no longer able to function on her own and the judge found for the defendants. The second case involved a young woman who had her car repossessed after she went to the dealer and threatened to blow it up because it was not working correctly. The finance company had decided that their secured prop-
410 erty was at risk and had picked up the car. The defendant in this case, the car dealer, explained to the judge that he had sought to honor the terms of his warranty and thus could not be faulted. The judge agreed. Obviously, the ability of these litigants to construct stories via the application of social rules and norms was impaired.

415 **CONCLUSION**

This research has been exploratory, and represents an initial step into the small claims courtroom. It does suggest, however, that this is a unique field for arguments because of the messages used by untrained conversational arguers in a rule governed and rule dominated
420 argument field. Future research should attempt to account for the strategic choices employed by these litigants, and should analyze the patterns of the messages to better understand the interpenetration of the fields. For example, follow-up studies which compare these argument strategies to those employed in other argument settings would
425 prove especially useful.

The resources which these advocates took with them into the courtroom varied greatly, but primarily they depended upon their skills as storytellers and their ability to create a story which would be believable to the judge.

430   The small claims court setting also made unique demands upon the judges. Specifically, the judges had to have a highly developed sense for the structures of "narrative probability"—what constitutes a coherent story—and "narrative fidelity"—whether the stories they hear ring true with stories they know to be true in their lives (Fisher, 435 p. 8). Since plaintiffs often came to court with minimal evidence, and defendants with almost none, the judges had to be attuned to the structure of the stories themselves. Furthermore, since neither the plaintiffs nor the defendants used much analysis or spent much time directly refuting their opponents' arguments, judges obviously had to 440 apply normative standards to evaluate the stories—legal rules transformed into guidelines for evaluating stories.

     Small claims court is an often confusing melange of diatribes, out-of-focus pictures, and responses of incredulity from the judge. The structuring patterns are continuously recreated primarily be- 445 cause the experience of "taking someone to court" seems to fulfill many plaintiffs' sense of justice, regardless of whether they ever collect on the judgments they win.

REFERENCES

Bennett, W. L. & Feldman, M. S. (1981). *Reconstructing reality in the courtroom.* New Brunswick, NJ: Rutgers University Press.

Farrell, T. B. (1976). Knowledge, consensus, and rhetorical theory. *Quarterly Journal of Speech, 62,* 1–14.

Fisher, W. R. (1984). Narration as a human communication paradigm: The case of public moral argument. *Communication Monographs, 51,* 1–22.

Giddens, A. (1979). *Central problems in social theory.* Berkeley: University of California Press.

Goodnight, G. T. (1982). The personal, technical, and public spheres of argument: A speculative inquiry into the art of public deliberation. *Journal of the American Forensic Association, 18,* 214–227.

Goodrich, C. (1983, July). Advising users of small claims court. *California Lawyer,* pp. 43–44.

Gronbeck, B. (1981). Sociocultural notions of argument fields: A primer. In G. Ziegelmueller & J. Rhodes (Eds.), *Dimensions of argument: Proceedings of the second summer conference on argumentation* (pp. 1–20). Annandale, VA: Speech Communication Association.

Hollihan, T. A., Riley, P., & Freadhoff, K. (1984, November). Arguing for justice: A content analysis of arguments made in small claims court. Paper presented at the meeting of the Speech Communication Association, Chicago, IL.

Hollingsworth, E., Feldman, W. B., & Clark, D. C. (1973). The Ohio small claims court: An empirical study. *Cincinnati Law Review, 42,* 469.

Knapp, M. S. (1979). Ethnographic contributions to evaluation research: The experimental schools program evaluation and some alternatives. In T. D. Cook & C. S. Reichardt (Eds.), *Quantitative and qualitative methods-in-evaluation research* (pp. 118–139). Beverly Hills: Sage.

Kronheim, M. S. (1951). Does the small claims branch of our municipal court measure up to the standards of our community? *Journal of the Bar Association of the District of Columbia, 18,* 113.

Kuhn, T. (1961). *The structure of scientific revolutions.* Chicago: University of Chicago Press.

Makau, J. M. (1984). The Supreme Court and reasonableness. *Quarterly Journal of Speech, 70,* 379–96.

McLaughlin, M. L., Cody, M. J., & O'Hair, H. D. (1983). The management of failure events: Some contextual determinants of accounting behavior. *Human Communication Research, 9,* 208–224.

Miller, C. R. (1983). Fields of argument and special topoi. In D. Zarefsky, M. Sillars, & J. Rhodes (Eds.), *Argument in transition: Proceedings of the third summer conference on argumentation* (pp. 147–158). Annandale, VA: Speech Communication Association.

Moulton, B. (1969). The persecution and intimidation of the low income litigant as performed by the small claims court of California. *Stanford Law Review, 21,* 1657.

Pagter, C., McCloskey, R., & Reinis, M. (1964). The California Small Claims Court. *The California Law Review, 52,* 876–898.

Poole, M. S., Siebold, D. R., & McPhee, R. D. (1985). Group decision-making as a structurationist process. *Quarterly Journal of Speech, 71,* 74–102.

Purdum, E. (1981). Examining the claims of a small claims court: A Florida case study. *Judicature, 65,* 25.

Rieke, R. D. (1981). Investigating legal argument as a field. In G. Ziegelmueller & J. Rhodes (Eds.), *Dimensions of argument: Proceedings of the second summer conference on argumentation* (pp. 152–158). Annandale, VA: Speech Communication Association.

Rieke, R. D. (1982). Argumentation in the legal process. In J. R. Cox & C. A. Willard (Eds.), *Advances in argumentation theory and research* (pp. 363–378). Carbondale: Southern Illinois University Press.

Riley, P. (1983). A structurationist account of political culture. *Administrative Science Quarterly, 28,* 414–437.

Riley, P. & Hollihan, T. A. (1981). The 1980 presidential debates: A content analysis of the issues and arguments. *Speaker and Gavel, 18,* 47–59.

Rowland, R. (1982). The influence of purpose on fields of argument. *Journal of the American Forensic Association, 18,* 228–245.

Sheppard, S. & Rieke, R. D. (1983). Categories of reasoning in legal argument. In D. Zaretsky, M. Sillars, & J. Rhodes (Eds.), *Argument in transition: Proceedings of the third summer conference on argumentation* (pp. 235–250). Annandale, VA: Speech Communication Association.

Siebold, D., McPhee, R. D., Poole, M. S., Tanica, N. E., & Canary, D. J. (1981). Argument, group influence, and decision outcomes. In G. Ziegelmueller & J. Rhodes (Eds.), *Dimensions of argument: Proceedings of the second summer conference in argumentation* (pp. 663–692). Annandale, VA: Speech Communication Association.

Spurrier, R. L. (1970). Use of counsel in Oklahoma small claims courts: Judicial perceptions, empirical data, and recommended reforms. *Tulsa Law Journal, 15*, 70–84.

Stauber, A. (1980). Small claims in Florida: An empirical study. *The Florida Bar Journal, 54*, 130-138.

Toulmin, S. (1958). *The uses of argument.* Cambridge: Cambridge University Press.

Toulmin, S. (1972). *Human understanding.* Princeton: Princeton University Press.

Wenzel, J. (1982). On fields of argument as propositional systems. *Journal of the American Forensic Association, 18*, 204–213.

Willard, C. A. (1981). Argument fields and theories of logical types. *Journal of the American Forensic Association, 17*, 129–145.

Willard, C. A. (1982). Argument fields. In J. R. Cox and C. A. Willard (Eds.), *Advances in argumentation theory and research* (pp. 24–77). Carbondale: Southern Illinois University Press.

Yngvesson, B. & Hennessey, P. (1975). Small claims, complex disputes: A review of small claims literature. *Law and Society Review, 9*, 219–274.

Zarefsky, D. (1981). Reasonableness in public policy argument: Fields as institutions. In G. Ziegelmueller and J. Rhodes (Eds.), *Dimensions of argument: Proceedings of the second summer conference on argumentation* (pp. 101–113). Annandale, VA: Speech Communication Association.

COMMENTS ON THE STUDY

Introduction, Review of the Literature, and Research Questions

The authors begin this article by explaining the concept of "fields of argument" (1–28). They contend that, "Universal standards cannot explain all successful argumentation or argument types because certain concepts are field-dependent" (5–7). This line of reasoning justifies doing ethnographic observations because an argument persuasive in this setting may be ineffectual in a different setting.

The authors justify their study further by arguing that the field of law is particularly appropriate for studying argumentation (29–34). Of course, it is made up of various subfields (34–40), so they chose just one, the small claims court, to study. They subsequently provide a detailed analysis of the small claims court as an argument field (98–165), which helps the reader understand this unique context.

The authors base their study of field-dependent argumentation on a particular theory, *structuration* (41–97), which claims that, "People draw on stores of knowledge to create and recreate the patterns of interaction that constitute the institution" (61–62). The arguments advanced in small claims courts, therefore, are consistent with what is customary there and thereby maintain the structure of those courts. Structuration theory justifies studying argument structures within particular institutions such as small claims court (142–156). For example, because litigants in small claims courts are advocates untrained and inexperienced in constructing legal arguments, structuration theory suggests they will use "typical" conversational strategies, such as excuses, justifications, and refusals (146–165).

The authors acknowledge, however, that we know little from previous research about the unique nature of the small claims court process or the argumentation that characterizes it (124–142). Further, what research does exist is based on court records, as opposed to actual observation (135–137). Since so little is known, the research inquiries (168–173) ask basic, descriptive questions about the types of arguments advanced in these courts and their relative degrees of success. In all, the authors provide the reader with substantive background information for understanding the goals of this particular study.

Method

The use of ethnographic observation in this study seems justified. The small claims court, in itself, is a worthwhile context for research, since it is a unique and important element in the American legal system. Descriptions of arguments used in small claims court might aid future litigants to advocate their viewpoints more effectively. Moreover, the small claims court is a useful setting for gathering data on how people are likely to defend their viewpoints wherever they may be speaking. From their attempts to persuade the judge to agree with them, the researchers garnered clues as to how people generally think and talk about problematic situations.

The researchers could not have interviewed the litigants or the judges about the nature of the arguments used, since they would not have been able to recall nor articulate them. Also, transcripts of small claims court proceedings are not available for a textual analysis.

Using a research team was helpful. Having three observers present (175) allowed for the oversights or biases of one individual to be recognized and corrected by the others. Observing 36 contested cases over a two-week period (176–183) also seems sufficient for discerning the argument patterns used in the small claims court context. Observations in more than one court location, however, would have enhanced the generalizability of the findings.

The researchers chose a *complete observer* role. This allowed them to observe, record, and take notes on the litigants' behavior unobtrusively (184–188). They might have acted as participant observers, perhaps by having one bring a case against another of them before the court to gain firsthand insight into the experience. However, this would have been an unethical waste of the court's time, may even have been illegal, and might not have added much to their knowledge.

Apparently, they operated *covertly*, not informing the litigants of their research activities. Since they did not mention names in their report, and the subjects would have been in that situation anyway, little harm was done. Had they been overt, their observations might have made the subjects self-conscious and influenced them to argue somewhat differently.

The observers appear quite capable. The three authors, all academic professionals in communication, presumably were the observers in the small claims court. They sat in the jury box facing the litigants (175–176), so they had full access to all their spoken messages. The comprehensiveness of the introduction to this article indicates that the authors were amply qualified to serve as observers—they were obviously familiar with the small claims court context and with a sufficient range of argument patterns to appropriately designate the types used by the people they observed. (They seem more skilled at tracking and identifying types of arguments than stories, however, since they acknowledge that, "While many of these stories appeared quite disjointed and confusing to the observers, the judges followed them without difficulty" [340–342]).

The position of the three observers, seated in the jury box, facing the litigants, and taking "comprehensive written notes" (188–191), may have caused some reactivity, but probably did not cause the litigants to alter their oral performance substantially, since they had so much at stake in the proceedings.

The researchers appear to have created the observational coding categories used for analyzing their data only after collecting them. During the trials, they noted everything said and done by the subjects, not sorting their behavior into categories until after the transcript was complete and checked for accuracy. This enabled them to sort the litigants' arguments into categories that fit them, rather than filing their statements in a system borrowed from, and perhaps better suited to, another context.

The researchers audiotaped the verbal arguments (184–185). Their notes included significant nonverbal acts (188–193) and the use of evidence in the form of "documents, photographs, witnesses, or material objects" (202–203). Using *triangulation*—comparing two data-gathering methods (their notes and the tape recordings), and then synthesizing what was learned from each—helped assure the accuracy and completeness of their data.

On some comments they could not reach consensus, nor could they obtain an accurate taped transcription, so these comments were not included in their analysis (196–200). Although they do not report the proportion of comments to which this problem applied, the thoroughness of their procedures suggests that little was missed.

We also must judge for ourselves how important nonverbal messages were in litigants' arguments. If someone flirted, limped, dressed shabbily, cried, or shook a fist to make a point, that behavior was not considered separately (191–193).

The researchers showed sensitivity to the link between past experience and observed behavior by reporting distinctive comments made by plaintiffs who they knew had appeared in small claims court before (279–293). This facet of their analysis would have been enriched if they had elicited from everyone observed, by interview or questionnaire, what information and experience they already had about the small claims court.

Results and Discussion

The observers provide no record of the raw data from which they drew their conclusions, which is typical in article-length ethnographic research. (Because ethnographers gather so much data, their findings are often reported in unusually lengthy articles, monographs, or books, allowing them to provide "thicker" descriptions than this relatively short piece contains.) They provide a synthesis of the kinds of arguments used (229–325), but no precise tally of how frequently each occurred. They do report that "appeals for 'fairness' were found in more than half the cases analyzed" (230–231). That rough figure still leaves a great many cases unaccounted for (up to 17 out of 36). Appeals to fairness are the only kind of arguments analyzed; while storytelling is analyzed, it is a mode of presentation, not an argument type. What kinds of appeals were used in the remaining cases? Lacking more complete data, the study leaves us unsure of how thoroughly and objectively the authors have paraphrased the litigants' messages (although their "quantitative analysis" paper, referred to [210–211], may provide that information).

The observers mention the interventions of the judges in the court proceedings (335–340), although their instructions, questions, and comments were not analyzed as thoroughly as were the litigants'. Perhaps the judges (or someone else involved in the court system) significantly shaped the litigants' comments before or during the proceedings.

As mentioned, the reliability of the observers' reports was enhanced when they checked their notes with each other and then reconciled them with the audiotaped version of the court proceedings. However, they report omitting from the "argument transcripts" statements on which they disagreed (199–200). These may have been dismissible, but they also might have represented statements not readily categorized, anomalies that should have been included nonetheless.

The authors also do not report how consistently they, as a group, categorized the argument transcripts into the five "fairness" themes identified (if indeed all three participated in this phase of their research). Ideally, each researcher would have first divided the statements into category types independently, and then they all would have met to compare their analyses and to reconcile their differences. (Such independent analysis helps assure that one person's biased viewpoint does not dominate and distort interpretation of the data.)

Weick (1985) states that validity in observational studies, "boils down to a question of credibility. And since credibility is audience specific . . . in the case of an audience of scientists, observers provide evidence that displays their reasoning process including summary statements, supporting and non-supporting anecdotes, and information on the range of variation in the phenomena observed" (p. 604). The researchers report their findings on the whole in a credible fashion. The validity of this study would have been stronger, however, had the researchers checked out their inferences by sharing their findings with the judges (or the litigants) themselves and asking them how accurately and completely they believed the arguments used in court had been categorized. They also might have reported instances of appeals that did not fit neatly into their five "fairness themes" category system.

Despite the aforementioned limitations, the conclusions reached regarding the forms of appeal used by litigants are supported with clear, illustrative examples. Several links are noted between the researchers' findings and those of other investigators (356–372), and these lend credence to their conclusions. These connections seem to have been made after their own conclusions were reached, and seem not to have biased their findings *a priori.*

The validity of their conclusions regarding what strategies and arguments lead to successful outcomes (383–390), however, is questionable. All but two of the 36 contested cases were won by the plaintiff (374–375), and those two losses were dealt to "emotionally unbalanced" individuals (391–414). Indeed, it seems that, in this small claims court, any reasonable story or argument *by a plaintiff* will result in victory.

Yet the authors state that, "The preponderance of plaintiff victories may be at least partially accounted for by the differences in the rate of evidence usage, with plaintiffs using seven times as much evidence (pictures, documents, legal precedents, etc.) as the defendants" (383–386). This conclusion would be more supportable if it were based on a comparison between a reasonable number of successful and unsuccessful plaintiffs, rather than just a comparison of plaintiffs and defendants. We cannot be sure success was due to the use of evidence and not to the role of plaintiff rather than defendant. In fact, attributing victory to evidence is also contradicted by another statement crediting most case outcomes to plausible storytelling: "Since few plaintiffs use evidence to support their claims—and virtually no defendants use evidence—the stories have to stand on their own merits," (363–365).

This study achieves the purposes of ethnographic observational research. Smith (1988) says that, "During the observational stage of inquiry . . . the researcher must discover the meanings communicators have in mind when they talk with others in particular contexts" (p. 9). What people mean by "fairness" and how they articulate it (via stories) in small claims court is made evident. Given the proportion of stories told, future researchers might analyze storytelling in small claims court with the same fine discernment that these authors applied to argumentation. Researchers can also build upon this study by determining whether people use the same five fairness themes and tell stories in other domains of everyday conversational talk when they want to explain why something is "fair" or "unfair," and whether in other legal contexts these fairness themes are included or excluded, as well as their effects on jury decisions.

CONCLUSION

Ethnographic observation is a powerful methodology for studying people's patterns of communication behavior in particular naturalistic settings. Hollihan, Riley, and Freadhoff's study illustrates many of the principles, strengths, and limitations of this type of research.

QUESTIONS AND ACTIVITIES TO CONSIDER

1. Do you believe the authors should have conducted observations in other court settings? If so, which ones?
2. Do you believe the observers in this study were obtrusive? Would their presence in the jury box have affected your behavior in that context? From what other position might they have conducted their observations? To what gain or loss?
3. Would interviewing the judge or litigants after the trials have provided any additional useful information? If so, what might they have been asked?
4. The researchers took the complete observer role. Might being a partici-

pant observer have helped them gain additional insight into the process? Would it have been ethical?

5. The researchers were covert observers. If you were one of their subjects, would you have been offended to learn your comments had been recorded and observed?

6. Should the researchers have brought their preliminary findings to the judge or to the litigants for comments before publishing them? If so, what questions might the researchers have asked them?

7. Conduct your own ethnographic observation of arguments used in a small claims or other kind of court in your town or city. Were the same types of argument advanced, or did you find some different lines of argument in your observations? Did the plaintiffs win the majority of the cases?

FURTHER READINGS ON ETHNOGRAPHIC OBSERVATIONAL RESEARCH

Bakeman, R., & Goteman, J. M. (1986). *Observing interaction: An introduction to sequential analysis.* Cambridge, England: Cambridge University Press.

Donaghy, W. (1989). Nonverbal communication measurement. In P. Emmert & L. L. Barker (Eds.), *Measurement of communication behavior* (pp. 296–332). New York: Longman.

Fetterman, D. (1989). *Ethnography: Step by step.* Newbury Park, CA: Sage.

Jorgenson, D. L. (1989). *Participant observation: A methodology for human studies.* Newbury Park, CA: Sage.

Sillars, A. (1991). Behavioral observation. In B. Montgomery & S. Duck (Eds.), *Studying interpersonal interaction* (pp. 197–218). New York: Guilford.

EXAMPLES OF ETHNOGRAPHIC OBSERVATIONAL RESEARCH

Darling, A. (1989). Signalling non-comprehensions in the classroom: Toward a descriptive typology. *Communication Education, 28,* 34–43.
This study was conducted to learn how students who do not understand what their teacher is saying indicate verbally their noncomprehension. The researcher observed three college classes—one large lecture class and two smaller discussion classes. She was introduced as "an individual interested in patterns of classroom interaction"; she then observed, but did not participate in, each 50-minute class three times a week for an academic quarter. She took fieldnotes on instances when students requested clarification, saying, for example, "I don't understand what you mean by _____," or, "Why isn't that an example of _____?" She recorded 68 examples and then content analyzed them into three different types of strategies.

Goodall, H. L., Jr. (1989). *Casing a promised land: The autobiography of an organiza-*

tional detective as cultural biographer. Carbondale, IL: Southern Illinois University Press.

This book contains five ethnographic studies (and a methodology chapter), each describing the significant symbols of a social setting in narrative terms. Most are about organizations in and around the aerospace industry in Huntsville, Alabama. Each ethnography is an example of a "confessional tale" because Goodall describes his own experiences as he learned about the contexts he describes. In the first one, for example, he describes (as a complete participant) his family's entry into the Huntsville community where he took his first university teaching job. In the second, he acts as a complete observer and takes the reader on a "tour" of a computer software company, with vivid descriptions of the objects observed along the way (such as the color and placement of cars in the parking lot, the signs and memorabilia in offices) and with interpretations of how they contribute to the corporate culture. This is a well written, perceptive set of ethnographic essays based on Goodall's acute observations of environmental clues to the nature of organizational life. This portrayal of the ethnographer as a "detective" provides a useful perspective on this approach to research.

Pacanowsky, M. (1988). Communication in the empowering organization. In J. A. Anderson (Ed.), *Communication yearbook 11* (pp. 356–379). Beverly Hills, CA: Sage.

This article describes communication in an organization known for having an "empowering" culture—W. L. Gore and Associates, makers of their patented product, Gore-Tex, a textile used in sportswear. Gore employs what they call a "lattice" structure, rather than a traditional organizational pyramid. People take on only the projects to which they are willing to make a personal commitment, and they are free to talk with whoever can help "get the job done." There is no fixed authority; leadership fluctuates with the specific problem at hand that needs most attention. Pacanowsky spent nine months with the organization as a participant observer. For the first four months, he just wandered around observing and chatting with people and taking notes. Later, he was called upon to lead a task force that was to improve communication in the plant. He used these opportunities to describe the culture of this organization in great detail and to interpret its empowering qualities.

Putnam, L., Van Hoeven, S. A., & Bullis, C. A. (1991). The role of rituals and fantasy themes in teachers' bargaining. *Western Journal of Speech Communication, 55,* 85–103.

These researchers studied symbolic interaction in the collective bargaining process in two Indiana school districts. They observed the negotiation sessions, planning meetings, and caucus interactions of both districts. For the first district, bargaining sessions covered a period of 11 days and included 40 hours of bargaining at the table, interspersed with an additional 14 hours of caucus meetings. The second district held its negotiation during one 10-hour marathon meeting that included caucuses. The observers took detailed fieldnotes (1,300 pages for District 1 and 325 pages for District 2) containing near-verbatim dialogue of interactions, as well as notes on the general atmosphere. They extracted all dramatic messages, examples, and digressions from the deliberations. They also identified activities such as opening and closing rituals, session formats and concession behaviors. Finally, they analyzed, tracked, and compared them for the two districts.

Snow, D., Robinson, C., & McCall, P. (1991). "Cooling out" men in singles bars and nightclubs: Observations on the interpersonal survival strategies of women in public places. *Journal of Contemporary Ethnography, 19,* 423–449.

This article attempts to advance understanding of the interactional survival strategies of women in public places by examining the manner in which they fend off men and parry their advances in singles bars and nightclubs. The data were gathered principally by participant observation in nine different nightclubs and drinking establishments over a three-month period. Each observer always stood or sat where she could hear or see other women, and usually observed and eavesdropped simultaneously. The observers recorded and analyzed the women's responses to unwanted, initial face-to-face requests or overtures, their handling of more persistent males, and the tactics they employed in hopes of avoiding the "cooling out" role and the whole encounter.

Chapter 10

Ethnographic Interview Research

INTRODUCTION TO THE METHOD

Ethnographic interviews provide information about communication not accessible through other research methods. They allow researchers to ask about communication events too *time-consuming* or too *private* to observe. A study of communication, for instance, in long-term, satisfying marriages would best be conducted by interviews. Observers could not spend years with such couples, nor could they observe their most intimate moments together. Consequently, asking the couples to recall and describe their interactions over the years would be the best way to discover communication characteristics common to satisfying marriages.

Ethnographic interviews are also essential for getting "below the surface" and discovering what people think and feel about particular communication events. Survey questionnaires can tell us what television shows families watch together, for example, but ethnographic interviews can help us understand *why* they chose each of those particular shows and *how* these choices are negotiated among family members.

Data from ethnographic interviews also help to enrich findings from other research methods. Most people are more comfortable speaking than writing, so interviews are useful for obtaining detailed accounts and specific examples that enable readers to picture the events and settings which aggregated quantitative findings explain.

Ethnographic interviews are a unique breed of human interaction, falling midway on a continuum between the highly structured interviews used most often in survey research and informal everyday conversations. Like structured interviews, their purpose is to obtain information from respondents. However, ethnographic interviews are more custom-tailored to particular respondents, rather than being consistent for everyone. Question sequences may be planned beforehand, but the anticipated wording and the order of questions are not necessarily followed in the actual interview. Ethnographers encourage respondents to speak frankly, at length, and in their own terms about the phenomena being investigated, not simply to answer uniform questions. Of course, the more homogeneous the respondent group, the more consistent the questions asked. When respondents are heterogeneous (such as a mix of doctors, nurses, patients, and orderlies in a hospital), questions naturally will vary more.

Consequently, the ethnographic interviewer's role is unique. Survey researchers usually dominate and control their interviews, channeling responses from subjects down desired tracks. In contrast, ethnographic interviewers want to empower respondents to speak freely, so they treat them more equally, often referring to them as "collaborators" or "consultants" (Werner & Schoepfle, 1987). This applies especially when the ethnographer is "working up"—interviewing people with higher social status than his or her own (as when a graduate student interviews a surgeon or a U.S. senator). Some ethnographers even prefer to take a subordinate stance, acting at times as supplicants or "handmaidens" to the people being interviewed in order to relieve respondents' anxiety, emphasize respondents' authority, and to assure that interviewer pressure has no effect whatsoever on what is said (Douglas, 1985).

Although the ethnographic interview is usually unstructured, it is rarely simply a haphazard conversation. Researchers plan beforehand the who, where, what and how of their interviews, and we will discuss each of these in turn.

Who: Subjects

Rather than trying to interview a random sample of individuals from the group being studied, most ethnographers seek out a nonrandom *purposive* sample. They decide upon the aspect of communication they wish to study, then seek out people who are able and willing to describe it to them. Sometimes they put out a call for interview volunteers; sometimes they go into the field and solicit the kinds of people with whom they wish to talk; and sometimes they start out by interviewing people they already know and get from them referrals to others with similar experiences or characteristics. These new contacts then refer others like them, and the subject pool "snowballs" until a substantial number are recruited.

For example, Baxter and Bullis (1986) wanted to learn about turning points in romantic relationships. They employed several methods to contact respondents, until they had interviewed partners from 40 relationships, a total of 80 individuals. First, a story about the project was placed in the weekly college newspaper. Next, volunteers were solicited from college classes taught by the researchers, and then **network sampling** was used. That is, the researchers trained student interviewers and asked them for the names of all the romantic pairs in their social networks. Then, upon completion of their interviews, these romantic couples were asked to identify other couples in their respective social networks who might be interested in participating.

Ethnographers usually set eligibility criteria to assure that the participants selected will provide data that apply to the research objectives; then they interview the eligible candidates. In the study mentioned above, for example, the duration of the respondents' romantic relationships had to exceed six months. People in newer relationships were less likely to have experienced the kinds of incidents being studied, so they were excluded.

Ethnographic interviewers usually contact fewer respondents than do survey researchers, so they must be careful to select a variety of people within the general category being investigated in order to obtain a full picture of the phenomenon being studied and to prevent reaching biased conclusions. Rawlins and Holl (1988), for instance, studied how teenagers interact with their parents and friends. They interviewed only 32 teenagers living in a "small city in the northeastern United States" (p. 30). To assure that their sample was varied, they selected half from a public high school and half from a private high school where students live away from home. They also asked guidance counselors at each school to help them select "half from each gender who were outgoing, visible and socially active and half who kept more to themselves and were less extroverted and socially involved" (p. 31). These selection procedures assured that their results would not be biased by extraneous socioeconomic, gender, or personality factors, and would be enriched by data from people who differed in all these characteristics.

When selecting people to interview, ethnographers usually start with individuals who are most informed, articulate, trustworthy, and comfortable speaking with them. These initial respondents are called **key informants.** They help interviewers become familiar with other members of the group they are studying and with factors like the environment, the social norms, and the jargon of that group. Morris and Coursey (1989) studied how managers perceive the "accounts" they receive from employees when problems occur. They interviewed 16 middle or high-level municipal managers. They began, however, by interviewing the city's personnel officer, asking his advice about which managers in the city they should contact. He also gave them details about city-wide procedures for handling problematic events. The personnel officer was a key informant in this study. He also acted as a "go-between," a valuable asset for securing subjects in many ethnographic studies.

How many people do ethnographers interview? When do they stop conducting interviews? A common rule of thumb is to keep seeking new respondents until they stop "hitting pay dirt," that is, stop learning anything new about the communication phenomenon being studied. A criterion for determining this point was articulated by Goodenough (1964), who argued that the researcher's objective is to learn "whatever it is one has to know or believe in order to operate in the manner acceptable to the group's members and to do so in any role that they accept for anyone of themselves" (p. 36). Researchers are done, in other words, when they have learned enough to act and think as members of the group being studied. Douglas (1985) recommends going a step further. He suggests that once ethnographers feel they have derived sufficient insight, they should "make an active search for negative instances—that is, for cases that do not fit the patterns you have already discovered" (p. 50). These exceptions should be incorporated into the findings.

Where: Setting

Ethnographic interviews occur in two basic settings, which Werner and Schoepfle (1987) call "grass huts" (where the respondents normally conduct their activities) or "white rooms" (somewhere apart from the field of action). Lozano (1989) studied interactions between home-based workers and their employers. She interviewed most of these "outside workers" at home where they do their work. A few she met in coffee shops and "another [interview] was conducted during a high-speed auto journey over Silicon Valley expressways, while my respondent drove to pick up several blueprints from a client" (p. 170). Interviews on-site are usually preferable, since the ethnographer can observe the context, and people are more likely to express themselves naturally on their "home turf." An important condition, however, is to be somewhat encapsulated, free from disruptions and the stares of others on the scene. However, sometimes respondents feel uncomfortable talking to a researcher around co-workers. For this reason, when Smith and Eisenberg (1988) studied communication among Disneyland staff, they interviewed workers in a nearby hotel lounge to assure confidentiality.

What and How: Interview Protocol

Some ethnographic interviews are very brief, informal conversations that take place amidst the researcher's *participant observation* while normal activities are going on. Other interviews are more formal—the parties meet explicitly for this purpose—and, therefore, are planned in advance.

The first preparatory step involves anticipating how the researchers will present themselves. To gain cooperation, ethnographers often begin with a brief "sales pitch" to motivate respondents to be disclosive. They usually introduce themselves as researchers and describe the purpose of the study, stressing its importance and crediting the respondents with being experts on the topic being investigated. Some respondents are paid; others contribute because they believe in the value of the research project, welcome an opportunity to tell their stories, or simply appreciate a break in the monotony of their ordinary activities.

Interviewers must be careful to take a neutral stance in their introduction to avoid any *demand characteristics* that might reveal their own expectations and thereby influence respondents' replies (see the researcher unintentional expectancy effect discussed in Chapter 2). Jorgenson (1989) says, "Explanation of the research should be general. It is sufficient in most instances to say something like 'I'm doing a study of so and so _____.' It usually is better to say too little rather than too much" (p. 86). Assurance of anonymity, consent to be interviewed, and permission to tape-record the interview are handled next.

Where trust is problematic, ethnographers usually do all the interviewing themselves. Occasionally they train a team of interviewers. Knapp, Hopper, and Bell (1984), for example, had 15 students conduct interviews to elicit examples of verbal "compliments" from a total of 58 respondents. Beforehand, each student interviewer conducted one training interview and was coached especially to get respondents to recall the exact wording of compliments and replies to them. This training assured that all 15 interviewers' data would be accurate and comparable.

People tend to confide more in others who are similar to themselves, so interviews are usually more effective when the investigator is of similar age, race, language and marital status. Therefore, having an interview team is helpful, not only to share the workload, but also to increase matches between investigators and respondents.

Interview questions are usually prepared in advance and are pilot-tested to check how understandable they are. The interview protocol is usually sequenced from open questions, asking for general information, to closed questions, eliciting specific details, and from questions seeking readily shared, public information to those inquiring about more personal or private material. To prod respondents' memory, ethnographers often start by asking them to recall incidents with strong emotional impact, and then to describe each incident they recall chronologically (Douglas, 1985). Spradley (1979) identifies several kinds of interview questions, including: (1) "grand-tour" questions—a request for an overview of some matter of interest; (2) "mini-tour" questions—a more detailed exploration of a particular matter; (3) example questions—requests for illustrations of general terms; (4) experience questions—queries about respondents' direct experiences (what actually happened to them); and (5) native language questions—requests for clarification of particular terms, phrases, and the like used by "insiders."

Just as important as the prepared questions is the process by which ethnographic interviewers encourage deeper, more extensive replies. They do this primarily by establishing warm rapport with their respondents, by being attentive and indicating continual interest in what they have to say, by remaining silent and nondirective during pauses so respondents can say everything they wish, and by gently probing for elaboration. The answers given by respondents influence subsequent questioning. That is, follow-up questions are formulated on the spot to suit the preferred direction for the respondent, or to fill in gaps in the interviewer's knowledge; thus, the ethnographic interview is more a dialogue than an interrogation, in contrast to many survey interviews. Its primary intent is to empower respondents to tell their stories in their own words (Mishler, 1986).

Some researchers use props, such as objects or photographs, when they wish to elicit more elaborated responses (Whyte, 1984). Others want more precise responses, so they use more focused prompts, such as incomplete sentences, rank-order tasks, rating scales, card sorting, and triadic comparisons (Weller & Romney, 1988). Researchers must be very careful when wording questions to avoid biasing responses. Loftus (1979) reports much research on this problem. For example, when studying headaches, she asked half of her subjects, "Do you get headaches frequently, and if so, how often?" Their mean response was 2.2 headaches per week. She asked the other half, "Do you get headaches occasionally, and if so, how often?," and their mean response was .7 times a week. This illustrates how just one word in a question can influence people's reports of past experiences.

Still other researchers conduct *group* interviews in which respondents encourage each other to share. These usually are termed "focus groups" because they address only one particular concern shared by the group's members (Morgan, 1988). Lederman (1983), for example, conducted focus groups with students who experienced communication apprehension and found that being together with people who shared that common concern enabled them to speak more freely about it. Pacanowsky (1988) gathered much of his data about communication in a particular "empowering organization" (W. L. Gore & Associates) by conducting 18 focus group interviews. To stimulate responses he simply asked each group just two questions: "What do you think of communication at Gore?" and "What do you think of the Gore culture?" (p. 360).

Analyzing Ethnographic Interview Data

Unlike other researchers who wait until all the data are in before analyzing them, ethnographers usually begin analyzing information gathered in interviews as soon as they obtain it. They look for clues to the communication patterns they are seeking, so they can check out their suspicions in subsequent interviews.

When the interviews are completed, ethnographers transfer their tapes into written form and read the transcripts over several times; or, if that is an overwhelming task, they listen repeatedly to the recordings. In doing so, they are immersing themselves in the data to discover categories or patterns implicit within the communicators' actions or thoughts.

After deriving those patterns, they usually go back through their interview data again to find examples of each. They might count those examples, as content analysts do; they might look for patterns within each category to further refine their analysis (they might discover, for example, that certain categories are more prevalent or take a different form under particular conditions); or, they might select representative examples under each category to report verbatim.

The conclusions derived from a study using ethnographic interviews usually provide thorough descriptions of what respondents reported. Often, they are also extrapolated into implications for people who will be experiencing similar communication events in that context and into tentative but "grounded" theoretical statements or "working hypotheses" about the general communication process being investigated.

QUESTIONS FOR EXAMINING ETHNOGRAPHIC
INTERVIEW RESEARCH

Besides the general questions used to evaluate all research, several issues are especially relevant when critiquing research based on ethnographic interviews. Keep the following questions in mind when reading the illustrative article, as well as any other research reports that use this research methodology.

A. The Interviewer's Role

1. Was the *interviewer method* applied appropriately, or could the information sought by the interviewer have been better obtained any other way, such as by observing the phenomenon of interest directly?

2. Is the interviewer sufficiently familiar with or similar to the respondents to elicit their *trust*, or was trust developed in another way?

3. How well did the *interviewer's self-introduction* to the respondents encourage their disclosure (perhaps relieving their anxiety and/or impressing them with the importance of the study and their own roles in it)— without biasing their responses?

4. Were the interviews conducted by the *primary investigator* (PI) or were *interviewers trained* to collect the data? If the PI conducted the interview-

ing, how assured are you that the data are unbiased? If an interviewing team did it, how assured are you that the data they collected are accurate and comparable?

5. Were the interviews conducted at a *time* and *place* conducive to a frank and complete exchange?

B. *Selection of Respondents*

1. Were the *people interviewed* varied and representative of the population being studied? Or, did most of them seem to be from a particular age, ethnic group, social status, ᴜr position in the target group, thereby limiting the validity of the study?

2. Were the criteria (or procedures) used to *select* respondents for this study sufficient to screen out inappropriate or biased individuals?

3. Were people *omitted* who should have been included to obtain complete understanding of the communication process being studied?

4. Was one or more *key informants* used? If so, do these individuals appear trustworthy, or might they have misdirected the researcher?

5. Were a sufficient *number* of interviews conducted? Were the number of respondents and the decision to conclude the interviewing process explained to your satisfaction?

C. *Interview Protocol*

1. Did the *interview plan* cover all the important bases, yet was it loose enough to follow up on unexpected leads?

2. Were the *questions* sequenced from general to specific, that is, to elicit first the respondents' own orientations to the interview topics before posing questions embedded with the interviewers' theories?

3. Were the respondents encouraged with *prompts* or other interview "tools" to speak freely, frankly, and at length?

4. Were the interviews conducted *one-to-one,* or were pairs or *groups* of people interviewed together? If together, do you believe other respondents' presence helped or distorted the interview?

D. *Interview Data Analysis*

1. How were the interview responses *recorded*? Were notes taken or was a tape recorder used? Was this method optimal?

2. How did the researcher *analyze* the data? What assurances are provided that inferences are grounded in the data, not imposed or biased by the researcher's *a priori* assumptions?

3. Did the researcher seek, report, and explain *"negative examples"* or exceptions to the generalizations made?

4. Do the article's *findings* put you in the respondents' "shoes," so that you

now have a better sense of how people in the group being studied act, think, speak, and/or react to others?

5. Did the article's findings yield *"grounded theory"* or *"working hypotheses"* that can be tested using other, more controlled research methods?

THE ILLUSTRATIVE STUDY

The study you will read used ethnographic interviews to investigate a dimension of nonverbal communication (touch) as it is perceived by women during a very stressful experience (labor and delivery of a child). This study contributes both to what we know about touch as a kind of message and to its role in a particular health care situation.

One of the researchers (Stolte) was a registered nurse who had worked in obstetrics and wanted to better understand the efficacy of using touch in that context from the recipient's viewpoint. Consequently, she decided to interview women shortly after their labor and delivery experiences to learn how they reacted to the touch they received.

Patients' Perceptions of Touch During Labor

Karen M. Stolte

Paul G. Friedman

1   Bodily contact is one of the main nonverbal signals used by man. Friends often greet or say goodbye by means of a handshake or hug, children are held when they have been hurt, and the elderly often seek contact through the touch of a hand. Additionally, touch is ac-
5   cepted more readily in some situations and environments than in others. Even in cultures where little physical contact occurs beyond ritualized handshakes, touch is used when one is in a dependent state, is in pain, or is seeking reassurance. Taboos regarding touch in this society are lessened when one is ill, bereaved, or undergoing some
10   type of suffering. Helping persons, such as nurses and doctors, are permitted to touch patients as a means of physical care, reassurance, and comfort.

Study of the role of touch in medical contexts can help to reveal the actual usefulness of this communication channel for indicating

Source: Stole, K. M., & Friedman, P. G. (1980). Patients' perceptions of touch during labor. *Journal of Applied Communications Research, 8,* 10–21. Reprinted by permission of the Speech Communication Association.

15   care and for relieving stress. Mystical writings refer to "the laying on
of hands" and recent nursing texts advocate touch as a means of
reassuring patients (1).

This advice is commonly followed. Barnett made observations of
"non-necessary touch" (defined as "primarily affective, a form of per-
20   sonal contact with the patient outside the realm of procedural duties")
given patients over a four week period in two hospitals. She found
that touch was used more often on the wards where the highest stress
potential existed, e.g., pediatrics, labor and delivery, recovery room,
and intensive care areas, than on other wards in the hospitals (2).

25   Indeed, touch does seem to have a positive effect. McCorkle
lightly touched the wrists of 60 seriously ill and control patients while
asking them three questions about their feelings and conditions. She
measured significantly more positive facial expressions and verbal
responses (using Bales Interaction Analysis) in the experimental
30   group (3).

However, reactions are not uniform. Day asked 10 medical and
10 surgical patients to describe eight slides of nurse-patient interaction involving touch, especially what they did or did not like about the
interaction. She found that age, severity of illness, number of pre-
35   vious hospital admissions, and the nurse-patient relationship affected
the patients' perceptions of the slides. For example, younger patients
(20–30 years of age) seemed more tolerant of the use of touch than
did older patients (4).

These general and promising findings merit further examina-
40   tion of the meaning to patients of various kinds of touch, especially
when administered spontaneously, in the course of an actual stressful
medical situation, such as the labor period preceding childbirth.
Hence, the following research questions were asked: 1) What are the
general perceptions that maternity patients have about the touch that
45   they received during labor? 2) What touch experiences during labor
do maternity patients describe as positive? What touch experiences do
they describe as negative? a) What is the relationship between who
touched and the patient and her perceptions of that touch? b) What is
the relationship between the part of the body touched and her per-
50   ceptions of that touch? c) What is the relationship between the meaning or purpose of the touch received (as described by the receiver)
and her perceptions of that touch?

METHOD

Sample

55   The setting for this study was the maternity ward of a large midwestern university medical center where a family-centered approach
to maternity care is used. Husbands (or substitute family members)

are encouraged to stay with their wives during labor and often attend
the delivery of their infants.

60   The population from which the sample was taken included all
patients delivered on the obstetrical service during a two month
period. The following criteria were used to define this sample: a) the
subject spoke English; b) she had a vaginal delivery; c) she had no
medical nor obstetrical complications during labor or pregnancy;
65   d) she delivered a normal full-term infant (infant weight was 5 lb. 3
oz. or more); and e) subjects who were taken to the delivery room
immediately upon admission were excluded from the sample. During
the period of data collection, 304 deliveries occurred. Subjects who
met the criteria were interviewed until 150 subjects had been ob-
70   tained. Many subjects had obstetrical or medical complications, premature infants, cesarean sections, or for some other reason did not
meet the sample criteria. Three subjects who met the criteria refused
to participate in the study.

        When approaching the subject to be interviewed, the researcher
75   introduced herself as a graduate student who was asking women questions about their labor. The length of labor of these women ranged
from one to 18 hours. They were having their first, second, third, or
fourth child. There were 109 clinic patients and 41 private patients in
the sample. Some women had been to childbirth education classes and
80   some had not. The sample consisted of 101 White, 44 Black, four
Spanish, and one Chinese and included married, separated, divorced,
and single women.

Interview

        The interview schedule consisted of ten questions related to the sub-
85   ject's feelings about labor and her perceptions of the touch she received during labor: 1) A description of the labor experience in their
own words (how they felt, what was thought, what was important
during labor, and what was helpful to them). 2) Whether the labor was
better than expected, about what was expected, or was worse than
90   expected. 3) Whether someone stayed with the patient and how long
during labor. 4) Things that women found useful during labor,
whether they were done, and if they were annoying, somewhat annoying, neutral, somewhat helpful, or helpful (rubbing of back, breathing
techniques, knowing someone was with them, being touched by an-
95   other person, and medication). (Only the answers related to "rubbing
your back" and "being touched by another person" were used for data
analysis). 5) Amount of touch (touched too much, the right amount,
or not enough touch during labor). 6) A description of a situation
during labor where the subjects felt that the touch received was a
100   positive (good) experience in terms of: a) who touched, b) what body

part was touched, c) why they were touched or why they thought they
were touched, d) what did the touch mean, and e) did being touched
help, hinder, or have no effect in terms of coping with labor. Question
7 was identical to question 6 except that the subject was asked to
105   describe a negative experience.

Questions 8 and 9 contained a list of 27 word pairs used to
describe separate perceptions about being touched during labor.
These word pairs were derived from a review of statements made
about touch in 60 articles, books, and theses by 45 different authors.
110   In this way, we hoped to ascertain face validity of some of the general,
ambiguous terms found in the literature as well as to learn subjects'
responses to the touch they received during labor. (See Table 4.) Each
pair of words was plotted on a five-point scale with a neutral position
in the center. The subject was asked to choose the position which best
115   described how she felt. For example, subjects were asked if they felt
accepted, somewhat accepted, neutral, somewhat unaccepted, or unaccepted when someone touched them during labor.

Question 10, stated "In general, would you say that your feelings
about the touch you received during labor were positive, somewhat
120   positive, neutral, somewhat negative, or negative?"

RESULTS AND DISCUSSION

The answers to the interview questions were analyzed in terms of
a) overall perceptions regarding being touched during labor, b) positive experiences regarding being touched during labor, and c) nega-
125   tive experiences regarding being touched during labor.

In response to question 10 on the interview schedule, "In general, would you say that your feelings about the touch you received
during labor were positive, somewhat positive, neutral, somewhat
negative, or negative?", 93 women replied positive, 31 replied some-
130   what positive, 14 women were neutral, 6 were somewhat negative, and
6 were negative. Thus, being touched, in general, was a positive experience for women in labor. The sample was examined in terms of age,
parity, length of labor, race, marital status, infant weight, classification, anesthesia, and attendance at childbirth education classes to see
135   if any significant difference in these variables existed among those
subjects who felt positive, neutral, or negative about being touched
during labor. Because the number of subjects who responded negatively about being touched was so small, the categories were combined
into one category as were the categories of positive and somewhat
140   positive. Thus, three categories of responses to being touched were
available for comparison. Chi Square values were computed for each
variable, yielding the following:

TABLE 1
Relationship Between Age and Perceptions of Touch Received During Labor

Age	Perceptions of Touch		
	Positive	Neutral	Negative
15–19	35	8	8
20–29	80	5	4
30–34	9	1	0

Age and Perceptions of Touch: The subjects in the age groups 20–29 and 30–34 perceived touch more positively ($\chi^2 = 11.12$, df = 4; p < .05) than did the subjects in the age group 15–19. (See Table 1.) One might assume that the younger age group was more likely to be having first children and that their labors were longer than those of the other age groups, thus contributing to the more negative feelings about the total labor situation. However, in this particular sample, neither the length of labor nor parity was significantly different among the groups who perceived touch as positive, neutral, or negative. In addition, no significant correlation between perceptions of labor and perceptions of touch existed. Also, there was no significance among age groups with regard to length of labor.

Race and Perceptions of Touch: There was a significant difference in the perceptions of touch between White and Nonwhite subjects ($\chi^2 = 26.82$; df = 2; p < .001). White subjects perceived touch more positively than did Nonwhite subjects (see Table 2). Although there were Nonwhite personnel on the delivery staff, the majority of the personnel were White. The labor and delivery room nursing staff consisted of 22 White and seven Black personnel. No conclusion about interracial contact can be made from the data gathered in this study, other than noting race as a significant variable, since no information was collected on the race of the person touching the subject.

Marital Status and Perceptions of Touch: As seen in Table 3, single or divorced subjects perceived touch more negatively than did married or separated subjects ($\chi^2 = 17.55$; df = 2; p < .001). This differ-

TABLE 2
Relationship Between Race and Perceptions of Touch Received During Labor

Race	Perceptions of Touch		
	Positive	Neutral	Negative
White	93	1	7
Nonwhite	31	13	5

TABLE 3
Relationship Between Marital Status and Perceptions
of Touch Received During Labor

	Perceptions of Touch		
Marital	*Positive*	*Neutral*	*Negative*
Married or separated	99	4	8
Single or divorced	25	10	4

ence may be due primarily to who was touching the subjects during labor. Almost all of the married women had their husbands with them
170 during labor and one separated woman had her husband with her. On the other hand, the single and divorced women had other family members or hospital personnel with them.

The other variables hypothesized to influence subjects' overall perceptions of touch during labor, namely infants' weight, subjects'
175 hospital classification (private or clinic), kind of anesthesia used, attendance at childbirth classes, subjects' comparison of their actual labor experience with their expectations regarding it, the length of time someone else was present during the labor period, subjects' perceptions of backrubs received during labor, and subjects' evaluations
180 of the amount of touch received, were not found to be significantly related.

Individual Perceptions of Touch and Overall Perceptions of Touch: Pearson Product Moment Correlations were computed between the subjects' responses to each pair of words in questions 8 and 9 and their over-
185 all perceptions of the touch they received during labor (see Table 4). Although all but two correlations were significant at the .01 level of confidence, none accounted for more than half of the variance from any variable, and therefore, none have a high predictive value. The population as a whole felt strongly positive about being touched. Had
190 there been more subjects who felt negatively about being touched during labor, the correlations might have been higher.

Positive and Negative Experiences: In interview questions 6 and 7, each subject was asked to describe a positive and a negative touch experience during labor; 115 subjects were able to do so. Of these, 53
195 described both a positive and a negative experience, 48 described only a positive experience, and 14 described only a negative experience. In all, 101 positive experiences and 67 negative experiences were described. Thirty-five subjects were unable to describe either a positive or a negative touch experience. Chi Square analysis of those subjects
200 who described experiences and those subjects unable to describe ex-

TABLE 4
Correlations Between Word Pairs and Overall Perceptions
of Touch Received During Labor

Word Pair	Correlation
Accepted—Unaccepted	.32
Reassured—Frightened	.47
Relaxed—Tense	.48
Understood—Misunderstood	.24
Closer to the Person Touching You—More Distant From the Person Touching You	.27
Cared For—That Your Privacy Was Invaded	.43
Supported By Another Person—Left Alone	.38
More Able to Follow Directions—Distracted	.51
Safe—Unsafe	.45
More Aware of What Was Happening—Less Aware of What Was Happening	.20 (ns)
Comforted—Rejected	.56
More Aware of What the Person Touching You Was Saying—Less Aware of What the Person Touching You Was Saying	.32
Respected as an Individual—Ignored as an Individual	.42
More Trusting of the Person Touching You—Less Trusting of the Person Touching You	.41
Secure—Threatened	.52
Calm—Irritated	.49
Encouraged—Restrained	.52
Able to Rely on the Other Person—Wish to be Left Alone	.66
Less Nervous—More Nervous	.43
Warmth—Frustration	.48
More Able to Tell the Person Touching You How You Felt—Less Able to Tell the Person Touching You How You Felt	.19 (ns)
Warm—Mechanical	.33
Gentle—Rough	.42
Supportive—Impersonal	.42
Lacking—Excessive	.37
Pleasant—Painful	.41
Expressed Genuine Concern—Routine Procedural Technique	.33

periences yielded no significant difference between the two groups in terms of the variables previously discussed in this study.

Who Touched the Subject and Perceptions of Touch: One of the research questions to be answered from the responses to questions 6 and 7 was, "Is there a relationship between who touched the patient

205

TABLE 5
Relationship Between Who Touched the Subject and Perceptions
of the Touch Experience

Person Touching the Subject	Negative Experience	Positive Experience
Doctor	49	13
Husband	8	48
Relative, Friend	1	15
Nurse	9	25

and whether the touch experience was perceived as positive or negative?" The Chi Square was used to derive an answer to this question. Table 5 shows the distribution of who touched the subject in terms of positive and negative experiences ($\chi^2 = 64.05$; df = 3; p < .001).

210   The doctor was the person who did the touching in most of the negative experiences. In general, the negative experiences which were described involved some type of procedure, i.e., pelvic examinations, abdominal palpations, etc. Since the physician performed most of these procedures, he was the source of most touch perceived as

215   negative. The largest group that did the touch in the positive experiences was the husband. The significance of who touched the subject may be confounded with the reason for the touch, i.e., subjects may have said their perceptions depended on who gave the touch when they were also dependent on the circumstances under which the

220   touch was given.

   Part of the Body Touched and Perceptions of Touch: Another research question to be answered from the data gathered in response to questions 6 and 7 was, "Is there a relationship between the part of the body that was touched and whether that touch was perceived as posi-

225   tive or negative?" Using Chi Square formula, a significant difference was found between where the subject was touched and her perception of the touch experience ($\chi^2 = 106.43$; df = 6; p < .001). (See Table 6.)

   The places touched most frequently during the negative experiences were the pelvic area and abdomen. Pelvic examinations and

230   abdominal palpation, to determine the quality and character of uterine contractions, were the most commonly described negative experiences. The area most frequently touched during positive experiences was the hand.

   No procedures were done which primarily involved touching

235   the hand. Consequently, subjects knew that this physical contact was not a necessary part of their care. Since it was a nonnecessary form of touch, touching the hand conveyed interest and concern.

TABLE 6
Relationship Between Where the Subject Was Touched and Perceptions
of the Touch Experience

Part of Body	Positive Experience	Negative Experience
Hand	59	3
Back	11	5
Arm, Shoulder	8	3
Abdomen	6	19
Pelvic Area	0	35
Head, Face	13	1
Other	4	1

     Effect of Touch and Perceptions of Touch: Another question to be
answered from the data gathered in response to questions 6 and 7
240 was, "Is there a relationship between the subject's perception of how
helpful the touch was and her perceptions of the touch she received
during labor?" Subjects were asked to state whether they thought the
touch experience that they described helped them, hindered them, or
had no effect on them in terms of coping with their labor. A signifi-
245 cant difference was found between the effect of touch and whether
the experience was positive or negative ($\chi^2 = 101.30$; df = 2; p <
.001). Subject responses are shown in Table 7. All the subjects who
described a positive experience stated that it helped them. There was
a fairly even distribution among the negative experiences in terms of
250 help, hindrance, or no effect. It is interesting to note that one-third of
the subjects stated that the negative experiences helped them. One
reason given for this perception of help was that knowing that they
had made progress in labor, as determined by a pelvic examination,
was helpful.

255   *Meaning of Touch:* In an attempt to answer the research question,
"What is the relationship between the meaning or purpose of the
touch received (as described by the receiver) and her perceptions of
the touch she received during labor?" subjects were asked, "What did

TABLE 7
Relationship Between Effects of Touch and Perceptions of Touch Experience

Effect	Positive Experience	Negative Experience
Helped	101	19
Hindered	0	22
No Effect	0	26

this touch mean to you?" and "Why did they touch you or why do you think you were touched?" as a part of interview questions 6 and 7. These open-ended questions gave the subjects an opportunity to describe touch as they wished rather than placing them in the constraints of a structured interview question. The literature uses words such as support, reassurance, and sustaining presence to describe the effects of touch. Since the subjects also described touch in these types of terms, some face validity for the terms used in the literature can be assumed.

A wide variety of responses were given by the subjects to these questions. To consider each response in detail would be tedious and confusing. Therefore, responses were grouped together when like or synonymous terms were used.

Meaning of Touch—Positive Experiences: One hundred and one subjects described a situation in which the touch they received was a positive experience for them. The most frequent response, given by 20 subjects, to the question "Why did they touch you or why do you think you were touched?" was "to help me." Some subjects were able to describe specific ways that they were helped such as "to help reassure me" or "to help me calm down." The second most common response for being touched, given by 13 subjects, was that they were touched because they asked for it or reached out for it. Nine subjects said they were touched for reassurance and eight subjects perceived touch as a means for comfort or a way to make them comfortable. The rest of the subjects' responses varied widely.

In the positive experience, the most frequent responses to the question "What did this touch mean to you?" were reassurance (17), caring (17), someone was there with me (16), security (8), pain relief (6), and comfort (5). A variety of other responses were given. This data suggests that the use of touch is one way to communicate reassurance and concern.

Meaning of Touch—Negative Experiences: Sixty-seven subjects described a situation in which the touch they received was a negative experience. In response to the question, "Why did they touch you or why do you think you were touched?" subjects often related this touch to the procedures performed during the course of labor. However, a few experiences had to do with supportive types of touch which had been used early in labor, but became annoying to the subjects as labor progressed. Assessing progress in labor, checking cervical dilation, and determining quality of contractions, accounted for over one-half of the responses (38). A small number of subjects (5) stated they were "touched" because the person touching them wanted "to help." Thus, even though an experience with touch may be described as negative, touch may still be perceived as a way to express a caring attitude.

Because a large proportion of the negative touch experiences dealt with procedures during labor, "it hurt," was the most frequent
305 response (26) given to the question, "What did this touch mean to you?" A variety of subjects (17) also expressed negative emotions such as irritation, annoyance, or dislike. On the other hand, some subjects perceived such touch as a way to show caring and concern and a few subjects stated that "it had to be done" (six each).

310 **SUMMARY**

The following statements present a summary of the major findings of the study:

As a whole, the maternity patients perceived the touch that they received during labor as positive. A significant difference was found
315 in age, race, and marital status. Younger subjects, ages 15–19, perceived touch more negatively than did the rest of the sample. Single or divorced subjects perceived touch more negatively than did married or separated subjects.

A significant difference was found between who touched the
320 subjects and their perceptions of the touch experiences. Doctors were responsible for most of the touch in the negative touch experiences and husbands were responsible for most of the touch in the positive touch experience.

A significant difference was found between the part of the body
325 that was touched and the subjects' perceptions of the touch experience. In the negative experiences, pelvic examinations and abdominal palpations accounted for the majority of the touches. Hand touches were mentioned most often by subjects when they described positive experiences.

330 The most frequent terms used to describe the meaning or purposes of the touch received in the positive experiences were "to help me," "I reached out for it," "I asked for it," "reassurance," "comfort," "caring," "someone was there with me," "security," and "pain relief." In the negative experiences, the most common reason given for being
335 touched related to procedures performed during labor. "It hurt" was the most frequent response given to the question, "What did this touch mean to you?"

This study contributes to the knowledge about the use of touch in human interaction in two ways. First, the findings support subjec-
340 tive remarks noted in the literature. Second, the study covers an area not included in previous research—the receiver's perceptions of his

touch experiences. Thus, it looks at the meaning of touch, not just its general effect, emphasizing variables related to the source and the receiver which influence perceptions of touch. Attitudes toward touch
345 are context-related. Tactile experience may be positive or negative depending on the relationship of the source to the receiver and what part of the body is touched.

Since being touched by her husband is, in general, a positive experience for the laboring woman, professional staff members
350 should provide opportunities for the husband to use physical contact with his wife during labor. In addition, guidance in the use of supportive touch can be given in expectant parents classes. In this way, couples might practice various types of touch before labor in order to increase the likelihood that it will be helpful to the wife when it is used
355 during the stress of labor. In addition, doctors and nurses could be encouraged to use touch as a means of providing reassurance and support to the laboring woman instead of only as a method by which various procedures are completed.

One of the purposes of this study was to generate hypotheses
360 which could be tested in future research. To broaden the implications of the findings in this study to other medical settings or to stressful situations in other contexts. The following hypotheses might be investigated:

Touch is perceived more positively if the source and receiver are of
365 the same race.

White subjects perceive touch more positively than do Nonwhite subjects.

Adolescent subjects perceive touch more negatively than do adult subjects.

370 Touch given by family members is perceived more positively than the touch given by hospital staff members.

Hand touches are perceived more positively than touches elsewhere on the body.

Supportive touch is conveyed most frequently by hand touches.

375 Married subjects perceive touch more positively than do nonmarried subjects.

In stressful situations, touch is perceived as a means of support and concern.

REFERENCES

1. M. A. Manfreda, *Psychiatric Nursing*, 9th ed., Philadelphia: Davis, 1973, pp. 183–186.

2. K. Barnett, "A Survey of the Current Utilization of Touch by Health Team Personnel with Hospitalized Patients," *International Journal of Nursing Studies*, 9 (1972), pp. 195–209.

3. M. R. McCorkle, "The Effects of Touch on Seriously Ill Patients," Thesis, University of Iowa, 1972.

4. F. A. Day, "The Patient's Perception of Touch," in *Current Concepts in Clinical Nursing*, IV, E. Anderson, B. S. Bergersen, M. Duffey, M. Lohr, and M. H. Rose (eds.), St. Louis: Mosby, 1973.

COMMENTS ON THE STUDY

Introduction, Review of the Literature, and Research Questions

The authors begin by explaining the importance of touch in everyday interactions (1–4). They point out that touch is more appropriate in some contexts than in others. In particular, taboos against touching are lessened when one is sick (4–12). They believe that studying touch in the medical setting will help people understand the role of touch in managing stress (13–17). This applied research study thus seems justified because it investigates an important, "real-world" communication problem.

The authors provide a sparse review of the relevant literature (18–38). They assume readers' knowledge of touch as a communication variable and focus only on studies dealing with touch in medical settings. A more thorough review of the touch-related literature would have been helpful, since they indicate later on (106–109) that this review was conducted.

The authors advocate studying the effects of touch in an actual stressful medical situation, and thus chose to focus on the labor period preceding childbirth (39–42). Undoubtedly, this situation is stressful for expectant mothers (and fathers), but there is no review of the research conducted on it. The authors could have justified the selection of this particular context more effectively.

However, the use of ethnographic interviews seems appropriate in this study. The communication phenomenon being investigated could not be studied through direct observation. Labor and childbirth are very private events at which an observer would not be welcome. Moreover, the researchers were more concerned with women's subjective reactions to touch than with the amount or kind of touch they receive. A comparable experimental study could not have been done—it would be unethical to subject people to discomfort equivalent to labor pain and to control the amount of touch they receive. Likewise, a survey would not have elicited the kind of rich responses these women were willing to share orally in an interview so soon after giving birth.

The research questions cover a variety of concerns (43–52). They range from general descriptions and perceptions of touch experiences during labor to understanding the relationship between various variables related to touch. The purpose of this ethnographic interview study thus appears to be a combination of description and explanation which can lead future researchers to test specific predictions.

Method

The first author, who conducted all the interviews, was well suited to this role, since she had been an obstetric nurse and, therefore, was familiar with the process and the context of the study. As a woman, she could also readily gain the respondents' trust.

She introduced herself as a graduate student seeking help with her dissertation research and explained its specific topic and overall purpose—to better understand the labor process (74–76). In this role, she disassociated herself from the hospital staff, so the women would feel freer to speak frankly about their labor experiences. The relevance of her purpose to the respondents, who had just been through labor, also motivated them to contribute. The women were interviewed while they were still hospitalized (55–57)—a convenient time for them to talk, and soon enough after their labor experience to still recall it vividly and be willing (often eager) to describe it.

The fact that Stolte conducted all the interviews herself and also participated in analyzing the results has some advantages, but also raises some doubts. Her personal interest in the topic may have biased how she presented the questions, responded to the women's answers, and content analyzed the results. Using other interviewers and independent data analysts (other than the co-author) would have provided more opportunities to check the reliability of her data and results.

To obtain respondents, Stolte interviewed everyone who gave birth in the maternity ward of a large midwestern medical center over a two-month period (with several exceptions) (60–62). The respondents varied by socioeconomic level (some were clinic patients and some were private), race, age, labor training and experience, and marital status (76–82). This setting apparently provided a good mix of subjects, contributing to our faith that her findings are relatively comprehensive and unlikely to be biased.

Criteria established for selecting respondents assured that all had had an equivalent experience (some labor and a vaginal birth, but no medical or obstetrical complications or premature delivery) and could provide information about it (could speak English) (62–67). These standards gave coherence to the study. However, they also eliminated about 50% of the women who gave birth during her study period (67–73), indicating that important subsets of the population were omitted. (Perhaps the word "Normal" should be inserted before "Labor" in the article's title.)

No key informant was used, since the setting was familiar and accessible to the researchers, although getting permission to conduct this study from the medical center's staff was a tedious process. The time period for gathering the data (two months) was ample and unlikely to bias the results, since childbirth is not affected by the time of year. The number of interviews (150) seems quite adequate and, in fact, is large for a study of this type. (Notice in the review of literature that related studies involved fewer subjects [25–38].)

The *interview protocol* used in this study proceeded from general, grand-tour questions to more specific, mini-tour and experience questions (84–120). It began by asking respondents to describe their labor experiences in their own words. Subsequent questions were targeted more precisely, but imposed no alien concepts. Not until question 8 (106–107) were terms incorporated that reflected previous researchers' orientations toward the research topic.

Some questions referred to objective variables, such as the people present and the types of touch used, but others also inquired about *subjective* responses (a primary strength of ethnographic interviews), such as the women's inferences about the toucher's intent and the meanings they ascribed to touch experiences, as well as their evaluations of how adequate and how helpful the touching was. The primary interview "tool" was a series of rating scales used to quantify the respondents' subjective impressions of their touch experiences.

On the whole, the interview protocol seems relatively standardized and rigid. Apparently, the interviewer took little initiative to pursue unexpected responses as the results do not indicate any findings outside the parameters established by the research questions and interview protocol. This constraint certainly contributes to the comparability of the interview findings—when everyone is asked the same things their answers can be readily aggregated and compared. However, standardization precludes a more freewheeling approach to interviewing which might uncover aspects of touch during labor that had not been foreseen. For example, when a difference between reactions to touch by the black and white respondents was first reported, subsequent respondents might have been asked to identify the race of the persons who touched them. This may have indicated whether discomfort with interracial touching or a more generalized attitude about being touched was the more likely explanation.

Finally, although not indicated in the article, the interviews were tape-recorded. Some responses (the short answer items) also were filled in on data-tabulation forms by the interviewer as the respondent spoke. These recording methods seem appropriate for this context and for achieving the objectives of this study.

Results and Discussion

The respondents' comments were analyzed rather straightforwardly. For example, the accounts of positive and negative experiences were analyzed in terms of who touched the person, what body part was touched, the inferred reason for the touch, the experienced meaning of the touch, and the evaluation of the touch's helpfulness. These content-analytic themes seem relatively easy to categorize. Nevertheless, no assurance is provided that the researchers' sorting process was reliable. Use of an independent data analyst would have been preferable. Also, the category headings seem to have been decided beforehand. Other categories might have arisen after hearing the women's responses, but none were reported. For example, the study might have distinguished between touch by physicians that seemed essential to the patient's medical care and touch that seemed extraneous. This distinction would have guided understanding of the frequent reports of negative touch from physicians.

The results section concentrates on reporting quantitative findings related to the research questions. The authors found significant relationships between the respondents' overall evaluation of the touch they received and several demographic variables: their age, race, and marital status (143–181; Tables 1–3), as well as several terms reported by others to influence touch perceptions (182–191; Table 4). For several other variables no differences were discovered (199–202). The authors also looked for contrasts in the accounts of particularly positive and negative touch experiences during labor and found them in regard to who touched the respondents, on what parts of their bodies, and the effects of touch on coping with labor pains (192–254; Tables 5–7). Finally, the authors reported common meanings ascribed to touch in the respondents' positive and negative experiences (255–309).

In several places (especially 330–337) snippets of respondents' comments are provided to give readers a direct report of the words they used when speaking about their touch experiences during labor. More verbatim reports would have been desirable, but including them would have lengthened the article considerably. Most ethnographic research reports are longer than this one for this reason.

At the end of the article, the findings from the study are extrapolated into several suggestions for reducing women's stress during labor (348–358) and into several "working hypotheses" worthy of future research (359–378). The relevance of this study to improving communication during an important life event is a strength, as is its generation of fresh and promising hypotheses for better understanding touch as a communication variable.

CONCLUSION

Ethnographic interviews enable researchers to study people's personal reports and interpretations of their communication behavior in particular contexts. Stolte and Friedman's article illustrates some of the methods, strengths, and limitations of conducting ethnographic interview research.

QUESTIONS AND ACTIVITIES TO CONSIDER

1. Would you have interviewed other people involved in these labor experiences, such as the attending family members, physicians, and/or nurses? If so, what would you have asked them?

2. Do you believe this study should be replicated in other birth settings? For other stressful medical procedures? In other stressful situations? If so, what would they be?

3. What interview questions, other than those posed in this study, would you have asked these respondents?

4. Should the interviews have been conducted in a focus group with several new mothers? What might that have added to or detracted from the data?

5. Many people now bring video cameras to their labor and delivery rooms. How might videotapes be incorporated in such a study?

6. What kind of a follow-up to this study do you believe should be done next? Design a study that continues to explore this same research theme.

FURTHER READINGS ON ETHNOGRAPHIC
INTERVIEW RESEARCH

Brenner, M. (Ed.) (1985). *The research interview.* London: Academic Press.

Douglas, J. (1985). *Creative interviewing.* Newbury Park, CA: Sage.

McCracken, G. (1988). *The long interview.* Newbury Park, CA: Sage.

Mishler, E. G. (1986). *Research interviewing: Context and narrative.* Cambridge, MA: Harvard University Press.

Morgan, D. L. (1988). *Focus groups as qualitative research,* Newbury Park, CA: Sage.

EXAMPLES OF ETHNOGRAPHIC INTERVIEW RESEARCH

Baxter, L. A., & Goldsmith, D. (1990). Cultural terms for communication events among some American high school adolescents. *Western Journal of Speech Communication, 54,* 377–394.

The authors studied the terms used to describe communication by interviewing a group of 16- and 17-year-old, middle-class, Caucasian adolescents enrolled in a six-week summer residential program at a university. Ten individuals (five males and five females), selected randomly from the group of 40, were interviewed for about an hour each. They were told to imagine that the interviewer was a foreigner who knew nothing about how American adolescents spend their days and were asked to provide their natural language labels and descriptions for the different types of talk they experienced in their daily lives. They were first asked a grand-tour question—to describe all the different types of communication events that had occurred on a recent typical day. Students were asked follow-up questions to elicit examples and to verify examples given by other respondents. They were also asked direct-language questions, such as "How do you refer to that kind of situation?" All interviews were tape-recorded, transcribed, and the terms they used were analyzed.

Carbaugh, D. (1988). Cultural terms and tensions in the speech at a television station. *Western Journal of Speech Communication, 52,* 216–237.

This study illustrates an ethnography of communication within a particular organization, a television station located in a western U.S. city. Carbaugh investigates the speech of its employees from a cultural perspective. He explains how communication events and the meanings ascribed to them structure and illuminate life within this particular social context. For example, his analysis reveals that the station employees label each other as (1) "the movers," "the shakers," or those on the "fast track"; (2) "the secure," "the stable," or "the satisfied"; and (3) the "paper movers" or "administration." To gain this information, Carbaugh spent nine months in extensive contact with station managers and interviewed employees at all levels and in each of the three buildings the station uses. He also drew upon participants' informal comments (both elicited and spontaneous). He scanned the data for potential commonalities or themes, and revised his findings when idiosyncratic and deviant episodes were noted.

Cissna, K., Cox, D., & Bochner, A. (1990). The dialectic of marital and parental relationships within the stepfamily. *Communication Monographs, 57,* 45–59.

This study was conducted to better understand communication processes involved in forming a stepfamily, particularly "metacommunication," or how family members talk with each other about their relationships. The authors took a dialectical perspective, assuming that couples would have to negotiate the tension between maintaining their spousal relationship and developing relationships with children from a previous marriage. They interviewed nine couples, all of whom had been married at least two years and had at least two school-aged children in their homes. The authors visited the families in their homes and first interviewed each spouse separately, posing a series of open questions regarding: 1) their relationships to previous spouses; 2) their visitation experiences with the nonresident parent; 3) their successes and failures in building relationships with and between the children; 4) their advice to other couples organizing a stepfamily; and 5) their overall satisfaction with their own stepfamily. That same evening, they interviewed the couple together about: 1) their most important problems in reorganizing a family; 2) their strategies for overcoming those problems; 3) their perceived resources; and 4) their perceptions of overall success in the reorganization process. The researchers first developed histories for each stepfamily and then recorded, summarized, and compared the metacommunicational statements from the interviews to discover the dominant themes associated with family reorganization. Of all the themes discovered, only the theme of perceived tension between marital and parental relationships was universal within the sample, so their analysis focused on that dimension.

Haefner, M., Metts, S., & Wartella, E. (1989). Siblings' strategies for resolving conflict over television program choice. *Communication Quarterly, 37,* 223–230. These researchers wanted to better understand how television show choices are negotiated within a family, particularly among siblings. They interviewed 115 pairs of siblings. The younger children in all the pairs were of elementary school age, and siblings were separated by no more than five years. The children attended four different schools from socioeconomically different neighborhoods, and they were interviewed individually in their schools. During the 10–12 minute interview, children were asked about the amount of time they spend with television and other media, about their relationships with their siblings, and about conflict with their siblings over program choices. They also were asked to respond to two open questions: 1) "Let's say you and _____ want to watch different television shows on TV. How do you get him/her to watch what you want to watch?"; and 2) "How does he/she get you to watch something he/she wants to watch?" Children's verbatim responses were coded and analyzed.

Smith, R., & Eisenberg, E. (1987). Conflict at Disneyland: A root-metaphor analysis. *Communication Monographs, 54,* 367–380.

The authors studied conflict in organizations by analyzing a labor-management dispute at Disneyland. They suspected that each side had a different view of the organization, which would be evidenced in the metaphors used to describe it—particularly their "root-metaphor," which reflects the basic framework or "world-view" used to interpret one's environment. Most of the interviews were conducted soon after a 22-day strike by a group of unionized employees. They interviewed eight managers, key figures in the strike, and 35 hourly employees. The interviews were conducted in three parts: 1) The researchers asked general questions, such as "What's it like to work at Disneyland?"; 2) Employees identified descriptions of the park from a list of metaphors used by management in previous interviews and documents; and 3) Employees completed the sentence, "Life at Disneyland is like. . . ," and discussed their attitudes toward the strike and the extent to which they thought the organization was changing. All the interviews were taped and transcribed. Root-metaphors were inferred from them. The authors discovered that employees were upset primarily because the traditional Disneyland root-metaphor of park employees as a "family" was being eroded by the corporations' emphasis on "drama" and "business" metaphors.

GLOSSARY

Alternative Causality Argument: A competing explanation for changes in a dependent variable other than the hypothesized effects of the independent variable(s) being studied.

Analysis of Variance (ANOVA; F–test): A statistical procedure used to determine whether there are significant differences between two or more groups.

Applied Research: Research conducted for the purpose of solving a particular, "real-world," socially relevant problem.

Basic Research: Research that develops, tests, clarifies, or refines theory.

Beta Score: A score in a regression analysis that indicates whether each independent variable significantly affects the dependent variable.

Blind Reviewers: Scholars who review manuscripts submitted for publication in a journal without knowing the identity of the author(s).

Case Study Approach: An educational tool designed to provide people with opportunities to apply the principles they study to, and answer questions about, specific situations or examples, called cases.

Causal Relationship: A relationship between variables in which one variable (the independent variable) is believed to produce changes in another variable (the dependent variable).

Census: A study of all the members of a population or universe of interest.

Closed Question: A question that asks respondents to choose between specified answer categories (such as yes or no).

Coders: Research assistants who code units into content categories.

Coding: The process of placing units into content categories.

Coefficient of Determination: A measure of the percentage of change in one variable explained by changes in another variable.

Communication: The management of messages for the purpose of creating meaning.

Complete Observer: A researcher who is a detached and uninvolved onlooker.

Complete Participant: A researcher who involves him or herself fully with the people or the process being observed.

Computer-assisted Telephone Interviewing (CATI): A computerized program that shows interviewers on a monitor the questions to be asked and enables them to enter responses to questions as they are being given.

Conceptualization: The first stage of research where researchers identify a topic worth studying, define the key concepts and variables, review the relevant literature on the topic, and ask a research question or pose a hypothesis.

Confederates: Research assistants who are trained to act consistently in pre-determined ways when interacting with research subjects.

Confidence Interval: The range of scores associated with the confidence interval.

Confidence Level: The degree of assurance that a statistic from a random sample can be used to infer a population or universe parameter.

Confounding Variables: Factors other than those studied that could explain the observed results.

Construct Validity: Establishing the accuracy of a measurement technique or research procedure from theoretical propositions and predictions.

Content Analysis: A research methodology used to identify, enumerate, and analyze occurrences of specific messages and message characteristics embedded primarily in mass-mediated texts.

Content Categories: The categories into which units are coded in content analysis and interaction analysis.

Continuous (Ordered) Variable: A concept that is assigned meaningful numbers to indicate some relative amount (such as degrees of temperature).

Control Group: A group of subjects in an experiment that do not receive a manipulation of an independent variable.

Convenience Sample: A nonrandom sample of subjects selected on the basis of availability.

Conversation Analysis: A qualitative research methodology used to analyze person-to-person communication.

Correlation Coefficient: A measure of the type and strength of a relationship between variables. A correlation coefficient ranges from $+1.00$ (a perfect positive relationship) to 0.00 (no relationship) to -1.00 (a perfect negative relationship). For intercoder reliability, the correlation coefficient ranges from $.00$ (no agreement) to 1.00 (perfect agreement).

Covert Observation: Observing subjects without their knowledge.

Criterion-related Validity: Establishing the accuracy of a measurement technique or research procedure by showing that it relates to a valid outcome.

Cross-sectional Survey: A survey that describes respondents' characteristics only at one point in time.

Cultural Communication: Communication that occurs between members of different cultures (intercultural communication) or between members of the same dominant culture who have slightly different values (intracultural communication).

Data: Information gathered by researchers.

Debriefing: Explaining the purposes and methods to subjects, and getting their opinions and insights, after they have completed a research study.

Decoding: The cognitive processes used to interpret messages we receive from others.

Deduction: The process whereby a researcher starts with a theory and then seeks to learn whether empirical (observable) data support it.

Dependent Variable: A variable that is thought to be changed by another variable (the independent variable).

Descriptive Statistics: Statistics used to summarize the information in data, such as by reporting the average score (the mean) or tabulating and displaying data on a graph.

Directional Hypothesis: A hypothesis that predicts the nature of the difference between groups or the type of relationship between variables.

Double-barreled Question: A question that asks about more than one issue.

Dramatistic Criticism: A rhetorical critical approach based on the work of

Kenneth Burke that analyzes persuasive messages primarily in terms of the elements in a dramatic event (act, purpose, agent, agency, and scene).

Ecological Validity: The extent to which research procedures reflect "real-life" circumstances.

Emic (Internal) Approach: An approach taken by ethnographers that relies on interviews to learn how their subjects think about their communication.

Encoding: The cognitive processes used to develop messages to send to others.

Ethnography: A research methodology used to describe and infer, as fully as possible and from research participants' viewpoint, people's patterns of communication in particular social contexts.

Etic (External) Approach: An approach taken by ethnographers in which they focus primarily on observable communication phenomena in a particular context and then infer a pattern from their data—the pattern being articulated by the researchers.

Experimental Research: A research methodology used to discover causal relationships between variables.

Exploratory Research: Research that investigates a topic about which little is known.

External Validity: The extent to which the findings from a study can be generalized to other populations (universes) and/or other settings.

Face Validity: Establishing the accuracy of a measurement technique or research procedure by a researcher's claim, perhaps based on a review of the literature or because others believe it is accurate.

Factorial Experiment: An experiment that studies the effects of two or more independent variables on a dependent variable(s).

Fantasy Theme Analysis: A rhetorical critical approach based on the work of Ernest Bormann that examines the common images used to portray narrative elements of situations described in a text.

Feminist Criticism: A rhetorical critical approach that analyzes how conceptions of gender are produced and maintained in persuasive messages.

Field Experiment: An experiment conducted in the natural environment of the people being studied, the field.

Field Research: Research that takes place on-site, in the natural environment.

Fieldnotes: The notes taken in the field by researchers, and used most often by ethnographers.

Fieldwork: Studying communication as it occurs naturally in an ongoing social context.

Focus Group Interview: An interview in which a facilitator leads a group of about five to seven people in a relatively unstructured discussion about a specific topic.

Full Experiments: Experiments that exercise the maximum amount of control by manipulating an independent variable, randomly assigning subjects to experimental conditions (which produces equivalent comparison groups), and accounting for the influence of extraneous variables.

Funnel Format: A question format that starts with broad, open questions and is followed by narrower, closed questions.

Generalizability: The extent to which findings can be applied to other people, texts, and settings.

Generic Criticism: A rhetorical critical approach that rejects using a single set of criteria to evaluate all persuasive messages, arguing instead that standards must apply to the particular type, or genre, of text being studied.

Group Communication: Communication that occurs among three or more (generally up to 15) people as they attempt to achieve shared goals.

Hawthorne Effect: The tendency for people to change their behavior when they know they are being observed.

Highly Structured (Scheduled) Interviews: Standardized interviews in which interviewers ask respondents the same questions, using the same wording, in a predetermined order, and respond in a consistent way to respondents' questions and answers.

Historical Criticism: A rhetorical critical approach that studies how important past events shape, and are shaped by, rhetorical messages.

Hypothesis: A prediction posed by a researcher.

Independent Variable: A variable that is thought to produce changes in another variable (the dependent variable).

Induction: The process whereby a researcher first gathers data and then develops a theory from them, often referred to as "grounded theory."

Inferential Statistics: Statistics used to estimate from a sample to a population (called estimation) and to test for significant differences between groups and significant relationships between variables.

Input Variables: Variables that pre-existed communication behavior (such as personality and situational characteristics).

Interaction Analysis: A quantitative research methodology used to analyze person-to-person communication.

Interaction Effect: A unique effect due to the combination of independent variables in a factorial experiment.

Intercoder (Interobserver) Reliability: The level of agreement demonstrated by independent coders (observers) about units and the coding of units into content categories.

Internal Validity: The extent to which research procedures lead to accurate conclusions.

Interpersonal Communication: Communication between at least two people that is characterized by the mutual awareness of the individuality of the other.

Intersubject Bias: An effect that occurs when subjects in a study influence one another's responses.

Interval Measurement: The measurement of a variable on a numerical scale where the distances between the points on the scale are equal.

Interview: The presentation of spoken questions to evoke oral responses from people.

Intragroup Baseline Comparison: Using multiple pretests and posttests in an experiment with only one group to establish the effects of an independent variable on a dependent variable.

Intrapersonal Communication: The internal messages we send to ourselves and the cognitive processes we use to develop messages to send to others and to process messages received.

Inverted Funnel Format: A question format that begins with narrow, closed questions and builds to broader, open questions.

Key Informant: A respondent in ethnographic research who is particularly well informed about the people or process being observed.

Laboratory Experiment: An experiment conducted in a setting created by a researcher.

Leading Question: A question that leads respondents to answer in certain ways.

Likert Scale: A measurement scale developed by psychologist Rensis Likert which measures on a rating scale (typically, 5 points) the extent of a person's feelings or attitudes toward a referent. Variations on Likert scales (such as the amount a statement applies to a person, using a scale of a lot, a little, not at all) are called Likert-type scales.

Longitudinal Survey: A survey administered more than once.

Main Effect: An effect due to a single independent variable in a factorial experiment.

Manipulation Check: A procedure used to check whether a manipulation of an independent variable in experimental research was successful.

Mass (Mediated) Communication: Communication that occurs through specialized communication media, such as newspapers, radio, film, and television.

Maturation: Internal changes that occur within subjects over the course of a study (such as growing tired) that may affect their responses.

Mean: The mathematical average score in a distribution.

Median: The score in a distribution at which half the scores fall above and half the scores fall below.

Metaphoric Criticism: A rhetorical critical approach that studies how rhetors' language represents reality, functioning as a metaphor, likening one thing to another.

Mode: The most frequently occurring score in a distribution.

Moderately Structured Interviews: Interviews in which researchers adhere to a standard set of questions in a predetermined order but also are allowed the freedom to probe for additional information in a more spontaneous manner than is allowed under a highly structured interview.

Multivariate Procedures: Statistical procedures that are used when there are two or more dependent variables in a study.

Narrative Criticism: A rhetorical critical approach that involves analyzing persuasive messages as stories that rhetors tell and evaluating how effective they are at shaping an audience's perception of reality.

Negative Relationship: A relationship between variables in which increases in one variable are associated with decreases in the other variable.

Neo-Aristotelian Criticism: A rhetorical critical approach based on Aristotle's writings that evaluates whether the most appropriate and effective means were used to create the rhetorical text(s) intended to influence a particular audience.

Network (Snowball) Sample: A nonrandom sample in which researchers ask subjects to provide them with the names of other people who can serve as subjects, who, in turn, are asked for additional names, and so on.

Nominal Measurement: A measurement of a variable by classifying it into different, mutually exclusive, symbolic categories (such as yes or no).

Nominal Variable: A concept differentiated on the basis of type or category, such as gender (male or female).

Nondirectional Hypothesis: A hypothesis that predicts, but does not specify the direction of, a difference between groups or a relationship between variables.

Nonrandom Sample: A sample in which each person (or text) in the population (or universe) of interest does not have an equal chance of being included.

Null Hypothesis: A hypothesis that predicts no differences between groups or no relationships between variables. Researchers always test the null hypothesis. If the null hypothesis is confirmed, then it must be accepted; if the null hypothesis is disconfirmed, then its alternative, the research hypothesis, can be accepted.

Open Question: A question that allows respondents to answer in their own words without using specific answer categories.

Operationalization: The procedure for the measurement or manipulation of a variable.

Ordinal Measurement: A measurement of a variable along a rank-order scale that does not possess equal distances between the points on the scale.

Organizational Communication: Communication that occurs within a social system composed of interdependent groups striving to accomplish commonly recognized goals.

Outputs of Communication: Texts produced by communicators themselves, such as letters, photographs, and graffiti.

Overt Observation: Observing subjects with their knowledge or consent.

Participant Observer: A researcher who functions both as a participant and as an observer with the people or in the process being observed.

Pilot Study: Testing the procedures of a study in a trial run prior to conducting the actual study.

Population: Everyone who possesses a certain characteristic of interest to a researcher.

Positive Relationship: A relationship between variables in which increases in one variable are associated with increases in the other variable.

Posttest: A measurement made in experimental research after a manipulation of an independent variable.

Pre-experiments: Experiments that demonstrate little or no control. Pre-experiments may or may not manipulate an independent variable, do not assign subjects randomly to conditions, and do not attempt to assess whether the experimental groups started off equivalent (which creates nonequivalent comparison groups).

Pretest: A measurement made in experimental research prior to a manipulation of the independent variable.

Primary Research: Research reported for the first time by the person who actually conducted it.

Probability Level: The confidence level (chance) set by researchers for rejecting a null hypothesis and accepting its alternative, the research hypothesis. The probability level typically is set at 95%, or .05, in the social sciences.

Probe: A neutral, nondirectional question designed to elicit an elaboration on an incomplete or ambiguous response, given in an interview in response to an open question.

Proprietary Research: Research conducted for, and available only to, a specific audience.

Public Communication: Communication by one person (or several) to a relatively large group of people.

Purposive Sample: A nonrandom sample in which people are chosen to participate because they possess a certain characteristic of interest.

Qualitative Data: Information in the form of words rather than numbers.

Quantitative Data: Information in the form of numerical indicators.

Quasi-experiments: Experiments that demonstrate a moderate amount of control. Quasi-experiments may or may not manipulate an independent variable, do not assign subjects randomly to experimental conditions, but attempt to determine whether the experimental groups started off equivalent by using pretests (which creates quasi-equivalent comparison groups).

Question Format: The strategic sequence of questions that a researcher uses. In an interview, this is called the interview protocol.

Questionnaire: The presentation of printed questions to evoke written responses from people.

Random Assignment of Subjects to Groups: A procedure that ensures that all research subjects in an experiment have an equal chance of being assigned to the different experimental conditions.

Random Digit Dialing (RDD): A technique in which telephone numbers are called at random.

Random Sample: A sample in which each person (or text) in the population (or universe) of interest has an equal chance of being selected. A random selection procedure produces a representative sample of the population/universe.

Rapport: The development of a cooperative relationship between an interviewer and an interviewee.

Ratio Measurement: A measurement of a variable on a scale with equal distance between the points that possesses an absolute zero point at which the variable ceases to exist (for example, weight).

Reconceptualization: The final stage of the research process where researchers use the findings from the previous stages to rethink the topic of inquiry.

Regression Analysis: A statistical procedure used to predict scores on one variable(s) on the basis of known scores on another variable(s).

Reliability: The extent to which a measurement technique, research procedure, or research finding is consistent.

Research: The systematic process of investigation. A disciplined form of inquiry that studies phenomena in a planned step-by-step manner.

Research Question: A question asked by a researcher which a research study is intended to answer.

Researcher-administered Questionnaire: A questionnaire given in person to subjects by researchers.

Researcher Personal Attribute Effect: A researcher effect that occurs when particular characteristics of the researcher affect subjects' behavior.

Researcher Unintentional Expectancy Effect: A researcher effect that occurs when researchers affect subjects' responses by inadvertently letting them know the desired responses.

Response Rate: The number of usable questionnaires or interviews divided by the total number of people sampled.

Response Set: A tendency for subjects to answer questions by choosing only one category of a measurement scale.

Rhetorical Criticism: A research methodology used to describe, analyze, interpret, and evaluate the persuasive uses of human communication.

Sample: A subgroup selected from a population or universe.

Sampling Error: The extent to which a random sample differs from its population or universe.

Sampling Frame: The part of the population or universe that actually can be reached. Ideally, this consists of all members of the population or universe of interest.

Scholarly Journals: Regular, often quarterly, publications, called periodicals, that print primary research and sometimes book reviews.

Scholarly Research: Research conducted to promote growth in public knowledge, and, therefore, is available to all members of society.

Secondary Research: Research reports presented for the second or subsequent time by the person who conducted the research or summaries of someone else's research, such as research findings reported in newspapers, textbooks, or on television.

Self-administered Questionnaire: A questionnaire completed by respondents at their own discretion.

Semantic Differential Scale: A measurement scale that has polar-opposite referents at each end of the scale and seven points in-between (for example, good ___: ___: ___: ___: ___: ___: ___ bad)

Semantic Validity: Establishing the accuracy of a measurement technique or research procedure by having persons familiar with the language and texts examine lists of words (or other units) placed in the same category and agreeing that these words have similar meanings or connotations.

Simple Random Sample: A random sample in which each person in the sampling frame is assigned a consecutive number and then individuals are selected from this list if their assigned numbers are chosen randomly until the desired sample size is obtained.

Societal Communication: Communication that occurs within and between social systems composed of interdependent organizations.

Spurious Relationship: A relationship between variables that is a mere coincidence.

Standard Deviation: The extent to which scores vary from the mean "on the average."

Statistical Power: The strength of a difference between groups or relationships between variables.

Statistical Regression: The tendency for subjects selected on the basis of extreme scores to "regress" back toward a more average level on a subsequent measurement.

Statistical Significance: The probability level set for rejecting a null hypothesis.

Stratification Sample: A random sample in which members of a population are categorized along a characteristic and then are sampled randomly from each category in proportion to its representation in the population.

Structured Observational Schemes: Predetermined, interpretive schemes that are used to code units into content categories.

Subject Mortality: The loss of subjects over the course of a study.

Summative Scales: A measurement instrument in which the scoring requires totaling responses to all the individual items.

Survey Research: A research methodology used to generalize about a population of interest based on responses from a relatively small number of representative individuals, called a sample.

Symbolic Interactionism: An orientation used by ethnographers that believes that what people do is influenced primarily by their interpretation of (or the meaning they ascribe to) themselves, others, and the situations they are in.

t-test: A statistical procedure used to assess differences between two groups. A one-tailed *t*-test is used when a directional hypothesis is advanced, and a two-tailed *t*-test is used when a nondirectional hypothesis is advanced.

Text: A recorded or visual message.

Textual Analysis: A research methodology used to study the messages embedded in documents or texts.

Theory: A generalization about a phenomenon, an explanation of how or why something occurs.

Transcripts of Communication: Verbatim written versions of what people actually say.

Treatment Group: A group of subjects in an experiment that receives a manipulation of the independent variable.

Triangulation: The use of multiple methodologies and/or techniques to study a phenomenon.

Tunnel Format: A question format that asks respondents a series of consistent or similarly organized questions.

Unitizing: The process of identifying appropriate units in content analysis and interaction analysis.

Univariate Procedures: Statistical procedures used when there is only one dependent variable in a study.

Universe: Every text that possesses a certain characteristic of interest to a researcher.

Unobtrusive Measures: Analyses of physical traces or artifacts to describe people and their communication behavior.

Unstructured Interviews: Interviews in which interviewers are given a general set of questions to ask, but are allowed maximum freedom in phrasing and ordering the questions and probing for additional information.

Variables: Concepts that take on two or more values.

Validity: The degree to which a measurement technique, research procedure, or research finding is accurate.

Variable Analytic Studies: Studies that collect information on many variables and test them all to see what might turn out to be significant.

Volunteer Sample: A nonrandom sample of subjects who choose to participate in a study.

BIBLIOGRAPHY

Agar, M. H. (1986). *Speaking of ethnography.* Newbury Park, CA: Sage.

Allen, J. L., & Shaw, D. H. (1990). Teachers' communication behaviors and supervisors' evaluation of instruction in elementary and secondary classrooms. *Communication Education, 39,* 308–322.

Andersen, P. A. (1989). Philosophy of science. In P. Emmert & L. L. Barker (Eds.), *Measurement of communication behavior* (pp. 3–17). New York: Longman.

Andrews, J. R. (1983). *The practice of rhetorical criticism.* New York: Macmillan.

Applebaum, R. L. (1985). Subject selection in speech communication research: A reexamination. *Communication Quarterly, 33,* 227–235.

Babbie, E. R. (1982). *Social research for consumers.* Belmont, CA: Wadsworth.

Babbie, E. (1989). *The practice of social research* (5th ed.). Belmont, CA: Wadsworth.

Babrow, A. S. (1989). An expectancy-value analysis of the student soap opera audience. *Communication Research, 16,* 155–178.

Babrow, A. S. (1990). Audience motivation, viewing context, media content, and form: The interactional emergence of soap opera entertainment. *Communication Studies, 41,* 342–361.

Bach, B. W. (1989). The effect of multiplex relationships upon innovation adoption: A reconsideration of Rogers' model. *Communication Monographs, 56,* 133–150.

Bales, R. F. (1950). *Interaction process analysis: A method for the study of small groups.* Reading, MA: Addison-Wesley.

Bantz, C. R., & Smith, D. H. (1974). A critique and experimental test of Weick's model of organizing. *Communication Monographs, 44,* 171–184.

Baxter, L. A., & Bullis, C. (1986). Turning points in developing romantic relationships. *Human Communication Research, 12,* 469–493.

Beach, W. A. (1989). Foreword: Sequential organization of conversational activities. *Western Journal of Speech Communication, 53,* 85–90.

Bell, R. A., & Daly, J. A. (1984). The affinity-seeking function of communication. *Communication Monographs, 51,* 91–115.

Benoit, W. L. (1991). Two tests of the mechanism of inoculation theory. *Southern Communication Journal, 56,* 219–229.

Berelson, B. (1952). *Content analysis in communication research.* New York: The Free Press.

Berger, C. R., & Calabrese, R. J. (1975). Some explorations in initiation interactions and beyond: Toward a developmental theory of interpersonal communication. *Human Communication Research, 1,* 99–112.

Bogart, L. (1985). How U.S. newspapers are changing. *Journal of Communication, 35,* 82–90.

Bormann, E. H. (1972). Fantasy and rhetorical visions: The rhetorical criticism of reality. *Quarterly Journal of Speech, 58,* 396–407.

Bormann, E. H. (1973). The Eagleton affair: A fantasy theme analysis. *Quarterly Journal of Speech, 59,* 143–159.

Bormann, E. H. (1982). Colloquy I. Fantasy and rhetorical vision: Ten years later. *Quarterly Journal of Speech, 68,* 288–305.

Bowers, J. W. (1970). Content analysis. In P. Emmert & W. D. Brooks (Eds.), *Methods of research in communication* (pp. 291–314). New York: Houghton Mifflin.

Bowers, J. W., & Courtright, J. A. (1984). *Communication research methods.* Glenview, IL: Scott, Foresman.

Brock, B. L., & Howell, S. (1988). The evolution of the PLO: A rhetoric of terrorism. *Central States Speech Journal, 39,* 281–292.

Burke, K. (1945). *A grammar of motives.* Englewood Cliffs, NJ: Prentice Hall.

Burke, K. (1950). *A rhetoric of motives.* Englewood Cliffs, NJ: Prentice Hall.

Burke, K. (1960). *Language as symbolic action.* Berkeley, CA: University of California Press.

Campbell, D. T., & Stanley, J. C. (1963). *Experimental and quasi-experimental designs for research.* Chicago: Rand McNally.

Campbell, K. K. (1972). *Critiques of contemporary rhetoric.* Belmont, CA: Wadsworth.

Campbell, K. K. (1974). Criticism: Ephemeral and enduring. *Speech Teacher, 23,* 10–11.

Cannell, C. F., & Kahn, R. L. (1968). Interviewing. In G. Lindzey & E. Aronson (Eds.), *Handbook of social psychology: Vol. II. Research methods* (2nd ed., pp. 526–595). Reading MA: Addison-Wesley.

Cappella, J. N. (1990). The method of proof by example in interaction analysis. *Communication Monographs, 57,* 236–242.

Chesebro, J. W. (1991). Communication, values, and popular television series—A seventeen year assessment. *Communication Quarterly, 39,* 197–225.

Christopher, F. S., & Frandsen, M. M. (1990). Strategies of influence in sex and dating. *Journal of Social and Personal Relationships, 7*, 89–106.

Comstock, G. (1975). *Television and human behavior: The key studies.* Santa Monica, CA: Rand Corporation.

Cook, T. D., & Campbell, T. D. (1979). *Quasi-experimentation: Design & analysis issues for field settings.* Boston: Houghton Mifflin.

Cragan, J. F., & Wright, D. W. (1990). Small group communication research of the 1980s: A synthesis and critique. *Communication Studies, 41*, 212–236.

Craig, J. R., & Metze, L. P. (1986). *Methods of psychological research* (2nd ed.). Monterey, CA: Brooks/Cole.

Deakins, A. H., Osterink, C., & Hoey, T. (1987). Topics in same sex and mixed sex conversations. In L. B. Nadler, M. J. Nadler, & W. R. Todd-Mancillas (Eds.), *Advances in gender and communication research* (pp. 89–108). Lanham, MD: University Press of America.

Dillard, J. P. (1990). Self-inference and the foot-in-the-door technique: Quantity of behavior and attitudinal mediation. *Human Communication Research, 16*, 422–447.

Douglas, J. (1985). *Creative interviewing.* Newbury Park, CA: Sage.

Dovring, K. (1954–1955). Quantitative semantics in 18th century Sweden. *Public Opinion Quarterly, 18*, 389–394.

Edelman, M. (1964). *The symbolic uses of politics.* Urbana, IL: University of Illinois Press.

Fetterman, D. M. (1990). *Ethnography: Step by step.* Newbury Park, CA: Sage.

Fink, A., & Kosecoff, J. (1985). *How to conduct surveys: A step-by-step guide.* Beverly Hills, CA: Sage.

Flesch, R. (1949). *The art of readable writing.* New York: Collier.

Foss, S. K. (1989). *Rhetorical criticism: Exploration & practice.* Prospect Heights, IL: Waveland.

Fowler, F. J., Jr. (1988). *Survey research methods* (rev. ed.). Newbury Park, CA: Sage.

Fowler, F. J., Jr., & Mangione, T. W. (1990). *Standardized survey interviewing: Minimizing interviewer-related error.* Newbury Park, CA: Sage.

Freimuth, V. S., Hammond, S. L., Edgar, T., & Monahan, J. L. (1990). Reaching those at risk: A content-analytic study of AIDS PSAs. *Communication Research, 17*, 775–808.

Frey, L. R., & Botan, C. H. (1988). The status of instruction in introductory undergraduate communication research methods. *Communication Education, 37*, 249–256.

Frey, L. R., Botan, C. H., Friedman, P. G., & Kreps, G. L. (1991). *Investigating communication: An introduction to research methods.* Englewood Cliffs, NJ: Prentice Hall.

Gerbner, G., Gross, L., Signorielli, N., Morgan, M., & Jackson-Beeck, M. (1979). The demonstration of power: Violence profile no. 10. *Journal of Communication, 29*(3), 177–196.

Gold, R. L. (1958). Roles in sociological field observations. *Social Forces, 36,* 217–223.

Goodenough, W. H. (1964). Cultural anthropology and linguistics. In D. Hymes (Ed.), *Language in culture and society: A reader in linguistics and anthropology* (pp. 36–39). New York: Harper & Row.

Grimshaw, A. D. (1974). Data and data use in an analysis of communicative events. In R. Bauman & J. Sherzer (Eds.), *Explorations in the ethnography of speaking* (pp. 419–424). London: Cambridge University Press.

Groves, R. M., & Kahn, R. L. (1979). *Surveys by telephone: A national comparison with personal interviews.* Orlando, FL: Academic Press.

Gubrium, J. (1988). *Analyzing field reality.* Newbury Park, CA: Sage.

Hammersley, M. (1989). *The dilemma of qualitative method: Herbert Blumer and the Chicago tradition.* London: Routledge.

Hansen, M. H., Hurwitz, W. N., Marks, E. S., & Maudlin, W. P. (1951). Response errors in surveys. *Journal of the American Statistical Association, 46,* 147–190.

Hecht, M. L., Ribeau, S., & Alberts, J. K. (1989). An Afro-American perspective on interethnic communication. *Communication Monographs, 56,* 385–410.

Heritage, J. (1989). Current developments in conversation analysis. In D. Roger & P. Bull (Eds.), *Conversation: An interdisciplinary perspective* (pp. 21–47). Clevedon, England: Multilingual Matter Ltd.

Hochstim, J. R. (1967). A critical comparison of three strategies of collecting data from households. *Journal of the American Statistical Association, 62,* 976–989.

Hyman, H. H. (1954). *Interviewing in social research.* Chicago: University of Chicago Press.

Jacobs, S. (1990). On the especially nice fit between qualitative analysis and the known properties of conversation. *Communication Monographs, 57,* 243–249.

Janis, I. L. (1982). *Victims of groupthink* (2nd ed.). Boston: Houghton Mifflin.

Janis, I. L., & Mann, L. (1965). Effectiveness of emotional role-playing in modifying smoking habits and attitudes. *Journal of Experimental Research in Personality, 1,* 84–90.

Johnson, J. C. (1990). *Selecting ethnographic informants.* Newbury Park, CA: Sage.

Jorgenson, D. L. (1989). *Participant observation: A methodology for human studies.* Newbury Park, CA: Sage.

Kahn, R., & Cannell, C. F. (1958). *Dynamics of interviewing.* New York: John Wiley.

Kerlinger, F. N. (1973). *Foundations of behavioral research* (2nd ed.). New York: Holt, Rinehart and Winston.

Kish, L., & Slater, C. W. (1960). Two studies of interviewer variance of socio-psychological variables. *Proceedings of the American Statistical Association, Social Science Section,* 66–70.

Knapp, M. L., Hopper, R., & Bell, R. A. (1984). Compliments: A descriptive taxonomy. *Journal of Communication, 34*(4), 12–29.

Kreps, G. L., Frey, L. R., & O'Hair, D. (1991). Applied communication research:

Scholarship that can make a difference. *Journal of Applied Communication Research, 19,* 71–87.

Kreps, G. L., & Lederman, L. C. (1985). Using the case study method in organizational communication education: Developing students' insight, knowledge, and creativity through experience-based learning and systematic debriefing. *Communication Education, 34,* 358–364.

Krippendorf, K. (1980). *Content analysis: An introduction to its methodology.* Newbury Park, CA: Sage.

Krueger, R. A. (1988). *Focus groups: A practical guide for applied research.* Newbury Park, CA: Sage.

Lavrakas, P. J., & Holley, J. K. (1989). The image of daily newspapers in their local markets. *Newspaper Research Journal, 10*(3), 51–60.

Lazarsfeld, P. (1959). Problems in methodology. In R. K. Merton (Ed.), *Sociology today* (pp. 39–78). New York: Basic Books.

Lederman, L. (1983). High communication apprehensives talk about communication apprehension and its effects on their behavior. *Communication Quarterly, 31,* 233–236.

Lewin, K. (1951). Problems of research in social psychology. In D. Cartwright (Ed.), *Field theory in social science: Selected theoretical papers by Kurt Lewin* (pp. 155–169). New York: Harper & Row.

Lincoln, Y. S., & Guba, E. G. (1985). *Naturalistic inquiry.* Beverly Hills, CA: Sage.

Loftus, E. (1979). *Eyewitness testimony.* Cambridge, MA: Harvard University Press.

Looney, R. (1991, February 5). Pollsters fret as Americans learn to say no. *Chicago Tribune,* Section 5, p. 1.

Lowry, D. T., Love, G., & Kirby, M. (1981). Sex on the soap operas: Patterns of intimacy. *Journal of Communication, 31*(3), 90–96.

Lozano, B. (1989). *The invisible work force.* New York: The Free Press.

Mackay, A. L. (1977). *The harvest of a quiet eye: A selection of scientific quotations.* London: Institute of Physics.

Margolis, J. (1991, February 3). Insufficient data: It's not that polls are wrong, they're just highly inadequate. *Chicago Tribune,* Section 4, pp. 1 & 5.

Marwell, G., & Schmidt, D. R. (1967). Dimensions of compliance-gaining behavior: An empirical analysis. *Sociometry, 30,* 350–364.

Matlon, R. J. (1987). *Index to journals in communication studies through 1985.* Annandale, VA: Speech Communication Association.

McGuire, W. J. (1964). Inducing resistance to persuasion: Some contemporary approaches. In L. Bekowitz (Ed.), *Advances in experimental social psychology* (pp. 191–229). New York: Academic Press.

Miles, M. B., & Huberman, A. M. (1984). *Qualitative data analysis: A sourcebook of new methods.* Newbury Park, CA: Sage.

Miller, G. (1987). Producing family problems: Organization and uses of family perspective and rhetoric in family therapy. *Symbolic Interaction, 10,* 245–265.

Miller, G. R., & Sunnafrank, M. J. (1984). Theoretical dimensions of applied communication research. *Quarterly Journal of Speech, 70,* 255–263.

Miller, K. I., Zook, E. G., & Ellis, B. H. (1989). Occupational differences in the influence of communication and stress and burnout in the workplace. *Management Communication Quarterly, 3,* 166–190.

Mishler, E. G. (1986). *Research interviewing: Context and narrative.* Cambridge, MA: Harvard University Press.

Moffett, E. A., & Dominick, J. R. (1987). Statistical analysis in the *Journal of Broadcasting,* 1970–1985. *Feedback, 28,* 13–20.

Mongeau, P. A. (1989). Individual differences as moderators of persuasive message processing and attitude-behavior relations. *Communication Research Reports, 6,* 3–8.

Morgan, D. L. (1988). *Focus groups as qualitative research,* Newbury Park, CA: Sage.

Morgan, M., Alexander, A., Shanahan, J., & Harris, C. (1990). Adolescents, VCRs, and the family environment. *Communication Research, 17,* 83–106.

Morris, G. H., & Coursey, M. (1989). Negotiating the meaning of employees' conduct: How managers evaluate employees' accounts. *Southern Communication Journal, 54,* 185–205.

Motley, M. T., & Smith, N. L. (1989). Effects of a temperament upon hiring decisions: A preliminary examination of global personality traits and communicator credibility. *Communication Reports, 2,* 22–29.

Murphy, J. M. (1990). "A time of shame and sorrow": Robert F. Kennedy and the American jeremiad. *Quarterly Journal of Speech, 76,* 401–414.

Pacanowsky, M. (1988). Communicating in the empowering organization. In J. A. Anderson (Ed.), *Communication yearbook 11* (pp. 356–379). Beverly Hills, CA: Sage.

Pomerantz, A. (1990). Conversation analytic claims. *Communication Monographs, 57,* 231–235.

Rawlins, W. K., & Holl, M. R. (1988). Adolescents' interaction with parents and friends: Dialectics of temporal perspective and evaluation. *Journal of Personal and Social Relationships, 5,* 27–46.

Ray, E. B. (1991). The relationship among communication network roles, job stress, and burnout in educational organizations. *Communication Quarterly, 39,* 91–102.

Reardon, K. K., Sussman, S., & Flay, B. R. (1989). Are we marketing the right message: Can kids "just say 'no'" to smoking? *Communication Monographs, 56,* 307–324.

Rose, D. (1987). *Black American street life: South Philadelphia, 1969–1971.* Gainesville, FL: University of Florida Press.

Rose, D. (1990). *Living the ethnographic life.* Newbury Park, CA: Sage.

Rosenthal, R. (1965). The volunteer subject. *Human Relations, 18,* 403–404.

Rowland, R. C., & Rademahcer, T. (1990). The passive style of rhetorical crisis management: A case study of the Superfund controversy. *Communication Studies, 41,* 326–341.

Rubin, R. B., Graham, E. E., & Mignerey, J. T. (1990). A longitudinal study of college students' communication competence. *Communication Education, 39,* 1–14.

Samter, W., & Burleson, B. R. (1984). Cognitive and motivational influences on spontaneous comforting behavior. *Human Communication Research, 11,* 231–260.

Sauceda, J. S. (1991). "His silvery incantation": Assessing James Joyce as a performer of his works. *Text and Performance Quarterly, 11,* 73–105.

Saville-Troike, M. (1989). *The ethnography of communication: An introduction* (2nd ed.). Oxford: Basil Blackwell.

Sillars, A. L., Coletti, S. F., Parry, D., & Rogers, M. A. (1982). Coding verbal conflict strategies: Nonverbal and perceptual correlates of the "avoidance-distributive-integrative" dimension. *Human Communication Research, 9,* 83–95.

Smith, C. D., & Kornblum, W. (1989). *In the field: Readings on the field research experience.* New York: Praeger.

Smith, M. J. (1988). *Contemporary communication research methods.* Belmont, CA: Wadsworth.

Smith, R. C., & Eisenberg, E. M. (1987). Conflict at Disneyland: A root-metaphor analysis. *Communication Monographs, 54,* 367–380.

Smith, V. (1990). *Managing in the corporate interest: Control and resistance in an American bank.* Berkeley, CA: University of California Press.

Snyder, M. (1974). Self-monitoring of expressive behavior. *Journal of Personality and Social Psychology, 30,* 526–537.

Socha, T. (1988). *Marital decision conversation: An investigation of spouses' perceptions of decision topics and relational communication control and support structures.* Unpublished doctoral dissertation, University of Iowa.

Sorensen, G., Plax, T. G., & Kearney, P. (1989). The strategy of selection-construction controversy: A coding scheme for analyzing teacher compliance-gaining message constructions. *Communication Education, 38,* 102–118.

Spradley, J. (1979). *The ethnographic interview.* New York: Holt, Rinehart and Winston.

Stempel, G. H., III. (1989). Content analysis. In G. H. Stempel III & B. H. Westly (Eds.), *Research methods in mass communication* (2nd ed., pp. 124–129). Englewood Cliffs, NJ: Prentice Hall.

Strauss, A., & Corbin J. (1990). *Basics of qualitative research: Grounded theory procedures and techniques.* Newbury Park, CA: Sage.

Survey Sampling, Inc. (1990). *A survey researcher's view of the United States* [Poster]. One Post Road, Fairfield, CT.

Sykes, R. E. (1983). Initial interaction between strangers and acquaintances: A multivariate analysis of factors affecting choice of communication partners. *Human Communication Research, 10,* 27–53.

Terkel, S. (1970). *Hard times.* New York: Avon Books.

Tracy, K. (1991). Discourse. In B. M. Montgomery & S. Duck (Eds.), *Studying interpersonal interaction* (pp. 179–196). New York: Guildford.

Tucker, R. K., Weaver, R. L., II, & Berryman-Fink, C. (1981). *Research in speech communication.* Englewood Cliffs, NJ: Prentice Hall.

Tukey, J. W. (1969). Analyzing data: Sanctification or detective work? *American Psychologist, 24,* 83–91.

Turner, D. N., & Saunders, D. (1990). Medical relabeling in Gamblers Anonymous: The construction of an ideal member. *Small Group Research, 21,* 59–75.

Van Maanen, J. (1983). Epilogue: Qualitative methods reclaimed. In J. Van Maanen (Ed.), *Qualitative methodology* (pp. 247–268). Beverly Hills, CA: Sage.

Van Maanen, J. (1988). *Tales of the field: On writing ethnography.* Chicago: University of Chicago Press.

Webb, E. J., Campbell, D. T., Schwartz, R. D., & Sechrest, L. (1973). *Unobtrusive measures: Nonreactive research in the social sciences.* Skokie, IL: Rand McNally.

Weber, R. P. (1990). *Basic content analysis* (2nd ed.). Newbury Park, CA: Sage.

Weick, K. (1969). *The social psychology of organizing.* Reading, MA: Addison-Wesley.

Weick, K. E. (1985). Systematic observational methods. In G. Lindzey & E. Aronson (Eds.), *Handbook of social psychology: Vol. I. Theory and methods* (pp. 567–634). New York: Random House.

Weller, S. C., & Romney, A. K. (1988). *Systematic data collection.* Newbury Park, CA: Sage.

Werner, O., & Schoepfle, G. M. (1987). *Systematic fieldwork, Volume I: Foundations of ethnography and interviewing.* Newbury Park, CA: Sage.

Wert-Gray, S., Center, C., Brashers, D. E., & Meyers, R. A. (1991). Research topics and methodological orientation in organizational communication: A decade in review. *Communication Studies, 42,* 141–154.

Wharton, C. S. (1991). Why can't we be friends?: Expectations versus experiences in the volunteer role. *Journal of Contemporary Ethnography, 20,* 79–106.

Whyte, W. F. (1984). *Learning from the field.* Newbury Park, CA: Sage.

Williams, C. L. (1989). *Gender differences at work: Women and men in nontraditional occupations.* Berkeley, CA: University of California Press.

Wilson, S. R. (1990). Development and test of a cognitive rules model of interaction goals. *Communication Monographs, 57,* 81–103.

Wimmer, R. D., & Dominick, J. R. (1991). *Mass media research: An introduction* (3rd ed.). Belmont, CA: Wadsworth.

Wolcott, H. F. (1990). *Writing up qualitative research.* Newbury Park, CA: Sage.

Yount, K. R. (1991). Ladies, flirts, and tomboys: Strategies for managing sexual harassment in an underground coal mine. *Journal of Contemporary Ethnography, 19,* 396–422.

Yu, J., & Cooper, H. (1983). A quantitative review of research design effects on response rates of questionnaires. *Journal of Marketing Research, 20,* 36–44.

Index